Table of Contents

★ **Introduction** **6**

Find out how to get the most out of this book and become a better student—while you have fun!

★ **Part I The Presidents** **7**

From George Washington's day to the twenty-first century—they're all here!

Games to Play—How to Use the Presidents Flash Cards 8
Flash Cards—Great pictures and lots of interesting facts 9
Election Tracker—Follow the election action and cast your vote 23

George Washington 26
John Adams 27
Thomas Jefferson 28
James Madison 29
James Monroe 30
John Quincy Adams 31
Andrew Jackson 32
Martin Van Buren 33
William H. Harrison 34
John Tyler 35
James K. Polk 36
Zachary Taylor 37
Millard Fillmore 38
Franklin Pierce 39
James Buchanan 40
Abraham Lincoln 41
Andrew Johnson 42
Ulysses S. Grant 43
Rutherford B. Hayes 44
James A. Garfield 45
Chester A. Arthur 46
Grover Cleveland 47
Benjamin Harrison 48

© 2001 McGraw-Hill. All Rights Reserved.

The Complete Book of Presidents & States

William McKinley 49
Theodore Roosevelt 50
William H. Taft 51
Woodrow Wilson 52
Warren G. Harding 53
Calvin Coolidge 54
Herbert C. Hoover 55
Franklin D. Roosevelt 56
Harry S. Truman 57
Dwight D. Eisenhower 58
John F. Kennedy 59
Lyndon B. Johnson 60
Richard M. Nixon 61
Gerald Ford 62
James E. Carter, Jr. 63
Ronald Reagan 64
George Bush 65
William Clinton 66
George W. Bush 67

First Ladies—The most famous first ladies from three centuries!
Eighteenth Century: Martha Washington and Abigail Adams 68
Nineteenth Century: Dolley Madison and Mary Todd Lincoln 70
Twentieth Century: Eleanor Roosevelt and Jacqueline Kennedy 72

Activities—Learn more about the presidents as you test your knowledge!
Time Lines 74
Compare and Contrast 76
Matching Games 78
Presidential Quiz 83

Part II Our Government and How It Came to Be 84

How the Founding Fathers created the longest lasting democracy on earth.

The American Colonies Under British Rule 85
Before the Declaration of Independence 86
The Declaration of Independence 87
The Articles of Confederation 89

Writing the Constitution 90
The Great Compromise 91
Signing the Constitution 92
The Three Branches of Government 93
Checks and Balances 94
The House of Representatives 95
The Senate 96
The Executive Branch—Presidency 97
Making Laws 98
Impeachment 99
The Judicial Branch 100
The Powers of the Federal Government 101
Ratifying the Constitution 102
The Bill of Rights 103
Amendments 105
Activities, Time Lines and Quizzes 106
Our Heritage 110

★ Part III The Fifty States 111

Fifty nifty United States—Maps, facts and fun. D.C. makes fifty-one.

Map of the United States—North, South, East AND West! 112
Games to Play—How to Use the States Flash Cards 114
Flash Cards—Great maps and lots of interesting facts! 115

Alabama 141
Alaska 144
Arizona 147
Arkansas 150
California 153
Colorado 156
Connecticut 159
Delaware 162
Florida 165

© 2001 McGraw-Hill. All Rights Reserved.   The Complete Book of Presidents & States

Georgia 168
Hawaii 171
Idaho 174
Illinois 177
Indiana 180
Iowa 183
Kansas 186
Kentucky 189
Louisiana 192
Maine 195
Maryland 198
Massachusetts 201
Michigan 204
Minnesota 207
Mississippi 210
Missouri 213
Montana 216
Nebraska 219
Nevada 222
New Hampshire 225
New Jersey 228
New Mexico 231
New York 234
North Carolina 237
North Dakota 240
Ohio 243
Oklahoma 246
Oregon 249
Pennsylvania 252
Rhode Island 255
South Carolina 258
South Dakota 261
Tennessee 264
Texas 267
Utah 270
Vermont 273
Virginia 276
Washington 279
West Virginia 282
Wisconsin 285
Wyoming 288
Washington, D.C. 291

Activities—Test your States I.Q. with these fun activities!
Riddles Across the USA 294
Abbreviate Those States! 299

© 2001 McGraw-Hill. All Rights Reserved.

Crossword Puzzles 300

Regional Geography—Put your knowledge to work!
The Northeast 304
The Southeast 305
The Midwest 306
The Southwest 307
The West 308

★ **Appendix** **309**

This could be the most important part of the whole book!

Bibliography and Resources 310
Glossary 313
Answer Key 319

© 2001 McGraw-Hill. All Rights Reserved.
The Complete Book of Presidents & States

Introduction

 Did you know that you cannot be president of the United States until you are at least 35 years of age? Were you aware that Alaska used to be part of Russia, and Michigan used to be called New France? Can you name the original 13 states and list the twentieth century presidents in order?

 When you are finished with this book, your answers will be yes, yes and yes! Contained in this book is a wealth of information about the history and culture of the place almost 300 million people call home—the United States of America. It is full of fun, too. You will build your knowledge and test your skill as you play the flash card games, solve the challenging puzzles and word games and answer the thought provoking questions.

Here are a few tips to help you get the most out of this book.

 Create your own learning path. Start with a topic that interests you. Perhaps you have heard about Andrew Jackson and would like to know more. If so, check out page 32. Maybe your favorite cousin lives in Kansas and you would like to impress her with your knowledge of her home state. Turn immediately to page 186. Getting ready to take an achievement or proficiency test? Review your knowledge of the Constitution starting on page 84.

 Once you are done learning, you can use the answer key. You will find answers to all the activities in the Appendix, found in the last section of the book. You can check your own work and monitor your own learning.

 Look up new words in the Glossary. So, you do not know what a treaty is? A handy glossary of terms is located in the Appendix for easy reference.

 Work with a friend. Many of the activities and flash card games are great for buddy work. Working with another person is often the best way to increase the value of the time you spend learning. And, it is more fun!

The Presidents

How to Use the Presidents Flash Cards

Cut apart the cards on the pages that follow to create your own set of Presidents Flash Cards. Then, use them to play games such as the ones described below. You'll learn a lot of fascinating information about the men who have held the most important office in the land—president of the United States.

SOLITAIRE GAMES

★ Select any three cards from your pile and place them faceup on the table. Arrange them left to right in the order in which they served.

★ Select any three cards and place them facedown on the table. Based on the information visible on the backs of the cards, name each president.

★ Separate out the cards for all the presidents who served in the twentieth century. Organize them into two groups, Democrats and Republicans.

GAME # 1 CONCENTRATION

★ Use 2 decks for this game. Shuffle the flash cards and place them facedown in an array of six columns and seven rows. Have a partner be the "caller." The caller draws a flash card from his or her deck and names the president shown on the face of the card. Based on the information visible on the backs of the cards, choose the card in your array that you think is the one for the president named. Turn it over. If you are correct, remove the card from the array and set it aside. If you are incorrect, replace the card facedown in its position. Keep track of the time it takes you to clear all thecards from the table.

★ To make the game more difficult, place the cards faceup instead of facedown. Then, the caller selects a card from his or her own deck and reads a fact from the back. Based on your knowledge of the facts about presidents, choose the matching card from your array.

★ Invite others to play along with their own arrays of cards displayed in front of them. The player who clears all the cards from his or her array first is the winner.

GAME # 2 RUMMY

★ Play this game with two or three players. Shuffle the deck and deal seven cards to each player. Hold the cards so you can see the information on the backs and your opponents can see the faces on the fronts. Place the remaining cards faceup in a draw pile. Turn the top card over to create a discard pile.

★ The object is to create a "run" of three or four presidents who served consecutively. For example, Washington, Adams, Jefferson and Madison were the 1st, 2nd, 3rd and 4th presidents. Buchanan, Lincoln and Andrew Johnson were the 15th, 16th and 17th. Grover Cleveland, who served twice, is a wild card and may be used to complete any run of three or four.

★ Play begins to the left of the dealer. The first player can choose the top card from the draw pile or select a card from an opponent's hand. If the chosen card is from the pile, the player discards one card from his or her hand and places it facedown in the discard pile. If the chosen card is from an opponent's hand, the player gives the opponent his or her discard. The first player to create a run of three and a run of four is the winner.

  © 2001 McGraw-Hill. All Rights Reserved.

© 2001 McGraw-Hill. All Rights Reserved.

The Presidents

The 6th President of the United States

- ★ served as an interpreter for a government diplomat at 14 years of age.
- ★ was the first child of a president who was later elected president.
- ★ was elected president by the House of Representatives.
- ★ did not enjoy entertaining or mixing with crowds.
- ★ married Louisa Johnson, daughter of an American diplomat, and had three children.
- ★ had a stroke while debating an issue in Congress and died 2 days later.

The 3rd President of the United States

- ★ founded the University of Virginia.
- ★ served as governor of Virginia.
- ★ designed his beautiful home, Monticello.
- ★ invented a special plow and a copying machine.
- ★ married Martha Wayles Skelton.
- ★ asked James Madison's wife, Dolley, to help him with social events at the White House after Martha died.
- ★ died on July 4, 1826, 50 years after signing the Declaration of Independence.
- ★ was known as "the Father of the Declaration of Independence."

The 5th President of the United States

- ★ came from Virginia, as did Presidents Washington, Jefferson and Madison.
- ★ was first elected to the Virginia government when he was 24 years of age.
- ★ encouraged the growth and expansion of the nation.
- ★ set aside land for Native Americans on the Great Plains.
- ★ married Elizabeth Kortright and had three children.
- ★ died on July 4, 1831, 5 years after Jefferson and Adams died and 55 years after the Declaration of Independence was signed.

The 2nd President of the United States

- ★ was the first vice president, serving under George Washington.
- ★ was the first president to live in the White House in Washington, D.C.
- ★ had a vice president, Thomas Jefferson, who belonged to a different political party.
- ★ married Abigail Smith and had five children.
- ★ had a son (John Quincy Adams) who also became president.
- ★ died on July 4, 1826, 50 years after signing the Declaration of Independence.

The 4th President of the United States

- ★ was the oldest of 12 children.
- ★ was the youngest delegate, at 29 years of age, to the Continental Congress.
- ★ had both of his vice presidents die in office.
- ★ was often called "the Father of the Constitution."
- ★ wrote political essays that were combined into a book titled The Federalist.
- ★ married a widow named Dolley Payne Todd—she helped Thomas Jefferson with social events after Martha died.

The 1st President of the United States

- ★ was educated by his father and his older brother.
- ★ belonged to the Federalist Party.
- ★ turned down an offer from his army to make him king of the United States.
- ★ was the only president to be elected unanimously by everyone who voted.
- ★ served as president in New York City and later Philadelphia.
- ★ kept the United States out of the French Revolutionary War in 1793 and avoided another war with Britain in 1794.
- ★ married Martha Custis, a wealthy widow, and helped raise her two children.

© 2001 McGraw-Hill. All Rights Reserved.

 William H. Harrison

 Zachary Taylor

 Martin Van Buren

 James K. Polk

 Andrew Jackson

 John Tyler

© 2001 McGraw-Hill. All Rights Reserved.

The Presidents

The 12th President of the United States

★ was known as "Old Rough and Ready" because of his military background.

★ never lost a battle.

★ let his favorite horse run loose on the White House lawn.

★ did not vote until he was 64 years old.

★ was the second president to die in office.

★ married Margaret Smith and had six children.

★ had a daughter who married Jefferson Davis. He later became president of the Confederate States.

The 9th President of the United States

★ was a soldier before becoming president.

★ gave the longest speech of any president when he was sworn in.

★ was the first president to die in office.

★ was the son of a signer of the Declaration of Independence.

★ was the grandfather of the twenty-third president, Benjamin Harrison.

★ married Anna Symmes, the daughter of a wealthy judge, and had 10 children.

The 11th President of the United States

★ was born in a log cabin on the North Carolina frontier.

★ was the oldest of 10 children.

★ could barely read or write when he started school at age 18.

★ learned quickly and graduated from college with honors.

★ became friends with Andrew Jackson and earned the nickname "Little Hickory."

★ was the first "dark horse" candidate for president—a person whom few people knew.

★ married Sarah Childress.

The 8th President of the United States

★ was called the "Little Magician" because of his size and political cleverness.

★ became a lawyer by 20 years of age.

★ had followers known as "Bucktails," because they wore deer tails on their hats when they attended political meetings.

★ headed a political group that later became the Democratic Party.

★ married Hannah Hoes in 1807 and had four sons.

The 10th President of the United States

★ was called "the president without a party."

★ was the first president to face impeachment.

★ had himself sworn in as president after Harrison died, instead of calling for a new election.

★ represented Virginia in the U.S. House of Representatives and the Senate.

★ served as governor of Virginia.

★ had 14 children by two wives.

The 7th President of the United States

★ was called "Old Hickory" by his soldiers because of his toughness.

★ had many supporters who were called "the mob" by his opponents.

★ gave parties at the White House and invited the public.

★ recognized Texas as an independent nation.

★ had a slogan, "Let the people rule."

★ married Rachel Donelson Robards before she had divorced her first husband; married her again after her divorce.

★ fought duels to defend his wife's honor, killing at least one man.

The Presidents 12

© 2001 McGraw-Hill. All Rights Reserved.

James Buchanan

Ulysses S. Grant

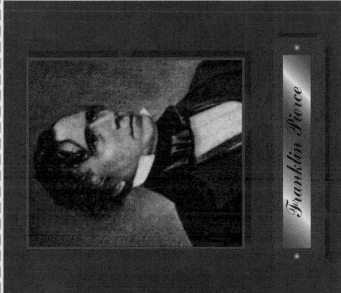

Franklin Pierce

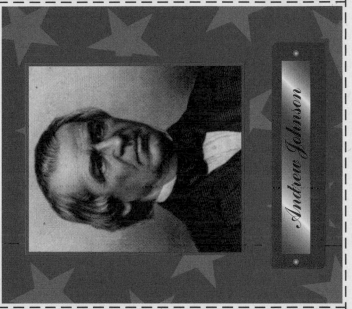

Andrew Johnson

Millard Fillmore

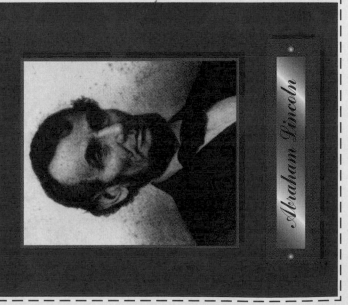

Abraham Lincoln

© 2001 McGraw-Hill. All Rights Reserved.

The Presidents

The 15th President of the United States

★ was nicknamed "Old Buck."
★ never married.
★ was thought of as a "lame duck" president.
★ was a foreign diplomat to Russia.
★ did little to prevent the Civil War.
★ lost seven southern states from the Union in a few months.
★ retired to his home, Wheatland.
★ handed the presidency over to Lincoln.

The 18th President of the United States

★ kept his mother's maiden name "Simpson" as his middle name.
★ did not like his real name "Hiram."
★ was nicknamed the "Hero of Appomattox."
★ served in the Mexican War.
★ was a Civil War hero.
★ married Julia Boggs Dent and had four children.
★ worked as a clerk in a leather goods store in Galena, IL.
★ owned a farm near St. Louis called Hard Scrabble.

The 14th President of the United States

★ at age 49, was the youngest president.
★ was friends with Nathaniel Hawthorne, the famous author.
★ was a close friend of Jefferson Davis, President of the Confederate States.
★ represented New Hampshire in the U.S. House of Representatives and the Senate.
★ served as a general in the Mexican War.
★ was the son of a two term governor of New Hampshire.
★ married Jane Appleton and had three sons, two died as children.

The 17th President of the United States

★ was an apprentice tailor as a young man.
★ was taught to write by his wife, Eliza.
★ had five children.
★ was Lincoln's vice president.
★ held pro-South views.
★ fired his Secretary of State, Edwin Stanton.
★ was impeached by Congress but found not guilty.
★ purchased Alaska, called "Seward's Folly."
★ served in the Senate after his presidency.

The 13th President of the United States

★ was born in a log cabin.
★ learned to be a cloth maker before deciding to study law.
★ represented New York in the U.S. House of Representatives.
★ was the second vice president to finish the term of a president.
★ started trade between the United States and Japan.
★ married Abigail Powers, a teacher, and had two children.
★ married a second wife, Caroline McIntosh.

The 16th President of the United States

★ was nicknamed "Honest Abe."
★ worked as a rail splitter as a young man.
★ traveled to his inauguration by train.
★ once said, "A house divided against itself cannot stand."
★ married Mary Todd and had four sons.
★ made the Emancipation Proclamation and freed the slaves.
★ delivered the Gettysburg Address.
★ led the country through the Civil War.

© 2001 McGraw-Hill. All Rights Reserved.

 Chester A. Arthur

 William McKinley

 James A. Garfield

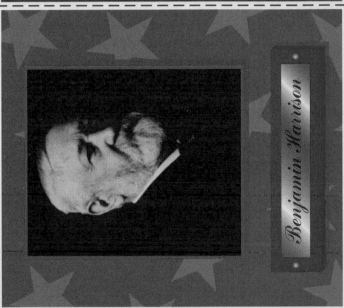 Benjamin Harrison

 Rutherford B. Hayes

 Grover Cleveland

© 2001 McGraw-Hill. All Rights Reserved.

The Presidents

The 21st President of the United States

★ graduated from Union College.
★ passed the Pendleton Act.
★ married Ellen Lewis Herndon and had three children.
★ asked his sister to serve as first lady when his wife died.
★ modernized the navy.
★ was known for acting honestly, rather than taking bribes.
★ was a private man who felt that the president's private life should be kept from the public.

The 25th President of the United States

★ was nicknamed the "Idol of Ohio."
★ defeated William Jennings Bryan twice.
★ had a campaign slogan, "Full Dinner Pail."
★ used a Spanish-American War slogan, "Remember the Maine," about a naval battle.
★ married Ida Saxton, who had epilepsy and needed much care.
★ had two children who died as infants.
★ won independence for Cuba.

The 20th President of the United States

★ was born in a log cabin.
★ was principal of Hiram College.
★ was nicknamed the "Dark Horse President."
★ came from Ohio.
★ once said, "Teaching is not the work in which a man can live and grow."
★ married Lucretia Rudolph and had seven children.
★ was president for less than 1 year.
★ was assassinated by a disappointed office seeker.

The 23rd President of the United States

★ was the grandson of William Henry Harrison, our ninth president.
★ was nicknamed "Little Ben."
★ had a campaign slogan, "Grandfather's Hat Fits Ben."
★ was a Civil War general.
★ built a stronger navy.
★ expanded the western states.
★ married Caroline Lavinia Scott (died 1892); married Mary Scott Lord Dimmick.
★ had three children.

The 19th President of the United States

★ had red hair and was nicknamed "Ruddy."
★ married Lucy Ware Webb from Delaware, Ohio.
★ once said, "He serves his party best who serves his country best."
★ ran for Congress after his term was up but lost.
★ retired to "Spiegel Grove," his family's home in Fremont, Ohio.
★ tried to guarantee the civil rights of all Americans.

The 22nd and 24th President of the United States

★ paid to have someone fight in the Civil War for him.
★ was the only president to serve two separate terms.
★ was defeated by Benjamin Harrison for a second back-to-back term in 1888.
★ was known as the "Veto Mayor" in Buffalo, NY.
★ married Frances Folsom and had five children.
★ fought the spoils system.
★ retired to Princeton, NJ.

© 2001 McGraw-Hill. All Rights Reserved.

Woodrow Wilson

Herbert C. Hoover

William H. Taft

Calvin Coolidge

Theodore Roosevelt

Warren G. Harding

© 2001 McGraw-Hill. All Rights Reserved.

The 28th President of the United States
★ lived through the Civil War as a child.
★ made reforms for sailors' work conditions and child labor.
★ almost declared war on Mexico.
★ promoted the League of Nations.
★ married Ellen Louise Axson (died 1914); married Edith Bolling Galt.
★ had three children.
★ earned the Nobel Peace Prize in 1919.
★ is buried at the Washington Cathedral.

The 27th President of the United States
★ was nicknamed "Willie."
★ was governor of the Philippines.
★ married Helen Herron and had three children.
★ survived a blizzard on his inauguration day.
★ proposed the Sixteenth Amendment that created an income tax.
★ started the tradition of throwing the first ball in the baseball season.
★ called the White House "lonesome."
★ was made chief justice after his presidency.

The 31st President of the United States
★ married his college sweetheart, Lou Henry.
★ was caught in the Boxer Rebellion in China in 1900.
★ gave some of the money he made to charity.
★ became an author and advised two presidents after his term in office.
★ worked on the St. Lawrence Waterways Commission to build the St. Lawrence Seaway.
★ served in the administrations of Wilson, Harding and Coolidge.

The 30th President of the United States
★ went by his middle name Calvin—his first name was John.
★ married Grace Anna Goodhue.
★ believed that the government should not act in domestic and foreign problems.
★ used the slogan "Keep Cool with Coolidge" when running in 1924.
★ wrote his autobiography in 1929.
★ held posts including city councilman, mayor, state senator, lieutenant governor and governor before he became president.

The 29th President of the United States
★ was born in Blooming Grove, Ohio.
★ had the middle name, Gamaliel.
★ married Florence Kling DeWolfe.
★ was elected in the first general election in which women were allowed to vote.
★ was voted into office by a 60.3 percent margin—the widest recorded to that time.
★ was the first president to have his election results broadcast by radio.
★ tried to reduce worldwide naval strength.

The 26th President of the United States
★ was nicknamed "Teddy."
★ had the first teddy bear named after him.
★ earned a Nobel Peace Prize.
★ became president after the assassination of William McKinley.
★ supported conservation efforts.
★ had a navy fleet that was called the "Great White Fleet."
★ married Alice Hathaway Lee (died 1884); married Edith Kermit Carow.
★ had six children.
★ died of jungle fever.

© 2001 McGraw-Hill. All Rights Reserved.

Dwight D. Eisenhower

Richard M. Nixon

Harry S. Truman

Lyndon B. Johnson

Franklin D. Roosevelt

John F. Kennedy

© 2001 McGraw-Hill. All Rights Reserved.

The Presidents

The 34th President of the United States

- ★ worked in his father's creamery to help pay for his brother's education.
- ★ loved golf and had a putting green on the White House lawn.
- ★ married Mamie Doud, whom he met when stationed in Texas as a second lieutenant.
- ★ was president of Columbia University after World War II.
- ★ wrote about desegregation, "There must be no second class citizens in the country."
- ★ remained as an adviser to other presidents even after he retired.

The 37th President of the United States

- ★ was the son of a grocer.
- ★ served as an aviation ground officer in the Pacific, in World War II.
- ★ married Thelma Catherine "Pat" Ryan.
- ★ served two terms as vice president under President Eisenhower.
- ★ was the first president to watch a rocket lift off into space, firsthand.
- ★ was the first president to visit Moscow.
- ★ was the first and only president to resign from office.

The 33rd President of the United States

- ★ married Elizabeth "Bess" Wallace in 1919.
- ★ fought bravely as a captain in World War I.
- ★ uncovered dishonesty in defense spending during World War II.
- ★ exposed the corruption of Tom Pendergast, an important boss in the Democratic Party.
- ★ introduced the Marshall Plan for rebuilding war-torn countries after World War II.
- ★ died in 1972 and is buried at the Truman Library grounds in Independence, Missouri.

The 36th President of the United States

- ★ was the oldest of five children.
- ★ was a teacher at Sam Houston High School in Houston, Texas.
- ★ married Claudia Alta "Ladybird" Taylor.
- ★ won the 1964 election by a record of more than 15 million votes.
- ★ appointed the first black cabinet member, Robert Weaver.
- ★ was the only president sworn into office on an airplane.
- ★ was the first president to be sworn in by a woman: U.S. District Court Judge Sarah T. Hughes.

The 32nd President of the United States

- ★ was the only president married to a woman with the same last name—her name was Anna Eleanor Roosevelt.
- ★ had polio that partially paralyzed his legs; he was often seen in a wheelchair.
- ★ was the first president to be sworn in on January 20.
- ★ was the first president to appoint a woman to his cabinet: Francis Perkins, Secretary of Labor.
- ★ was the first president to appear on television.
- ★ enjoyed sailing and collecting stamps.

The 35th President of the United States

- ★ was injured when a Japanese destroyer sank his boat in World War II.
- ★ married Jacqueline Lee Bouvier on September 12, 1953.
- ★ never lost an election.
- ★ is the only president who has won a Pulitzer Prize for a biography.
- ★ was the youngest man and first Roman Catholic ever elected president.
- ★ enjoyed his greatest foreign triumph when Russia and Great Britain signed the Nuclear Test-Ban Treaty.
- ★ was assassinated in Dallas, Texas, in 1963.

© 2001 McGraw-Hill. All Rights Reserved.

 *Ronald Reagan*

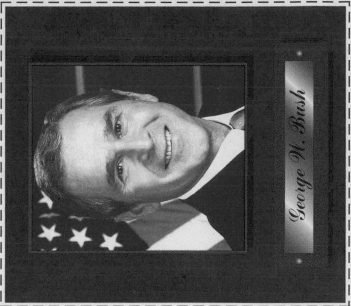 *George W. Bush*

 *James E. Carter, Jr.*

 *William Clinton*

 *Gerald Ford*

 *George Bush*

© 2001 McGraw-Hill. All Rights Reserved.

The Presidents

The 40th President of the United States

- ★ is the son of a shoe salesman.
- ★ worked to help pay for his college education.
- ★ appeared in about 50 motion-picture films.
- ★ is the only president who was an actor before entering office.
- ★ is married to Nancy Davis Reagan (born Ann Frances Robbins).
- ★ became a spokesman for the General Electric Company when his movie career declined.
- ★ ended the Cold War with Russia.

The 43rd President of the United States

- ★ served as a pilot in the Texas Air National Guard.
- ★ owned an oil and gas business.
- ★ was managing general partner of the Texas Rangers baseball team.
- ★ married Laura Welch and had twin daughters.
- ★ was the first Texas governor to be elected to consecutive four-year terms.
- ★ became president in one of the closest elections in U.S. history.
- ★ was the second son of a president and later was elected president.
- ★ calls himself a "compassionate conservative."

The 39th President of the United States

- ★ opened Georgia's government offices to African-Americans and women while serving in that state.
- ★ is the son of a woman who had been a Peace Corps volunteer.
- ★ beat Ford in the 1976 election by a million votes.
- ★ was in the submarine program while in the Navy.
- ★ he and his wife, Rosalynn, now live in their hometown of Plains, Georgia.
- ★ developed treaties to allow Panama to control the Panama Canal in 1999.

The 42nd President of the United States

- ★ was born William Jefferson Blythe III but was renamed when his widowed mother remarried.
- ★ once taught law at the University of Arkansas.
- ★ directed the presidential campaigns of George McGovern in 1972 and Jimmy Carter in 1976.
- ★ reformed the Arkansas educational system.
- ★ was inspired by President Kennedy while in high school.
- ★ married Hillary Rodham and had one daughter.
- ★ enjoys playing the saxophone.

The 38th President of the United States

- ★ was born with the name Leslie Lynch King, but it was changed after his mother remarried.
- ★ once worked as a football coach at Yale.
- ★ married Elizabeth "Betty" Bloomer Warren.
- ★ was the only person who was vice president and president without being elected to either office.
- ★ ordered an evacuation of 237,000 Vietnamese refugees at the end of the Vietnam War.
- ★ was the first person to be nominated for vice president under the Twenty-Fifth Amendment.

The 41st President of the United States

- ★ grew up in Greenwich, Connecticut, and Andover, Massachusetts.
- ★ won the Distinguished Flying Cross for heroism in World War II.
- ★ was once a salesman of oil field supplies in Texas.
- ★ was appointed to be a liaison to China.
- ★ married Barbara Pierce.
- ★ was appointed head of the Central Intelligence Agency (CIA).
- ★ once told the nation that he would not eat broccoli.

The Presidents

22

© 2001 McGraw-Hill. All Rights Reserved.

Follow a National Election

Who is running for the House of Representatives from your district? Who is running for the Senate? Who is running for president? Choose a race and follow the candidates as they compete to win. Complete the chart below.

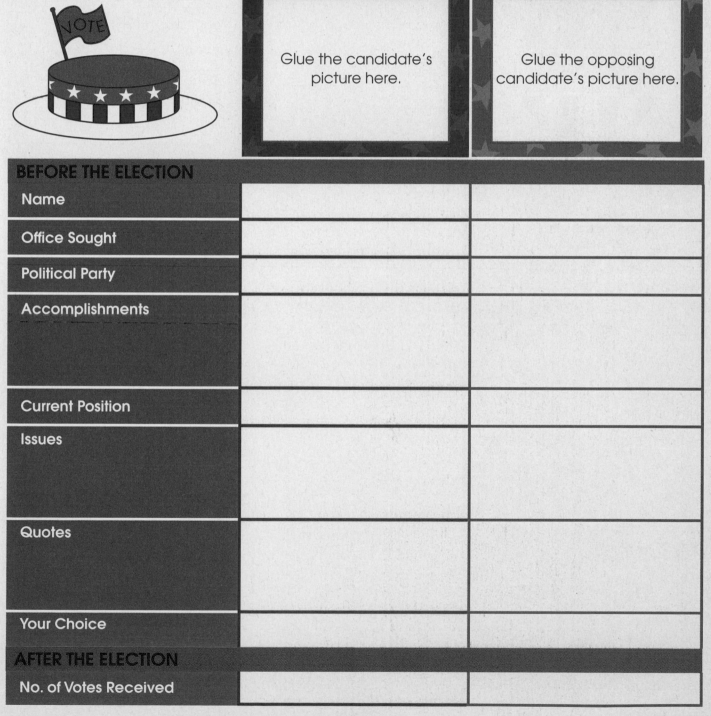

	Glue the candidate's picture here.	Glue the opposing candidate's picture here.
BEFORE THE ELECTION		
Name		
Office Sought		
Political Party		
Accomplishments		
Current Position		
Issues		
Quotes		
Your Choice		
AFTER THE ELECTION		
No. of Votes Received		

© 2001 McGraw-Hill. All Rights Reserved.

The Presidents

Follow a Statewide Election

Who is running for the Statehouse from your district? Who is running for a seat in the Upper House? Who is running for governor? Choose a race and follow the candidates as they compete to win. Complete the chart below.

	Glue the candidate's picture here.	Glue the opposing candidate's picture here.
BEFORE THE ELECTION		
Name		
Office Sought		
Political Party		
Accomplishments		
Current Position		
Issues		
Quotes		
Your Choice		
AFTER THE ELECTION		
No. of Votes Received		

© 2001 McGraw-Hill. All Rights Reserved.

Follow a Local Election

Who is running for mayor? Who is running for City Council? Who is running for a judgeship? Choose a race and follow the candidates as they compete to win. Complete the chart below.

VOTE

Glue the candidate's picture here.

Glue the opposing candidate's picture here.

BEFORE THE ELECTION		
Name		
Office Sought		
Political Party		
Accomplishments		
Current Position		
Issues		
Quotes		
Your Choice		
AFTER THE ELECTION		
No. of Votes Received		

© 2001 McGraw-Hill. All Rights Reserved.

The Presidents

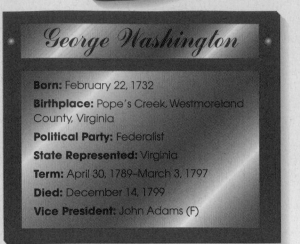

George Washington

Born: February 22, 1732

Birthplace: Pope's Creek, Westmoreland County, Virginia

Political Party: Federalist

State Represented: Virginia

Term: April 30, 1789–March 3, 1797

Died: December 14, 1799

Vice President: John Adams (F)

George Washington was a leader long before he became our first president. In 1755, at the age of 23, Washington led the Virginian forces to victory in the French and Indian War. However, Washington and the other colonists soon grew tired of British rule. By 1775, Washington became the commander of the Continental Army. His army defeated the British in 1783. George Washington also helped write our new Constitution, making sure the states had a strong role in the government. By 1789, Washington was the most popular man in the United States. He was also tired after serving our country for many years. Still, he knew a new nation needed strong leadership. When George Washington agreed to run for president, everyone voted for him. Washington served two terms as president of the United States. He died two years after his retirement, at his farm in Virginia.

★ SHOW WHAT YOU KNOW

Write in the missing words on the lines below.

Washington led British troops in the French and Indian __ __ __ .
　　　　　　　　　　　　　　　　　　　　　　　　　　　　　　1　2　3

Then, he led the __ __ __ __ __ __ __ __ __ __ __ __ __ __ __ __ against
　　　　　　　　　7　　　　　　　　　　　　　　　　　　　　6

the __ __ __ __ __ __ __ .
　　　　　　9

Washington __ __ __ __ __ __ his __ __ __ __ __ __ in many ways.
　　　　　　10　　　　　　　　　　　11

He was then elected __ __ __ __ __ __ __ __ __ .
　　　　　　　　　　　4　12　5　14　　　　8　　13

Match the letters to the numbers under each line. Write the letters on the lines below to learn what people said about George Washington.

"First in __ __ __ , first in __ __ __ __ __ , and first in the __ __ __ __ __ __ of
　　　　　1　2　3　　　　　　4　5　6　7　8　　　　　　　　　9　10　11　12　13　14
his countrymen."

★ FIND OUT MORE

Who was the king of Britain when the
United States won its freedom from British rule? _____

　　　　© 2001 McGraw-Hill. All Rights Reserved.

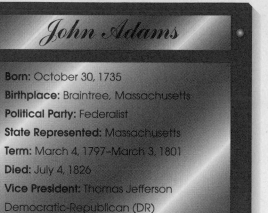

John Adams

Born: October 30, 1735

Birthplace: Braintree, Massachusetts

Political Party: Federalist

State Represented: Massachusetts

Term: March 4, 1797–March 3, 1801

Died: July 4, 1826

Vice President: Thomas Jefferson Democratic-Republican (DR)

John Adams began his long career as a lawyer in the colony of Massachusetts. A fiery speaker, Adams strongly opposed the unfair taxes that Britain forced on the colonists. He also tried to convince Britain to give the colonies more freedom. He did not succeed. Instead, Adams asked George Washington to organize the Continental Army to fight the British. In 1776, Adams helped write the Declaration of Independence. In 1783, he helped write the Treaty of Paris. This treaty ended the Revolutionary War and created the United States. When Washington became president of the United States in 1789, Adams became the first vice president. However, Adams was not pleased with the office or the appointment. He called the vice presidency "the most insignificant office" ever created. He was elected president in 1797. During his service to his country, John Adams's wife, Abigail, gave birth to a son, John Quincy. Abigail was not only a president's wife but became the mother of a future president.

SHOW WHAT YOU KNOW

Answer each of the following questions, then circle the answers in the word search.

Adams was George Washington's _____ president.

Adams helped write the Treaty of _____ , which ended the Revolutionary War.

Adams's wife was named _____ .

They had a _____ who was also elected president.

```
L A P K L O E
A B S R E I N
N I K O A R K
T G L C N V H
N A P A R I S
B I B I H C U
O L V C D E N
```

FIND OUT MORE

What was the White House called when Adams lived there?

© 2001 McGraw-Hill. All Rights Reserved.

Thomas Jefferson

Born: April 13, 1743

Birthplace: Goochland, Virginia

Political Party: Democratic-Republican

State Represented: Virginia

Term: March 4, 1801–March 3, 1809

Died: July 4, 1826

Vice President: (1) Aaron Burr (DR)

(2) George Clinton (DR)

Thomas Jefferson led the colonies' fight for freedom, but he was not a soldier. Jefferson was the main author of the two documents that helped form our nation—the Declaration of Independence and the Bill of Rights. Jefferson strongly believed that the states should have a strong role in the new government of the United States. The main political party at that time, the Federalists, disagreed. So Jefferson formed a new political party, the Democratic-Republicans. Before becoming president, Jefferson was the U.S. ambassador to France. As president, he bought the Louisiana Territory for $15 million, doubling the size of the United States. He then sent the explorers, Lewis and Clark, to explore this large unknown area. Jefferson was a politician, an educator, an architect, an inventor, a pioneer in scientific farming, a musician and a writer. Before and after becoming president, Jefferson contributed to the new nation in lasting ways.

★ SHOW WHAT YOU KNOW

Write the answer to each clue on the lines below.

Jefferson was the ambassador to _____.

Jefferson sent _____ and _____ to explore the unknown territory.

Jefferson helped write the Bill of _____.

Jefferson called his home _____.

Jefferson had no interest in becoming a _____.

★ FIND OUT MORE

What is the Louisiana Territory?

_____

_____

_____

 © 2001 McGraw-Hill. All Rights Reserved.

James Madison

Born: March 16, 1751

Birthplace: Port Conway, Virginia

Political Party: Democratic-Republican

State Represented: Virginia

Term: March 4, 1809–March 3, 1817

Died: June 28, 1836

Vice President: (1) George Clinton (DR)

(2) Elbridge Gerry (DR)

James Madison was a small person—only 5 feet, 4 inches tall and weighed about 100 pounds. However, few people contributed as much as he did to our nation. Madison believed that Americans should be free to live and worship as they pleased. As Virginia's representative to the Continental Congress, Madison helped write the Constitution. He was often referred to as "the Father of the Constitution." Madison was elected president in 1809. At this time, Britain and France were at war. After Britain attacked American ships, Madison reluctantly led our nation into war against Britain. During the War of 1812, the British captured Washington, D.C. and large areas of the Midwest. Madison escaped from the White House just before the British burned it. In 1814, he signed the Treaty of Ghent. This treaty ended the war and returned the captured land to the United States. Madison was praised for leading our nation through this difficult time.

★ SHOW WHAT YOU KNOW

Answer the following questions. Write your answers on the lines.

Madison was called "the Father of the _____."

He was _____ representative to the Continental Congress.

Madison was concerned about a person's freedom to live and _____.

Madison signed the Treaty of _____ to end the war.

Madison declared war on Britain in the War of _____.

★ FIND OUT MORE

When and why was "The Star Spangled Banner" written? Who wrote it?

_____

_____

© 2001 McGraw-Hill. All Rights Reserved.

The Presidents

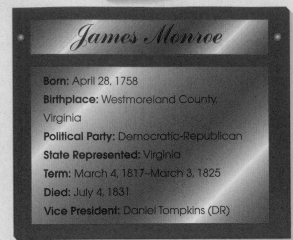

James Monroe

Born: April 28, 1758

Birthplace: Westmoreland County, Virginia

Political Party: Democratic-Republican

State Represented: Virginia

Term: March 4, 1817–March 3, 1825

Died: July 4, 1831

Vice President: Daniel Tompkins (DR)

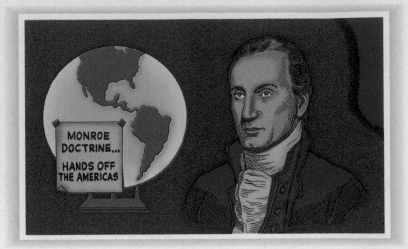

MONROE DOCTRINE... HANDS OFF THE AMERICAS

James Monroe was well prepared to be president of the United States. He had fought beside George Washington in the Revolutionary War. He had also helped his friend President Jefferson complete the Louisiana Purchase. Monroe held several positions in the Virginia government, including governor. Then, President Madison named him as secretary of state. Later, during his first term as president, Monroe was very popular. Only one vote was cast against him when he ran for his second term. His two terms were known as the time of "good feelings." Monroe made good use of this time. He bought Florida from Spain and established the Canadian border. He accepted Maine into the nation as a free state and Missouri as a slave state. And most importantly, he wrote the Monroe Doctrine. This document warned nations in Europe not to take over land or set up colonies in North and South America.

★ SHOW WHAT YOU KNOW

Write the answer to each clue in the puzzle.

Across

1 President for whom Monroe was secretary of state
2 Position in Virginia government
3 The number of votes cast against Monroe during his second term
4 The state Monroe bought from Spain
5 Admitted as a slave state
6 Admitted as a free state

What is the surprise vertical word? _____

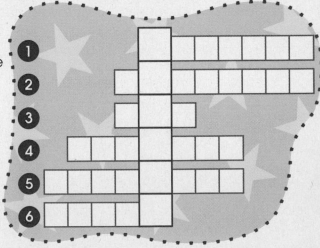

★ FIND OUT MORE

What is the Missouri Compromise? Why was it written?

_____

_____

The Presidents   **30**   © 2001 McGraw-Hill. All Rights Reserved.

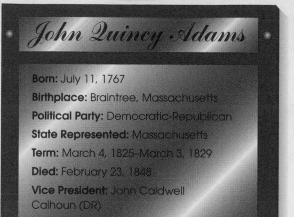

John Quincy Adams

Born: July 11, 1767

Birthplace: Braintree, Massachusetts

Political Party: Democratic-Republican

State Represented: Massachusetts

Term: March 4, 1825–March 3, 1829

Died: February 23, 1848

Vice President: John Caldwell Calhoun (DR)

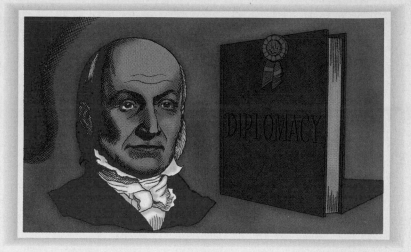

John Quincy Adams often traveled with his father, President John Adams. This experience helped the younger Adams serve as a U.S. diplomat to the Netherlands, Prussia, Russia and Great Britain. He was also elected to the U.S. Senate and served as secretary of state under President Monroe. In the 1824 presidential election, Adams ran against three men. In the end, no one candidate won a majority of the votes. The House of Representatives had to decide who had won the election. Although Andrew Jackson had received the most votes, the House chose John Quincy Adams as president. During his term, Adams was often opposed by Jackson. Adams was frustrated by the politics of the presidency. He thought that people's abilities were more important than their political parties. He even appointed his enemies to offices when he thought they would do a good job. After his term, Adams spent 17 years as Massachusetts's representative to Congress.

★ SHOW WHAT YOU KNOW

Complete the crossword puzzle.

Across

4 _____ received more votes than Adams in the 1824 presidential election.

6 Adams was elected by the _____ of Representatives.

Down

1 The sixth president was the son of John _____.

2 Adams was a diplomat in the Netherlands, Britain, Prussia and _____.

3 Later, Adams served 17 years in _____.

5 Adams served as president for _____ years.

★ FIND OUT MORE

Which political party did Adams first belong to? Which party did he switch to?

_____

© 2001 McGraw-Hill. All Rights Reserved.

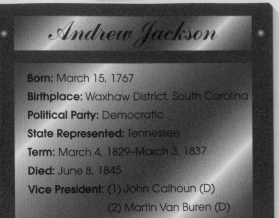

Andrew Jackson

Born: March 15, 1767

Birthplace: Waxhaw District, South Carolina

Political Party: Democratic

State Represented: Tennessee

Term: March 4, 1829–March 3, 1837

Died: June 8, 1845

Vice President: (1) John Calhoun (D)

(2) Martin Van Buren (D)

Andrew Jackson was a new kind of president. He was born to a poor mother in a log cabin on the South Carolina frontier. His father had already died. As a young man, Jackson fought in the Revolutionary War and later became a lawyer. He was elected to the U.S. House of Representatives and later became a senator for Tennessee. In the War of 1812, Jackson led an army that defeated the British in the Battle of New Orleans. Then, Jackson moved the Native American tribes—the Cherokee, Choctaw, Creek and Chickasaw—from their homes in the eastern United States to the area now called Oklahoma. He also fought the Seminole tribe in Florida. Jackson was elected president due to his reputation as an "Indian fighter." He was also known for upholding the rights of "ordinary Americans."

★ SHOW WHAT YOU KNOW

Find the letters that spell the four Native American groups that Jackson moved. Cross out the letters as you write the names below.

_____

_____

_____

_____

Find the letters that spell the Native American group that Jackson did not move. Write their name on the line below.

_____

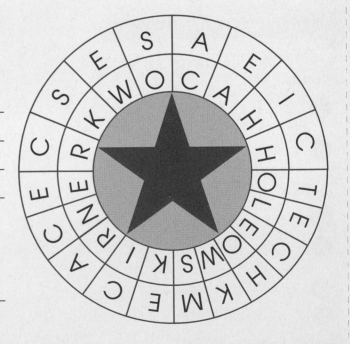

★ FIND OUT MORE

In which state did the Cherokee live before Jackson moved them?

_____

© 2001 McGraw-Hill. All Rights Reserved.

Martin Van Buren

Born: December 5, 1782

Birthplace: Kinderhook, New York

Political Party: Democratic

State Represented: New York

Term: March 4, 1837–March 3, 1841

Died: July 24, 1862

Vice President: Richard Johnson (D)

Martin Van Buren learned about politics from the politicians who stopped at his father's inn. The inn was on the way to Albany, the capital of New York. Van Buren began working in a law office when he was only 14 years of age. At age 21, he was already a lawyer. Van Buren served as a U.S. senator for New York. By 1829, he was governor of New York. Van Buren had helped Andrew Jackson win the presidency. In return, Jackson appointed him secretary of state, then vice president in 1833. Van Buren became president in 1837—the same year that the United States entered a major depression. Many people lost their jobs and turned to the government for help. Van Buren did not think the government should get involved. When he ran for his second term in 1840, he lost. He ran a third time in 1848 and lost again.

★ SHOW WHAT YOU KNOW

Complete the time line with either the date or the event.

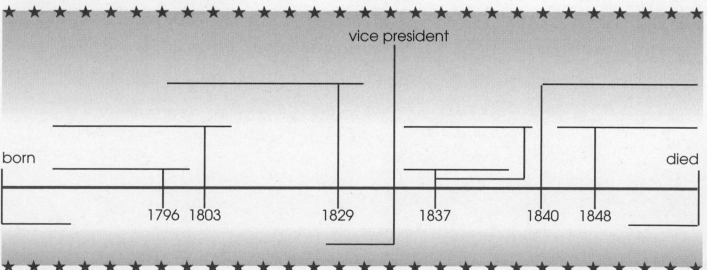

vice president

born

died

1796   1803   1829   1837   1840   1848

★ FIND OUT MORE

What was the name of Van Buren's political party the last time he ran for president? What did the party fight against? _____

© 2001 McGraw-Hill. All Rights Reserved.

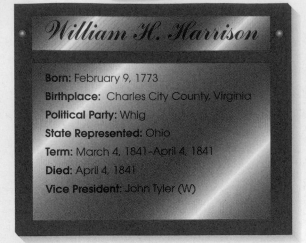

William H. Harrison

Born: February 9, 1773

Birthplace: Charles City County, Virginia

Political Party: Whig

State Represented: Ohio

Term: March 4, 1841–April 4, 1841

Died: April 4, 1841

Vice President: John Tyler (W)

The Morning News

PRESIDENT DIES AFTER ONLY 32 DAYS IN OFFICE

William H. Harrison helped shape our nation before his election as president. As a young man, Harrison became known as a fearless military leader. He studied medicine for a while but left college to fight in the Indian Wars. In time, he became governor of the territory of Indiana. Harrison took millions of acres of land from Native Americans by battle or by treaty. He was named "Old Tippecanoe" after defeating the Shawnee at the Battle of Tippecanoe. During the War of 1812, he recaptured Detroit from the British. Later, Harrison represented Ohio in the U.S. House of Representatives and the Senate. He ran for president in 1836 but lost. Harrison later succeeded when he became president of the United States in 1841. During the inauguration ceremony, Harrison gave a very long speech. The weather that day was cold and wet. Harrison talked so long that he caught pneumonia and died 32 days later.

★ SHOW WHAT YOU KNOW

Write F for false and T for true for the following statements.

_____ Harrison never went to college.

_____ Harrison was called "Old Tippecanoe" because of his military record.

_____ Harrison fought for the rights of Native Americans.

_____ Harrison was known for his wealth.

_____ Harrison ran for president twice.

_____ Harrison had the shortest term of any president.

★ FIND OUT MORE

When Harrison ran for president, why did he use the slogan "Tippecanoe and Tyler, Too"?

_____

_____

 © 2001 McGraw-Hill. All Rights Reserved.

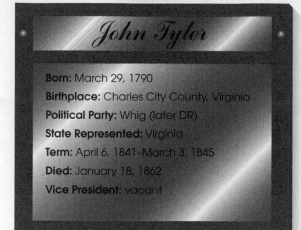

John Tyler

Born: March 29, 1790

Birthplace: Charles City County, Virginia

Political Party: Whig (later DR)

State Represented: Virginia

Term: April 6, 1841–March 3, 1845

Died: January 18, 1862

Vice President: vacant

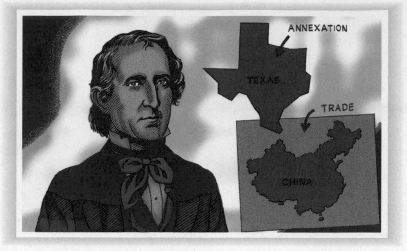

*J*ohn Tyler unexpectedly became president when William H. Harrison died after 1 month in office. Tyler showed that a vice president can smoothly take over when a president dies. Tyler then surprised his political party, the Whigs, by opposing them. Tyler supported states' rights, while the Whigs wanted a strong central government. He vetoed, or cancelled, the bills the Whigs sent him from Congress. The Whigs were so angry that they tried to impeach Tyler and remove him from office. They were not successful and Tyler continued as president. Tyler added Texas as a state. He also helped the United States begin selling and buying products with China and other countries in Asia. Tyler, who was from Virginia, always supported the southern states. In 1861, after his presidency and just before the Civil War, he was elected to the Confederate States Congress. He voted for Virginia to withdraw from the United States.

★ SHOW WHAT YOU KNOW

Answer the following questions. Write your answers on the lines.

Tyler belonged to the _____ political party.

Tyler _____ bills that the Whigs in Congress sent to him.

His own party tried to _____ him.

Tyler served as president for _____ term.

Tyler had been the vice president under President _____.

Tyler served as vice president for one _____.

Tyler favored the _____ states.

★ FIND OUT MORE

What political office did both Tyler and his father hold?

_____

© 2001 McGraw-Hill. All Rights Reserved.   The Presidents

James K. Polk

Born: November 2, 1795

Birthplace: Near Pineville, Mecklenburg County, North Carolina

Political Party: Democratic

State Represented: Tennessee

Term: March 4, 1845–March 3, 1849

Died: June 15, 1849

Vice President: George Dallas (D)

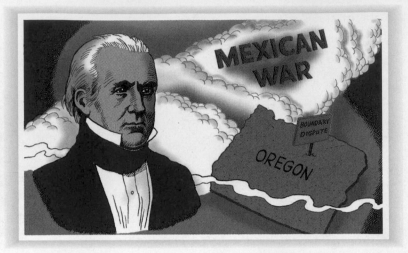

James K. Polk was one of our most important presidents. As a young man, Polk studied law. However, he soon decided that politics was more exciting. Polk was elected to many positions in the Tennessee government, including governor. In 1844, the Democrats had trouble choosing someone to run for president. They finally chose Polk, and he won the election. President Polk added a huge amount of land to our nation. Polk believed that the United States should stretch from the Atlantic Ocean to the Pacific Ocean. Mexico owned most of the land along the Pacific Ocean, so Polk tried to buy it. Mexico did not want to sell the land. Polk then went to war with Mexico to gain the California and the New Mexico Territories. However, Polk worked peacefully with Britain to gain the Oregon Territory. James Polk served only one term, just as he had promised voters.

★ SHOW WHAT YOU KNOW

Draw a line from each clue in Column A to the answer in Column B.

Column A	Column B
Polk's political party	Jackson
A friend whom Polk supported as president	California
The number of terms that Polk served	Oregon
The territory Polk obtained from Britain	one
The territory Polk won from Mexico	Democrats

★ FIND OUT MORE

Which congressman objected when Polk went to war against Mexico? Hint: This congressman would later become our president. _____

 36

© 2001 McGraw-Hill. All Rights Reserved.

Zachary Taylor

Born: November 24, 1784

Birthplace: Orange County, Virginia

Political Party: Whig

State Represented: Louisiana

Term: March 4, 1849–July 9, 1850

Died: July 9, 1850

Vice President: Millard Fillmore (W)

Zachary Taylor was a soldier for most of his life. He led U.S. troops to victory during the War of 1812 and the Mexican War and became known as "Old Rough and Ready." He was so popular that the Whigs asked him to run for president in 1848. Taylor was one of the first military leaders to become president of the United States without first holding a political office (although he was a cousin of James Madison's). Some people thought that this ex-military president was too eager to go to war. During this time, the nation was divided by the slavery issue. Taylor wanted to use the army to prevent any states from withdrawing from the United States. He was 64 years of age when he became president and served only 16 months. Taylor became sick during a ceremony for the Washington monument and died soon afterward.

★ SHOW WHAT YOU KNOW

Unscramble a word from the Word Bank to answer each question. Write the word on the line.

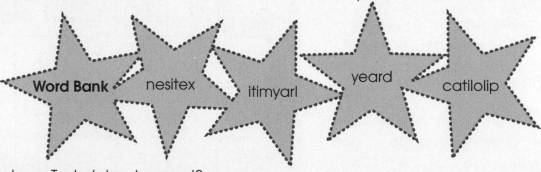

Word Bank   nesitex   itimyarl   yeard   catilolip

★ What was Taylor's background? _____

★ How many months was Taylor president? _____

★ Taylor's nickname was "Old Rough and _____."

★ Before he became president, Taylor had never held a _____ office.

★ FIND OUT MORE

What was happening in California while Taylor was president? _____

© 2001 McGraw-Hill. All Rights Reserved.   The Presidents

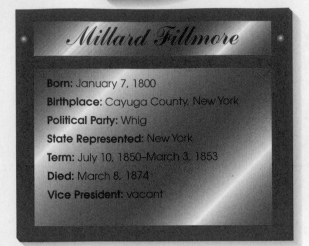

Millard Fillmore

Born: January 7, 1800

Birthplace: Cayuga County, New York

Political Party: Whig

State Represented: New York

Term: July 10, 1850–March 3, 1853

Died: March 8, 1874

Vice President: vacant

JAPAN

After Zachary Taylor died in office, Vice President Millard Fillmore took his place. By that time, slavery was dividing the nation. Taylor had added a large piece of land to the western United States. As president, Fillmore had to decide whether the new land would become slave states or free states. This decision was difficult as Fillmore was against slavery. However, he offered a compromise—part of the new land would be free, and part would allow slavery. Fillmore then approved a law that returned escaped slaves to their owners. Fillmore's party, the Whigs, were strongly against slavery and Fillmore's choice angered them. The Whigs did not support Fillmore for a second term in 1853. Instead, the Know-Nothings supported Fillmore's nomination for president in 1856. Fillmore lost the 1856 election. Yet he still tried to prevent the Civil War. He urged the northern and southern states to agree on a settlement. Sadly, his efforts were not successful.

★ SHOW WHAT YOU KNOW

The names of the two political parties that supported Millard Fillmore are hidden in this puzzle. Start at the arrow. Then, move in any direction to connect the letters that spell these two parties.

The letters in the first two words are connected for you. Write the names of the parties on the lines.

	T	N	O	H	I
E	H	W	O	T	N
S	K	N		G	A
E	A	P	I	D	N
I	T	R	G	H	W

_____

_____

★ FIND OUT MORE

What was the main goal of the Know-Nothings party?

_____

_____

The Presidents

38

© 2001 McGraw-Hill. All Rights Reserved.

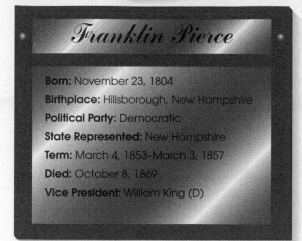

Franklin Pierce

Born: November 23, 1804

Birthplace: Hillsborough, New Hampshire

Political Party: Democratic

State Represented: New Hampshire

Term: March 4, 1853–March 3, 1857

Died: October 8, 1869

Vice President: William King (D)

Franklin Pierce became president 8 years before the Civil War began. His vice president, William King, died before their term even started. During his presidency, Pierce bought parts of Arizona and New Mexico from Mexico. He also tried to buy Cuba from Spain. Although Pierce was from the North, he sided with the South on slavery. Pierce tried not to anger the southern states. At the time, the southern states threatened to leave the Union. Pierce wanted to keep the Union together. He signed a bill that allowed voters in Kansas and Nebraska to decide whether to be free or slave states. Pierce's party, the Democrats, did not like his views on slavery. They did not support Pierce for a second term, and he returned to New Hampshire. Many people now consider Pierce to be a weak president, even though he was well meaning and honest.

★ SHOW WHAT YOU KNOW

Write F for false and T for true for the following statements.

_____ Pierce fought against slavery.

_____ Pierce did not want a Civil War.

_____ Pierce bought Cuba from Spain.

_____ People thought Pierce was well meaning and honest.

_____ Pierce was well thought of in his party, the Democrats.

_____ William King completed his term in office.

_____ Pierce served in the Mexican War.

★ FIND OUT MORE

While in office, Pierce voted against a bill to build the National Road. What is this road now called?

© 2001 McGraw-Hill. All Rights Reserved.

The Presidents

James Buchanan

Born: April 23, 1791

Birthplace: Cove Gap, Pennsylvania

Political Party: Democratic

State Represented: Pennsylvania

Term: March 4, 1857–March 3, 1861

Died: June 1, 1868

Vice President: John Breckinridge (D)

When James Buchanan became president, the country was ready for a civil war. Buchanan arrived in the United States after serving as a foreign minister in Russia, then Britain. Buchanan was the only candidate who was not caught up in the arguments between the North and the South. He appeared to provide a new point of view. However, in office, James Buchanan was known as a "lame duck" president. He is remembered most for leading the country into the Civil War. In the last few months of Buchanan's presidency, seven southern states had left the Union. Buchanan handed over the presidency to Abraham Lincoln. Lincoln became the president of a country ready to begin a war with itself. Nicknamed "Old Buck," Buchanan was also unlucky in love. He was once engaged to Ann Coleman, but the marriage never took place. Buchanan never married. After leaving office, Buchanan retired to his home named Wheatland.

★ SHOW WHAT YOU KNOW

Write the answers to each clue on the lines.

★ ★

Name of Buchanan's home __ __ __ __ __ __ __ __ __

Country where he was first a foreign minister __ __ __ __ __ __

Buchanan's nickname "__ __ __   __ __ __ __"

The country was ready for a __ __ __ __ __   __ __ __.

Buchanan handed the presidency over to __ __ __ __ __ __ __.

★ ★

★ FIND OUT MORE

Find out more about the term "lame duck."

_____

_____

 © 2001 McGraw-Hill. All Rights Reserved.

Abraham Lincoln

Born: February 12, 1809

Birthplace: Hardin County, Kentucky

Political Party: Republican

State Represented: Illinois

Term: March 4, 1861–April 15, 1865

Died: April 15, 1865

Vice President: (1) Hannibal Hamlin (R)
(2) Andrew Johnson (D)

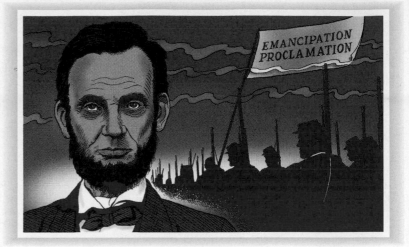

Abraham Lincoln is remembered as the greatest president of the United States. As a young man, Lincoln worked in many different jobs, including cutting wood and serving in the military. Even before he became president, Lincoln knew that the country must stay united to become a powerful nation. However, Lincoln's ideas were not shared and he was not a popular candidate. The South viewed Lincoln as an enemy who did not care about their issues. Despite these problems, Lincoln was elected president. Shortly after his inauguration in 1861, the Civil War began. Lincoln guided the country through the Civil War. His Gettysburg Address inspired the weary North to continue fighting for freedom. He also declared freedom for the slaves in the Emancipation Proclamation. Lincoln lived to see the end of the Civil War with General Robert E. Lee's surrender in 1865. However, Lincoln was assassinated 5 days later at a performance of *Our American Cousin* at Ford's Theatre in Washington, D.C.

★ SHOW WHAT YOU KNOW

Answer the following questions. Write your answers on the lines.

What are two jobs Lincoln held as a young man? _____

Why was the Gettysburg Address important? _____

_____

When did the Civil War begin? _____

What is a famous statement of Lincoln's? What was it about? _____

_____

_____

Who surrendered and ended the Civil War? _____

★ FIND OUT MORE

How did people communicate with each other over long distances during Lincoln's time as president?

_____

© 2001 McGraw-Hill. All Rights Reserved. The Presidents

Andrew Johnson

Born: December 29, 1808

Birthplace: Raleigh, North Carolina

Political Party: Democratic

State Represented: Tennessee

Term: April 15, 1865–March 3, 1869

Died: July 31, 1875

Vice President: vacant

JOHNSON ESCAPES CONVICTION IN IMPEACHMENT TRIAL

Andrew Johnson was born to a poor family in Raleigh, North Carolina in 1808. Johnson did not have a formal education. Instead, he became an apprentice tailor. His wife, Eliza, later taught him to read and write. As a young man, Johnson became interested in politics. Johnson supported the States' Rights position and believed that government should not interfere in people's private lives. His pro-South views helped balance Abraham Lincoln's pro-North views, and Johnson became Lincoln's vice president. After Lincoln's assassination in 1865, Johnson became president. He had a difficult time as president. Johnson struggled with Congress and fought against new laws that would protect the rights of ex-slaves. Johnson was later tried by Congress for "high crimes and misdemeanors," and was impeached. The Senate found him not guilty by only one vote. His main accomplishment was the purchase of Alaska, known as "Seward's Folly." Johnson returned to politics in 1874 to serve in the Senate.

★ SHOW WHAT YOU KNOW

Write F for false and T for true for the following statements.

_____ Johnson was impeached and convicted by one vote.

_____ Johnson was an apprentice tailor.

_____ Eliza taught Johnson to write.

_____ The purchase of Alaska was called "Seward's Folly."

_____ Johnson felt that the government should not interfere with people's private lives.

_____ Johnson served as president before Lincoln.

_____ Lincoln was Johnson's vice president.

_____ Secretary of State Stanton was fired by Johnson.

★ FIND OUT MORE

Why was Alaska's purchase called "Seward's Folly"? _____

_____

_____

© 2001 McGraw-Hill. All Rights Reserved.

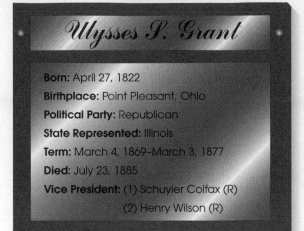

Ulysses S. Grant

Born: April 27, 1822

Birthplace: Point Pleasant, Ohio

Political Party: Republican

State Represented: Illinois

Term: March 4, 1869–March 3, 1877

Died: July 23, 1885

Vice President: (1) Schuyler Colfax (R)

(2) Henry Wilson (R)

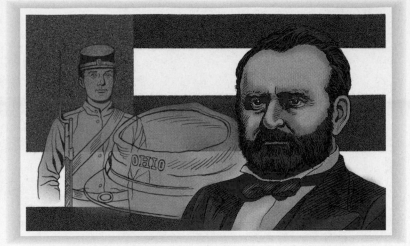

Born Hiram Ulysses Grant, an error in his enrollment at West Point listed his name as Ulysses Simpson Grant. Grant liked the new name and he kept it. As a young man, Ulysses S. Grant thrived during his service in the Mexican War. After the war, Grant struggled to make a living, taking jobs as a farmer, real estate salesman and finally a clerk in his father's leathergoods store in Galena, Illinois. The Civil War brought a new opportunity for Grant, and he impressed President Lincoln with his courage and leadership. Grant was promoted to general in chief of all the federal armies. On April 9, 1865, General Robert E. Lee surrendered the Confederacy to Grant at the town called Appomattox Court House. Grant became known as the "Hero of Appomattox." After the Civil War, Grant served briefly as secretary of war. Grant's Civil War fame made him a popular choice for president. Off the battlefield, however, Grant was not the greatest leader. His presidency was known for corruption and scandal.

★ SHOW WHAT YOU KNOW

Write the answer to each clue on the lines below.

Grant's nickname _____

Grant fought in this war before the Civil War _____

Grant went to this college _____

Grant worked as a clerk in this town _____

Grant's administration had corruption and _____ .

★ FIND OUT MORE

What major event involving transportation happened during Grant's first year as president?

_____

© 2001 McGraw-Hill. All Rights Reserved.

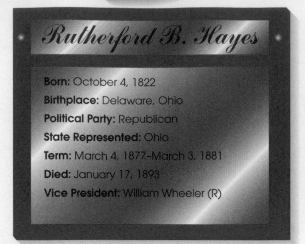

Rutherford B. Hayes

Born: October 4, 1822

Birthplace: Delaware, Ohio

Political Party: Republican

State Represented: Ohio

Term: March 4, 1877–March 3, 1881

Died: January 17, 1893

Vice President: William Wheeler (R)

Rutherford B. Hayes set serious goals for himself when he was young. One of his goals was to "…acquire a character distinguished for energy (and) firmness…." He even once decided to stop laughing so he could be more serious. He did not stop laughing, but he did grow up to be a serious president who fought for voting rights for African-Americans and against fraud in government. Hayes was a "dark horse" nominee at the Republican Convention of 1876. No one expected him to be the candidate that year, but he was the only one acceptable to everyone. The election itself was very close—many people thought Samuel Tilden, his opponent, received more votes. In the end, Congress decided for Hayes. His most important accomplishment was ending Reconstruction— the period after the Civil War during which the southern states were reorganized and made part of the Union once again.

★ SHOW WHAT YOU KNOW

The motto by which Hayes lived is hidden in the puzzle to the right. Start in the box where the arrow is pointing. Move from left to right without jumping a letter. Write his motto on the lines below.

_____

_____

_____

H	E	S	E	R	V	E	S
H	I	S	P	A	R	T	Y	B
E	S	T	W	H	O	S	E	R
V	E	S	H	I	S	C	O	U
N	T	R	Y	B	E	S	T

★ FIND OUT MORE

Explain the term "dark horse."

_____

_____

© 2001 McGraw-Hill. All Rights Reserved.

James A. Garfield

Born: November 19, 1831

Birthplace: Orange, Ohio

Political Party: Republican

State Represented: Ohio

Term: March 4, 1881–September 19, 1881

Died: September 19, 1881

Vice President: Chester A. Arthur (R)

James A. Garfield was the last president to be born in a log cabin. Despite growing up in a poor family, Garfield received an excellent education. He graduated from Williams College in 1856, then became principal of Hiram College. After 4 years at Hiram, Garfield said, "Teaching is not the work in which a man can live and grow." Garfield joined the Army and served bravely in the Civil War battles at Shiloh and Chickamauga. After the war, Garfield served nine terms in Congress. While running for president, Garfield was nicknamed a "dark horse" candidate. Once in office, bribery and political favors blackened Garfield's one year as president. On July 2, 1881, Garfield was shot by Charles J. Guiteau, a disappointed office seeker who had not been appointed to Garfield's cabinet. A bullet remained in Garfield's body, and he lived in great pain for 11 weeks before dying in Elberon, New Jersey.

★ SHOW WHAT YOU KNOW

Write F for false and T for true for the following statements.

_____ Garfield was born in a hospital.

_____ Garfield served nine terms in Congress.

_____ Garfield's reputation was blackened by bribes.

_____ Garfield did not serve in the Civil War.

_____ Garfield graduated from college.

_____ Garfield was from Ohio.

_____ Garfield died during his second term.

★ FIND OUT MORE

What might doctors use today to help find a bullet lodged in a person's body?

© 2001 McGraw-Hill. All Rights Reserved.

The Presidents

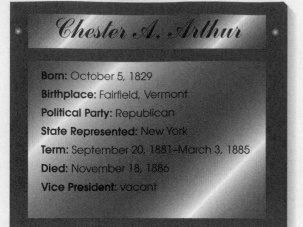

Chester A. Arthur

Born: October 5, 1829

Birthplace: Fairfield, Vermont

Political Party: Republican

State Represented: New York

Term: September 20, 1881–March 3, 1885

Died: November 18, 1886

Vice President: vacant

CIVIL SERVICE ACT

POLITICAL APPOINTMENTS

Chester A. Arthur was a Civil War veteran and a defender of civil rights for slaves. He became president at a time when the public had lost respect for the office. Scandal and the "spoils system" had blackened the presidency of Garfield. The American public expected Arthur to follow Garfield's example and choose friends and political supporters for his cabinet members. As a Union College graduate and the son of a clergyman, Arthur brought values back to the presidency. Arthur acted honestly during his term as president. He passed the Pendleton Act, which helped to eliminate the corruption of political favors. Arthur was a private man who believed that the president's private life should be kept from the public. When his wife died, his sister took over the duties of the first lady. Arthur's main accomplishment was the modernization of the navy. He did not win the Republican Party's nomination for re-election in 1884.

★ SHOW WHAT YOU KNOW

Circle the hidden words in the puzzle using the clues below. Write the answers on the lines.

Name of act passed _____

Wife's name _____

College name _____

Person who took over first lady's duties _____

Branch of the armed service he modernized _____

O	G	A	C	I	H	C	N	N
G	O	N	T	H	R	E	E	O
Y	T	R	H	A	U	N	D	T
E	L	L	E	N	A	V	Y	E
N	A	Y	I	T	H	E	D	L
D	S	O	S	H	S	T	I	D
I	N	E	Y	A	V	I	K	N
K	C	O	C	N	A	H	S	E
E	V	I	T	I	G	U	F	P

★ FIND OUT MORE

How did Arthur modernize the navy? What does modernized mean?

_____

_____

 © 2001 McGraw-Hill. All Rights Reserved.

Grover Cleveland

Born: March 18, 1837

Birthplace: Caldwell, New Jersey

Political Party: Democratic

State Represented: New York

Terms: March 4, 1885–March 3, 1889
March 4, 1893–March 3, 1897

Died: June 24, 1908

Vice President: (1) Thomas Hendricks (D)
(2) Adlai Stevenson (D)

Grover Cleveland dropped out of school when he was 16 years of age to care for his mother and sisters after the death of his father. As a young man, Cleveland worked as a lawyer. He started his career in politics as mayor of Buffalo, NY, and later as governor of New York. Cleveland was known as the "Veto Mayor" and fought corruption throughout his career. Cleveland lost his re-election campaign for president in 1888 to Benjamin Harrison. Four years later, Cleveland ran for president again. This time the public welcomed Cleveland's ideas. Cleveland reversed the Sherman Silver Purchase Act and helped protect the value of gold currency. Cleveland did not support the expansion of the United States into Hawaii and Cuba. The Democratic Party was pro-expansion and Cleveland lost the nomination for a third term. He retired to Princeton, New Jersey, where he practiced law and served on Princeton University's Board of Trustees.

★ SHOW WHAT YOU KNOW

Write F for false and T for true for the following statements.

_____ Cleveland served two terms in a row as president.

_____ He helped protect the value of gold currency.

_____ Benjamin Harrison defeated him in 1888.

_____ He paid a soldier to fight in the Civil War for him.

_____ He was known as the "Veto Mayor."

_____ He encouraged corruption.

_____ He retired to Princeton, New Jersey.

★ FIND OUT MORE

What did France give the United States during Cleveland's first term?

© 2001 McGraw-Hill. All Rights Reserved.

Benjamin Harrison

Born: August 20, 1833

Birthplace: North Bend, Ohio

Political Party: Republican

State Represented: Indiana

Term: March 4, 1889–March 3, 1893

Died: March 13, 1901

Vice President: Levi P. Morton (R)

Benjamin Harrison was the son of a patriotic family. His grandfather was William H. Harrison, the ninth president of the United States. Harrison was a successful lawyer from Ohio who earned the position of general in the Civil War. His soldiers nicknamed him "Little Ben." "Grandfather's Hat Fits Ben" was a popular slogan for Harrison's presidential campaign. As president, Harrison built a stronger Navy and strengthened trade policies overseas. Harrison also pushed for western statehood. The states of Montana, Idaho, Washington, North and South Dakota and Wyoming were admitted to the Union during his term as president. Harrison tried to acquire Hawaii, but the Senate did not sign the treaty before his term ended. When President Cleveland returned for his second term, Cleveland withdrew the Hawaiian proposal from the Senate. Hawaii eventually entered the Union in 1959.

★ SHOW WHAT YOU KNOW

Find the letters that spell the names of the states that joined the Union during Harrison's term. Cross them out as you write the names on the lines below.

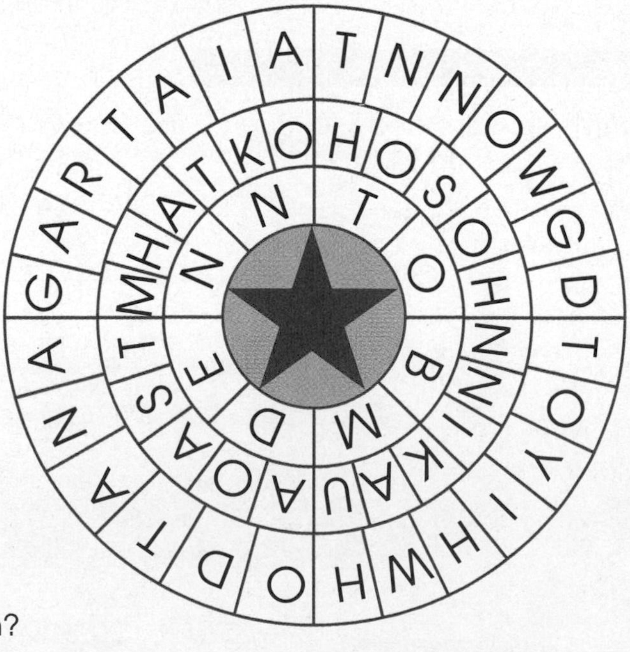

_____   _____

_____   _____

_____   _____

Use the remaining letters to complete Harrison's slogan below.

★ FIND OUT MORE

Why did Harrison use the slogan "Grandfather's _____ Fits _____" during his campaign?

_____

_____

_____

© 2001 McGraw-Hill. All Rights Reserved.

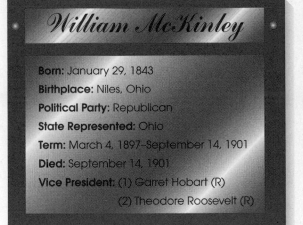

William McKinley

Born: January 29, 1843

Birthplace: Niles, Ohio

Political Party: Republican

State Represented: Ohio

Term: March 4, 1897–September 14, 1901

Died: September 14, 1901

Vice President: (1) Garret Hobart (R)

(2) Theodore Roosevelt (R)

William McKinley was a popular president, nicknamed the "Idol of Ohio." As a young man, he served in the Civil War, then studied law. McKinley led the country into his second term with the campaign slogan, the "Full Dinner Pail." He advertised the fact that the country enjoyed a good economy under his leadership. McKinley was also a devoted husband. His wife, Ida, suffered from epilepsy and needed special attention. As president, McKinley guided the country through the Spanish-American War. McKinley used the war slogan, "Remember the Maine" to encourage the public to support the war. The war lasted 100 days. As a result of the war, Cuba gained its independence from Spain. McKinley's other accomplishments were the signing of the Treaty of Paris and the Gold Standard Act. He also signed a bill to annex Hawaii. McKinley was assassinated in September 1901 by a man who wanted to get rid of all leaders.

★ SHOW WHAT YOU KNOW

Write the answer to each clue. Unscramble the circled letters on the lines below to state McKinley's campaign slogan.

The Spanish-American War slogan

Ida McKinley suffered from this disease

The country that gained its independence from Spain

This man lost to McKinley twice

McKinley promised that a dinner pail would be like this

McKinley's campaign slogan: __ __ __ __   D __ __ __ __ __ __ __   __ __ __ __

★ FIND OUT MORE

Why did McKinley use the slogan "Remember the Maine"? What was "the Maine"? _____

_____

_____

© 2001 McGraw-Hill. All Rights Reserved.

The Presidents

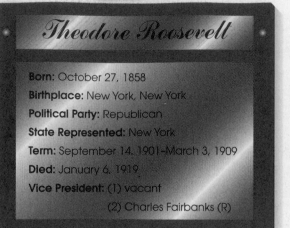

Theodore Roosevelt

Born: October 27, 1858

Birthplace: New York, New York

Political Party: Republican

State Represented: New York

Term: September 14, 1901–March 3, 1909

Died: January 6, 1919

Vice President: (1) vacant

(2) Charles Fairbanks (R)

Theodore "Teddy" Roosevelt was an adventurer and a hunter. Once, while hunting with some friends, he came across a bear cub. Roosevelt did not kill the cub because it looked so cute. A toy maker heard about the bear cub and made a stuffed bear, calling it "Teddy's Bear," in honor of Roosevelt's kindness. Roosevelt allowed the toy maker to use his name. The "teddy bear" was born. Teddy Roosevelt became governor of New York in 1898. Roosevelt became president in 1901, after the assassination of William McKinley. He was awarded a Nobel Peace Prize for helping to bring peace between Japan and Russia. Roosevelt wanted the world to know that the United States was a world power. His motto was "Speak softly and carry a big stick." This meant that the U.S. should be friendly with other countries but should also be ready to use force when needed. He sent the Great White Fleet on a tour to demonstrate the strength of the U.S. Navy. He and his son toured South America in 1914 where Roosevelt caught a type of jungle fever. He died in 1919.

★ SHOW WHAT YOU KNOW

Write the answer to each clue in the boxes below. Then, use the red boxes to finish Roosevelt's famous motto.

1 The peace prize Roosevelt won

2 U.S. Navy ships that made a tour

3 A fever he caught in South America

4 Roosevelt's motto told how he worked with other

5 This toy is named after him

6 He helped bring peace to Japan and this country

7 He refused to kill this animal

8 The president before Roosevelt

"Speak softly and carry a _____   _____."

★ FIND OUT MORE

Roosevelt created the Progressive Party. What did it stand for? _____

_____

_____

© 2001 McGraw-Hill. All Rights Reserved.

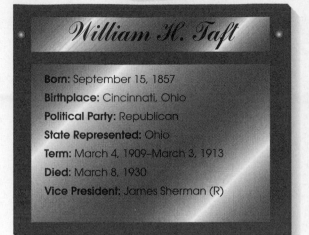

William H. Taft

Born: September 15, 1857

Birthplace: Cincinnati, Ohio

Political Party: Republican

State Represented: Ohio

Term: March 4, 1909–March 3, 1913

Died: March 8, 1930

Vice President: James Sherman (R)

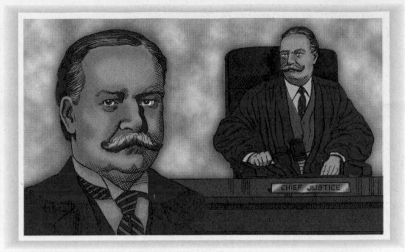

William H. Taft was known to his family as "Willie." Before becoming president, Taft held many legal and political positions. One position was governor of the Philippines. This fun-loving president began the presidential tradition of throwing out the first ball of the baseball season each spring. Sadly, Taft found his time at the White House disappointing and "lonesome"—the slump began with a blizzard on his inauguration day. Taft had a difficult time following in the footsteps of Teddy Roosevelt. While in office, Taft helped to create the Sixteenth Amendment to the Constitution. This would later establish an income tax. However, Taft's administration was filled with controversy and turmoil. His Republican Party split while he was president. In 1912, Theodore Roosevelt challenged Taft for the Republican nomination. The result was a party split that weakened the Republicans and gave the presidency to Woodrow Wilson. Later in life, Taft was appointed chief justice by President Harding.

★ SHOW WHAT YOU KNOW

Complete the crossword puzzle.

Across

3 The thing he threw each spring

4 President who made Taft chief justice

6 He thought the White House was like this

Down

1 Where he was governor

2 Weather at his inauguration

5 The tax he helped create

★ FIND OUT MORE

Where is the Philippines? When was Taft governor? _____

_____

_____

© 2001 McGraw-Hill. All Rights Reserved.

The Presidents

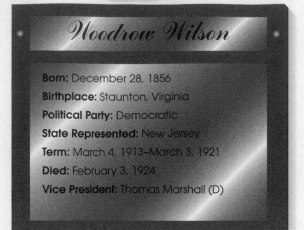

Woodrow Wilson

Born: December 28, 1856

Birthplace: Staunton, Virginia

Political Party: Democratic

State Represented: New Jersey

Term: March 4, 1913–March 3, 1921

Died: February 3, 1924

Vice President: Thomas Marshall (D)

Woodrow Wilson's childhood was shaped by the Civil War. As a young man, he studied law and practiced in Georgia. As president, Wilson reduced tariffs and created an income tax. Wilson also passed laws to improve the working conditions of sailors and limit the number of hours that children could work. In 1916, the United States was on the verge of war with Mexico. Soon after, the United States was in another foreign war—the Germans had ambushed and sunk the *Lusitania*. The United States entered World War I when Wilson declared war on Germany. Wilson stated that "the world must be made safe for democracy." He presented his famous "14 Points" that explained the United States' war goals. After the war, the League of Nations became Wilson's main interest. Wilson was awarded the Nobel Peace Prize in 1919. He had a stroke while on a speaking tour to promote the League of Nations. He is buried at the Washington National Cathedral.

★ SHOW WHAT YOU KNOW

Answer the questions. Write your answers on the lines.

★ ★

Whose work conditions did Wilson improve? _____

Which war was fought when Wilson was a child? _____

Wilson almost declared war on which country in 1916? _____

What was the name of Wilson's war goals? _____

Which war was fought during his presidential term? _____

What organization was Wilson promoting when he had a stroke? _____

Where is he buried? _____

★ ★

★ FIND OUT MORE

What was the *Lusitania* and what happened to it? _____

_____

 © 2001 McGraw-Hill. All Rights Reserved.

Warren G. Harding

Born: November 2, 1865

Birthplace: Blooming Grove, Ohio

Political Party: Republican

State Represented: Ohio

Term: March 4, 1921–August 2, 1923

Died: August 2, 1923

Vice President: Calvin Coolidge (D)

Warren G. Harding began his working career at the newspaper, the *Marion Daily Star* in Marion, Ohio. Later, Harding became the director of many local Ohio businesses and joined many clubs. Harding participated in Republican Party campaigns and made many political friends. In 1920, the Republicans nominated Harding to be their candidate. When Harding was elected president in 1921, he appointed many of his friends from Ohio. They were called the "Ohio Gang." In office, Harding worked hard to make a budget system for the federal government and to reduce the number of immigrants to the United States. Unfortunately, the Ohio Gang blackened the Harding presidency. Some of these men were dishonest and there were many scandals. In the "Teapot Dome Scandal," federal oil reserves were illegally rented to private businesses. President Harding was not involved, but he was criticized for putting his friends in office. Harding died in the second year of his term.

★ SHOW WHAT YOU KNOW

Complete each sentence. Write your answers on the lines.

★ ★

In the _____ Scandal, federal oil reserves were illegally leased to private businesses.

Harding started out by working on a _____.

Harding's political work mates were called the _____.

Harding tried to reduce the number of _____ entering the United States.

The 1920 election was the first general election where _____ could vote.

The election results were broadcast on _____.

★ ★

★ FIND OUT MORE

Harding was elected after what "great" war? _____

© 2001 McGraw-Hill. All Rights Reserved.

The Presidents

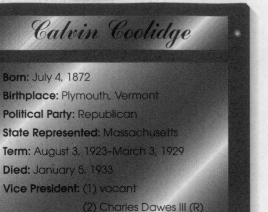

Calvin Coolidge

Born: July 4, 1872

Birthplace: Plymouth, Vermont

Political Party: Republican

State Represented: Massachusetts

Term: August 3, 1923–March 3, 1929

Died: January 5, 1933

Vice President: (1) vacant

(2) Charles Dawes III (R)

Calvin Coolidge had experienced tragedy early in his life. Calvin's mother died when he was 12 years old. As a young man, Coolidge attended Amherst College. He graduated and became a lawyer in Massachusetts in 1897. Coolidge was involved in politics when he married Grace Goodhue in 1905. Coolidge was elected governor of Massachusetts in 1918 and stopped a police strike the following year. This earned him national attention. Coolidge was nominated for vice president and became president after Harding's death. Coolidge successfully dealt with the scandals left behind by President Harding. He restored honesty to the government. Coolidge believed that government should not interfere with private business. He vetoed bills for farm relief and a bonus for World War I veterans. He also believed that America should not get involved with other nations. Coolidge chose not to run for another term in 1928. He died in 1933.

★ SHOW WHAT YOU KNOW

Complete the time line with either the date or the event.

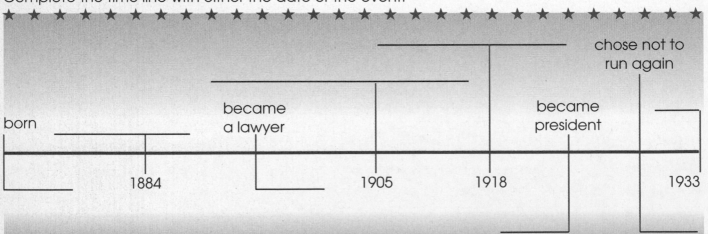

chose not to run again

born

became a lawyer

became president

1884   1905   1918   1933

★ FIND OUT MORE

The first winter Olympics were held during Coolidge's term as president. Where and when were they held? Did the United States attend? _____

_____

© 2001 McGraw-Hill. All Rights Reserved.

Herbert C. Hoover

Born: August 10, 1874

Birthplace: West Branch, Iowa

Political Party: Republican

State Represented: California

Term: March 4, 1929–March 3, 1933

Died: October 20, 1964

Vice President: Charles Curtis (R)

Herbert C. Hoover was an orphan before he was 9 years old. Then, he was raised by several relatives. Hoover attended Stanford University and graduated as a mining engineer. After college, Hoover was known for his work as the head of the Allied Relief Program in Europe during World War I. Hoover then joined the political world and served under Presidents Wilson, Harding and Coolidge. In 1921, Hoover became secretary of commerce. In office, he worked to improve the standards of radio broadcasting, aviation, housing and highway safety. Hoover was elected president in 1929. Soon after his election, the stock market crashed. This caused the Great Depression. Many people lost their jobs. Some people became homeless. President Hoover felt that the government should not help the public. Instead, he believed that charities should help the poor. Under Hoover's leadership, the Depression got worse. Hoover lost the 1932 election by a landslide vote.

★ SHOW WHAT YOU KNOW

Answer the following questions, then circle the answers in the word search.

Where Hoover went to college

_____

Hoover's wife's name (2 words)

_____

The crash of the stock market caused this
The Great _____

Hoover was this by the age of nine

_____

Hoover felt that these groups should help
the poor _____

```
D C H A R I T I E S D
I A M L B O N T L H I
L U K O R P H A N T V
N D A U B M E O C U I
Y F G H E R S P B D S
E J H E K F S C I O I
S T A N F O R D D E O
D E P R E S S I O N M
A Q R Y I G J L P R S
```

★ FIND OUT MORE

What famous dam is named after President Hoover? Where is this dam located? _____

_____

© 2001 McGraw-Hill. All Rights Reserved. The Presidents

Franklin D. Roosevelt

Born: January 30, 1882

Birthplace: Hyde Park, New York

Political Party: Democratic

State Represented: New York

Term: March 4, 1933–April 12, 1945

Died: April 12, 1945

Vice President:

(1) John Garner (D)   (3) Henry Wallace (D)

(2) John Garner (D)   (4) Harry Truman (D)

Franklin D. Roosevelt, or "FDR," was president during hard times. He was elected for four terms and became our longest serving president. In 1933, when Roosevelt first became president, the United States was suffering under the Great Depression. Many banks had failed, industries produced less than half of their normal production and more than 13 million people were out of work. FDR was determined to make things better. Roosevelt introduced a program called the "New Deal." It created work, built roads and provided electricity to rural areas. As time went on, the United States became involved in another great struggle—World War II. In 1941, the United States entered World War II and helped fight the Axis powers of Japan, Germany and Italy. Roosevelt led the United States during most of World War II. Roosevelt died while still in office in 1945.

★ SHOW WHAT YOU KNOW

A famous saying of FDR's is hidden in the puzzle. Start with the first box. Move from left to right. Write down every other letter. Then, start at the end and go backwards to the beginning. Write his saying on the lines below.

T	F	H	L	E	E	O	S	N	T
L	I	Y	R	T	A	H	E		
I	F	N	S	G	I	W	R		
E	A	H	E	A	F	V	O	E	T

_____ _____ _____ _____ _____

_____ _____ _____ _____ _____ _____ .

★ FIND OUT MORE

Which twentieth-century president was Franklin D. Roosevelt's cousin? When was he president?

 © 2001 McGraw-Hill. All Rights Reserved.

Harry S. Truman

Born: May 8, 1884

Birthplace: Lamar, Missouri

Political Party: Democratic

State Represented: Missouri

Term: April 12, 1945–January 20, 1953

Died: December 26, 1972

Vice President: (1) vacant

(2) Alben Barkley (D)

*H*arry S. Truman was vice president when Franklin D. Roosevelt died. Truman had been vice president for only 82 days when he became president. Truman quickly adopted FDR's programs, renaming them the "Fair Deal." This son of a mule trader and farmer also carried out Roosevelt's plans to establish the United Nations. However, Truman became a great leader in his own right. He helped arrange Germany's surrender in 1945. And in September of 1945, Truman used the atomic bomb on the Japanese cities of Hiroshima and Nagasaki to end World War II. After the war, he worked for equal rights for all people in the United States. Truman did not run again after he finished his second term in 1953. Truman's hard work and honesty made him one of our strongest presidents.

★ SHOW WHAT YOU KNOW

Match the Items In each column. Write the correct letter on the line.

_____ The president before Truman   **a** World War II

_____ Truman was president at the end of this war   **b** FDR

_____ Truman's decision to use this weapon ended World War II   **c** equal rights

_____ An important ideal Truman worked for   **d** atomic bomb

★ FIND OUT MORE

What are the goals of the United Nations today? _____

_____

_____

© 2001 McGraw-Hill. All Rights Reserved. The Presidents

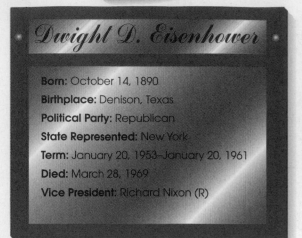

Dwight D. Eisenhower

Born: October 14, 1890

Birthplace: Denison, Texas

Political Party: Republican

State Represented: New York

Term: January 20, 1953–January 20, 1961

Died: March 28, 1969

Vice President: Richard Nixon (R)

$\mathcal{A}$s a young man, Dwight D. Eisenhower excelled in sports. Everyone called him "Ike." After high school, he attended the Military Academy at West Point. He fought in World War I and became a hero for helping to win World War II. When he ran for president in 1952, he used the slogan, "I like Ike." He won by more votes than anyone before him. As a soldier, he had fought to win a war. As president, he fought to keep the peace. In 1953, Eisenhower ended the Korean War. During Ike's term, Khrushchev, the leader of the Soviet Union, began to threaten world peace. This was the beginning of the Cold War, a time when countries fought with each other without firing shots or using deadly weapons. Ike had problems at home, too. Schools were being racially integrated, some for the first time. This meant that children of different races went to school together. Integration tried to promote unity. After his second term, Eisenhower retired to his farm in Pennsylvania.

★ SHOW WHAT YOU KNOW

Write the answer to each clue in the boxes. The circled letters spell out Eisenhower's first presidential slogan.

1 College Eisenhower attended

2 Eisenhower fought in this war

3 Wife's first name

4 Name of Soviet leader

5 Policy that tried to promote unity between people

6 Eisenhower ended America's conflict with this country

Eisenhower's first presidential slogan: "___   __ __ __ __   __ __ __."

★ FIND OUT MORE

The "Space Race" was part of the Cold War with the Soviet Union. Find two interesting facts about our race into space with the Soviet Union. _____

_____

© 2001 McGraw-Hill. All Rights Reserved.

John F. Kennedy

Born: May 29, 1917

Birthplace: Brookline, Massachusetts

Political Party: Democratic

State Represented: Massachusetts

Term: January 20, 1961–November 22, 1963

Died: November 22, 1963

Vice President: Lyndon Johnson (D)

John F. Kennedy came from a well-known, Irish-American family. After college, he joined the Navy and fought in World War II. Later, Kennedy served three terms in Congress before being elected to the Senate. While running for president, Kennedy joined Richard Nixon in a series of four debates on television. Kennedy's charm helped him win. As president, Kennedy dealt with many problems with other countries. For example, when the Soviets sent nuclear missiles to Cuba, Kennedy forced Khrushchev, the Soviet leader, to remove them. Kennedy did not enjoy his success for long. On November 22, 1963, he was assassinated in Dallas, Texas. Kennedy is best remembered for starting the Peace Corps and inspiring Americans to work hard for their country.

⭐ SHOW WHAT YOU KNOW

Match the letters to the numbers to find out what President Kennedy said in his inaugural speech.

A	B	C	D	E	F	G	H	I	J	K	L	M	N	O	P	Q	R	S	T	U	V	W	X	Y	Z
1	2	3	4	5	6	7	8	9	10	11	12	13	14	15	16	17	18	19	20	21	22	23	24	25	26

"Ask not what your country can do for you.

$\overline{1}\ \overline{19}\ \overline{11}\quad \overline{23}\ \overline{8}\ \overline{1}\ \overline{20}\quad \overline{25}\ \overline{15}\ \overline{21}\quad \overline{3}\ \overline{1}\ \overline{14}\quad \overline{4}\ \overline{15}$

$\overline{6}\ \overline{15}\ \overline{18}\quad \overline{25}\ \overline{15}\ \overline{21}\ \overline{18}\quad \overline{3}\ \overline{15}\ \overline{21}\ \overline{14}\ \overline{20}\ \overline{18}\ \overline{25}$."

⭐ FIND OUT MORE

Which of President Kennedy's brothers was elected to the Senate in 1962 and still holds that seat today?

_____

© 2001 McGraw-Hill. All Rights Reserved.

The Presidents

Lyndon B. Johnson

Born: August 27, 1908

Birthplace: Stonewall, Texas

Political Party: Democratic

State Represented: Texas

Term: November 22, 1963–January 20, 1969

Died: January 22, 1973

Vice President: (1) vacant

(2) Hubert Humphrey (D)

Lyndon B. Johnson grew up in a three-room house in southwest Texas. As a young man, Johnson became interested in politics and went to work in Washington, D.C. Later, Johnson served as a member of both the House of Representatives and in the Senate for a total of 24 years. President Kennedy chose Johnson to be his running mate, and he became vice president in 1961. Two years into his term as vice president, Johnson was sworn into office aboard the presidential jet, *Air Force One*, after Kennedy's assassination. Johnson tried to calm the nation after Kennedy's death. He passed Kennedy's bills on civil rights, poverty and conservation. Johnson then created a program called the "Great Society." The Great Society promoted equal rights for all, helped African-Americans with their right to vote and provided health insurance for the elderly. However, because of the turmoil of the Vietnam War, Johnson decided not to run for re-election in 1968. He retired to his ranch in Texas.

★ SHOW WHAT YOU KNOW

Complete each sentence. Write your answers on the lines.

★ ★

Johnson's program was called the _____.

He worked in _____ before becoming a member of the House of Representatives.

Johnson was Kennedy's _____.

Johnson helped get _____ rights for all.

The _____ War put the country in turmoil.

★ ★

★ FIND OUT MORE

Robert Weaver became the first African-American to join a president's cabinet. What position did he hold? _____

_____

© 2001 McGraw-Hill. All Rights Reserved.

Richard M. Nixon

Born: January 9, 1913

Birthplace: Yorba Linda, California

Political Party: Republican

State Represented: California

Term: January 20, 1969–August 9, 1974

Died: April 22, 1994

Vice President: (1, 2) Spiro Agnew (R)

(2) Gerald Ford (R)

Richard M. Nixon began his political career soon after graduating from law school. In 1942, Nixon joined the Navy and fought in World War II. After the war, Nixon was a member of both the House and the Senate. Eisenhower asked Nixon to run as his vice president in 1952 and he served two terms with Eisenhower. Nixon was elected president in 1968. The Vietnam War was raging. Nixon began bringing United States troops home from Vietnam. In his second term, the war ended with the victory of North Vietnam. Later, Nixon rebuilt ties with China after 21 years of silence between the two countries. Despite his successes, scandal ruined Nixon. In 1973, the *Washington Post*, a newspaper, investigated the illegal activities of Nixon and his aides during the 1972 election campaign. In 1974, faced with almost certain impeachment, Nixon resigned. He left Washington, D.C. in disgrace and retired to his estate in San Clemente, California.

★ SHOW WHAT YOU KNOW

Write the answers to each clue. Unscramble the letters in the circles to write the name of the scandal during Nixon's term on the lines below.

1 Nixon joined the Navy to fight in this war

2 Nixon served two of these as vice president

3 Nixon did this in 1974

4 Nixon rebuilt ties with this nation

5 Nixon retired to this city

The scandal that caused Nixon to resign is known as ___ ___ ___ ___ ___ ___ ___ ___ ___ ___.

★ FIND OUT MORE

Who was president when Richard Nixon was born? How long was his term in office?

© 2001 McGraw-Hill. All Rights Reserved.

The Presidents

Gerald Ford

Born: July 14, 1913

Birthplace: Omaha, Nebraska

Political Party: Republican

State Represented: Michigan

Term: August 9, 1974–January 20, 1977

Died:

Vice President: Nelson Rockefeller (R)

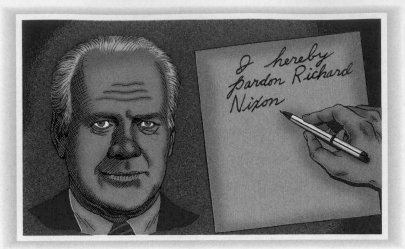

Young Gerald Ford was a good student. He studied hard and played football in high school and college. Ford then earned his law degree and joined the Navy during World War II. After the war, he ran for a seat in Congress and won. In 1973, after the resignation of Vice President Spiro T. Agnew, President Nixon asked Ford to be the new vice president. Ford became president in 1974 when Nixon resigned. Ford was the first vice president and president to take office without having been elected. As president, Ford gave Nixon a pardon "for all offenses against the United States." This act made him unpopular with many people. Ford, who was a Republican, had many differences with the Democrat-controlled Congress. He vetoed over 50 bills. Despite Ford's friendly manner and strong efforts to pull the nation together, he lost his bid for a second term in 1976.

★ SHOW WHAT YOU KNOW

Write the answer to each clue. The circled letters spell two important words.

1 Gerald Ford was this kind of student

2 After college, he earned his law

3 He joined this branch of the armed forces

4 Ford became vice president even though he wasn't this

5 He played this in high school and college

6 He gave this to Nixon

Write the two words here : ___ ___ ___ ___ ___ ___   ___ ___ ___ ___

★ FIND OUT MORE

The Bicentennial was celebrated during Ford's term as president. What is a bicentennial? When was it celebrated in the United States? _____

_____

© 2001 McGraw-Hill. All Rights Reserved.

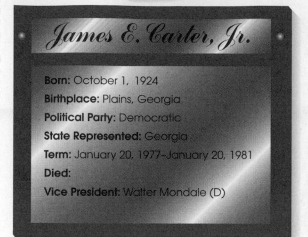

James E. Carter, Jr.

Born: October 1, 1924
Birthplace: Plains, Georgia
Political Party: Democratic
State Represented: Georgia
Term: January 20, 1977–January 20, 1981
Died:
Vice President: Walter Mondale (D)

James Earl Carter, Jr., better known as "Jimmy," is the son of a Georgia peanut farmer. He went to the U.S. Naval Academy at Annapolis and graduated in 1946. After serving in the Navy for 7 years, Carter resigned to run the family business. As a young man, Carter was active in defending civil rights. In 1962, he was elected state senator and later governor of Georgia. Carter ran for president in 1976. He presented himself as a man of the people and won the election. As president, Carter improved our ties with China and helped to write a peace treaty between Egypt and Israel. However, his success was to change. The economy was bad. In 1979, a group of Iranian students took the U.S. embassy staff hostage. Carter tried to get the hostages released, but he was unsuccessful. The public saw this as a weakness, and Carter became very unpopular. Carter was defeated in the 1980 election. After his term as president, Carter was an unofficial diplomat to Nicaragua, Ethiopia, North Korea, Haiti and Serbia.

★ SHOW WHAT YOU KNOW

Answer the questions. Write your answers on the lines.

★ ★

What was the family business? _____

What two government posts did Carter hold in Georgia? _____

Between which two countries did Carter make peace while president? _____

Students in which country kidnapped the U.S. embassy staff? _____

In which countries did Carter work as an unofficial diplomat? _____

_____

★ ★

★ FIND OUT MORE

How long did the Iran hostage crisis last? When were the hostages freed? _____

_____

© 2001 McGraw-Hill. All Rights Reserved.

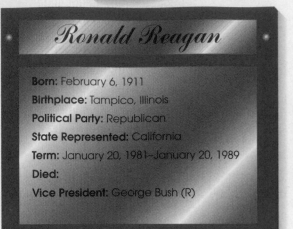

Ronald Reagan

Born: February 6, 1911

Birthplace: Tampico, Illinois

Political Party: Republican

State Represented: California

Term: January 20, 1981–January 20, 1989

Died:

Vice President: George Bush (R)

*R*onald Reagan went to school in Illinois where he studied economics and sociology. After college, he was a sportscaster in Chicago before beginning a long career as an actor. Reagan later became active in politics as a Democrat in 1948, but he became a Republican in 1962. His first public office was governor of California in 1966. In 1980, at the age of 69, Reagan won the Republican nomination for president. He promoted traditional American values and won a landslide victory over Jimmy Carter. Reagan then set out to strengthen military defense, stop inflation and improve business growth. Reagan won a second term by a landslide. During his second term, terrorism rose worldwide. In 1986, it was discovered that the Reagan administration had shipped guns to Iran in an effort to get American hostages released. Reagan was criticized from around the world. Reagan finished his second term in poor health.

★ SHOW WHAT YOU KNOW

Write the answer to each clue. The circled letters spell the name of a famous comet seen during Reagan's term.

1. Reagan was a sportscaster in this city
2. Besides politics, Reagan had a long career as this
3. He went to school in this state
4. Reagan studied this subject related to how people behave
5. Reagan became this in 1962
6. When first inaugurated, he was this age
7. He also studied this subject

The name of the comet seen in 1986 is ___ ___ ___ ___ ___ ___ ___ .

★ FIND OUT MORE

In 1994, Reagan wrote a letter to the American people telling them about his ill health. What did the letter say? _____

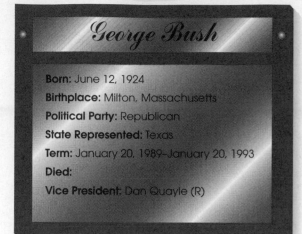

George Bush

Born: June 12, 1924

Birthplace: Milton, Massachusetts

Political Party: Republican

State Represented: Texas

Term: January 20, 1989–January 20, 1993

Died:

Vice President: Dan Quayle (R)

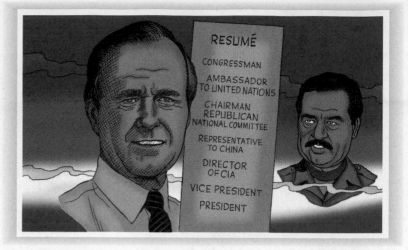

George H. W. Bush was born into a successful New England family. Before finishing his degree in economics at Yale University, Bush spent over 2 years as a Navy pilot during World War II. After the war, Bush was awarded the Distinguished Flying Cross for his bravery. Bush began his political career when he represented Texas in the House of Representatives in 1966. Bush then served as the ambassador to the United Nations and head of the Central Intelligence Agency (CIA). In 1980, Bush became vice president under Reagan. Bush was later elected president in 1988. President Bush quickly made his mark upon the office. In 1989, Bush ordered an invasion of Panama to remove the country's leader, General Manuel Noriega. In 1990, Iraq invaded Kuwait. President Bush led the worldwide forces against Iraq in the Persian Gulf War. Bush earned much praise for his leadership during the Persian Gulf War.

★ SHOW WHAT YOU KNOW

Answer the questions. Write your answers on the lines.

What did Bush do during World War II? _____

What college did Bush attend? _____

What award did Bush receive for his World War II service? _____

When did Bush first enter politics? Where? _____

_____

Which country did Bush invade? _____

What was the war in 1990 called? _____

★ FIND OUT MORE

The Bush family has a long political history. George Bush's father, Prescott S. Bush, was a United States senator from Connecticut. Find out two interesting facts about George Bush's son, George W. Bush.

_____

_____

© 2001 McGraw-Hill. All Rights Reserved.

The Presidents

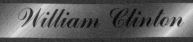

William Clinton

Born: August 19, 1946

Birthplace: Hope, Arkansas

Political Party: Democratic

State Represented: Arkansas

Term: January 20, 1993–January 20, 2001

Died:

Vice President: Al Gore (D)

William Clinton grew up in Arkansas. A well-educated young man, Clinton graduated from Georgetown University and Yale Law School. He also spent 2 years studying in England on a Rhodes scholarship. Clinton returned to Arkansas to become attorney general, then governor. Later, Clinton won the Democratic nomination in 1992 and was elected president. As president, Clinton successfully reduced the national debt and promoted trade between the United States, Canada and Mexico. In foreign policy, Clinton was successful in restoring the presidency of Haiti's Jean-Bertrand Aristide after he was forcefully removed from office. Clinton also sent peace keeping forces to the war-torn areas of Bosnia and Herzegovina. In 1999, Clinton supported NATO forces to end the Serbian occupation of Kosovo, Yugoslavia. Clinton was re-elected in 1996. During his second term, Clinton became involved in a scandal over court testimony and was impeached by the House of Representatives. Clinton was acquitted of the charges by the U.S. Senate.

★ SHOW WHAT YOU KNOW

Answer the questions. Write your answers on the lines.

Clinton was governor of which state? _____

Which president inspired Clinton as a young man? _____

Where did Clinton attend university?_____

_____

Clinton sent peace keeping forces to which areas? _____

What musical instrument does Clinton play?_____

How many other presidents have been impeached? _____

★ FIND OUT MORE

What is a Rhodes scholarship? _____

_____

_____

© 2001 McGraw-Hill. All Rights Reserved.

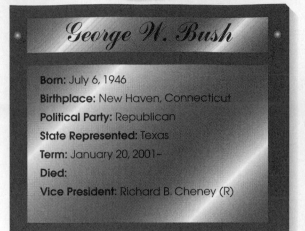

George W. Bush

Born: July 6, 1946

Birthplace: New Haven, Connecticut

Political Party: Republican

State Represented: Texas

Term: January 20, 2001–

Died:

Vice President: Richard B. Cheney (R)

George Walker Bush was named after his father, the 41st President, George Herbert Walker Bush. George Walker grew up in Midland, Texas, graduated from Yale University in 1968, and served as a pilot in the Texas Air National Guard. After receiving a degree from Harvard Business School in 1975, he began working in the oil business. In the late 1980's, Bush helped manage his father's presidential campaign and later became the managing general partner of the Texas Rangers baseball team. Elected governor of Texas in 1994 and reelected in 1998, Bush was the first Texas governor to be elected to consecutive four-year terms. While governor, he decided to run for president. The 2000 presidential election was one of the closest in U.S. history. Bush received a smaller number of popular votes than Democrat Al Gore but won more votes in the Electoral College. The outcome of the election was in doubt until five weeks later, when a decision by the U.S. Supreme Court ended vote recounts in Florida, and Bush became the 43rd president. A "compassionate conservative," Bush's platform included limiting government, cutting taxes, and improving education.

★ SHOW WHAT YOU KNOW

Answer the questions. Write your answers on the lines.

What college did Bush attend? _____

What did he do in the Texas Air National Guard? _____

_____

Bush was governor of what state? _____

Bush was managing general partner of what baseball team? _____

Who won the most popular votes in the 2000 presidential election? _____

★ FIND OUT MORE

Bush's election was the fourth in U.S. history in which the winner received fewer popular votes than his opponent. Who were the other three? _____

_____

© 2001 McGraw-Hill. All Rights Reserved.

Famous First Ladies

Born: 1731

Birthplace: Williamsburg, Virginia

Husband/Political Affiliation:
George Washington/Federalist

Term: 1789–1797

Died: 1802

Significant fact: Mrs. Washington, our nation's first first lady, set the standard in entertaining for future first ladies.

Martha Dandridge Custis Washington

Born Martha Dandridge in Virginia, our first lady was a quiet, gentle woman. Martha was raised as a cultured, eighteenth century lady and learned how to run a busy household. She once wrote that she would "much rather be at home" than live as a public person. But this was soon to change. Martha bravely followed her husband throughout the Revolutionary War. And when George Washington took his oath of office in 1789, Martha moved with him to the nation's capital in New York City. Later, they moved to Philadelphia when the nation's capital was moved there. As first lady, Martha Washington put aside her shyness. She entertained formally and often, so that the new Republic could show Europe that it was a "civilized" nation.

★ SHOW WHAT YOU KNOW

Answer the following questions. Write your answers on the lines.

Martha Washington lived in which two capital cities before Washington, D.C. became the

capital city? _____

How did Mrs. Washington entertain? _____

During which war did Martha Washington follow her husband? _____

Mrs. Washington wrote that she would "much rather be at home." Write a sentence about what her statement suggests she was like.

_____

★ FIND OUT MORE

After Washington retired from the presidency, George and Martha moved to Mount Vernon, their

beloved home. Mount Vernon is close to what city? _____

68

© 2001 McGraw-Hill. All Rights Reserved.

Famous First Ladies

Born: 1744

Birthplace: Weymouth, Massachusetts

Husband/Political Affiliation:
John Adams/Federalist

Term: 1797–1801

Died: 1818

Significant fact: Abigail Adams was the wife of one president and the mother of another—John Quincy Adams.

Abigail Smith Adams

Abigail Smith was born into a well-known, New England family. Her father, a Congregational minister, encouraged his daughter to read often. When Abigail met the young lawyer and Harvard graduate, John Adams, their love of books and learning brought them together. Their long marriage was very happy and eventful. When John Adams served in the Revolutionary War, his wife ran their Massachusetts farm in what is now Quincy, Massachusetts, and raised their four children. Abigail traveled with John to his diplomatic posts in Paris and London. Abigail also served as a hostess when Adams was vice president. Later, as first lady, she entertained often in the new capital city of Washington, D.C. This was no small achievement, as Washington was a swampy wilderness and the new home for the president was not finished.

★ SHOW WHAT YOU KNOW

Write the missing words on the lines below.

Abigail Adams ran the family farm in __ __ __ __ __ __, Massachusetts, alone during the
Revolutionary War.   1   2   3   4

Mrs. Adams was born Abigail __ __ __ __ __.
                            5   6   7

John Adams studied at __ __ __ __ __ __ __ __.
                      8   9   10

The Adamses lived in both Paris and __ __ __ __ __.
                                    11   12

Abigail Smith and __ __ __ __ Adams both loved books and learning.
                  13

Match the numbered letters above to those below to learn the name of John and Abigail Adams' son. Some numbered letters may be used twice.

__ __ __ __   __ __ __ __ __ __ __   __ __ __ __ __
13 11 8 12   1 2 7 12 3 4   9 10 9 6 5

★ FIND OUT MORE

What was the White House called in 1800? _____

_____

© 2001 McGraw-Hill. All Rights Reserved.

The Presidents

Famous First Ladies

Born: 1768

Birthplace: Piedmont, North Carolina

Husband/Political Affiliation:
James Madison/Republican

Term: 1809–1817

Died: 1849

Significant fact: The cultured and charming Mrs. Madison served as an informal hostess for President Thomas Jefferson, a widower.

Dolley Payne Todd Madison

*F*un-loving and beautiful, Dolley Payne grew up in a North Carolina community of Quakers. Her family returned to their home colony of Pennsylvania when Dolley was a teenager. Philadelphia briefly became the capital of the United States during the period of 1777 to 1788. During this time, Dolley met and married representative James Madison of Virginia. Their long and happy marriage included his years as secretary of state to President Thomas Jefferson. When her husband became president in 1809, the Madisons hosted the first Inaugural Ball. Dolley Madison loved to entertain and dressed so finely that one of her friends said that "she looked a Queen. . . ." When the British Army burned the capital city and forced everyone to flee during the War of 1812, the President's House was left in ruins. Undaunted, Dolley Madison returned and began renovating the house and entertaining once again.

★ SHOW WHAT YOU KNOW

Complete each of the following sentences, then circle the answers in the word search.

Dolley Payne grew up in a _____ community.

_____ was the capital city of the United States for a short time.

Dolley Madison was hostess of the first Inaugural _____.

James Madison was a state representative from _____ when he met Dolley.

```
V B A B I O G I N I A E
H P A A H N Q U A K E R
P H I L A D E L P H I A
V O R L V I R G I N I A
P H D M N K Q U M Q W B
```

★ FIND OUT MORE

What started the War of 1812? Who won the war? _____

_____

_____

© 2001 McGraw-Hill. All Rights Reserved.

Famous First Ladies

Born: 1818

Birthplace: Lexington, Kentucky

Husband/Political Affiliation:
Abraham Lincoln/Republican

Term: 1861–1865

Died: 1882

Significant fact: Mrs. Lincoln was seated next to her husband when he was shot at Ford's Theater.

Mary Todd Lincoln

A young man once called Mary Todd "the very creature of excitement," and her lively personality certainly got her noticed. However, it also caused her to be misunderstood. Mary Todd was her husband's complete opposite in personality. Born in Kentucky, she spent many years with Lincoln in Springfield, Illinois, while he was building a career in politics. Later, when Lincoln was elected president in 1860, Mary felt her faith in him had been proven. Mary also loved to entertain and enjoyed her role as first lady. However, the Lincolns arrived in Washington, D.C. at a time when the nation was divided. Early into Lincoln's term, the arguments over slaves' rights and states' rights exploded and began the Civil War. Mrs. Lincoln, born in the South yet married to the Union's president, was seen by some as a traitor to the South and by others as a threat to the North.

★ SHOW WHAT YOU KNOW

Answer the questions. Write your answers on the lines.

Some people thought Mary Todd Lincoln was a _____ to the South.

Arguments over states' rights and slaves' rights caused the _____.

Mary Lincoln had a _____ personality.

The Lincolns spent many years in Springfield, _____.

Abraham Lincoln was the _____ president.

★ FIND OUT MORE

How many terms did President Lincoln serve? Did he complete each of his terms? _____

_____

_____

_____

© 2001 McGraw-Hill. All Rights Reserved.

The Presidents

Famous First Ladies

Born: 1884

Birthplace: New York City

Husband/Political Affiliation:
Franklin D. Roosevelt/Democrat

Term: 1933–1945

Died: 1962

Significant fact: When Eleanor and Franklin
Roosevelt were married, her uncle, former president,
Theodore Roosevelt, gave away the bride.

Anna Eleanor Roosevelt Roosevelt

Eleanor Roosevelt was born into a wealthy family but lacked love and attention. Her mother, Anna, called her awkward, shy daughter "Granny." Eleanor's parents died before she was 10 years old. She was then raised by her very strict grandmother. Eleanor was later sent to an English boarding school. There she grew into a lady. During her debut season in 1905, Eleanor met and married her distant cousin, Franklin. They had a busy life, with six children born in 11 years—Franklin's political career grew at a similar rate. He was first a New York State senator, then served as secretary of the Navy. Mrs. Roosevelt was active in her own way, serving on the State Democratic Committee and learning about social conditions in America. When her husband was elected president, Eleanor Roosevelt began to change the role of first lady. She traveled, lectured, wrote a newspaper column and entertained heads of state. Eleanor continued her work throughout the rest of her life.

★ SHOW WHAT YOU KNOW

Answer the questions. Write your answers on the lines.

What did Eleanor Roosevelt's mother call her? _____

What was the family connection between Eleanor and Franklin? _____

What was Franklin Roosevelt's first state office in New York? _____

How many children did the Roosevelts have? _____

What did Eleanor write? _____

Where did Eleanor go to boarding school? _____

★ FIND OUT MORE

President Roosevelt contracted polio when he was a young man. When was the polio vaccine discovered? Who discovered it?

_____

 © 2001 McGraw-Hill. All Rights Reserved.

Famous First Ladies

Born: 1929

Birthplace: South Hampton, New York

Husband/Political Affiliation:
John Fitzgerald Kennedy/Democrat

Term: 1961–1963

Died: 1994

Significant fact: The Kennedys met when Senator John F. Kennedy was interviewed by inquiring photographer, Jacqueline Bouvier.

Jacqueline Lee Bouvier Kennedy

Jacqueline Kennedy was one of the twentieth century's most famous women. As a child, "Jackie" Bouvier rode horses, studied ballet and received an excellent education. She brought culture to her duties as first lady. Jacqueline wanted to make the White House a national museum of American antiques and decorative arts. She later asked Congress to declare the White House a national museum. The Kennedy children, John Jr. and Caroline, were the youngest to live in the White House in half a century. Mrs. Kennedy gave most of her time and energy to their and her husband's care and well being. President Kennedy was assassinated in 1963 while visiting Dallas, Texas. Jacqueline Kennedy's courage and dignity through this tragedy was admired around the world. Jacqueline later married Aristotle Onassis in 1968. Later, she became an editor for Doubleday.

★ SHOW WHAT YOU KNOW

Complete the crossword puzzle.

Across

3 The name of the Kennedys' daughter.

4 The U.S. city where John F. Kennedy was assassinated.

Down

1 The kind of dance that Jacqueline Kennedy studied.

2 Jacqueline wanted to fill the White House with these.

★ FIND OUT MORE

Mrs. Kennedy was very interested in historical furniture. What do the following three terms have in common: Chippendale, Hepplewhite and Duncan Phyfe?

© 2001 McGraw-Hill. All Rights Reserved.

73

The Presidents

Time Line

Name these early nineteenth century presidents. Put them in the correct order by numbering the pictures from 1 to 4.

#_____   #_____   #_____   #_____

Name these late nineteenth century presidents. Put them in the correct order by numbering the pictures from 1 to 4.

#_____   #_____   #_____   #_____

© 2001 McGraw-Hill. All Rights Reserved.

Time Line

Name these early twentieth century presidents. Put them in the correct order by numbering the pictures from 1 to 4.

#_____   #_____   #_____   #_____

Name these late twentieth century presidents. Put them in the correct order by numbering the pictures from 1 to 4.

#_____   #_____   #_____   #_____

© 2001 McGraw-Hill. All Rights Reserved.

The Presidents

Compare and Contrast

Write the name of each president under his picture.

Name the presidents pictured above that match these statements.

★ We were born in Ohio. _____

★ I served as governor of a state. _____

★ Our vice presidents became president after us. _____

_____

★ The three of us were in office on the first day of a new century. _____

_____

★ I was born in the eighteenth century but died in the nineteenth. _____

★ I was born in the nineteenth century but died in the twentieth. _____

★ We were both assassinated while in office. _____

_____

★ We both have the same first name. _____

 © 2001 McGraw-Hill. All Rights Reserved.

Compare and Contrast

Write the name of each president under his picture.

Name the presidents pictured above that match these statements.

★ We were both born in New York. _____

★ The two of us served as governors of states. _____

_____

★ We both served as vice president. _____

★ The three of us were in office during times of economic trouble. _____

_____

★ The three of us served only one term each. _____

_____

★ We were both elected as Republicans. _____

★ We were both elected as Democrats. _____

© 2001 McGraw-Hill. All Rights Reserved.

Presidents and Wars

Write the name of each president under his picture. Then, draw a line to the name of the war with which he is most closely associated.

Revolutionary War

War of 1812

Civil War

Spanish-American War

World War I

World War II

Vietnam War

Persian Gulf War

© 2001 McGraw-Hill. All Rights Reserved.

Who's Who

Write the name of each president under his picture. Then, draw a line to another name by which each president was known.

Old Rough and Ready

Old Buck

Hero of Appomattox

Old Hickory

Little Magician

Ike

FDR

William Jefferson Blythe III

© 2001 McGraw-Hill. All Rights Reserved.

The Presidents

Slogans and Quotations

Write the name of each president under his picture. Then, draw a line to the slogan or quotation with which he is associated.

"He serves his party best who serves his country best."

"First in war, first in peace, first in the hearts of his countrymen."

"Remember the Maine."

"Ask not what your country can do for you — ask what you can do for your country."

"A house divided against itself cannot stand."

". . . the world must be made safe for democracy."

© 2001 McGraw-Hill. All Rights Reserved.

Presidents and Important Events

Write the name of each president under his picture. Then, draw a line to match each president with an important event with which he is associated.

The end of slavery

The end of Reconstruction

The end of the Cold War

The end of World War II

The Watergate scandal

The Teapot Dome scandal

The Lewis and Clark Expedition

The founding of the League of Nations

© 2001 McGraw-Hill. All Rights Reserved.

The Presidents

Presidents and Programs

Write the name of each president under his picture. Then, draw a line to match each president with an important program with which he is associated.

14 Points

The New Deal

The Fair Deal

The Great Society

The Time of Good Feelings

The Full Dinner Pail

© 2001 McGraw-Hill. All Rights Reserved.

Presidential Quiz

★ ★

Which two presidents died on the same day? _____

What is interesting about the date? _____

_____

Which three men served as president during 1841? _____

_____

Which three men served as president during 1881? _____

_____

Name the two presidents who were father and son. _____

_____

Name the two presidents who were grandfather and grandson. _____

_____

Which man gave up the presidency? _____

Which two presidents graduated from West Point? _____

_____

Name three successive presidents who were born in Ohio. _____

_____

Which two presidents helped write the U.S. Constitution? _____

_____

Which man had the shortest presidency? _____

Which man had the longest presidency? _____

Name two sets of presidents who were distant cousins. _____

_____

Which president is called "the Father of His Country"? _____

Which president is called "the Father of the Declaration of Independence"? _____

Which president is called "the Father of the Constitution"? _____

★ ★

© 2001 McGraw-Hill. All Rights Reserved.   The Presidents

Our Government and How It Came to Be

The American Colonies Under British Rule

$\mathcal{D}$uring America's first 150 years, most settlers came from Great Britain. These colonists built settlements up and down America's Atlantic coast. The settlements eventually became the states we now call the original Thirteen Colonies.

British settlers worked hard creating homes, farms and towns. Yet these places were not their own. They still lived under the rule of the King of England. Through their labors, the colonists eventually came to desire a larger role in making decisions about their land and lives.

The British tightened their control when they saw the colonists wanted independence. By the mid-1770s, King George III and the British government had imposed heavy taxes on everyday goods like tea. These taxes made it difficult for the colonists to afford their basic necessities.

New York
New Hampshire
Massachusetts
Rhode Island
Connecticut
Pennsylvania
New Jersey
Maryland
Delaware
Virginia
North Carolina
South Carolina
Georgia

On June 7, 1776, Richard Henry Lee, a delegate to the Second Continental Congress, presented a new idea. He proposed that the colonies should be free and independent of Great Britain. As a result of Lee's proposal, a committee was appointed to write the Declaration of Independence.

★ SHOW WHAT YOU KNOW

Circle the names of the thirteen colonies in the puzzle. They may be forward, backward, up, down or diagonal. Write them on the lines to the right of the puzzle.

```
D A H O R E G O N I N D I A N A E
L O R I D A D N A L S I E D O H R
A N I L O R A C H T U O S M R Y I
I C C O N N E C T I C U T A T O H
N A N G R I V E R M O N T I H K S
A L E R I H S P M A H W E N C E A
V I W M W E N E V A D A S E A N I
L F J O A D E L A E N T U E R T G
Y O E N I S N S L K E E H S O U R
S R R T N I A A H R W X C S L C O
N N S A I H W S L O Y A A E I K E
N I E N G A E E N Y O S S N N Y G
E A Y A R Y W Y R A R H S N A E N
P V R E I G E O M G K A A E O W J
W E S T V I R G I N I A M T R S Y
```

_____
_____
_____
_____
_____
_____
_____
_____
_____
_____
_____
_____
_____

© 2001 McGraw-Hill. All Rights Reserved.

Our Government and How It Came to Be

Before the Declaration of Independence

*R*ichard Henry Lee's call for free states led directly to the writing of the Declaration of Independence. However, earlier events played a role in the Declaration of Independence, too. Ten years before it was written, the colonies asked the King of England to allow them a more active role in lawmaking. The King denied that request, and England continued to make the laws for the colonies. The more the states asked for freedom, the more and higher taxes the British government made them pay.

For example, the Stamp Act required taxes on legal and business papers. The British also taxed tea, a very popular drink. Tea was not grown in the 13 colonies; it was imported into the colonies from overseas. One of the most famous events before the Revolutionary War was the Boston Tea Party, a protest against the British tax on tea.

During the First Continental Congress, all but one colony agreed not to trade with England any more. But this had no effect on the King's policies. By the time of the Second Continental Congress, the colonists felt they needed to take drastic action.

SHOW WHAT YOU KNOW

Fill in the blanks below to learn which colony did not agree to stop trading with England. Its name will appear down in the boxes.

Write the name of the king that levied high taxes. ☐ __ __ __ __ __ __ __ __

How many years before the Declaration was written did America ask to be a part of the law-making process? __ ☐ __ __

Where was the "tea party" held? __ ☐ __ __ __ __ __

Goods sent into America from another country are __ __ __ __ ☐ __ __ __ __ .

With what country did America want to share the lawmaking process? __ __ ☐ __ __ __ __

Which Continental Congress voted not to trade with England? __ __ ☐ __ __

What act taxed many legal and business papers? __ __ ☐ __ __ __ __ __

Which colony did not agree to stop trade with England? _____

　　© 2001 McGraw-Hill. All Rights Reserved.

The Declaration of Independence

*B*y the time the Second Continental Congress met to discuss stronger action for independence, tensions in the American colonies were very high. Colonists who did not wish to remain British subjects declared themselves Patriots; those who remained faithful to England called themselves Loyalists. The Revolutionary War broke out on April 19, 1775, at the Battle of Lexington and Concord.

The Second Continental Congress appointed a committee of five men to write a Declaration of Independence from British Rule. Those five men were Thomas Jefferson, John Adams, Benjamin Franklin, Robert Livingston and Roger Sherman. Jefferson wrote the first draft. The committee declared it to be almost perfect. After making a few corrections, the committee presented the document to the Congress. After a few more small changes, Thomas Jefferson's work was approved. Church bells rang out on July 4, 1776, the day the Declaration of Independence was adopted and our nation was officially born.

★ SHOW WHAT YOU KNOW

Find and circle the first and last names of the five men who created the Declaration of Independence.

© 2001 McGraw-Hill. All Rights Reserved.

Our Government and How It Came to Be

The Declaration of Independence, Part II

*T*he Declaration of Independence has five parts. They are the Preamble, the Statement of Human Rights, Charges Against the King and Parliament, the Statement of Separation and Signatures. The main purpose was to announce the colonies' separation from England. In doing so, they also expressed the ideals they held that caused them to seek independence. The Declaration of Independence states that all men are created equal and are entitled to "life, liberty, and the pursuit of happiness." These ideals would be expressed again in the new republic's Constitution. They form the basis of our beliefs in our government's role in our lives today.

★ SHOW WHAT YOU KNOW

Complete the puzzle below. Unscramble the circled letters to find out how many people signed the Declaration of Independence.

★★

Across

1 The main author

3 Another member of the committee who wrote the Declaration

Down

1 The month in which it was completed

2 The parts in the Declaration and the number of people on the committee that wrote it

4 177__ is the year it was completed

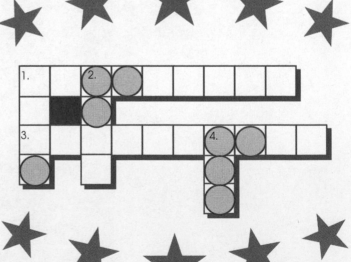

How many people signed the Declaration of Independence? _____

★★

© 2001 McGraw-Hill. All Rights Reserved.

The Articles of Confederation

*D*uring the Revolutionary War, the Continental Congress wrote the Articles of Confederation. These were meant to give the colonies some sense of a unified government. However, once the thirteen colonies became thirteen states, each one began to act alone in its own best interest. In order for these new states to act together, a new governing document was needed. In September 1786, delegates from Maryland, New York, New Jersey, Virginia, Pennsylvania and Delaware met in Annapolis, Maryland. At the Annapolis Convention, these delegates discussed states' rights. Recognizing the need for a stronger central government, they recommended that a convention be held with the purpose of changing the Articles of Confederation.

The Constitutional Convention of May 1787 was held in Philadelphia, Pennsylvania. Delegates from 12 of the 13 states were present. The state of Rhode Island refused to send a delegate because it was afraid of losing its states' rights. For 4 months, the delegates worked behind the closed doors of the statehouse to draft a new document, which would be known later as the Constitution.

SHOW WHAT YOU KNOW

Circle the letter of the correct answer for each question.

★ When did the Continental Congress write the Articles of Confederation?
  a. before the Declaration of Independence
  b. after the Revolutionary War
  c. during the Revolutionary War
  d. after the Constitution

★ Which state refused to send a delegate to the Constitutional Convention?
  a. New York
  b. Rhode Island
  c. Maryland
  d. Georgia

★ City in which the Constitutional Convention was held.
  a. Rhode Island
  b. Philadelphia
  c. Annapolis
  d. Maryland

★ Which was NOT a concern of the delegates to the Constitutional Convention?
  a. to discuss states' rights
  b. to create a stronger central government
  c. to create a weaker central government
  d. to save the Articles of Confederation

© 2001 McGraw-Hill. All Rights Reserved.
Our Government and How It Came to Be

Writing the Constitution

As commander of the Continental Army, George Washington won the respect of his countrymen. Because of the high esteem in which they held him, Washington's fellow delegates elected him president of the Constitutional Convention. As President of the Convention, Washington's job was to keep the meetings orderly and effective. Considering the many different points of view among the delegates, this was no small task. When President Washington broke in to make a contribution, the delegates listened carefully.

Before the Convention began its work, a rules committee decided how the process would work. Each state was given only one vote, no matter how many delegates that state had sent. If a state sent more than one delegate, they all had to come to an agreement about their state's one vote. Any delegate could voice an opinion, but all proceedings would be kept secret until the Convention presented a finished Constitution.

★ SHOW WHAT YOU KNOW

Complete the crossword puzzle.

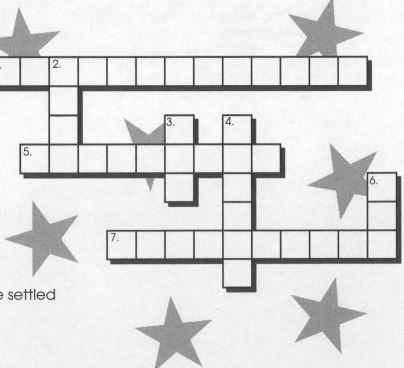

Across

1 Washington commanded the army in this war

5 They elected Washington president of the convention.

7 Where the convention took place.

Down

2 The means by which different laws are settled

3 The month the convention began

4 The meetings were held in _____.

6 The number of votes allowed per state

 © 2001 McGraw-Hill. All Rights Reserved.

The Great Compromise

I propose a two house legislature! The House & the Senate

Agreed!

Agreed!

VIRGINIA

CONNECTICUT

NEW JERSEY

Delegates to the Constitutional Convention had different backgrounds and political views. There were naturally areas of disagreement among them. One argument was about how many representatives each state should be allowed. The larger states favored the Virginia Plan in which the number of representatives for each state would be different, according to the state's population. The smaller states favored the New Jersey plan in which the number of representatives would be the same for each state.

Roger Sherman of Connecticut proposed a two-house legislature, consisting of a Senate and a House of Representatives. The Senate would have an equal number of representatives from each state, satisfying states with smaller populations. The House of Representatives would include one representative for each 30,000 individuals in a state, which pleased states with larger populations. Because this plan worked for all the states, it became known as the Great Compromise.

★ SHOW WHAT YOU KNOW

Answer each of the following questions, then circle the answers in the word search.

★ What was the first name of the man who proposed the two-house legislature?_____

★ What was the last name of the man who proposed the two-house legislature?_____

★ Which legislative body has an equal number of representatives from each state? _____

★ Which states favored the Virginia Plan?_____

★ Which states favored the New Jersey Plan?_____

★ Which plan was based on equal representation?

_____

★ Which plan was based on population to determine representation? _____

A	I	N	I	G	R	I	V
E	S	E	D	M	U	R	L
N	H	W	D	R	E	L	A
E	E	J	N	G	A	D	O
T	R	E	O	M	L	P	L
A	M	R	S	H	W	A	I
N	A	S	L	L	R	I	A
E	N	E	M	G	P	A	T
S	E	Y	E	R	S	O	N

© 2001 McGraw-Hill. All Rights Reserved.

Our Government and How It Came to Be

Signing the Constitution

$\mathcal{T}$he Constitutional Convention met over a period of 4 months. Because the weather was bad and travel was difficult, the 55 delegates were seldom all together at once. For most of the process of writing the Constitution, about 35 delegates were present.

These delegates had been selected by their states. They were educated, patriotic and experienced men who ranged in age from under 50 to 81. The oldest was Benjamin Franklin. Some men were landowners, some were lawyers or judges and all had held at least one public office. This group is sometimes referred to as the "Founding Fathers."

In all, 39 delegates signed the Constitution. William Jackson, secretary of the Constitutional Convention, also signed. Both the state with the smallest delegation (New Hampshire) and the state with the largest delegation (Pennsylvania) shared the distinction of having all their delegates sign this historic document.

★ SHOW WHAT YOU KNOW

Write F for false and T for true for the following statements.

_____ No delegate to the Constitutional Convention was older than 81.

_____ The Constitution was written quickly over a few days.

_____ Delegates nominated themselves to come to the Constitutional Convention.

_____ Forty men signed the Constitution.

_____ Benjamin Franklin is considered a "Founding Father."

_____ It was difficult for all of the delegates to meet at the same time.

_____ The smallest delegation came from Pennsylvania.

_____ Some of the delegates had never held public office.

 © 2001 McGraw-Hill. All Rights Reserved.

The Three Branches of Government

$\mathscr{D}$elegates to the Constitutional Convention first designated which powers would be given to the federal government. They needed to decide how these powers would be divided, since they did not want them to all be controlled by one man or group alone. The delegates feared that if any small group was given too much power, the United States would once again be under the rule of another tyrant.

To avoid the threat of tyranny, the group divided the new government into three parts, or branches: the executive branch, the legislative branch and the judicial branch.

Legislative Branch: Headed by Congress, which consists of the House of Representatives and the Senate. The main task of these two bodies is to make the laws by which our government operates. Its powers include passing laws, originating spending bills (House), impeaching officials (Senate) and approving treaties (Senate).

Executive Branch: Headed by the president. The president carries out federal laws and recommends new ones, directs national defense and foreign policy, and performs ceremonial duties. Powers include administering government, commanding the Armed Forces, dealing with international powers, acting as chief law enforcement office and vetoing laws.

Judicial Branch: Headed by the Supreme Court, its powers include interpreting the Constitution, reviewing laws and deciding cases involving states' rights.

★ SHOW WHAT YOU KNOW

Match the power with the branch that is responsible for it.

_____ Interprets the law

_____ Performs ceremonial duties

_____ Makes the laws

_____ Settles states' disputes

_____ Directs foreign policy

A Executive Branch

B Legislative Branch

C Judicial Branch

© 2001 McGraw-Hill. All Rights Reserved.

Our Government and How It Came to Be

Checks and Balances

$\mathcal{T}$he delegates built a "check and balance" system into the Constitution, so that no one branch of our government could become too powerful. Each branch is controlled by the other two in several ways. For example, the president may veto a law passed by Congress. However, Congress can override that veto with a vote of two-thirds of both houses. Another example is that the Supreme Court may check Congress by declaring a law unconstitutional. This power is balanced by the fact that members of the Supreme Court are appointed by the president, but those appointments have to be approved by Congress.

SHOW WHAT YOU KNOW

Use the information here and on the previous page to complete the chart.

POWER	HOW IT CAN BE CHECKED
Congress passes a law.	The president may _____ OR the president may _____ THEN, the Supreme Court may _____ _____
The president vetoes a law passed by Congress.	Congress may _____ _____
The president appoints a Supreme Court judge.	The Senate may _____ _____
The president makes a treaty with another country.	The Senate may _____ _____
The president enforces a law.	The Supreme Court may _____ _____

 © 2001 McGraw-Hill. All Rights Reserved.

The House of Representatives

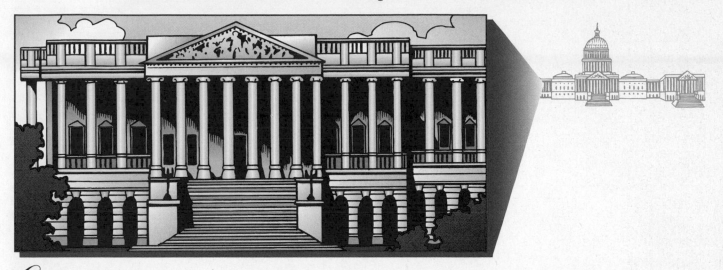

$\mathcal{O}$ne of the two lawmaking bodies established as a result of the Great Compromise was the House of Representatives. This pleased states with large populations, since they would have more representatives than the small states. Representatives would be elected to serve for a period of 2 years.

The House is larger than the Senate. The Constitution gave Congress the power to determine the size of the House and to divide representation according to state population. The Constitution also provided for at least one representative for each state. Originally, there was one representative for every 30,000 people. Today, there is one representative per several hundred thousand people. Six states have just one representative each. They are Alaska, Delaware, North Dakota, South Dakota, Vermont and Wyoming. California has the most representatives, with 45. Every 10 years, the Constitution requires a census to be taken, so that if state populations change, their number of representatives can, too. At the first session of the House of Representatives, there were 59 members. Today there are 435.

★ **SHOW WHAT YOU KNOW**

Answer the following questions.

★ Which state has the most representatives? _____

★ What does the Constitution use to determine the number of representatives?

_____

★ How many representatives were in the first House session? _____

★ How many representatives sit in the House today? _____

★ What tool is used to determine when the number of representatives should change?

_____

© 2001 McGraw-Hill. All Rights Reserved.

Our Government and How It Came to Be

The Senate

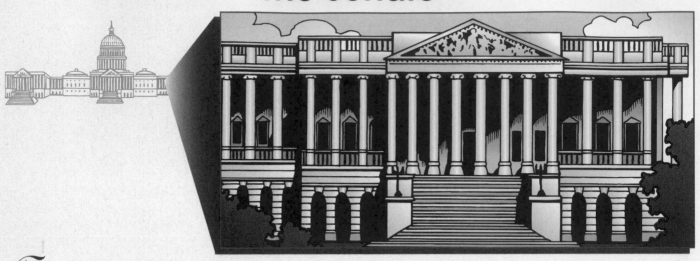

The other lawmaking body in our country's legislative branch, or Congress, is called the Senate. Voters elect two senators from each state, regardless of population size. There is equal representation from each state in the Senate, whether the state is big or small, densely or sparsely populated and no matter where it is located. Senators are elected every 6 years, although the elections are staggered so that both senators from a state are not elected at the same time.

Like the House of Representatives, the Senate can introduce different types of legislation. Only the House can introduce spending bills, while only the Senate can approve or reject treaties and presidential nominations for government offices.

The Constitution states the qualifications for being a senator: a person must be at least 30 years old, a U.S. citizen for at least 9 years and have fulfilled the requirements for residency in the state that person wishes to represent.

★ SHOW WHAT YOU KNOW

Find out who the two senators from your state are and place their pictures in the spaces below. Write their names below the pictures. Add a sentence telling something interesting about each person.

Glue the senator's picture here.

Glue the senator's picture here.

_____

_____

© 2001 McGraw-Hill. All Rights Reserved.

The Executive Branch—Presidency

$\mathcal{N}$ew laws are first introduced as "bills" in the two bodies of Congress. A bill has to be approved by both the House and the Senate through a series of votes and debates. Once a bill has been approved by Congress, it is sent to the president, who heads the Executive Branch. The president has several options about what to do with a bill. He may sign it into law, send it back to Congress to be changed or veto the bill.

These presidential powers are designed to keep Congress from taking too much control. In Article II of the Constitution, the president's qualifications and powers are detailed: The president will be elected for a term of 4 years at a time. A vice president of the same political party will be elected for the same term. In order to be considered for the office, a presidential candidate must be at least 35 years old, a natural-born U.S. citizen and have at least 14 years of residence in the United States.

SHOW WHAT YOU KNOW

Write F for false and T for true for the following statements.

_____ The president may negotiate treaties.

_____ The president is elected for 8 years.

_____ The president must approve all bills from Congress.

_____ The president can be older than 35.

_____ The president can come from England or Canada.

© 2001 McGraw-Hill. All Rights Reserved.

Our Government and How It Came to Be

Making Laws

$\mathscr{W}$hen a member of Congress decides to create a new law, he or she introduces a "bill." Any member of Congress can introduce a bill, but only members of the House may introduce bills that deal with taxes or spending. Both houses of Congress must pass identical versions of a bill before it can become law.

Once a bill is introduced in either house, it goes through almost the same process.

Each bill is first assigned to a committee for review. If the committee decides the bill is not worthy, the bill is tabled, or set aside. If the committee decides the bill is worthy of further action, it sends the bill to the entire house for debate.

If the bill passes, it is sent to the other house. Any differences the two houses of Congress have concerning a bill are worked out by a joint committee. When both houses agree on a bill, it is signed by the speaker of the house and the vice president before being sent to the president.

★ SHOW WHAT YOU KNOW

Write a complete sentence to answer each question.

★ ★

Who may introduce a bill? _____

_____

What is the only exception? _____

_____

What is the first thing that happens to a bill when it is introduced? _____

_____

What happens to a bill when the committee thinks it is not worthy? _____

Who signs a bill for Congress? _____

_____

★ ★

 © 2001 McGraw-Hill. All Rights Reserved..

Impeachment

When a new president takes office, he or she takes an oath that lists many heavy responsibilities. Abuse of power or failure to uphold these responsibilities cannot be tolerated and the Constitution gives the House of Representatives the right to impeach the president. Impeachment means that a charge of misconduct is filed against the president. To bring these charges, a majority of the members of the House must vote for them.

The Senate, then, has the power to try impeachment cases like a court. Two-thirds of the senators must vote for conviction. If an official is found guilty, he or she may be removed from office and never allowed to hold a government position again.

Andrew Johnson, our 17th president, was impeached while in office. He was found guilty by 35 senators, which was just one vote short of the two-thirds vote necessary to convict him. In 1974, President Richard Nixon resigned from office rather than face impeachment charges in the Watergate scandal. In 1998, President Clinton became the second president to be impeached by the House. Later, he was found not guilty by the Senate.

SHOW WHAT YOU KNOW

Circle the letter of the correct answer for each question.

★ Who brings impeachment charges?

    a. the Senate

    b. the Supreme Court

    c. the House

★ What vote is need for conviction?

    a. one-half

    b. two-thirds

    c. one-third

★ Which president was not impeached?

    a. Clinton

    b. Nixon

    c. Johnson

★ Which body tries impeachment cases?

    a. the Senate

    b. the Supreme Court

    c. the House

© 2001 McGraw-Hill. All Rights Reserved.

Our Government and How It Came to Be

The Judicial Branch

he Supreme Court heads the judicial branch of the United States government. It is the only court established by the Constitution. Decisions made by the Supreme Court are usually of national importance. Because the wording of the Constitution is complex, it must be studied and interpreted carefully. Interpreting the Constitution is one of the main duties of the justices who make up the Supreme Court.

Once the justices of the Supreme Court reach a decision, all other courts in the United States must follow that ruling. The Constitution also gives the Supreme Court the power to judge whether federal, state and local governments are acting within the law. The Supreme Court can also decide if a president's action is unconstitutional.

★ SHOW WHAT YOU KNOW

Answer the questions below. Write the letter above each number on its matching blank to find out who heads up the Supreme Court.

The Supreme Court usually only hears cases of __ __ __ __ __ __ __ __ importance.
       1

What guides Supreme Court decisions?

__ __ __   __ __ __ __ __ __ __ __ __ __ __
 2   3   4

What branch of the government does the Supreme Court head?

__ __ __ __ __ __ __ __ __
5   6

Which other U.S. courts must follow Supreme Court decisions?

__ __ __ __ __ __ __ , __ __ __ __ __ A N D __ __ __ __ __
7   8   9

What is the title of a member of the Supreme Court? __ __ __ __ __ __ __
                                                    10 11 12

T H E __ __ __ __ __   __ __ __ __ __ __ __
      11 2 6 12 7   5 4 3 1 10 9 8

          © 2001 McGraw-Hill. All Rights Reserved..

Powers of the Federal Government

*T*he Constitution of the United States divides powers between the federal, or national, government and the 50 states. In writing the Constitution, the Founding Fathers knew they had to leave enough powers with the states, or the Constitution would never be approved by the delegates. All states were granted the right to control certain things within their borders, as long as they did not interfere with the rights of other states or the nation.

★ FIND OUT MORE

Below is a list of the powers granted by the Constitution to Congress. Choose three of the bold words you do not know or would like to learn about more. Look in a dictionary or other reference source and write a phrase or sentence telling what each one means.

★ **Levy** and collect taxes

★ Borrow money

★ Regulate **commerce**

★ Set rules for **naturalization** and bankruptcy

★ Coin money and regulate its value

★ Provide punishment for **counterfeiting**

★ Establish post offices and postal roads

★ Promote copyright laws

★ Establish a court system

★ Punish crimes at sea

★ Declare war

★ Maintain an army

★ Maintain a navy

★ Regulate the military

★ Allow president to use **militia** for emergencies

★ Maintain state militias

★ Govern the capitol and **U.S. possessions**

★ Make laws needed to carry out duties above

★ ★

_____

_____

_____

_____

_____

_____

_____

© 2001 McGraw-Hill. All Rights Reserved.

Our Government and How It Came to Be

Ratifying the Constitution

$\mathcal{B}$efore the Constitution was adopted, it had to be sent to each state for approval. Before it could be sent to the states, it had to be rewritten so it was easier to read. The delegates asked a man named Morris of New Jersey to do this. Morris, an excellent writer, completed 4,300 words in two days. On September 17, 1787, 39 of the 55 delegates signed the Constitution and sent it to the states for special conventions. Nine states had to approve the Constitution before it could become law.

Some delegates to the Constitutional Convention, including George Mason and Patrick Henry, were afraid it would not guarantee individual states' rights. Alexander Hamilton, James Madison and John Jay wrote 85 letters supporting its passage. These advocates of the Constitution believed that the checks and balances system would allow a strong central government to preserve states' rights.

★ FIND OUT MORE

Find out more about each person listed below. Write a sentence telling something interesting about each.

★★★★★★★★★★★★★★★★★★★★★★★★★★★★★★★★

George Mason _____

Patrick Henry _____

Alexander Hamilton _____

James Madison _____

John Jay _____

_____

    © 2001 McGraw-Hill. All Rights Reserved.

The Bill of Rights

When the Constitution was sent to the states for ratification, some delegates would not approve it until it included a bill of rights listing the individual rights of every citizen. So, the Convention promised a bill of rights would be attached to the final version. When the first Congress met in 1789, it immediately considered several amendments. James Madison wrote 12 of them, which were presented to the states for final approval. Ten were approved. Those ten make up the Bill of Rights. They are also the first 10 Amendments to the Constitution.

The First Amendment:

> Congress shall make no law establishing a religion, or prohibiting the free exercise thereof; or **abridging** the freedom of **speech**, or of the **press**; or the right of the people to assemble peaceably, and to **petition** the Government for a **redress** of **grievances**.

★ SHOW WHAT YOU KNOW

Look at the bold words above. Match each to a word or phrase in the list below that has a similar meaning.

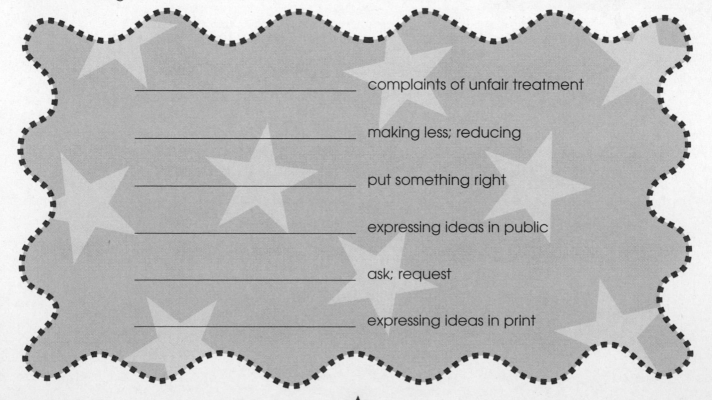

_____ complaints of unfair treatment

_____ making less; reducing

_____ put something right

_____ expressing ideas in public

_____ ask; request

_____ expressing ideas in print

© 2001 McGraw-Hill. All Rights Reserved.

Our Government and How It Came to Be

More About the Bill of Rights

*T*he authors of the Bill of Rights could not list every individual right, so they put in the Ninth and Tenth Amendments to cover all those not listed. For example, one right not specifically listed is privacy. Many people consider privacy to be covered under the Ninth and Tenth Amendments.

The Ninth Amendment:

> The **enumeration** in the Constitution of certain rights shall not be **construed** to deny or **disparage** others **retained** by the people.

★ This amendment means that nothing written in the Constitution can be used to cancel amendments to it.

The Tenth Amendment:

> The powers not **delegated** to the United States by the Constitution nor **prohibited** by states, are reserved to the states respectively or to the people.

★ This amendment means that anything the Constitution does not mention can be considered by states as part of their powers if they wish to do so.

★ SHOW WHAT YOU KNOW

Look at the bold words above. Match each to a word or phrase in the list below that has a similar meaning.

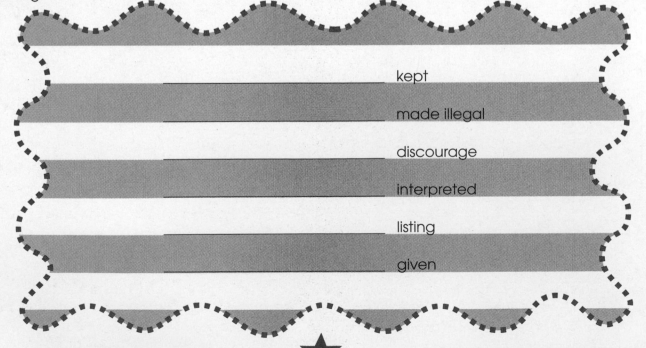

_____ kept

_____ made illegal

_____ discourage

_____ interpreted

_____ listing

_____ given

© 2001 McGraw-Hill. All Rights Reserved.

Amazon Amendments

Amendments

*N*othing is perfect, and very few things last long without change. The writers of the Constitution realized this when they provided for amendments to the Constitution. Amendments to the Constitution can be either additions or changes to the original text. It is not easy to change the Constitution. Over 9,000 amendments have been proposed since 1787, but only 27 have been approved.

Listed below are the rest of the Amendments that have been made so far to the Constitution. On the right are brief descriptions of what those Amendments are about, in scrambled order. Read a copy of the Amendment section of the Constitution. Use it to help you match the Amendment number with its definition.

Amendment 11 (1798)

Amendment 12 (1804)

Amendment 13 (1865)

Amendment 14 (1868)

Amendment 15 (1870)

Amendment 16 (1913)

Amendment 17 (1913)

Amendment 18 (1919)

Amendment 19 (1920)

Amendment 20 (1933)

Amendment 21 (1933)

Amendment 22 (1951)

Amendment 23 (1961)

Amendment 24 (1964)

Amendment 25 (1967)

Amendment 26 (1971)

Amendment 27 (1992)

_____ Repealed the Eighteenth Amendment but allowed states that wanted, to keep it

_____ Described rights of citizens, representation and voting, and defined the obligation of oath takers and Civil War debts

_____ Says no one may be kept from voting because of non-payment of a tax

_____ Abolished slavery

_____ Gave the vote to citizens 18 and older

_____ Gave women the right to vote

_____ Limited the length of presidential term

_____ Changed how senators are elected

_____ Provided for succession to the presidency and presidential disability

_____ Gave everyone otherwise eligible the right to vote, regardless of race

_____ Changed the dates of the president and vice presidents' term in office

_____ Would not allow alcohol to be made or sold

_____ Gave people who live in Washington, D.C. the right to vote in presidential elections

_____ Explained what kind of cases federal courts could try

_____ Established the income tax

_____ Changed how the Electoral College voted

_____ Congressional members may not raise their own salaries

© 2001 McGraw-Hill. All Rights Reserved.

Our Government and How It Came to Be

Know Your Constitution

Circle the correct answer to each of the following questions.

★ How many delegates signed the Constitution?

   a. 50

   b. 40

   c. 39

   d. 55

★ What had to be done to ratify the Constitution?

   a. A Bill of Rights had to be written

   b. The delegates had to sign it

   c. Eighty-five letters were written to support it

   d. Nine states had to approve it

★ Who was not a delegate but signed the Constitution?

   a. William Jackson

   b. Benjamin Franklin

   c. George Mason

   d. Gouverneur Morris

★ Who was considered the author of the Declaration of Independence?

   a. George Washington

   b. James Madison

   c. Thomas Jefferson

   d. Roger Sherman

★ Which part of the Constitution has seven parts?

   a. Bill of Rights

   b. Amendments

   c. Articles

   d. Preamble

★ Who may introduce all kinds of bills?

   a. The Supreme Court justices

   b. Members of the House of Representatives

   c. Members of the Senate

   d. The vice president

★ Who can veto a bill?

   a. A senator

   b. A justice

   c. A representative

   d. The president

★ What document did the Constitution replace?

   a. Declaration of Independence

   b. Articles of Confederation

   c. Bill of Rights

   d. The Magna Carta

★ Who tries impeachment charges against a government official?

   a. The Senate

   b. The Supreme Court

   c. The Executive Branch

   d. The House of Representatives

Matching Constitutional Facts

Write the number of the item in the top box next to the phrase in the bottom box that tells more about it.

1. A candidate for the Senate
2. George Washington and Thomas Jefferson
3. Passed the Bill of Rights
4. Benjamin Franklin
5. Slavery
6. Philadelphia
7. Adopted on July 4, 1776
8. Senators
9. Constitutional Convention
10. Supreme Court justices
11. Annapolis Convention
12. House of Representatives

_____ The Declaration of Independence

_____ City where the Constitutional Convention was held

_____ It was abolished with Amendment 13

_____ Every state is allowed two

_____ Needs to be 30 years old and a U.S. citizen for 9 years

_____ Introduces all bills having to do with money

_____ Was the oldest delegate at the Constitutional Convention

_____ Became presidents

_____ Events of this convention were kept secret

_____ There are nine of them

_____ One of the first things Congress did

_____ Representatives from five states attended this convention

© 2001 McGraw-Hill. All Rights Reserved.

Our Government and How It Came to Be

Constitutional Vocabulary

Write the definitions for the following words as they relate to the Constitution of the United States.

abolish _____

amendment _____

ballot _____

bill _____

census _____

chief justice _____

civil rights _____

compromise _____

delegate _____

due process _____

elector _____

federal _____

impeach _____

lame duck _____

legislature _____

majority _____

petition _____

preamble _____

president pro tempore _____

quorum _____

ratify _____

reapportion _____

seizure _____

treason _____

veto _____

 © 2001 McGraw-Hill. All Rights Reserved.

Complete the Time Line

An important event in the making of our government occurred on each of the dates listed in the time line below. Write a phrase or sentence to complete the information for each date.

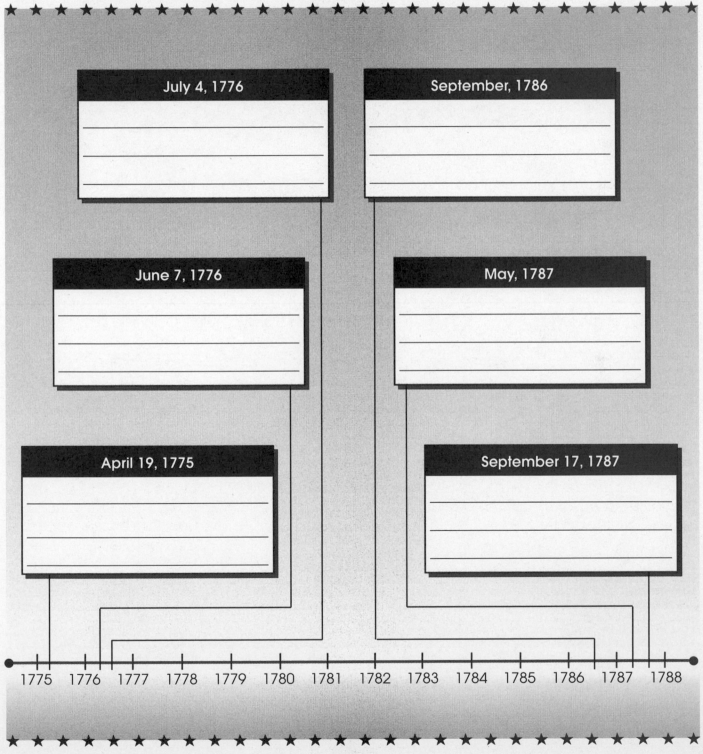

July 4, 1776

_____
_____
_____

September, 1786

_____
_____
_____

June 7, 1776

_____
_____
_____

May, 1787

_____
_____
_____

April 19, 1775

_____
_____
_____

September 17, 1787

_____
_____
_____

1775 1776 1777 1778 1779 1780 1781 1782 1783 1784 1785 1786 1787 1788

© 2001 McGraw-Hill. All Rights Reserved.

Our Government and How It Came to Be

Our Heritage

Written in the box below are names of some symbols of our heritage. Below the box are pictures of these symbols. Write the name for each symbol on the line under its picture. Color each picture as you are directed.

Liberty Bell	Washington Monument	Statue of Liberty
The White House	United States Capitol	Mount Rushmore
Flag	Jefferson National Expansion Memorial	Eagle

_____
Color me silver.

_____
Color me red, white and blue.

_____
Color me brown.

_____
Color me white.

_____
Color me tan.

_____
Color me brown, white and yellow.

_____
Color me green.

_____
Color me gray.

_____
Color me white.

© 2001 McGraw-Hill. All Rights Reserved.

The Fifty States

United States Map

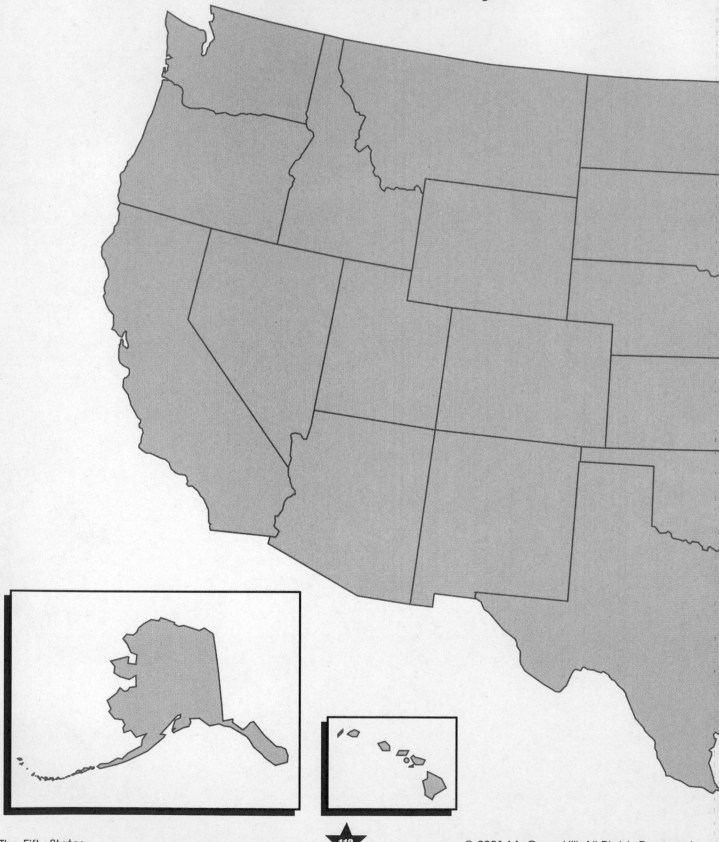

© 2001 McGraw-Hill. All Rights Reserved.

© 2001 McGraw-Hill. All Rights Reserved.

The Fifty States

How to Use the States Flash Cards

Cut apart the cards on the pages that follow to create your own set of States Flash Cards. Then, use them to play games such as the ones described below. You'll learn a lot of fascinating information about the states that make up the United States of America.

★ SOLITAIRE GAMES

★ Select any three cards from your pile and place them faceup on the table. Arrange them left to right in the order in which they became part of the United States.

★ Select any three cards and place them facedown on the table. Based on the information visible on the backs of the cards, name each state.

★ Copy the states flash cards to make a second deck. Place one set map down and one set map up. Match each map with the information that goes with it.

★ GAME #1 CONCENTRATION

★ Use 2 decks for this game. Shuffle the flash cards and place them facedown in an array of seven columns and seven or eight rows. Have a partner be the "caller." The caller draws a flash card from his or her deck and names the state shown on the face of the card. Based on the information visible on the backs of the cards, choose the card in your array that matches the state named. Turn it over. If you are correct, remove the card from the array and set it aside. If you are incorrect, replace the card facedown in its position. Keep track of the time it takes you to clear all of the cards from the table.

★ To make the game more difficult, place the cards faceup instead of facedown. Then, the caller selects a card from his or her own deck and reads a fact from the back. Based on your knowledge of the facts about the states, choose the matching card from your array.

★ To add an element of competition, invite others to play along with their own arrays of cards displayed in front of them. The player who clears all of the cards from his or her array first is the winner.

★ GAME #2 RUMMY

★ Play this game with two or three players. Shuffle the deck and deal seven cards to each player. Hold the cards so that you can see the information on the backs and your opponents can see the maps on the fronts. Place the remaining cards faceup in a draw pile. Turn the top card over to create a discard pile.

★ The object is to create a "run" of three or four states that are connected by at least one common border. For example, Washington, Oregon, California and Arizona make a run. Vermont, New York, Pennsylvania and West Virginia also make a run. Hawaii and Alaska are wild cards and may be used to complete any three or four card run.

★ Play begins to the left of the dealer. The first player can choose the top card from the draw pile or select a card from an opponent's hand. If the chosen card is from the pile, the player discards one card from his or her hand and places it facedown in the discard pile. If the chosen card is from an opponent's hand, the player gives the opponent his or her discard. The first player to create a run of three and a run of four is the winner.

 © 2001 McGraw-Hill. All Rights Reserved.

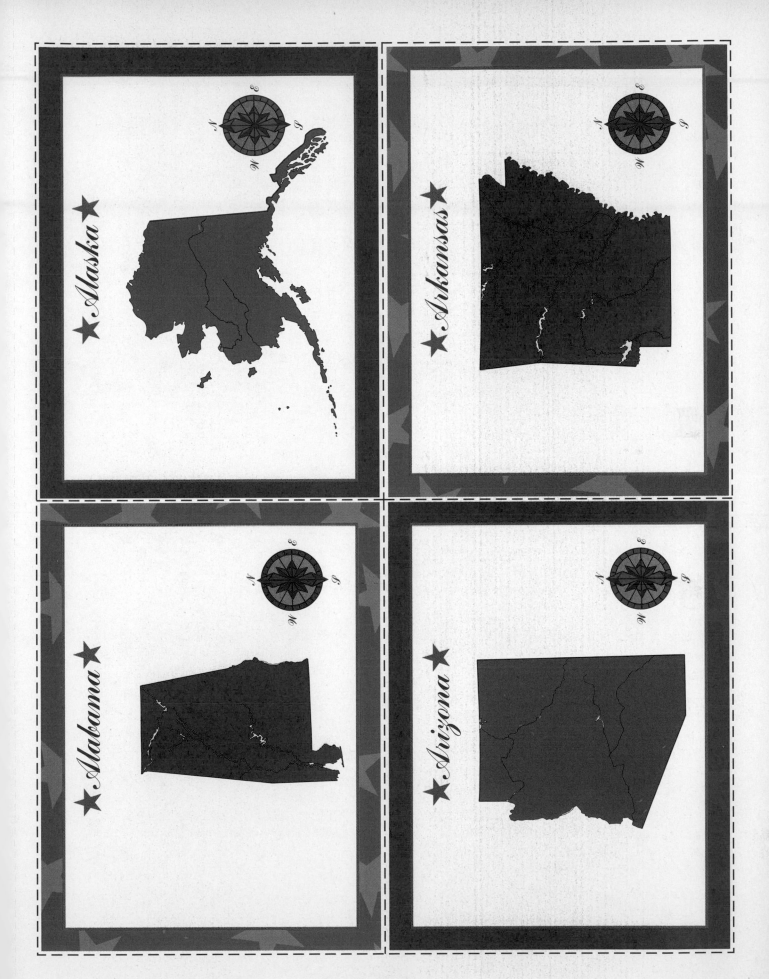

© 2001 McGraw-Hill. All Rights Reserved.

The Fifty States

The forty-ninth state

★ has two nicknames, "America's Last Frontier" and "Land of the Midnight Sun."

★ is home to Mount McKinley, the highest point in North America.

★ is home to Point Barrow, the northernmost point in the United States.

★ is the largest of America's states.

★ is only 50 miles from Russia at its westernmost point.

★ shares a border with no other states in the United States.

★ was once called "Seward's Folly" because many people thought Secretary of State William Seward was wasting America's money when he bought Alaska.

The twenty-second state

★ is where, in 1886, the first electric streetcars in the United States began operating.

★ rates cotton and soybeans as its main cash crops.

★ is called the "Heart of Dixie" because it was the home of the first capital of the Confederate States of America.

★ is where, in 1881, Booker T. Washington founded Tuskegee University for African-American students.

★ is where, in 1955, the Civil Rights Movement began when Rosa Parks refused to give up her seat on a city bus to a white person.

The twenty-fifth state

★ is nicknamed the "Land of Opportunity."

★ borders the Mississippi River along its eastern flank.

★ was part of the huge land parcel known as the Louisiana Purchase.

★ is the birthplace of Bill Clinton, the forty-second president, who was its governor.

★ was visited in 1541 by Spanish explorer Hernando de Soto, who was the first European to see it.

The forty-eighth state

★ is where, in 1150, the Hopi people built the village now called Old Oraibi.

★ is where, in 1888, the first organized rodeo took place.

★ was once part of Mexico.

★ is the new home of the London Bridge, which was taken apart, brought to the United States and reconstructed in the desert.

★ is the location of the Grand Canyon.

© 2001 McGraw-Hill. All Rights Reserved.

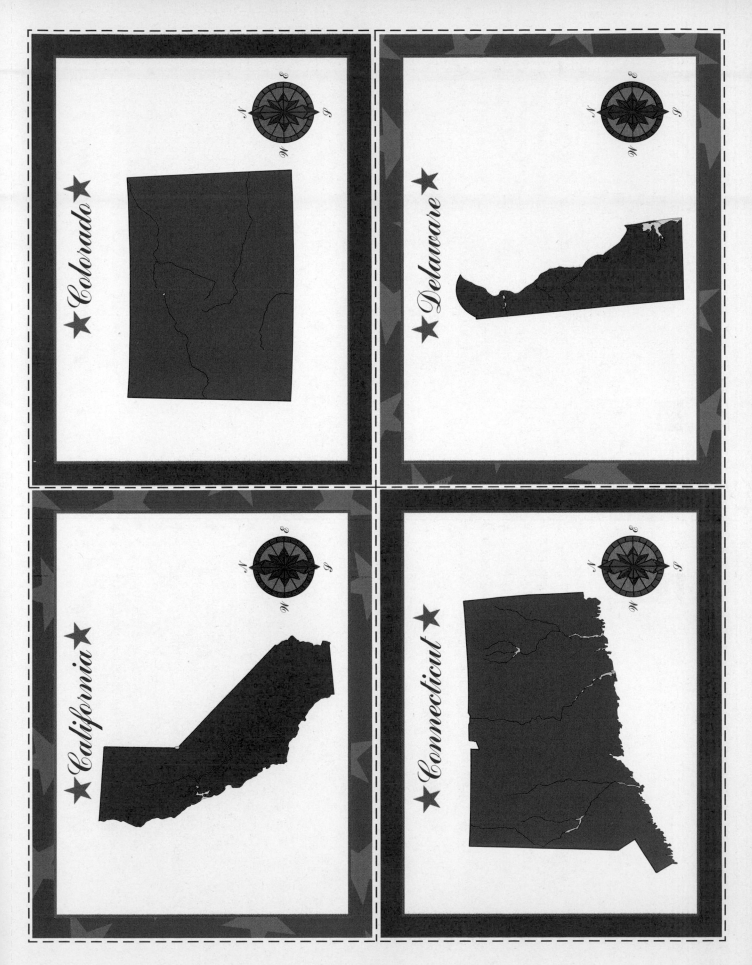

© 2001 McGraw-Hill. All Rights Reserved.

The thirty-eighth state

★ is the most mountainous state, with the highest average elevation of any state.

★ is a great place to search for dinosaur bones.

★ is the home of the United States Air Force Academy.

★ is the location of the world's highest suspension bridge.

★ is where, around 750 A.D., the Anasazi people built pueblos at Mesa Verde and lived for the next 550 years.

The first state

★ is known as the "First State" because it was first to join the Union.

★ is also nicknamed the "Diamond State."

★ is named after Thomas West, who was Lord De La Warr.

★ is bordered on the east by the Atlantic Ocean.

★ is a leading producer of broiler chickens.

★ was first seen by a European when Henry Hudson explored it in 1609.

The thirty-first state

★ is the most populated state in the nation.

★ was claimed for England in 1579 by Sir Francis Drake.

★ belonged to Mexico until 1848.

★ is the home of the world's largest living thing, a tree found in Sequoia National Park.

★ is the location of Death Valley, the lowest point in North America.

★ is the home state of Ronald Reagan, the fortieth president, who was its governor.

The fifth state

★ is known as the "Constitution State."

★ chose "Yankee Doodle" as its state song.

★ is a leading producer of helicopters and submarines.

★ is the birthplace of mass-production manufacturing, thanks to Eli Whitney, inventor of the cotton gin.

★ is the home of many Native American groups such as the Pequot, the Mohegan and the Niantic.

© 2001 McGraw-Hill. All Rights Reserved.

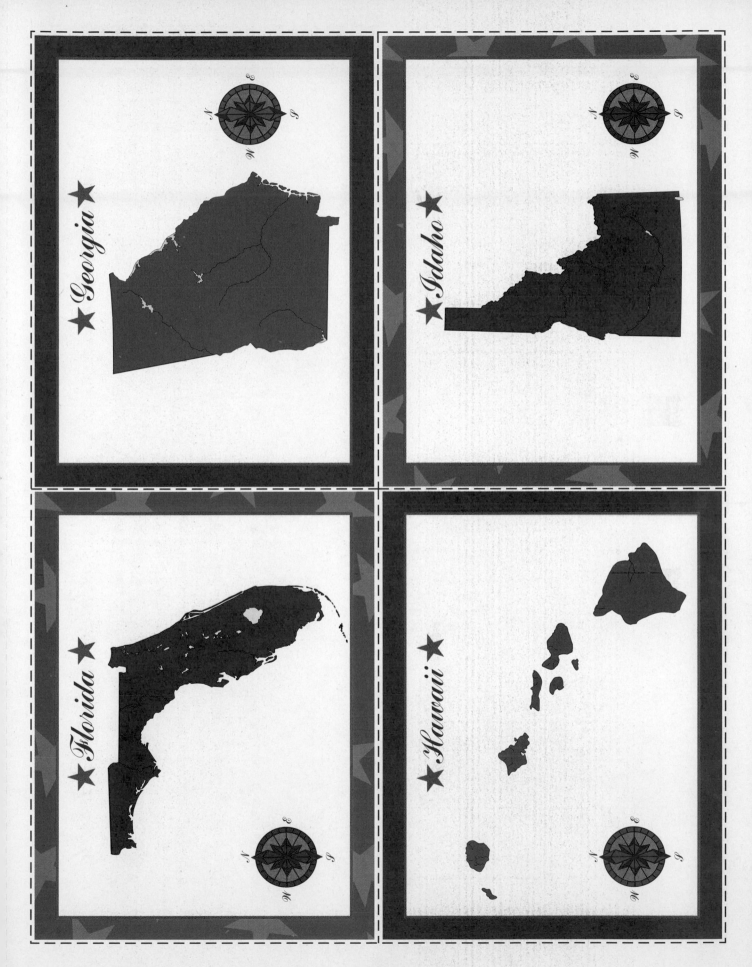

The fourth state

- is known as the "Peach State" and the "Empire State of the South."
- is the largest state east of the Mississippi River.
- is the location of Stone Mountain, a popular tourist attraction.
- is the nation's leading producer of peanuts.
- is the birthplace of James Earl Carter, Jr., the thirty-ninth president, who was its governor.

The forty-third state

- is best known for its potatoes.
- is the nation's leading producer of silver.
- is the home of Hell's Canyon, which is deeper than the Grand Canyon.
- is the home of Lewiston, a Pacific port city that is almost 500 miles inland.
- was explored in 1805 by Lewis and Clark on their Journey of Discovery.

The twenty-seventh state

- is known as the "Sunshine State."
- has a name that means "feast of flowers" in Spanish.
- is the theme park capital of the world.
- is the location of Saint Augustine, founded in 1565, the oldest city in the United States.
- is a large peninsula; no point in this state is more than 70 miles from open water.
- is the location of the Kennedy Space Center where the Space Shuttle is launched.

The fiftieth state

- is the only state not on the mainland of North America.
- is bordered on all sides by the Pacific Ocean.
- is where Pearl Harbor is located; the bombing of the Navy base led to the involvement of the United States in World War II.
- was once ruled by King Kamehameha.
- is the location of Haleakala Crater, the world's largest dormant (sleeping) volcano.

© 2001 McGraw-Hill. All Rights Reserved.

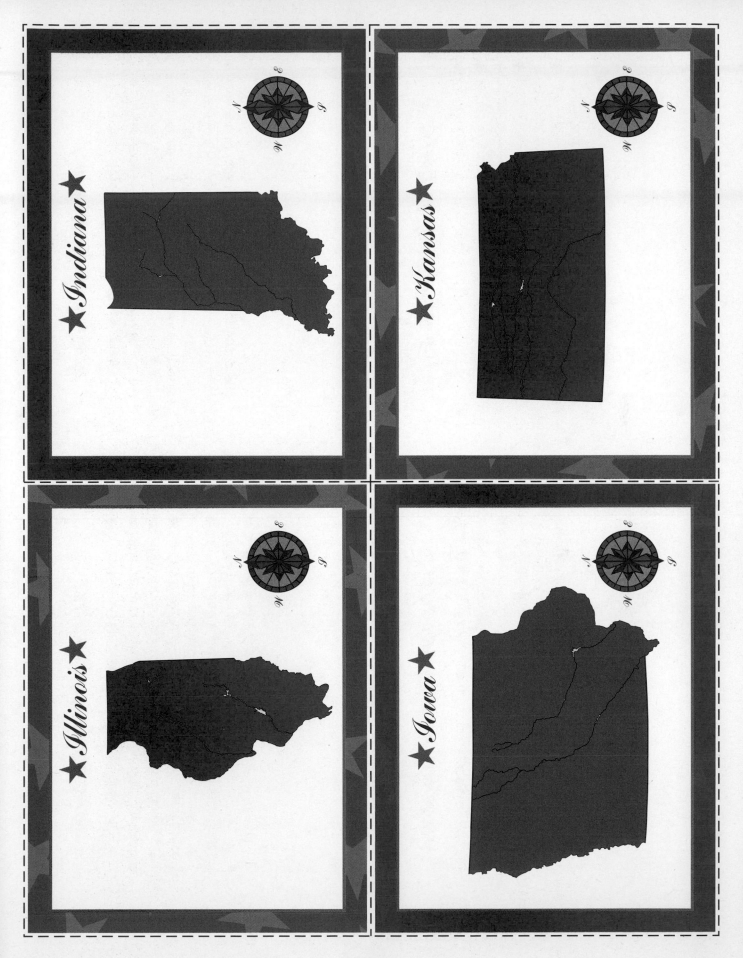

© 2001 McGraw-Hill. All Rights Reserved.

The Fifty States

The nineteenth state

★ is called the "Hoosier State" by many people.
★ is bordered on the south by the Ohio River.
★ is the home of the "Greatest Spectacle in Sports," the Indy 500, an auto race held in its capital city every Memorial Day weekend.
★ is the place where, in 1914, Raggedy Ann was created.
★ was first explored in 1673 by the French explorer Robert Cavelier, sieur de La Salle.

The thirty-fourth state

★ is often called the "breadbasket of America."
★ lies in the geographic center of North America.
★ traditionally leads the nation in wheat production.
★ is the childhood home of Dwight D. Eisenhower, the thirty-fourth president.
★ was part of the "Dust Bowl" during the great depression of the 1930s.

The twenty-first state

★ is bordered on the west by the Mississippi River.
★ is the home of Sears Tower, one of the world's tallest buildings.
★ is the birthplace of Ronald Reagan, the fortieth president.
★ is the place where Abraham Lincoln, the sixteenth president, lived most of his life.
★ was explored by Jacques Marquette and Louis Joliet in 1673.
★ is known as the "Land of Lincoln."

The twenty-ninth state

★ is called "the land where the corn grows tall."
★ is mostly flat and was once covered by glaciers.
★ is the nation's leading producer of hogs and corn.
★ is bordered on the east by the Mississippi River and on the west by the Missouri River.
★ is the birthplace of Herbert Hoover, the thirty-first president.

© 2001 McGraw-Hill. All Rights Reserved.

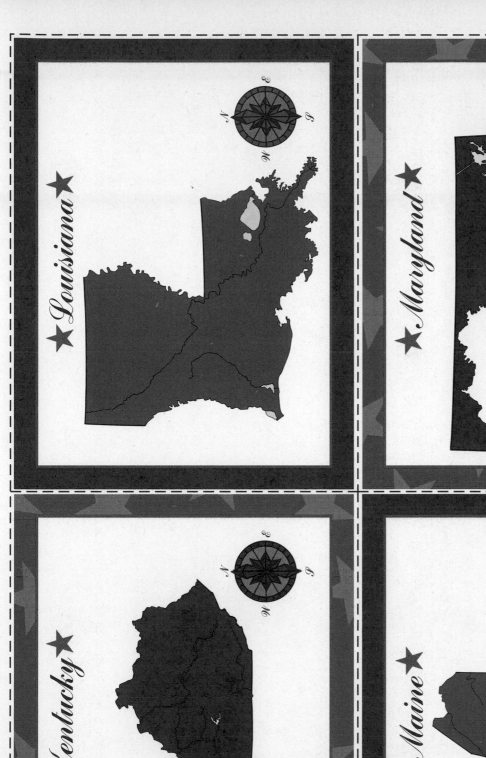

Louisiana

Maryland

Kentucky

Maine

© 2001 McGraw-Hill. All Rights Reserved.

The Fifty States

The eighteenth state

★ accounts for almost 90 percent of all crayfish produced in the United States.

★ was the site of the final battles of the War of 1812.

★ was once claimed for France by the French explorer Robert Caveller, sieur de La Salle.

★ was part of the Louisiana Purchase, a huge land parcel purchased from Napoleon of France in 1803.

★ is important to everyone who loves jazz music, Cajun and Creole cooking, and Mardi Gras.

★ has New Orleans, a city built where the Mississippi River empties into the Gulf of Mexico.

The fifteenth state

★ is the location of the United States Gold Depository at Fort Knox.

★ is the location of the Cumberland Gap, an important passageway for early explorers.

★ is the nation's leading producer of bituminous coal.

★ sided with the Union during the Civil War, even though it is a southern state.

★ is the birthplace of Abraham Lincoln, the sixteenth president, and Jefferson Davis, president of the Confederate States of America during the Civil War.

The seventh state

★ was named for Queen Henrietta Maria, the wife of Charles I of England.

★ is almost cut in half by the Chesapeake Bay.

★ was explored in 1608 by Captain John Smith.

★ is the home of the United States Naval Academy at Annapolis.

★ is where Francis Scott Key wrote "The Star-Spangled Banner" while watching the British bombard Fort McHenry at Baltimore.

The twenty-third state

★ is known as "Down East."

★ once belonged to Massachusetts.

★ is bordered on the north by Canada.

★ is famous for its lobsters.

★ was probably visited by the first European when Leif Ericson, a Viking leader, arrived around 1000 A.D.

★ is the home state of Margaret Chase Smith, the first woman to have been elected to both houses of the United States Congress.

© 2001 McGraw-Hill. All Rights Reserved.

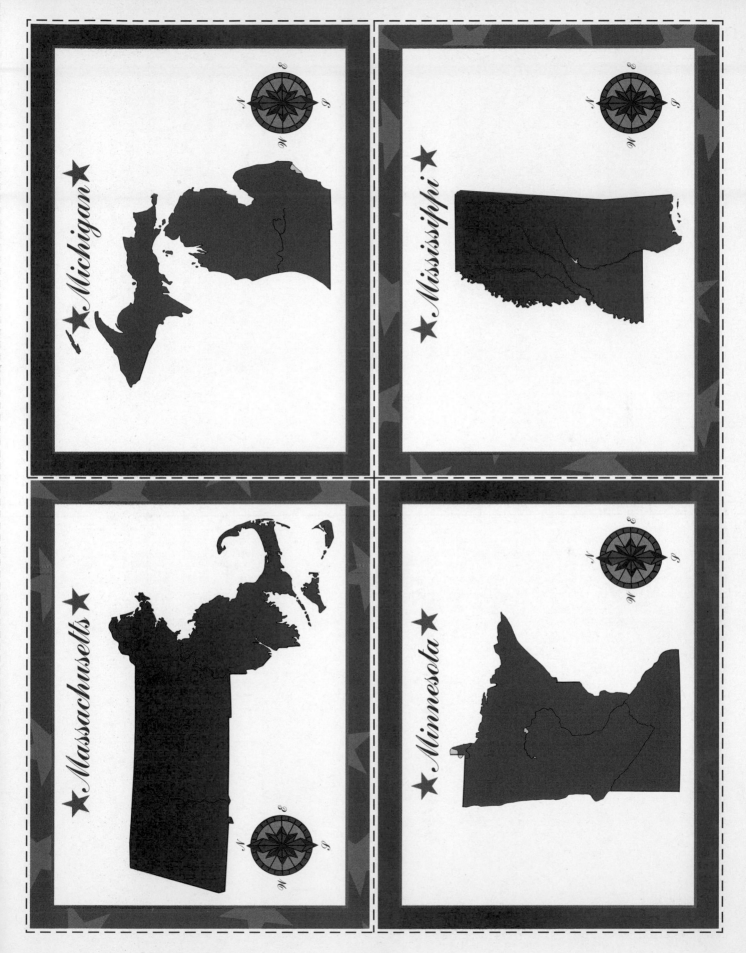

Michigan

Mississippi

Massachusetts

Minnesota

© 2001 McGraw-Hill. All Rights Reserved.

The Fifty States

The twenty-sixth state

★ has two nicknames, the "Wolverine State" and the "Great Lakes State."

★ shares a border with Canada.

★ is home to Greenfield Village, where visitors can see Henry Ford's birthplace and Thomas Edison's laboratory.

★ once fought with Ohio over the land around what is now the city of Toledo, Ohio.

★ has 2 separate sections—the Upper Peninsula and the Lower Peninsula.

The sixth state

★ is the location of Salem, the site of the infamous witchcraft trials of 1692.

★ is the location of Plymouth, the place where the Pilgrims landed in 1620.

★ is the birthplace of John F. Kennedy, the thirty-fifth president, who was a senator from this state.

★ is where, in April of 1775, the Revolutionary War began when patriots fought the British at Lexington and Concord.

The twentieth state

★ is where Coca-Cola was first bottled.

★ is the birthplace of Elvis Presley, one of the most popular singers of the 1900s.

★ is the ancestral home of the Chickasaw and the Natchez, two Native American nations.

★ became the second state to leave the Union at the start of the Civil War in 1861.

The thirty-second state

★ is known as the "Land of 10,000 Lakes."

★ is the location of the northernmost point in the continental United States.

★ is said to have been the home of fabled lumberjack, Paul Bunyan.

★ is the location of Duluth, the busiest freshwater port in North America.

★ boasts the Mall of America, the largest shopping mall in the United States.

 © 2001 McGraw-Hill. All Rights Reserved.

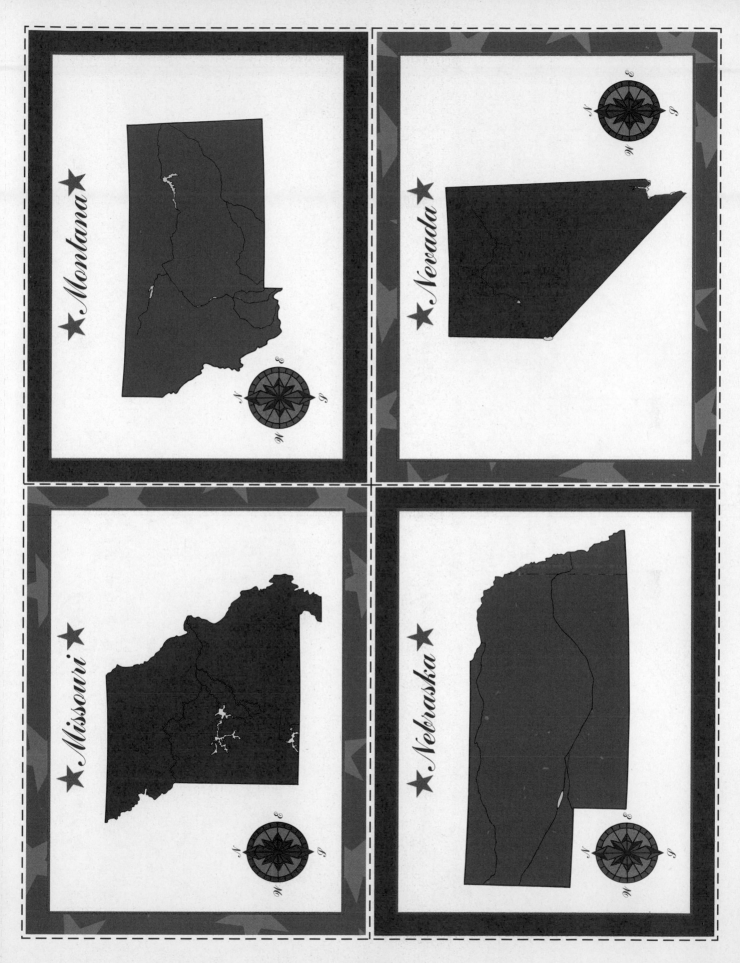

© 2001 McGraw-Hill. All Rights Reserved.

The Fifty States

The forty-first state

★ is the location of Glacier National Park.

★ is the home of Pompey's Pillar, a famous landmark used by pioneers in their migration to the West.

★ is where, at the Battle of Little Bighorn in 1876, Custer's Last Stand was fought.

★ is where, in 1842, Jesuit missionaries established St. Mary's mission, the first attempt at a permanent settlement in the state.

The twenty-fourth state

★ is known as the "Show Me State."

★ is the location of the famous Gateway Arch.

★ is the place where Mark Twain, creator of Tom Sawyer and Huckleberry Finn, lived.

★ is the home state of Harry S. Truman, the thirty-third president.

★ was the starting point for Lewis and Clark's 1804 Journey of Discovery.

★ was the eastern destination of the Pony Express, which connected the eastern United States with California.

The thirty-sixth state

★ is the driest of the 50 states.

★ is the location of Lake Mead and Lake Tahoe.

★ is the location of Las Vegas, one of the fastest growing cities in the United States.

★ was once part of Mexico; the treaty of Guadalupe Hidalgo, which ended the Mexican War, granted the area to the United States.

The thirty-seventh state

★ is the location of Chimney Rock in the North Platte River Valley, an important landmark for early pioneers traveling along the Oregon Trail.

★ has a greater percentage of farmland than any other state.

★ is the birthplace of Gerald Ford, the thirty-eighth president.

★ once contained the Dakota and Colorado territories.

© 2001 McGraw-Hill. All Rights Reserved.

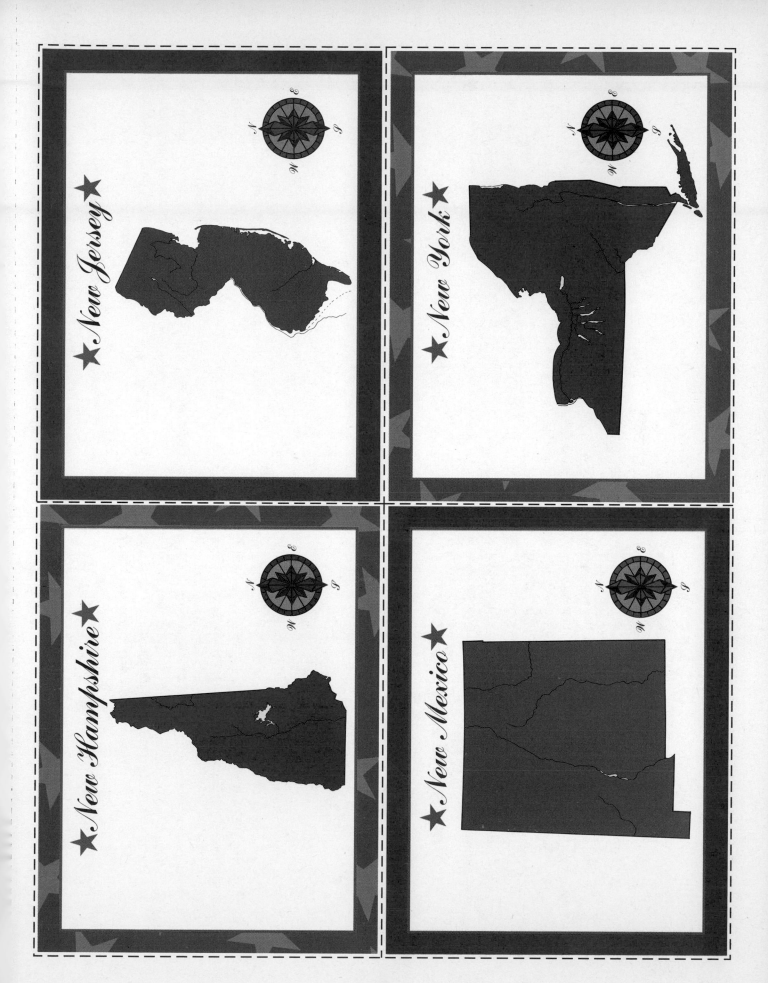

New Jersey

New York

New Hampshire

New Mexico

© 2001 McGraw-Hill. All Rights Reserved.

The Fifty States

The third state

★ is nicknamed the "Garden State."

★ is where Thomas Edison set up his laboratory and made many astounding discoveries and inventions.

★ is the home state of Woodrow Wilson, the twenty-eighth president of the United States.

★ is where, in 1524, Giovanni de Verrazzano explored the coast.

★ is where, on June 6, 1933, the first drive-in movie theater in the United States opened.

The eleventh state

★ is the home of Lake Placid, site of the 1932 and 1980 Winter Olympic games.

★ is the home of the United States Military Academy at West Point.

★ is the "birthplace" of baseball and home of the National Baseball Hall of Fame at Cooperstown.

★ is where President McKinley was assassinated while attending the Pan American Exposition in 1901.

★ is where George Washington first took the oath of office as the nation's president.

The ninth state

★ has the motto "Live Free or Die."

★ is known by its official trademark: the Old Man of the Mountain, a natural granite formation on Profile Mountain.

★ is the state where, since 1920, the earliest presidential primary election has been held.

★ is the home state of Franklin Pierce, the fourteenth president.

★ is the birthplace of Alan Shepard, America's first astronaut in space.

The forty-seventh state

★ is separated from Mexico by the Rio Grande River.

★ is the home of Carlsbad Caverns National Park.

★ is the site of El Camino Real, the oldest road built by Europeans in the United States.

★ was explored by Coronado, the Spanish explorer who searched for a legendary lost city of gold, in 1540–1542.

★ is where, on July 16, 1945, the world's first atomic bomb exploded.

© 2001 McGraw-Hill. All Rights Reserved.

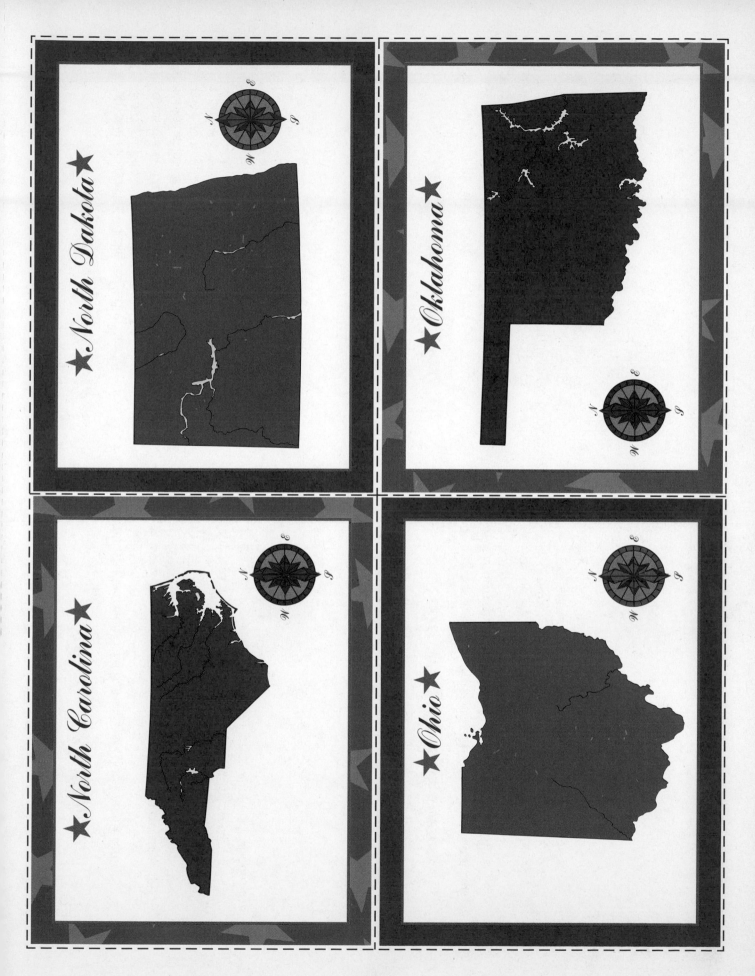

North Dakota

Oklahoma

North Carolina

Ohio

© 2001 McGraw-Hill. All Rights Reserved.

The Fifty States

The thirty-ninth state

★ has two nicknames, "Flickertail State" and "Peace Garden State."
★ leads the nation in the production of barley and wheat.
★ ranks first in the nation in total coal reserves.
★ is home to several Native American groups including the Sioux, Hidatsa, Ojibwa and Cheyenne.

The forty-sixth state

★ is named after words from the Native American Choctaw language that mean "red people."
★ is the home of the National Cowboy Hall of Fame.
★ is the location of the Chisholm Trail, which was used by cowboys to drive millions of cattle from Texas to Kansas to sell there.
★ has working oil wells on the grounds of the state capitol building.

The twelfth state

★ is the location of both the Blue Ridge and the Great Smoky Mountains.
★ is the location of Cape Hatteras, sometimes called the "graveyard of the Atlantic"—many shipwrecks have occurred nearby.
★ is where, in 1903, the Wright Brothers launched the world's first successful airplane flight near Kitty Hawk.
★ is the location of Ocracoke Island, where Blackbeard the pirate had a hideout.

The seventeenth state

★ was named after an Iroquois word meaning "beautiful."
★ is known as the "Buckeye State" after a tree of the same name.
★ was the first state admitted to the Union from the Northwest Territory.
★ is the birthplace of seven presidents.

© 2001 McGraw-Hill. All Rights Reserved.

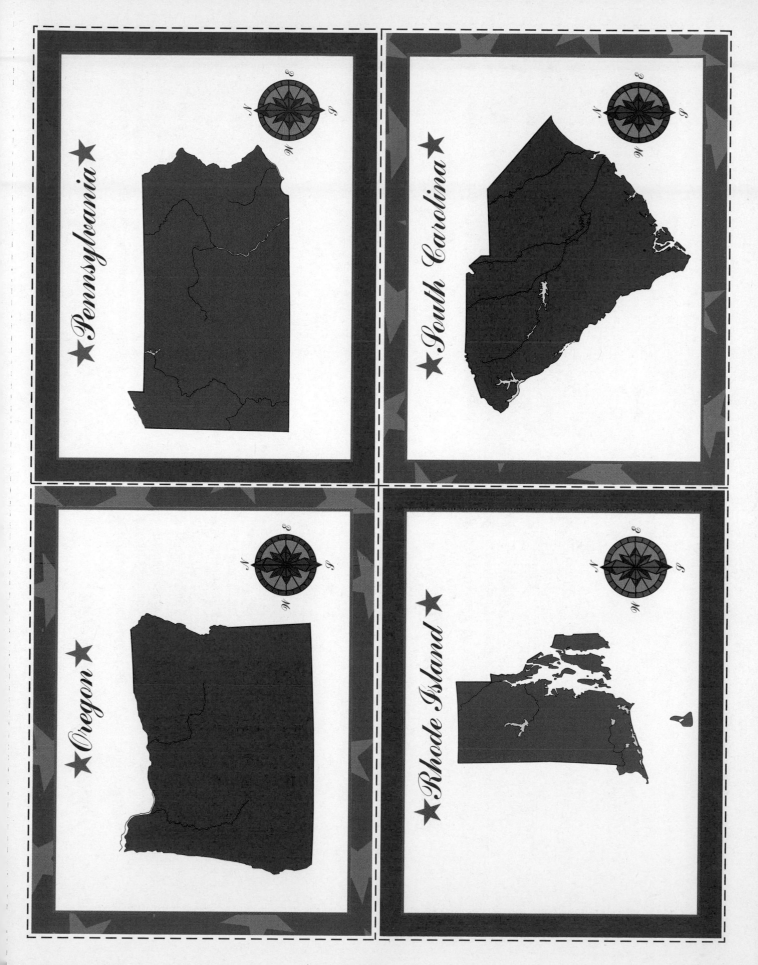

© 2001 McGraw-Hill. All Rights Reserved.

The second state

★ has two nicknames, the "Keystone State" and the "Quaker State."

★ is the location of the world's largest chocolate factory.

★ is where the Declaration of Independence was signed in 1776.

★ was, in 1681, a large land grant offered by King Charles II to William Penn.

The thirty-third state

★ is bordered on the north by the Columbia River.

★ is the location of Crater Lake—at 1,932 feet deep, it is the deepest lake in the United States.

★ is the location of Deschutes National Forest, which has the largest forest of lava-cast trees in the world.

★ is the location of Fort Clatsop, where Lewis and Clark and their band of explorers spent the terrible winter of 1805–1806.

The eighth state

★ was originally named after King Charles II of England.

★ is nicknamed the "Palmetto State."

★ is the location of popular resorts including Myrtle Beach and Hilton Head.

★ was first seen by a European, Francisco Gordillo, in 1521.

★ is where the first shots of the Civil War were fired.

The thirteenth state

★ is the smallest of the 50 states.

★ is cut almost in half by Narragansett Bay.

★ ranks first in the nation in the production of costume jewelry.

★ is where a permanent European settlement was founded, in 1636, by Roger Williams.

★ was first to declare its independence from Britain on May 4, 1776.

 © 2001 McGraw-Hill. All Rights Reserved.

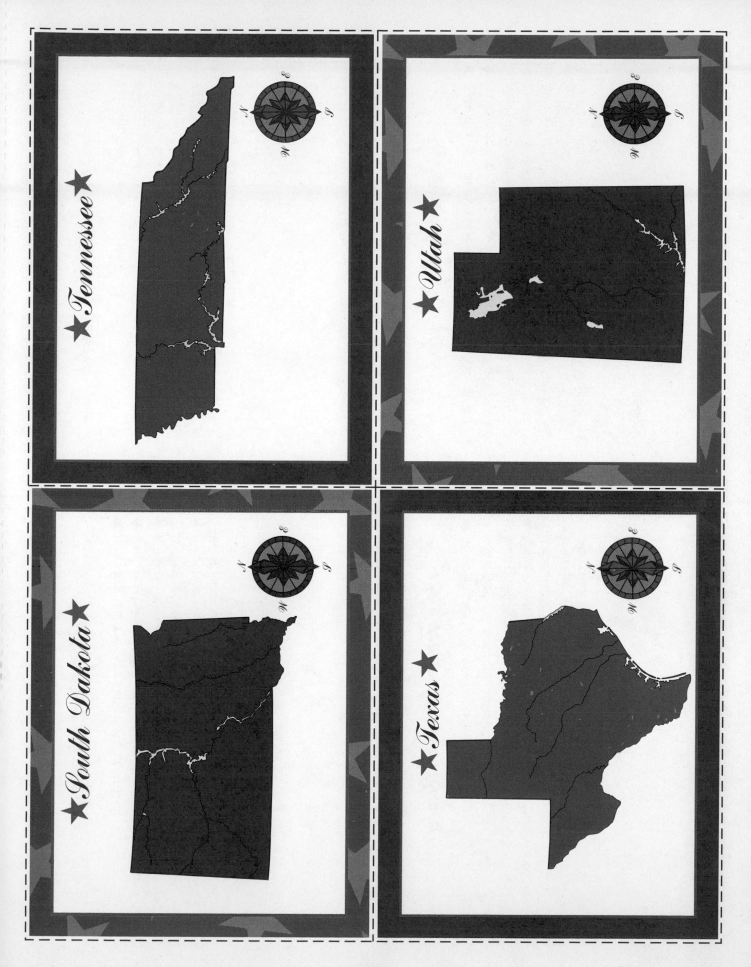

★ *Tennessee* ★

★ *Utah* ★

★ *South Dakota* ★

★ *Texas* ★

© 2001 McGraw-Hill. All Rights Reserved.

The Fifty States

The sixteenth state

★ is nicknamed the "Volunteer State."

★ is the location of the Grand Ole Opry, the most famous country music center in the world.

★ is the location of Graceland, the estate of Elvis Presley, which attracts thousands of visitors each year.

★ is the birthplace of three presidents, Andrew Jackson, James K. Polk and Andrew Johnson.

★ is where the Battle of Shiloh, an important battle of the Civil War, was fought.

The forty-fifth state

★ is divided in half by the spine of the Rocky Mountains.

★ is the location of the Great Salt Lake, the largest salt lake in North America.

★ is where, at Promontory Point in 1869, the first transcontinental railroad system in the United States was completed.

★ was settled by Mormon leader Brigham Young and his band of followers.

The fortieth state

★ is nicknamed the "Mount Rushmore State."

★ is roughly divided in half by the Missouri River.

★ is the location of Mount Rushmore, the famous monument to four presidents.

★ is the home of Homestake Mine, the oldest continuously operating gold mine in the world.

The twenty-eighth state

★ is known as the "Lone Star State."

★ is our nation's second largest state.

★ was an independent republic before statehood.

★ is the location of the Alamo, perhaps the state's most important historical site.

★ is where, in 1963, President John F. Kennedy was assassinated.

© 2001 McGraw-Hill. All Rights Reserved.

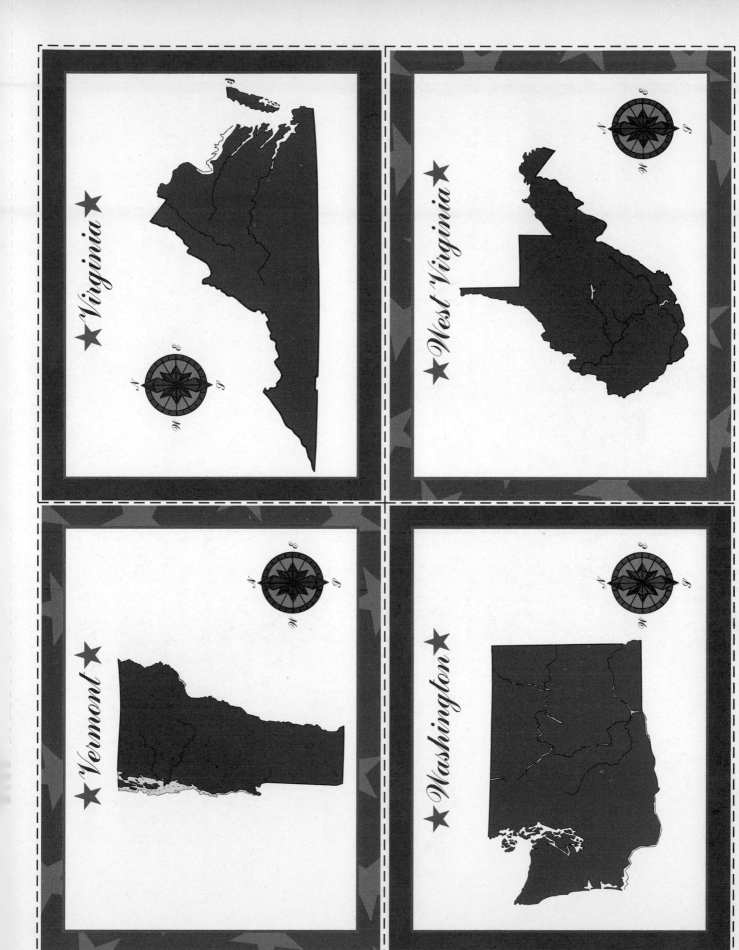

Virginia

West Virginia

Vermont

Washington

© 2001 McGraw-Hill. All Rights Reserved.

The Fifty States

The tenth state

★ is known as "Old Dominion."

★ is the location of Mount Vernon, once the home of George Washington.

★ is the birthplace of eight presidents.

★ is where, at Jamestown in 1607, the first permanent English settlement in North America was established.

★ is where, at the town called Appomattox Court House on April 9, 1865, General Lee surrendered to General Grant, bringing an end to the Civil War.

The thirty-fifth state

★ was part of Virginia until the Civil War. They broke off to remain in the union while Virginia joined the South.

★ is the only state with two panhandles.

★ is the glass and marble manufacturing center of the United States.

★ is completely covered by the Appalachian Mountains.

★ is the location of Harpers Ferry where, in 1850, John Brown made his famous raid.

★ is the location of Romney, a town that changed hands between the Union and the Confederacy no fewer than 56 times during the Civil War.

The fourteenth state

★ is nicknamed the "Green Mountain State."

★ is bordered on the east by the Connecticut River.

★ is the only New England state without a seacoast.

★ has the lowest percentage of city dwellers of any state.

★ leads the nation in the production of maple syrup.

★ is the birthplace of Calvin Coolidge, the thirtieth president.

★ was explored by Samuel de Champlain who, in 1609, became the first European to set foot on its soil.

The forty-second state

★ is known as the "Evergreen State."

★ is the location of Grand Coulee Dam, the largest concrete dam in the United States.

★ is where, in 1980, the volcano Mount Saint Helens erupted.

★ is the home of the Space Needle, a unique tower over 600 feet tall.

★ is where, in 1962, the first municipal monorail service in the United States began operating.

The Fifty States

© 2001 McGraw-Hill. All Rights Reserved.

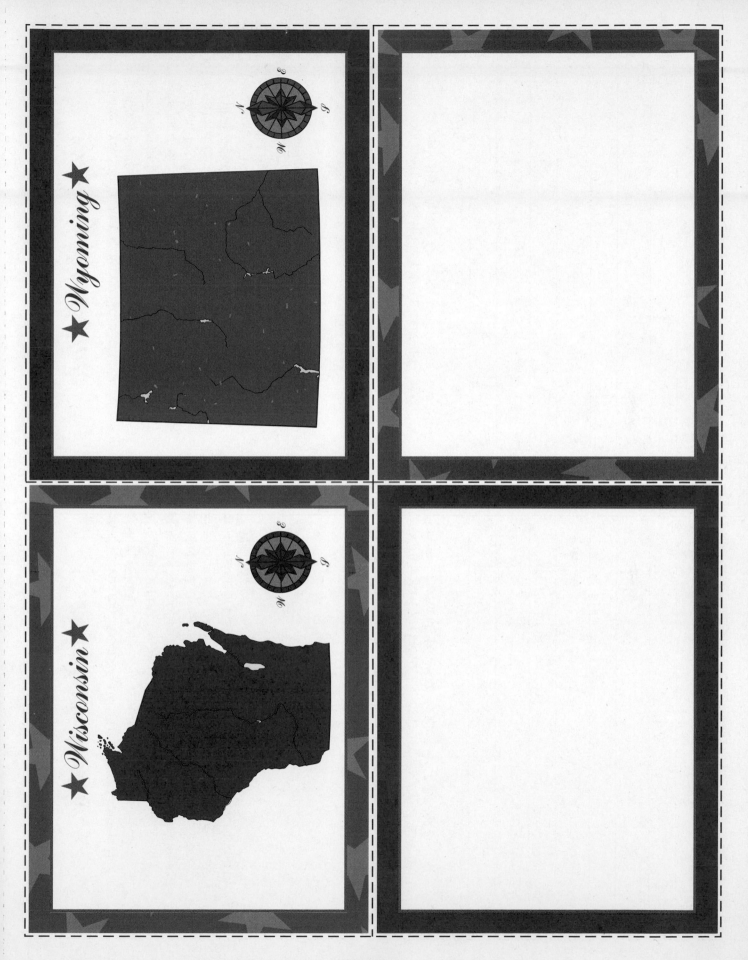

© 2001 McGraw-Hill. All Rights Reserved.

The Fifty States

The forty-fourth state

★ has two nicknames, the "Cowboy State" and the "Equality State."

★ is the least populated of all the states.

★ is the location of Devil's Tower, set aside by Congress in 1906 as the nation's first national monument.

★ is the location of Old Faithful, the most famous geyser in the United States.

★ became, in 1869, the first state in the nation to grant women the right to vote.

★ became, with the election of Nellie Tayloe Ross in 1924, the first state to choose a woman as its governor.

Create your own state. List its points below. Draw a picture of your state on the back.

★ _____
_____
★ _____
_____
★ _____
_____
★ _____
_____

The thirtieth state

★ is named for an Ojibway word meaning "gathering of the waters."

★ is nicknamed the "Badger State."

★ leads the nation in the production of milk and cheese.

★ is where, at Green Bay in 1634, Jean Nicolet, a French explorer, became the first European to set foot on its soil.

★ is where, at Racine in 1887, malted milk was created by William Horlick.

Create your own state. List its points below. Draw a picture of your state on the back.

★ _____
_____
★ _____
_____
★ _____
_____
★ _____
_____

The Fifty States

140

© 2001 McGraw-Hill. All Rights Reserved.

Welcome to Alabama

*I*n 1519, Native American tribes, such as the Choctaw and Creek, greeted the Spanish explorer Alonso Alvarez de Pineda. He was the first European to arrive on the land that became Alabama. Hernando de Soto also explored the land in 1540. De Soto fought with the Choctaw and defeated their chief, Tuscaloosa. But the explorers did not stay very long in the New World. It was not until 1702 that the French brothers Pierre and Jean-Baptiste Moyne started the first French settlement. This settlement would become the modern-day city of Mobile, Alabama.

In 1763, England and France signed the Treaty of Paris. The countries agreed that England would take most of the northern part of Alabama. This land went to the United States after the War of Independence. In 1814, General Andrew Jackson won the rest of the land from the Creek Indians. On December 14, 1819, Alabama became the twenty-second state in the Union.

State Flag

Yellowhammer State Bird

Camellia State Flower

FAMOUS ALABAMANS

★ Coretta Scott King was a civil rights leader and is the widow of Martin Luther King, Jr.

★ Hank Aaron hit more home runs than any other baseball player.

★ Nat "King" Cole was a popular singer.

★ Helen Keller, although blind and deaf, became a public speaker and author.

★ Rosa Parks was a civil rights activist who refused to give up her seat to a white person on a city bus.

★ Jesse Owens was an Olympic gold medal winner in track and field.

★ Harper Lee wrote novels and won a Pulitzer prize.

STATE GREATS

★ Russell Cave, in Bridgeport, is a national monument. People lived in the cave more than 9,000 years ago.

★ NASA's first headquarters was in Huntsville, Alabama.

★ Selma, Alabama was the site of Rosa Parks' civil rights protest of the 1960s.

★ The Tuskegee Institute, one of the first African-American schools, is in Tuskegee, Alabama.

★ The Tenn-Tom Waterway links the Tennessee and Tombigbee Rivers. The project moved more dirt than the building of the Panama Canal, a large waterway connecting the Atlantic and Pacific oceans.

© 2001 McGraw-Hill. All Rights Reserved.

The Fifty States

Alabama: The Heart of Dixie

Look at an atlas or map of Alabama. Add the names of the following places to the map below.

★ the capital of Alabama

★ the site of Rosa Parks' civil rights protest

★ the large body of water to the south of Alabama

★ the city that shares the name of the Tuskegee Institute

★ the city named after Andrew Jackson

★ the river named after the state

★ the cave where humans lived more than 9,000 years ago

★ the site of NASA's first headquarters

★ the first French settlement

★ the town named after a Choctaw chief

Size: 51,705 square miles
Population: 4,283,000

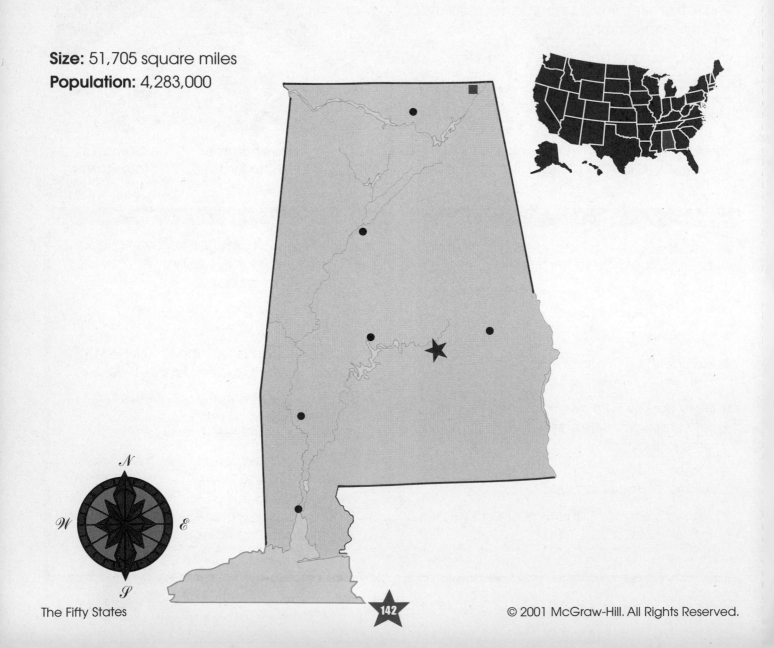

142

© 2001 McGraw-Hill. All Rights Reserved.

Alabama: **The Heart of Dixie**

Read the clues. Circle the answers in the word search below.

Across

★ the capital of Alabama

★ the name of the city near Russell Cave

★ this crop is grown in Alabama

Down

★ the state flower

★ General Jackson's first name

★ the city that had the first major civil rights protest

```
F G C X Y C L E A N D R E W
B A A H M C W P S H O P Z T
T S M Y W Z A R Q E A S L T
P E E X M O N T G O M E R Y
A Q L K G H D T Z Y X L W B
E X L K M B R O I B C M X F
B R I D G E P O R T Y A N V
Y P A W B X W D C O T T O N
```

Unscramble the circled letters to find the name of the first settlement in Alabama.

— — — — — —

The Alabama state motto reads: *Audemus jura nostra defendere.*

In Latin, this means: "We dare defend our rights."

Write about how people in Alabama have defended their rights and why this is important.

_____

_____

_____

_____

_____

© 2001 McGraw-Hill. All Rights Reserved.

The Fifty States

Welcome to Alaska

HOW ALASKA BECAME A STATE

*B*efore the Russian explorers and a Danish scientist, Vitus Bering, landed on the coast in 1741, Alaska was home to several groups of Native Americans including the Tlingit, Haida, Athabascan, Aleut and Inuit. Later, the Russians explored Alaska's long coastline and hunted seals for their fur. They built their first settlement on Kodiak Island and made their trading headquarters near Sitka.

In 1867, Secretary of State William H. Seward bought Alaska from Russia for $7.2 million. Few people believed the land had any value, and they called the purchase, "Seward's Folly." But this idea would soon change. In 1896, gold was discovered in Canada's Klondike River and the stream beds of Alaska. Thousands of people rushed to make their fortunes in places like Juneau, Nome and Fairbanks, Alaska's second largest city. After the gold rush, some settlers stayed. Alaska became the forty-ninth state in 1959. Alaska is also rich in oil, fishing, minerals and timber.

State Flag

Willow Ptarmigan
State Bird

Forget-Me-Not
State Flower

FAMOUS ALASKANS

★ William Egan was the first elected governor of Alaska.

★ Benny Benson, at 13 years old, designed the state flag.

★ Elizabeth Peratrovich supported and worked for Alaska's Anti-Discrimination Act.

★ Mary Antisarlook protected and herded reindeer.

★ Chief Kowee found the first gold strike at Juneau.

★ Edward Lewis "Bob" Bartlett was the first state senator.

★ Ernest Gruening is known as "the father of Alaskan statehood."

STATE GREATS

★ Alaska is the largest state in the United States.

★ Alaska has more coastline than all of the other states combined.

★ Mt. McKinley, in Denali National Park, is the highest mountain in North America.

★ Point Barrow is the United States' most northern point.

★ Alaska also contains Amatignak Island—the westernmost point, and Semisopochnoi Island—the easternmost point in the United States. Both islands are in the Aleutian Islands chain.

★ The Trans Alaska Pipeline takes oil from Prudhoe Bay across Alaska to the port of Valdez.

 © 2001 McGraw-Hill. All Rights Reserved.

Alaska: **The Last Frontier**

Look at an atlas or map of Alaska. Add the names of the following places to the map below.

★ a chain of islands crossing into the eastern hemisphere

★ the highest mountain in North America

★ a gold rush town and Alaska's second largest city

★ the state capital where Chief Kowee first found gold

★ a narrow waterway between Alaska and Russia, named for a Danish scientist

★ the northern beginning of the Trans Alaska Pipeline

★ the northernmost point in the United States

★ the Trans Alaska Pipeline ends at Valdez and this large area of water

★ the island first settled by Russians

★ the city named after the man who purchased Alaska

Size: 591,004 square miles
Population: 551,947

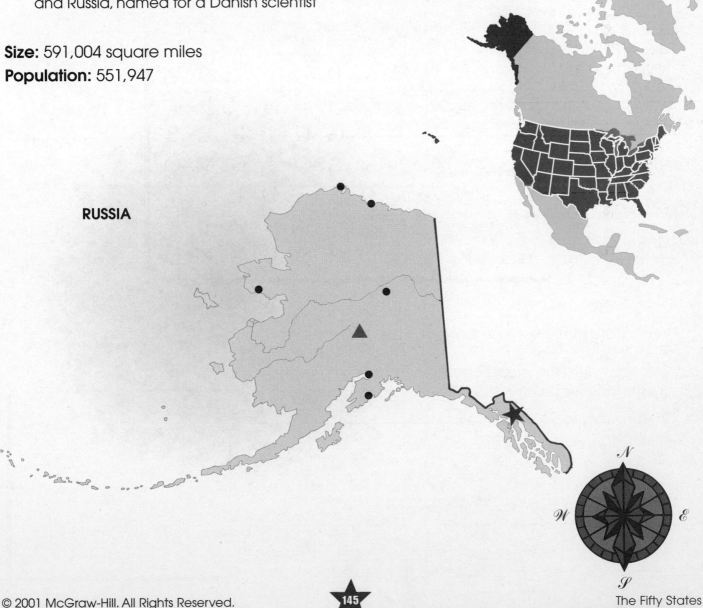

RUSSIA

© 2001 McGraw-Hill. All Rights Reserved.

The Fifty States

Alaska: The Last Frontier

Use the words in the Word Bank to find and circle words about Alaska in the word search below.

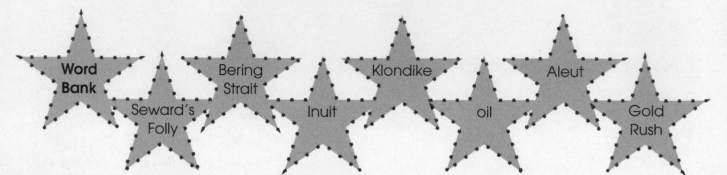

Word Bank

Bering Strait

Klondike

Aleut

Seward's Folly

Inuit

oil

Gold Rush

K	B	T	N	I	A	O	I	L	H	J	Z
L	E	A	N	U	M	K	X	L	S	A	M
O	B	U	K	T	U	E	L	A	U	K	L
T	I	A	R	T	S	G	N	I	R	E	B
T	D	F	O	L	I	A	O	T	D	M	O
S	E	W	A	R	D	S	F	O	L	L	Y
G	O	L	W	E	K	I	D	N	O	L	K
Y	D	H	B	G	O	H	S	U	G	K	D

Alaska's state motto is: *North to the Future.*

Write about what the motto means. Then, design a new state seal with your own image of *North to the Future.*

_____

_____

_____

_____

_____

_____

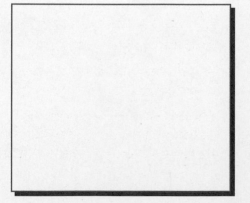

  146

© 2001 McGraw-Hill. All Rights Reserved.

Welcome to Arizona

HOW ARIZONA BECAME A STATE

*N*ative Americans, including the Navajo, Apache and Pueblo, lived in Arizona's deserts for hundreds of years before the Europeans came. One of the first Spanish explorers, Marcos de Niza, arrived in 1539. He came looking for gold. In 1692, Father Eusebio Kino also came looking for gold. He did not find gold either, but he helped start 24 missions. It was another 60 years before the first European settlement was built at Tubac.

Arizona belonged to many countries before it became part of the United States. In 1821, Mexico won its independence from Spain. Arizona was part of Mexico at the time. From 1846 to1848, the United States and Mexico fought a war for ownership of the territory. The United States won most of Arizona and bought the rest in 1862. Next, Arizona belonged to the Confederacy for 1 year during the Civil War. Finally, in 1863, Arizona belonged to the United States as just a territory. In 1912, it became the forty-eighth state.

State Flag

Cactus Wren
State Bird

Saguaro Blossom
State Flower

FAMOUS ARIZONANS

★ Charles D. Poston served in Congress and worked to make Arizona a territory. He is called "the father of Arizona."

★ Geronimo was an Apache leader who fought, surrendered and died at Fort Sill, Oklahoma.

★ Chief Cochise was another Apache leader. He was never captured.

★ Wyatt Earp was the deputy U.S. marshal at Tombstone.

★ Bill Williams was a settler who lived with the Osaga tribe.

★ Sandra Day O'Connor was Arizona's assistant attorney general and became the first woman Supreme Court justice.

STATE GREATS

★ Hopi Village, on the Hopi Indian Reservation, is the oldest village in the United States.

★ Arizona State University, in Tempe, is a leading university.

★ The Gila lizard that lives in Arizona's deserts is the only poisonous lizard found in the United States.

★ The Grand Canyon is the largest canyon in the United States.

★ The Sonoran Desert is one of the hottest places in the United States. Summer temperatures average 103 degrees Fahrenheit.

★ The Hoover Dam is one of the largest hydroelectric plants in the United States. It was named after President Herbert Hoover.

© 2001 McGraw-Hill. All Rights Reserved.

The Fifty States

Arizona: The Grand Canyon State

Look at an atlas or map of Arizona. Add the names of the following places to the map below.

★ the river named for the state of Colorado

★ the country to the south that once owned Arizona

★ the town where Wyatt Earp was deputy U.S. Marshall

★ the river named after the poisonous lizard

★ the city named after a flag pole

★ the capital of Arizona

★ the largest canyon in the United States

★ the place where the corners of four states meet

★ the dam named after Herbert Hoover

★ the Indian reservation that has the oldest village

★ the city that is home to Arizona State University

Size: 114,000 square miles
Population: 3,677,985

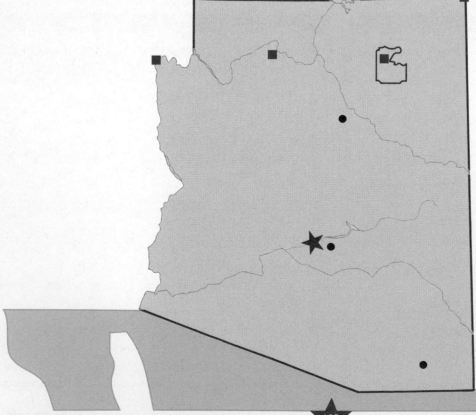

 © 2001 McGraw-Hill. All Rights Reserved.

Arizona: The Grand Canyon State

Match the Arizona words with their definitions. Each time you make a match, your line should cross out a letter. You can cross out a letter more than once.

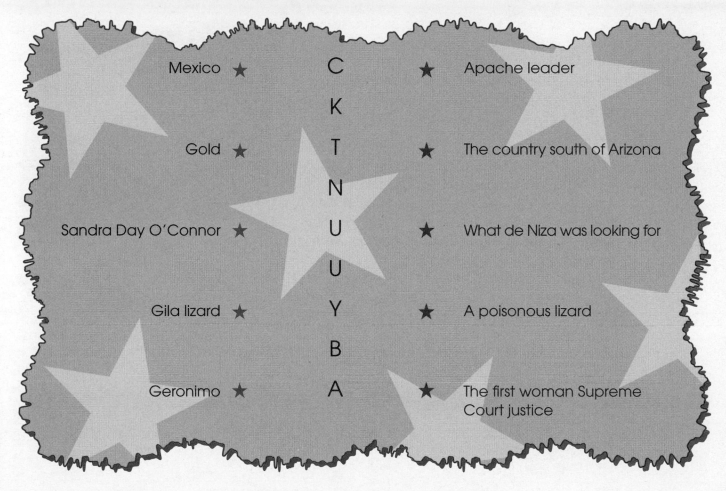

Mexico ★   C   ★ Apache leader

      K

Gold ★   T   ★ The country south of Arizona

      N

Sandra Day O'Connor ★   U   ★ What de Niza was looking for

      U

Gila lizard ★   Y   ★ A poisonous lizard

      B

Geronimo ★   A   ★ The first woman Supreme Court justice

You should have five letters left over. Unscramble the five letters to find where the first white settlement was built in Arizona.

___ ___ ___ ___ ___

When Lt. Joseph Ives visited Arizona in 1858, he saw a big desert. He told the United States Congress that Arizona was "altogether valueless." He was wrong. What interesting things can you see in Arizona today? Write about what you might see in Arizona.

_____

_____

_____

© 2001 McGraw-Hill. All Rights Reserved.

Welcome to Arkansas

HOW ARKANSAS BECAME A STATE

*I*n 1682, the Frenchman, La Salle, traveled through the wilderness that would become Arkansas. La Salle claimed the whole territory for France. This territory made up most of the land west of the Mississippi River. But few settlers stayed to live in this land. It was not until 1686 that Henri de Tonti, one of La Salle's men, started a fur trading village named Arkansas Post.

In 1803, President Jefferson bought Arkansas from France as part of the Louisiana Purchase. A monument in Marianna marks the place where surveyors began mapping the territory. At this time, there were fewer than 1,000 settlers. Most of the people living in the Louisiana territory were Native Americans from the Quapaw, Osage or Caddo tribes. In the 1820s and 1830s, settlers from the eastern United States began to move into the new land. Many were farmers or fur traders looking for good land and forests. In the 1830s, the number of settlers in Arkansas grew to more than 50,000. Arkansas became the twenty-fifth state on June 15, 1836.

State Flag

Mockingbird State Bird

Apple Blossom State Flower

FAMOUS ARKANSANS

★ William Jefferson Clinton was born in Hope, Arkansas, and became the forty-second president of the United States.

★ Maya Angelou is a writer who often writes about her home in Stamps, Arkansas.

★ Douglas MacArthur was an important military leader during World War II.

★ Sam M. Walton founded the Wal-Mart Stores.

★ Leroy "Eldridge" Cleaver was a civil rights activist.

★ Hattie Ophelia Wyatt Caraway was the first woman elected to the U.S. Senate.

★ William Grant Still was the first African-American to conduct an American professional symphony.

STATE GREATS

★ The Buffalo River was the United States' first national river.

★ Crater of Diamonds State Park, near Murfreesboro, is the only diamond mine in North America.

★ The University of Arkansas is located in Fayetteville.

★ Ozark folk music and crafts entertain tourists at the Ozark Folk Center in Mountain View.

★ Magazine Mountain is the highest point in the state. It is 2,753 feet above sea level.

★ Hot Springs is known for the healing waters of its natural springs.

© 2001 McGraw-Hill. All Rights Reserved.

Arkansas: The Land of Opportunity

Look at an atlas or map of Arkansas. Add the names of the following places to the map below.

★ the river that has the same name as the state

★ the nation's first national river

★ the river that runs down the east side of the state

★ the location of the University of Arkansas

★ the city on the border of Texas and Arkansas that takes its name from the two states

★ the capital of Arkansas

★ the tourist town named after its many natural hot springs

★ the town where the Ozark Folk Center was built

★ the birthplace of Maya Angelou

★ the town where surveyors began mapping the Louisiana territory

★ the town where President Clinton was born

Size: 53,187 square miles
Population: 2,473,000

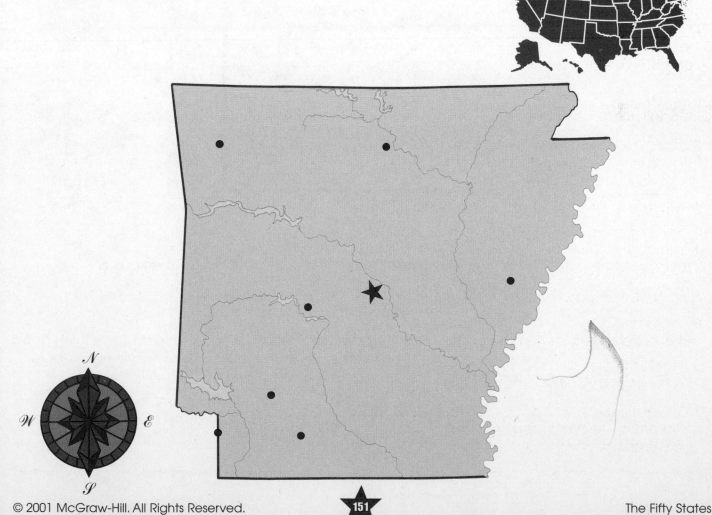

© 2001 McGraw-Hill. All Rights Reserved.

The Fifty States

Arkansas: **The Land of Opportunity**

Read the clues and unscramble the words. Then, find and circle them in the word search below.

★ President Clinton's first name   LBIL   __ __ __ __

★ A national river   FFULBOA   __ __ __ __ __ __ __

★ First explorer of Arkansas   LLLAASE   __ __ __ __ __ __ __

★ Founder of Arkansas Post   TINTO   __ __ __ __ __

★ President Clinton's home town   EOPH   __ __ __ __

★ A writer who lives in Stamps   AAYM   __ __ __ __

A	Y	A	M	X	P	B	V
A	R	K	A	N	S	H	A
B	U	F	F	A	L	O	X
I	A	S	P	O	S	P	K
L	A	S	A	L	L	E	Y
L	T	T	O	N	T	I	W

Now, use some of the left over letters to write the name of the first village in Arkansas.

__ __ __ __ __ __ __ __ __ __ __

Arkansas is called the "Land of Opportunity." Opportunity means a chance to do something good. What kinds of opportunities do people have in Arkansas? Write about the good things people could do or see in Arkansas.

_____

_____

 © 2001 McGraw-Hill. All Rights Reserved.

Welcome to California

HOW CALIFORNIA BECAME A STATE

When Portuguese explorer Juan Cabrillo sailed by the Californian coast for Spain in 1542, he claimed the area for Spain. At that time, more than 100 Native American tribes were living in California. In 1579, the British explorer Sir Francis Drake claimed California for England. The Spanish soon realized that they must settle California or lose their land. However, it was not until almost 200 years later, in 1769, that Father Junipero Serra built a mission in San Diego. It was the first of 21 missions.

California was ruled by Spain until 1821, when Mexico won its independence. California was then a province of Mexico. American trappers and settlers settled in California around this time. Later, the United States declared war against Mexico and, in 1848, California became a United States territory. That same year, gold was found at Sutter's Mill near Sacramento. The gold rush brought people from all over the world to search for gold. In 1850, California became the thirty-first state.

State Flag

CALIFORNIA REPUBLIC

California Valley Quail
State Bird

Golden Poppy
State Flower

FAMOUS CALIFORNIANS

★ Richard Nixon was the thirty-seventh president.

★ John Steinbeck was a writer who set most of his novels in California.

★ Sally Ride was the first woman in space.

★ Shirley Temple Black was a child actress and ambassador to the United Nations.

★ General George S. Patton, Jr., was a famous military leader during World War II.

★ Ronald Reagan was our fortieth president and also governor of California. He had been an actor in films as well.

STATE GREATS

★ Disneyland, Walt Disney's first theme park, is located in a suburb of Los Angeles.

★ Hollywood is the movie capital of the world.

★ San Francisco is famous for its Golden Gate Bridge.

★ Sequoia National Park's giant sequoia trees are the largest living things.

★ Yosemite National Park is home to Yosemite Falls, the nation's highest waterfall.

★ Death Valley contains the lowest point in the Western Hemisphere.

★ Mount Whitney is the highest peak in the United States outside of Alaska.

© 2001 McGraw-Hill. All Rights Reserved.

The Fifty States

California: **The Golden State**

Look at an atlas or map of California. Add the names of the following places to the map below.

* ★ the capital city of California
* ★ the place near where the Gold Rush started
* ★ the city where Disneyland is located
* ★ the place where the first mission was built
* ★ the city where the Golden Gate Bridge is located

* ★ the location of Yosemite Falls
* ★ the highest mountain in the lower 48 states
* ★ the location of the giant sequoia trees
* ★ the lowest point in the Western Hemisphere
* ★ the country that owned California in 1821

Size: 158,706 square miles
Population: 29,839,250

The Fifty States

154

© 2001 McGraw-Hill. All Rights Reserved.

California: The Golden State

Read the clues. Unscramble the words about California.

★ the state flower   YPPOP   __ __ __ __ __

★ the tallest mountain in California   TYHNIWE   __ __ __ __ __ __ __

★ the lowest place in California   EATDH AYLLVE   __ __ __ __ __ __ __ __ __ __

★ a famous national park   OSMTYEIE   __ __ __ __ __ __ __ __

★ the Spanish built 21 of them   SISMNIOS   __ __ __ __ __ __ __ __

★ the movie capital of the world   LLDOOHYOW   __ __ __ __ __ __ __ __ __

★ the state nickname   OGDLNE   __ __ __ __ __ __

In the past, California was known as "The Bear Flag Republic." There is a grizzly bear on California's state seal and flag today. Draw a picture of the flag and write about why a grizzly bear might have been chosen.

_____

_____

_____

_____

The state seal has the word "Eureka" on it which means "I have found it." Write about the things that were found in California.

_____

_____

_____

_____

© 2001 McGraw-Hill. All Rights Reserved.

The Fifty States

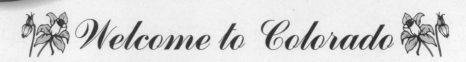

Welcome to Colorado

*B*efore Europeans arrived, Colorado was home to many Native American tribes. One tribe built its houses into the sides of cliffs. These cliff dwellings are now part of the Mesa Verde National Park. In 1706, Juan de Ulibarri claimed Colorado for Spain. Much of Colorado was later included in the Louisiana Purchase of 1803. By the end of the war with Mexico in 1848, all of Colorado belonged to the United States. Thousands of people rushed to Colorado in the middle and late 1800s, hoping to find gold or silver. Several mining communities grew into towns. Colorado's capital of Denver was once two mining villages.

Colorado's borders were created in 1861. The state is almost a perfect rectangle. Colorado first tried to become a state in 1864. But it would have to wait until August 1, 1876 to become the thirty-eighth state. Colorado is called the Centennial State because it became a state the same year the United States celebrated its one-hundredth anniversary.

State Flag

Lark Bunting
State Bird

Rocky Mountain Columbine
State Flower

FAMOUS COLORADIANS

★ M. Scott Carpenter from Boulder was one of America's first astronauts.

★ Patricia Schroeder was the first woman from Colorado elected to Congress.

★ Florence Rena Sabin was the first woman named to the National Academy of Sciences.

★ William Harrison "Jack" Dempsey was the world heavyweight boxing champion.

★ Ouray was an Ute chief.

★ Ben Nighthorse Campbell was the first Native American elected to the U.S. Senate.

STATE GREATS

★ Pikes Peak inspired Katharine Lee Bates to write "America the Beautiful" after a hiking trip.

★ Colorado Springs is the home of the United States Air Force Academy.

★ Skiers from around the world visit Colorado in the winter. The winter population of Vail is up to five times higher on weekends than on weekdays.

★ Leadville is the highest city in the United States.

★ Dinosaurs once roamed the state of Colorado. Scientists found so many fossils in one area that it was turned into Dinosaur National Monument.

 © 2001 McGraw-Hill. All Rights Reserved.

Colorado: The Centennial State

Look at an atlas or map of Colorado. Add the names of the following places to the map below.

- ★ an astronaut's hometown
- ★ the state capital
- ★ the Colorado River
- ★ the highest city in America
- ★ the site that inspired "America the Beautiful"
- ★ the home of the U.S. Air Force Academy

- ★ the national park that preserves the cliff dwellings
- ★ a ski community whose population grows by almost five times on winter weekends
- ★ the mining town of Pueblo
- ★ the Rio Grande
- ★ Dinosaur National Monument

Size: 104,091 square miles
Population: 3,307,912

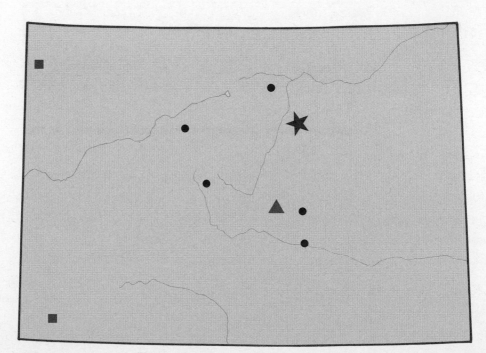

© 2001 McGraw-Hill. All Rights Reserved.

The Fifty States

Colorado: The Centennial State

Use the words in the Word Bank to find and circle the words about Colorado in the word search below.

Word Bank

Dempsey Denver gold Mesa

Bates Pikes Peak Leadville

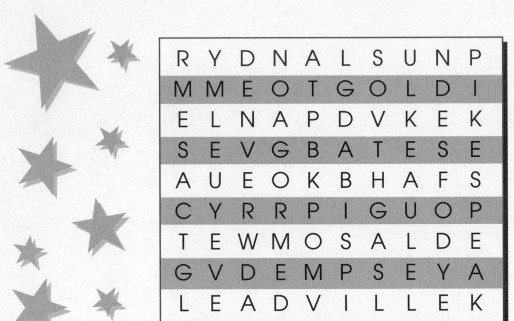

R	Y	D	N	A	L	S	U	N	P
M	M	E	O	T	G	O	L	D	I
E	L	N	A	P	D	V	K	E	K
S	E	V	G	B	A	T	E	S	E
A	U	E	O	K	B	H	A	F	S
C	Y	R	R	P	I	G	U	O	P
T	E	W	M	O	S	A	L	D	E
G	V	D	E	M	P	S	E	Y	A
L	E	A	D	V	I	L	L	E	K

Colorado is the nation's highest state. High in the mountains snow storms can occur, even in early autumn and late spring. Write about how this affects the people of the state.

_____

_____

_____

 © 2001 McGraw-Hill. All Rights Reserved.

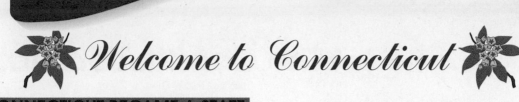

Welcome to Connecticut

★ HOW CONNECTICUT BECAME A STATE

A Dutch explorer named Adriaen Block sailed up the Connecticut River and became the first European to see Connecticut. Later, English settlers from Massachusetts came to the area in the 1630s. Thomas Hooker is called "Connecticut's Founder." He and a small group of settlers built a settlement called Hartford, which later became the state capital. The Connecticut settlers and the Algonquian tribe lived peacefully together.

In the early days of the colony, not everyone supported the American fight for independence. Many people were loyal to the British King George III. However, when fighting began in 1775, Connecticut supported the American cause. The state provided the Army with most of its supplies including food, tents, gunpowder, soap and candles. Connecticut became the fifth state to join the country in 1788.

State Flag

Robin State Bird

Mountain Laurel State Flower

FAMOUS CONNECTICUTERS

★ Nathan Hale was a Revolutionary War hero.

★ Eli Whitney invented the cotton gin.

★ Harriet Beecher Stowe wrote *Uncle Tom's Cabin,* a book about slavery.

★ Noah Webster gave us our Webster's Dictionary.

★ P.T. Barnum called his circus "The Greatest Show on Earth."

★ Charles Goodyear developed a process for making rubber.

★ Dean Acheson was a senator who helped write the Marshall Plan and the Truman Doctrine.

STATE GREATS

★ The first helicopter was developed in Stratford in 1939.

★ Visitors to Groton can tour the first nuclear-powered submarine, the *U.S.S. Nautilus.*

★ Yale University, the third oldest university in the nation, is located in New Haven.

★ Mystic Seaport is a popular vacation spot.

★ Hartford is called "America's Insurance Capital" since the oldest insurance company in the United States is located there.

★ Bridgeport is sometimes called "Park City" because it has many open spaces.

★ A large hurricane called the "Great Hurricane" hit New London in 1938.

© 2001 McGraw-Hill. All Rights Reserved.

The Fifty States

Connecticut: The Constitution State

Look at an atlas or map of Connecticut. Add the names of the following places to the map below.

★ the place where visitors can tour the *U.S.S. Nautilus*

★ the site of Yale University

★ the town where the first helicopter was developed

★ the state capital

★ Long Island Sound

★ the Connecticut River

★ the town known as "Park City"

★ a city that takes its name from London, England

★ Block Island Sound

★ the former fishing town of Norwalk

★ a popular vacation spot

Size: 5,018 square miles
Population: 3,296,000

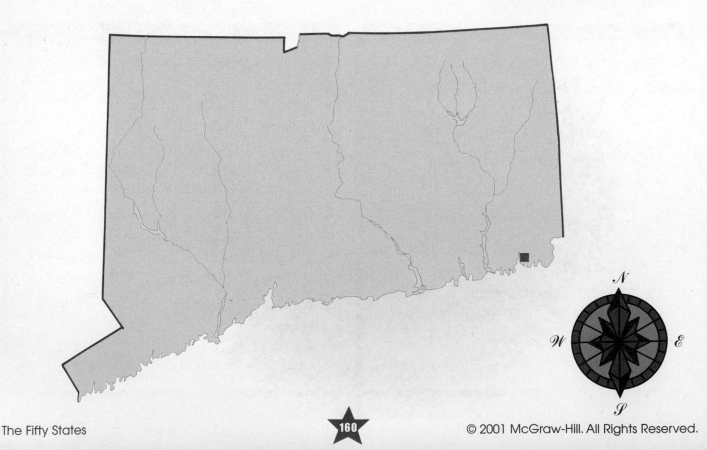

 © 2001 McGraw-Hill. All Rights Reserved.

Connecticut: The Constitution State

Complete the crossword puzzle.

Across

1 The man who invented the cotton gin

4 A university located in New Haven

6 The town where the first helicopter was developed

Down

2 First name of author of *Uncle Tom's Cabin*

3 First nuclear-powered submarine

5 He discovered Connecticut

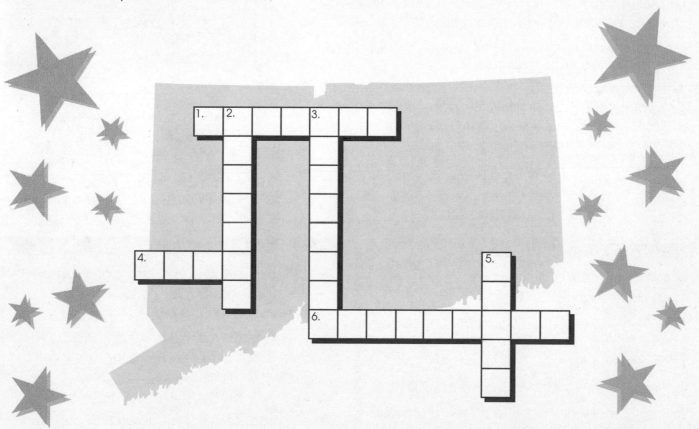

Hartford is called the "Insurance City." Explain why this is so.

_____

_____

_____

© 2001 McGraw-Hill. All Rights Reserved.

The Fifty States

Welcome to Delaware

State Flag

DECEMBER 7, 1787

Blue Hen Chicken
State Bird

Peach Blossom
State Flower

*N*ative Americans called the Lenni Lenape lived in Delaware before the first Europeans arrived. The Dutch were the first Europeans to settle the area, but they struggled. The Lenni Lenape destroyed many early settlements. Unlike the other states, Delaware first belonged to Sweden and Holland. One settlement was called New Amstel, later, called New Castle. The British took control of Delaware in 1664. Delaware was also part of Pennsylvania until 1704.

Delaware was eager to join the other colonies in their fight against England. When it came time to vote for independence, a Delaware man made the difference. One more vote was needed to adopt the Declaration of Independence. It is said that Caesar Rodney rode his horse 86 miles almost non-stop from his home in Dover to Philadelphia. He arrived in time to cast the deciding vote. Delaware became the first state in 1787.

FAMOUS DELAWARIANS

★ Oliver Evans was an inventor, scientist and researcher.

★ Henry Heimlich developed the "Heimlich maneuver," a method used to help choking victims.

★ Annie Jump Cannon discovered 300 stars.

★ Frank Stephens began a small community named Arden in 1900.

★ Richard Allen created the African Methodist Episcopal Church.

★ John Phillips Marquand won the Pulitzer Prize for his novel *The Late George Apley.*

STATE GREATS

★ Wilmington is home to the world's largest maker of chemicals—E.I. du Pont de Nemours and Company.

★ Settlers from Holland, Sweden and England all built settlements along the Delaware River. This is the only area in the country where all three countries built settlements.

★ A reproduction of the Town Hall of Hoorn from the Netherlands was built in Lewes.

★ Two communities are in both Delaware and Maryland: Delmar and Marydel.

★ Delaware is the only state with a rounded border.

© 2001 McGraw-Hill. All Rights Reserved.

Delaware: The First State

Look at an atlas or map of Delaware. Add the names of the following places to the map below.

★ the home of E.I. du Pont de Nemours and Company

★ the place where the Town Hall of Hoorn was built

★ the state capital

★ the river where three countries started settlements

★ Nanticoke River

★ the state that shares a rounded border with Delaware

★ the ocean that borders Delaware to the east

★ the two communities that are in both Delaware and Maryland

★ the bay that is named for Delaware

★ the town that was once called New Amstel

Size: 2,045 square miles
Population: 669,000

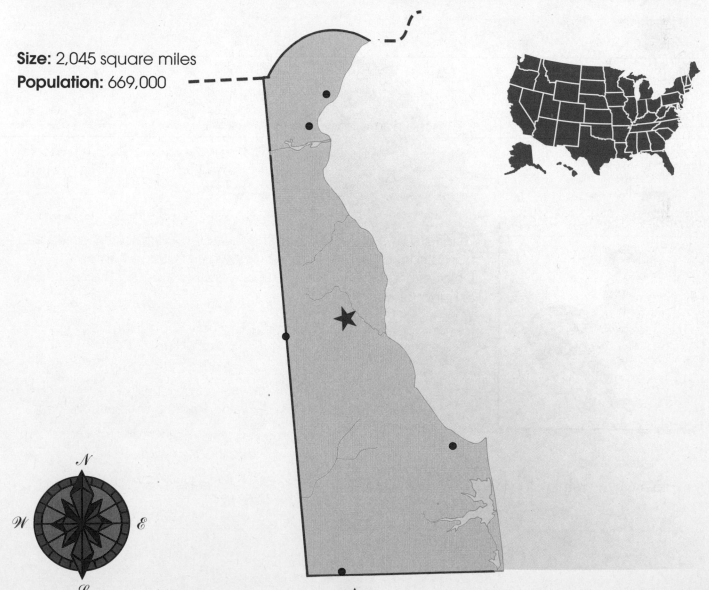

© 2001 McGraw-Hill. All Rights Reserved.

The Fifty States

Delaware: The First State

Unscramble the words to complete the sentences.

★ Delaware was the __ __ ◯ __ __ state to enter the Union.　　　SRFIT

★ ◯◯ __ __ __ is the state capital of Delaware.　　　OREDV

★ There are two towns that are located on the border of Delaware

and __ __ __ ◯ __ __ __ __.　　　YLNMAARD

★ Richard __ __ __ ◯◯ created the African Methodist Episcopal Church.　　　EANLL

Rearrange the circled letters to form the name of a Delaware hero.

__ __ __ __ __ __

The state bird of Delaware is the Blue Hen. Originally, the name came from a type of blue hen known as a fierce fighter. Delaware's revolutionary soldiers were nicknamed the "Blue Hens" in honor of these birds.

Explain why you think the people of Delaware would choose the Blue Hen as their state bird.

_____

_____

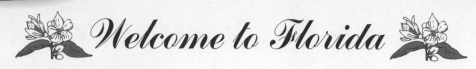

Welcome to Florida

★ HOW FLORIDA BECAME A STATE

*E*very spring, young people travel to Florida to soak up the sun in the Florida Keys, play in the Atlantic Ocean, watch baseball near Tampa and visit amusement parks in Orlando. You could say, there is a fountain of youth in Florida. And that is just what the explorer Juan Ponce de Leon was looking for nearly 500 years ago.

Ponce de Leon had heard the Native Americans speak of a "Fountain of Youth." They said it could keep people young forever. Ponce de Leon never found the Fountain of Youth, but he did claim the land for Spain. Spain built a fort, now the city of St. Augustine, and ruled the peninsula for about 300 years. Spain agreed to give Florida to the United States in 1819. Florida was quickly organized into a territory, thanks to a general named Andrew Jackson. In 1845, Florida became the twenty-seventh state with its capital, Tallahassee. Known as the "Sunshine State," Florida is known as much for its oranges, grapefruit and tangerines as it is for its tourist sites.

State Flag

Mockingbird State Bird

Orange Blossom State Flower

FAMOUS FLORIDIANS

★ Mary McLeod Bethune was a famous African-American teacher who later served as a presidential advisor.

★ Gloria Estefan is a singer. She used to head a group called the Miami Sound Machine.

★ Chris Evert is a tennis player who won Wimbledon in 1974, 1976 and 1981.

★ Sidney Poitier is an actor best known for the movie, *Guess Who's Coming to Dinner.*

★ John Ringling ran a circus which is still running today.

★ Clarence Thomas is a Supreme Court justice.

STATE GREATS

★ The Kennedy Space Center launched the first man to land on the Moon.

★ Disney World, in Orlando, covers 28,000 acres and has Florida's largest hotel with more than 1,500 rooms.

★ Most of Florida is less than 100 feet above sea level.

★ The Everglades is the only place in the world where crocodiles and alligators live together naturally.

★ Florida adopted its sixth and most recent constitution in 1969.

© 2001 McGraw-Hill. All Rights Reserved.

The Fifty States

Florida: **The Sunshine State**

Look at an atlas or map of Florida. Add the names of the following places to the map below.

★ the ocean that borders Florida

★ the space shuttle is launched from this spot

★ this is Florida's largest lake

★ the capital of Florida

★ a long bridge links these islands called the Florida Keys

★ the body of water Florida shares with Alabama

★ Gloria Estefan was in a group with this city's name

★ a city near where many baseball teams train

★ the first permanent Spanish settlement

★ Mickey Mouse lives here

★ this area is known for its alligators and crocodiles

Size: 58,664 square miles
Population: 13,003,362

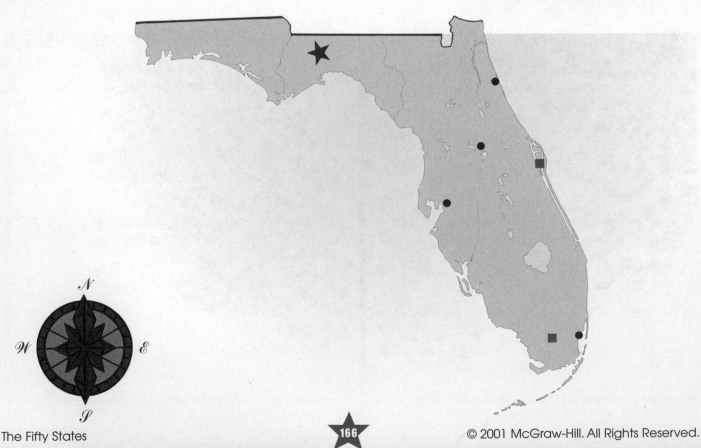

 © 2001 McGraw-Hill. All Rights Reserved.

Florida: The Sunshine State

Complete the sentences about Florida.

★ Big reptiles live in the __ __ __ __ __ __ __ __ __ .

★ The state flower is the __ __ __ __ __ __ __ __ __ __ __ __ __ .

★ Ponce de Leon was looking for a __ __ __ __ __ __ __ __ of youth when he arrived in Florida.

★ Lake __ __ __ __ __ __ __ __ __ __ is the largest lake in Florida.

★ Tallahassee is Florida's __ __ __ __ __ __ __ .

★ St. __ __ __ __ __ __ __ __ __ __ was founded by the Spanish.

Florida is well known for its oranges. What other fruits are grown in Florida?

_____

_____

© 2001 McGraw-Hill. All Rights Reserved.

The Fifty States

Welcome to Georgia

★ HOW GEORGIA BECAME A STATE

*I*n the 1500s, Spanish explorers came to Georgia. The Native American tribes of the Cherokee and Creek soon had to share their land. In 1733, the first English settlement, Savannah, was founded. Not much later, Georgia, named after King George II of England, became the fourth state to sign the Declaration of Independence. Although Georgia joined the Union early, it was the fifth southern state to leave the Union. During the Civil War, Union General William Sherman marched through Georgia and burned Atlanta, now Georgia's capital, to the ground.

Georgia is now an important part of the United States. Atlanta is a big city boasting the big businesses of CNN and Coca-Cola. Other big cities include Columbus and Macon. Georgia is a beautiful state. The Okefenokee Swamp was named by Native Americans to mean the "Land of the Trembling Earth." The Blue Ridge mountains tower in the north. Tourists visit Stone Mountain to see three confederate heroes carved into the side of the mountain.

State Flag

**Brown Thrasher
State Bird**

**Cherokee Rose
State Flower**

FAMOUS GEORGIANS

★ Jimmy Carter was governor of Georgia and the thirty-ninth president of the United States.

★ Ty Cobb was one of the greatest baseball players of all time.

★ Martin Luther King, Jr., was a civil rights leader. He was assassinated in 1968.

★ Elijah Muhammad was a leader of the African-American Muslim movement.

★ Jackie Robinson was the first black baseball player in the Major Leagues.

★ Flannery O'Connor was a writer whose books include *Wise Blood*.

STATE GREATS

★ The first steamship to cross the Atlantic Ocean, the *S.S. Savannah*, sailed from Savannah to Liverpool, England, in 1819.

★ 1.5 billion pounds of peanuts are harvested every year in Georgia.

★ A pharmacist named John Styth Pemberton invented Coca-Cola.

★ Georgia is a leading grower of peaches.

★ The Girl Scouts was founded by Juliette Gordon Low in Savannah in 1912.

 © 2001 McGraw-Hill. All Rights Reserved.

Georgia: The Empire State of the South

Look at an atlas or map of Georgia. Add the names of the following places to the map below.

★ capital of Georgia

★ Girl Scouts were founded in this city

★ you can swim in this ocean

★ the state to the south of Georgia

★ Georgia shares these mountains with South Carolina

★ Georgia's eastern border is shared with this state

★ the big city in central Georgia

★ "Land of the Trembling Earth"

★ a city on the border with Alabama

★ you can see confederate heroes here

Size: 58,910 square miles
Population: 7,184,000

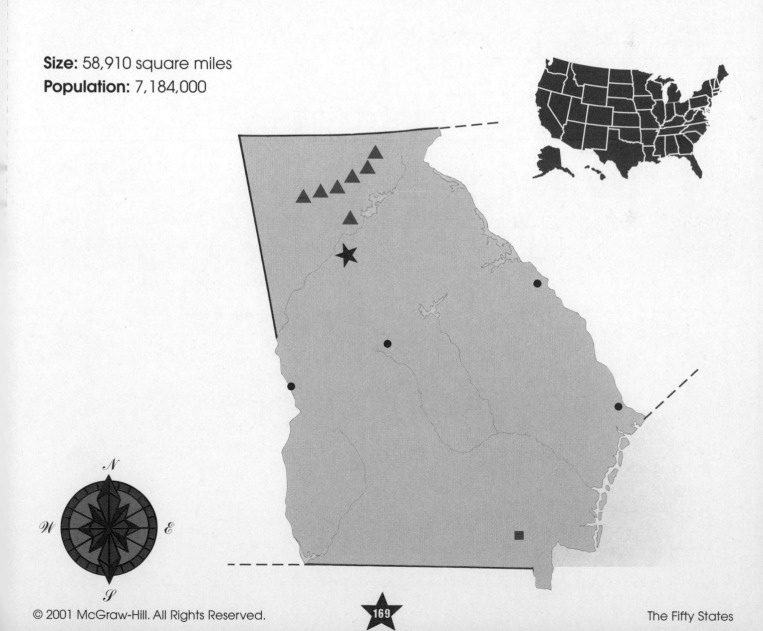

© 2001 McGraw-Hill. All Rights Reserved.

The Fifty States

Georgia: The Empire State of the South

Complete the crossword puzzle.

Across

3 Home of Coca-Cola and CNN

5 Famous civil rights leader

6 Peanut farmer and former president

Down

1 Columbus is on the border with this state

2 The first English colony in Georgia

4 This city's name sounds like a summer month

6 One of the greatest baseball players

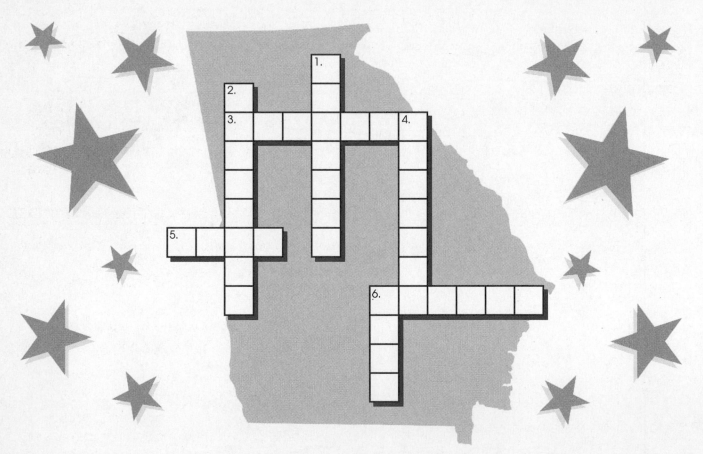

Which do you think is more popular in Georgia, Coke or Pepsi?

_____

_____

_____

© 2001 McGraw-Hill. All Rights Reserved.

Welcome to Hawaii

★ HOW HAWAII BECAME A STATE

Hawaii is our nation's youngest state. Its first inhabitants came from the Polynesian Islands. Fifteen hundred years ago, they traveled 2,000 miles in open canoes to reach Hawaii. Since then, Hawaii has been ruled by many groups. In 1778, James Cook, a British sea captain, arrived in the islands. In 1790, after a bloody 10-year war, the islands were ruled by King Kamehameha. Over 100 years later, a group of American planters and businessmen removed Queen Liliuokalani from power. In 1900, the United States established the Territory of Hawaii. In 1903, Hawaii tried to become a state, but the attempt failed.

In 1941, during World War II, the Japanese attacked the United States' large naval base at Pearl Harbor on the island of Oahu. The United States then declared war on Japan. In 1959, almost 60 years after the first attempt to make Hawaii a state, it became our fiftieth state.

State Flag

Nene (Hawaiian Goose)
State Bird

Yellow Hibiscus
State Flower

FAMOUS HAWAIIANS

★ King Kamehameha the Great formed Hawaii into a peaceful kingdom and expanded trade with other countries.

★ Queen Liliuokalani was the last royal leader, her reign ending in 1893.

★ Luther Gulick was the founder of the Camp Fire Girls.

★ Lois Lowry is a children's author.

★ Don Ho is a singer and entertainer.

★ Duke Kahanamoku was a famous Olympic swimmer who made surfing and Hawaiian shirts popular.

★ Father Damien, a missionary, worked with people with leprosy (Hansen's disease), even after contracting the disease himself.

STATE GREATS

★ The Arizona Memorial floats above where the battleship *Arizona* was sunk on December 7, 1941, during the attack on Pearl Harbor, Oahu.

★ Hawaii's Volcanoes National Park contains Mauna Loa, the world's largest active volcano.

★ Kauai's Waimea Canyon has brilliantly colored walls and is half a mile deep.

★ The Polynesian Cultural Center, on the island of Oahu, has Polynesian music and dance performances. It also has seven reconstructed native villages.

★ Diamond Head, an extinct volcano, overlooks famous Waikiki Beach.

★ Hawaii is the only state that is made up entirely of islands.

© 2001 McGraw-Hill. All Rights Reserved.

The Fifty States

Hawaii: **The Aloha State**

Look at an atlas or map of Hawaii. Add the names of the following places to the map below.

- ★ Honolulu, the capital city of the islands
- ★ Hawaii, the "big island"
- ★ the island of Maui
- ★ the "Garden Isle" where Waimea Canyon is located
- ★ the location of Volcanoes National Park

- ★ the island where the Polynesian Cultural center is located
- ★ Pearl Harbor
- ★ the "Pineapple Island" of Lanai
- ★ the "Friendly Island" of Molokai
- ★ the "Forbidden Island" of Niihau

Size: 6,471 square miles
Population: 1,243,000

© 2001 McGraw-Hill. All Rights Reserved.

Hawaii: **The Aloha State**

Use the words in the Word Bank to find and circle the words about Hawaii in the word search below.

Word Bank

Hawaii	pineapple	volcano	Polynesian	aloha
hibiscus		Oahu	Lanai	Pearl Harbor
island	nene		flag	canoes	Mauna Loa

S	H	T	M	U	R	B	A	L	F	E	C	G	E	A	I
C	I	A	B	A	O	Q	W	L	A	N	A	I	H	L	S
Y	B	D	W	M	V	E	D	V	E	D	N	D	I	O	L
A	I	F	L	A	G	S	F	O	G	C	O	B	J	H	A
N	S	U	T	U	I	P	O	L	Y	N	E	S	I	A	N
X	C	S	V	N	K	I	J	C	I	H	S	C	A	O	D
M	U	P	E	A	R	L	H	A	R	B	O	R	K	P	B
C	S	R	Q	L	M	L	P	N	E	N	E	O	N	H	F
Z	B	W	L	O	A	H	U	O	U	G	M	J	P	X	L
P	I	N	E	A	P	P	L	E	K	A	Z	G	I	N	Y

The state seal of Hawaii has a picture of a king on it. Write about who you think it is. Then, tell why you think the state flag has a British "Union Jack" in the corner. Draw a picture of the state flag. Can you also find the meaning of the word "Aloha?"

© 2001 McGraw-Hill. All Rights Reserved.

The Fifty States

Welcome to Idaho

*B*efore Europeans claimed Idaho, it was the home to many Native Americans including the Bannock, the Shoshone, the Nez Percé, the Kootenai, the Pen d'Oreille and the Coeur d'Alenes. The people lived in the mountains and valleys of Idaho for thousands of years.

Two American explorers, Lewis and Clark, reached Idaho in 1805. At this time, both England and the United States claimed Idaho as their own. Not long after, fur traders, trappers and missionaries began settling in Idaho. David Thompson started a trading post on Lake Pend Oreille. The Mormons started Idaho's oldest town, called Franklin. In 1846, England gave up Idaho. Soon after, Elias Pierce found gold at Orofino Creek. Thousands of people came to Idaho to look for gold. Later, the Homestead Act of 1862 encouraged settlers to move to Idaho and settle the land. About this time, Colonel Patrick Conner and his soldiers attacked the Shoshone Indians at Bear River, killing hundreds of people. In July of 1890, Idaho became a state.

State Flag

Mountain Bluebird
State Bird

Syringa
State Flower

FAMOUS IDAHOANS

★ Sacajawea, a Shoshone woman, helped Lewis and Clark explore the Louisiana Territory.

★ Moses Alexander became the first Jewish governor in the U.S.

★ Gutzon Borglum, the artist who designed and sculpted the Mt. Rushmore Memorial, was born near Bear Lake, Idaho.

★ Lana Turner of Wallace, Idaho, was one of the world's greatest movie stars.

★ Carol Ryrie Brink, author of the Newbery Medal winning book, *Caddie Woodlawn*, was born in Moscow, Idaho.

★ Famous poet and author, Ezra Pound, was born in Hailey, Idaho.

STATE GREATS

★ The Powerbar International Women's Challenge is the world's biggest bike race for women.

★ Philo Farnsworth invented the television in Rigby, Idaho, in 1922.

★ The Amalgamated Sugar Company, the largest sugar refinery in the United States, is in Boise.

★ The biggest nesting place of hawks and eagles in the Unites States is at the Snake River Birds of Prey Natural Area.

★ Idaho is the second largest silver mining state in the country.

★ Arco, Idaho, was the first town in the world that used nuclear energy to generate electricity.

 © 2001 McGraw-Hill. All Rights Reserved.

Idaho: **The Gem State**

Look at an atlas or map of Idaho. Add the names of the following places to the map below.

- ★ the city where Philo Farnsworth invented the television
- ★ the oldest town in Idaho
- ★ the capital of Idaho
- ★ site of the first trading post in Idaho
- ★ the site of the Bear River Massacre

- ★ Coeur d'Alene Lake
- ★ Craters of the Moon National Park
- ★ Birds of Prey Natural Area is on this river
- ★ Borah Peak, Idaho's tallest mountain
- ★ Hells Canyon National Park

Size: 83,564 square miles
Population: 1,164,000

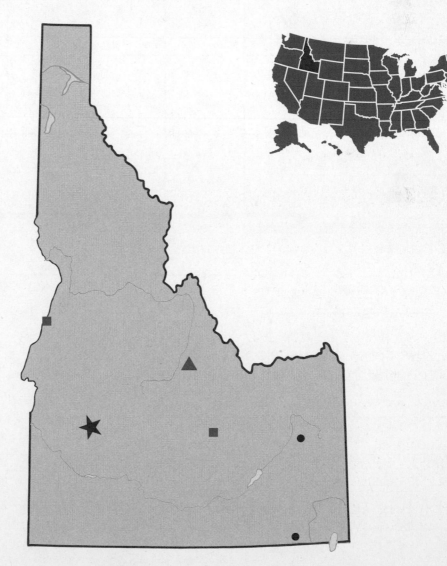

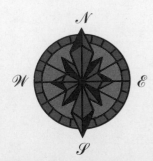

© 2001 McGraw-Hill. All Rights Reserved.

The Fifty States

Idaho: **The Gem State**

Find five names related to the Gem State in the word puzzle below. Some letters are together, but others are mixed up. You will use each box only once. The first letters are already there for you.

EW	L	GL	H	O
L	D	J	I	EA
SA	B	M	O	K
I	U	A	AW	S
C	CA	A	R	R

L _____   C _____

I _____   Sa _____   B _____

The governor of Idaho is holding a contest to find a new nickname for the state of Idaho. Look for four things that Idaho is known for and write a new nickname.

_____

_____

_____

_____

_____

© 2001 McGraw-Hill. All Rights Reserved.

HOW ILLINOIS BECAME A STATE

*I*llinois has always been an important place, even before it became a state. On one side of Illinois are the Great Lakes. On another is the Mississippi River. Native Americans used to hunt deer and bear that roamed in Illinois. They built large structures like Monk's Mound. Shortly before the Revolutionary War, Chicago was settled on Lake Michigan. Chicago grew quickly because ships could reach the city through the Great Lakes or the Illinois-Michigan Canal. By 1818, Illinois was the twenty-first state.

The state is known as the "Land of Lincoln" because Abraham Lincoln lived in Illinois. However, Lincoln was not born in Illinois. Lincoln first lived near Decatur in central Illinois, and also lived in Illinois' capital, Springfield. In fact, the Old State Capitol displays Lincoln's original Gettysburg address. Although Chicago is very large, most of Illinois is rural. After Chicago, Rockford, in the north, and Peoria, on the Illinois River, are the next biggest cities. But both Rockford and Peoria have less than 5 percent of the population of Chicago.

State Flag

ILLINOIS

Cardinal State Bird

Native Violet State Flower

FAMOUS ILLINOISANS

★ Black Hawk was a Sauk Indian chief at age 21. He fought in two wars against American settlers.

★ Ernest Hemingway was a world-famous author.

★ Jackie Joyner-Kersee was an Olympic champion in the long jump and other track and field events.

★ Former actor, Ronald Reagan, the fortieth president and governor of California, was the only president born in Illinois.

★ Walt Disney created Mickey Mouse and began Disneyland.

★ Frank Lloyd Wright was one of America's most famous architects.

STATE GREATS

★ The original Ferris Wheel was built in Chicago in 1893 by George W. G. Ferris.

★ Ronald Reagan spent his early days as a radio announcer for the Chicago Cubs.

★ Chicago is known as the "windy city" because a writer from New York thought people from Chicago bragged too much, so he called them "windy."

★ One of the world's tallest buildings, the Sears Tower, is in Chicago.

★ The city of Pekin was named after Peking, China, because an early settler thought it was directly opposite from the Chinese city. It is not.

© 2001 McGraw-Hill. All Rights Reserved.

The Fifty States

Illinois: The Land of Lincoln

Look at an atlas or map of Illinois. Add the names of the following places to the map below.

★ this city has one of the world's tallest skyscrapers

★ this city sits on the Illinois river

★ one settler thought this city was opposite from China

★ this river links the Mississippi to the Illinois-Michigan Canal

★ this lake is the largest wholly within the United States

★ the capital of Illinois

★ where Native Americans built a large structure

★ this river forms the western border of Illinois

★ a large city in the north

★ Abraham Lincoln lived here as a boy

★ boats use this man-made waterway to reach Chicago

Size: 56,345 square miles
Population: 11,467,000

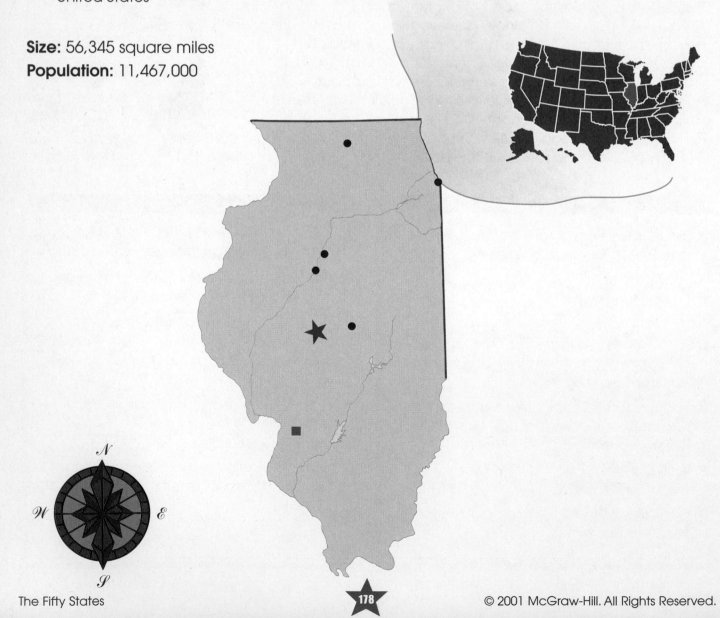

178 © 2001 McGraw-Hill. All Rights Reserved.

Illinois: **The Land of Lincoln**

Complete the clues. Then, use the clues to find words in the word search below.

★ Illinois is called the Land of _____ .

★ A Native American who fought against settlers _____

★ The lake that borders Chicago _____

★ The northernmost city _____

★ An amusement ride invented in Illinois was the _____ wheel.

★ The state bird of Illinois is the _____ .

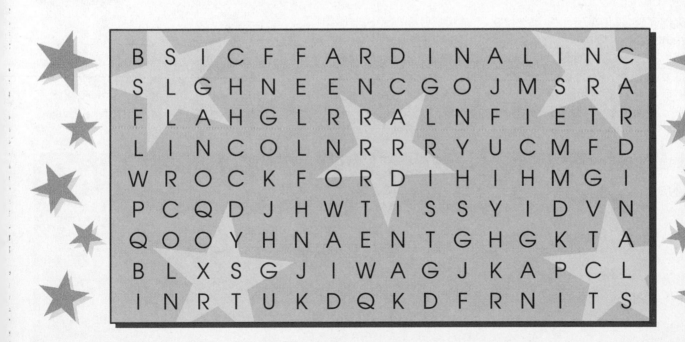

```
B  S  I  C  F  F  A  R  D  I  N  A  L  I  N  C
S  L  G  H  N  E  E  N  C  G  O  J  M  S  R  A
F  L  A  H  G  L  R  R  A  L  N  F  I  E  T  R
L  I  N  C  O  L  N  R  R  R  Y  U  C  M  F  D
W  R  O  C  K  F  O  R  D  I  H  I  H  M  G  I
P  C  Q  D  J  H  W  T  I  S  S  Y  I  D  V  N
Q  O  O  Y  H  N  A  E  N  T  G  H  G  K  T  A
B  L  X  S  G  J  I  W  A  G  J  K  A  P  C  L
I  N  R  T  U  K  D  Q  K  D  F  R  N  I  T  S
```

Why did Chicago become such a big city? When was the Illinois-Michigan Canal built?

_____

_____

_____

© 2001 McGraw-Hill. All Rights Reserved.   The Fifty States

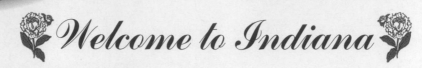

Welcome to Indiana

★ HOW INDIANA BECAME A STATE

*I*ndiana was home to Native American tribes such as the Miami, Potawatomi, Shawnee and Kickapoo when the French first arrived. The French built forts near present day Fort Wayne. Fort Wayne was named for the Revolutionary War hero General "Mad" Anthony Wayne. Vincennes was the first permanent French settlement in Indiana. After the French and Indian War of 1754, England gained all the French land east of the Mississippi. Later, during the American Revolution, Lieutenant Colonel George Rogers Clark led an attack on the British-held Vincennes. The American victory ended British control in the Ohio Valley.

Hoping to regain their territories, several Native American tribes joined together under Shawnee chief Tecumseh. In 1811, Governor William Henry Harrison and his forces fought with Tecumseh's forces a few miles south of the junction of the Tippecanoe and Wabash Rivers. The battle became known as the Battle of Tippecanoe. Indiana became the nineteenth state in 1816.

State Flag

**Cardinal
State Bird**

**Peony
State Flower**

FAMOUS INDIANANS

★ William Henry Harrison, whose home was in Indianapolis, was the ninth president.

★ Virgil Grissom was an astronaut and has an air force base named after him.

★ Kurt Vonnegut, Jr., is a famous science fiction writer.

★ J. Danforth Quayle served as vice president during the term of President George Bush.

★ Eli Lilly founded a pharmaceutical company.

★ James Whitcomb Riley was a poet who wrote "When the Frost is on the Punkin."

★ David Letterman hosts a late night talk show.

★ Abraham Lincoln worked on a family farm in Indiana as a boy.

STATE GREATS

★ The Indianapolis Motor Speedway hosts the Indianapolis 500 and the Brickyard 400.

★ The Indianapolis Children's Museum is the largest in the world.

★ The first professional baseball game was played in Fort Wayne in 1871.

★ Santa Claus, Indiana, receives over 500,000 letters and requests at Christmastime.

★ Indiana is home to both the Indiana Pacers and Indianapolis Colts.

★ The Studebaker automobile was built in South Bend.

© 2001 McGraw-Hill. All Rights Reserved.

Indiana: The Hoosier State

Look at an atlas or map of Indiana. Add the names of the following places to the map below.

★ the capital of Indiana

★ the first permanent French settlement

★ the river that flows along the southern border of Indiana

★ the Studebaker automobile was built here

★ the Great Lake that borders Indiana

★ the location of the Indianapolis Motor Speedway

★ the city named for a Revolutionary War General

★ a city near the junction of the Wabash and Tippecanoe Rivers

★ the states which border Indiana

Size: 36,185 square miles
Population: 5,841,000

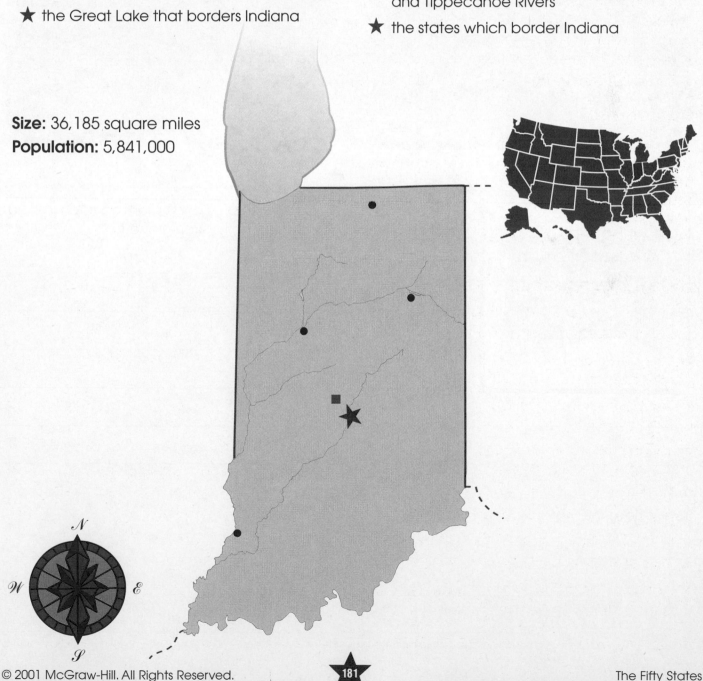

© 2001 McGraw-Hill. All Rights Reserved.

The Fifty States

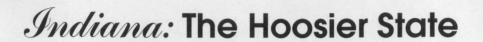

Indiana: The Hoosier State

Read the clues and unscramble the words about Indiana.

Lincoln's first name   __ __ __ __ ◯ __ ◯   M A B A R A H

a car made in South Bend   __ __ ◯ __ ◯ __ __ __ ◯ __   K R A T U S E B D E

Indianapolis's football team   ◯ __ __ ◯◯   S L O C T

Unscramble the boxed letters to find the name of the Indian chief who was defeated at the Battle of Tippecanoe.

__ __ __ __ __ __ __ __ __

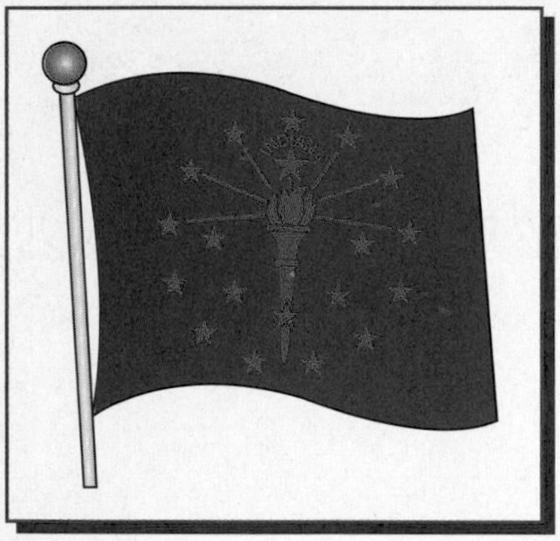

The Indiana flag is blue with 19 stars and a flaming torch in gold. What does the arrangement of the stars stand for?

_____

_____

_____

_____

_____

_____

What does the word "Hoosier" mean?

_____

_____

_____

© 2001 McGraw-Hill. All Rights Reserved.

Welcome to Iowa

HOW IOWA BECAME A STATE

Millions of years ago, giant sheets of ice called glaciers inched over Iowa and created three areas: the Drift Plains, Till Plains and Driftless Area. The first people to come to Iowa were Native Americans called the Iowa. These hunters also gathered nuts and berries, which grew well in the rich Iowa soil. One of the first European settlers was a French-Canadian named Julien Dubuque. Dubuque came to Iowa in 1788 to mine for lead. Later, a town was named after him.

In the mid-1800s, many people heard about the rich soil and moved to Iowa to farm the land. In 1846, Iowa became the twenty-ninth state. Since then, Iowa has been known for producing food. Its farms grow tons of corn to feed livestock. Many of Iowa's cities are on the riverbanks. In the west is Sioux City, on the Missouri River. In central Iowa, on the Des Moines River, is the city of Des Moines, the capital. Even Dubuque is on a river, the Mississippi.

State Flag

Eastern Goldfinch
State Bird

Wild Rose
State Flower

FAMOUS IOWANS

★ Bob Feller is a Hall of Fame pitcher who played for the Cleveland Indians.

★ Fred Maytag sold washing machines and created the largest washing machine company in the world.

★ John Wayne won an Academy Award for his movie, *True Grit*, but was most famous for his many Westerns.

★ Jacob Schick grew up in Des Moines and invented the electric razor.

★ Herbert Hoover served as the thirty-first president of the United States.

★ Glenn Miller led the famous Glenn Miller Orchestra.

STATE GREATS

★ More than 90 percent of Iowa's land is farmland.

★ Sioux City produces more popcorn than any other city in the country.

★ More than 50 insurance companies have their headquarters in Des Moines.

★ In 1890, William Morrison built the first car in the United States. It was electric and traveled at 20 miles per hour.

★ The Star Trek character Capt. James T. Kirk was said to have been born in Iowa. The town of Riverside holds a birthday party for him every year.

© 2001 McGraw-Hill. All Rights Reserved.

The Fifty States

Iowa: The Hawkeye State

Look at an atlas or map of Iowa. Add the names of the following places to the map below.

★ this city is known for making popcorn

★ the capital of Iowa

★ mined lead could be sent down this eastern river

★ the state to the south of Iowa

★ the river that shares the same name as the capital

★ this town celebrates Capt. James T. Kirk's birthday each year

★ a city where early settlers came to mine lead

★ this river makes up Iowa's western border

★ an area in southern Iowa

★ the state to the north of Iowa

Size: 56,275 square miles
Population: 2,865,000

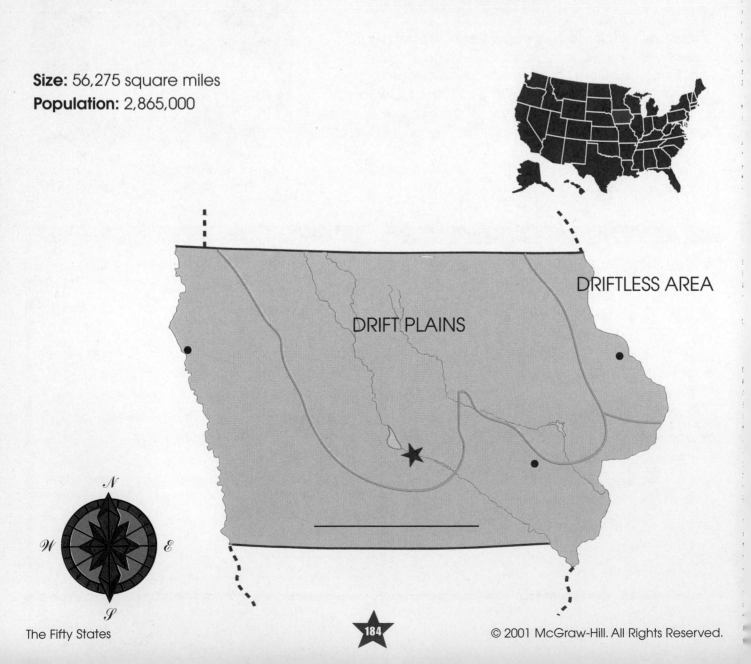

DRIFTLESS AREA

DRIFT PLAINS

N

W   E

S

© 2001 McGraw-Hill. All Rights Reserved.

Iowa: **The Hawkeye State**

Read the clues. Unscramble the words about Iowa.

this is produced in Sioux City __ Ⓞ __ __ __ __ Ⓞ __   R P O C P O N

he invented the electric razor Ⓞ __ __Ⓞ __ __   K S C C H I

he'll wash your clothes Ⓞ __ __ __ __ __ __   Y A M A T G

lead was mined in this city Ⓞ __ __ __ __ __Ⓞ   Q U E B U D U

the famed birthplace of Kirk __ __ __ __ __ __Ⓞ __ __Ⓞ S R I V E I D E R

Unscramble the circled letters to find Iowa's capital.

__ __ __ __   __ __ __ __ __ __

Iowa produces a lot of food. What is it about Iowa that makes it good for farming?

_____

_____

_____

_____

© 2001 McGraw-Hill. All Rights Reserved.

The Fifty States

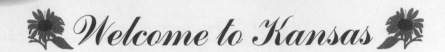 Welcome to Kansas

★ HOW KANSAS BECAME A STATE

The Spanish explorer, Francisco Vasquez de Coronado, first visited the area in 1541. At that time, Native American tribes including the Kansa, the Wichita, the Osage and the Pawnee lived in Kansas. Today, in central Kansas, small pieces of chain mail armor worn by Spanish explorers are sometimes found.

Kansas joined the United States as part of the Louisiana Purchase in 1803. In 1854, treaties were made with some of the Native American tribes and the land was given to the new settlers. These good times did not last long. In 1854, Kansas was given the right to decide if it was a free or slave state. Soon after, in 1855, over a thousand pro-slavery Missourians crossed the border and demanded to vote at gunpoint. This was the beginning of "Bleeding Kansas"—a term given to the state because of the violence over the slavery issue. On January 29, 1861, Kansas, the thirty-fourth state in the Union, was admitted as a free state, and Topeka became the state capital.

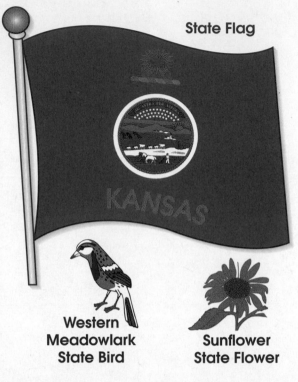

State Flag

Western Meadowlark State Bird

Sunflower State Flower

FAMOUS KANSANS

★ Melissa Etheridge, a popular singer, was born in Leavenworth.

★ Amelia Earhart was the first woman to fly across the Atlantic Ocean. She was born in Atchison.

★ "Wild Bill" Hickock was a scout and frontier marshal in the Old West.

★ Bob Dole was a United States senator for many years.

★ Charlie "Bird" Parker was born in the 1920s. He is one of the greatest jazz musicians in American history.

★ Wilt Chamberlain played on the basketball team of the University of Kansas located in Lawrence.

STATE GREATS

★ The first American salt was produced in Hutchinson in 1888.

★ The Kansas railroads in Abilene and Dodge City made it possible to ship cattle and agricultural products to the East.

★ The Dwight D. Eisenhower Museum and Library is located in Abilene.

★ Factories in Wichita lead the nation in the production of small aircraft.

★ Kansas is in the center of the original 48 states.

★ Lawrence was a key point in the Underground Railroad to help slaves escape from the South.

 © 2001 McGraw-Hill. All Rights Reserved.

Kansas: The Sunflower State

Look at an atlas or map of Kansas. Add the names of the following places to the map below.

★ the state capital

★ the city that has the same name as the state

★ the river that separates Kansas and Missouri

★ the place where salt was first produced

★ the birthplace of Melissa Etheridge

★ the states that border Kansas

★ the birthplace of Amelia Earhart

★ the city that was an important site in the Underground Railroad

★ the location of the Dwight D. Eisenhower Museum and Library

★ the city that produces small aircraft

Size: 82,277 square miles
Population: 2,591,000

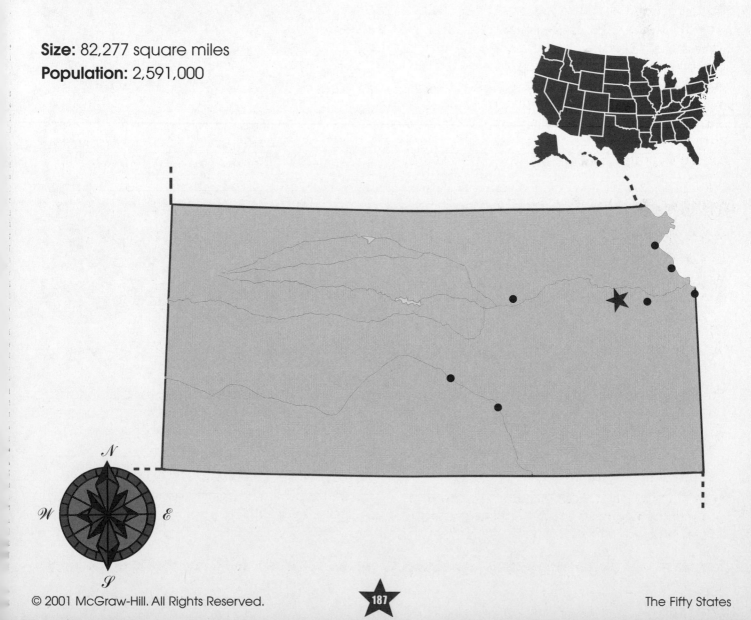

© 2001 McGraw-Hill. All Rights Reserved.

The Fifty States

Kansas: The Sunflower State

The motto of Kansas is: *Ad astra per aspera.*

Unscramble the letters below to find what the motto means.

OT   HET   SRAST   GHROUHT

"__ ___ _____ _____

FICIDUTFILES

_____."

Rewrite the motto in your own words. What do you think it means?

_____

_____

Think of a personal motto for yourself. Write it below.

_____

★★★★★★★★★★★★★★★★★★★★★★★★★★★★★★★★★★★★★★

The Jayhawkers were a very important part of Kansas history. Today, the athletic teams at Kansas University are called Jayhawks. Find out who the original Jayhawkers were. Explain their importance.

_____

_____

_____

★★★★★★★★★★★★★★★★★★★★★★★★★★★★★★★★★★★★★★

© 2001 McGraw-Hill. All Rights Reserved.

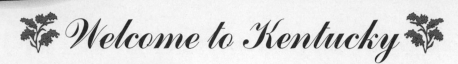

Welcome to Kentucky

Kentucky was not explored by Europeans until the mid-1700s. Kentucky was not settled until after the English had won the French and Indian War of 1754 to1763. Daniel Boone was among the first colonists to explore Kentucky. He passed through the Cumberland Gap and followed a Native American path.

The first permanent settlement was built in Kentucky in 1774. During the next year, Daniel Boone settled Boonesborough on the Kentucky River. When the Kentucky settlers tried to become a state, they failed. Virginia then decided to declare Kentucky a county of Virginia. After the Revolutionary War, many settlers moved into Kentucky. The settlers again tried to gain their independence from Virginia. In 1792, Virginia dropped its claim to Kentucky. Within a few months, Kentucky was admitted to the Union as the fifteenth state. Kentucky was the first state west of the Appalachian Mountains.

State Flag

**Cardinal
State Bird**

**Goldenrod
State Flower**

FAMOUS KENTUCKIANS

★ Abraham Lincoln was born in Kentucky.

★ Jefferson Davis was the president of the Confederacy.

★ Carry Nation was the leader of the temperance movement.

★ Muhammad Ali was a boxer.

★ Diane Sawyer is a broadcast journalist.

★ Rosemary Clooney is a singer and actress who appeared in the movie *White Christmas*.

★ Loretta Lynn is a country and western singer.

STATE GREATS

★ All Chevrolet Corvettes are made in Bowling Green.

★ The Kentucky Derby, run at Churchill Downs in Louisville, is the oldest continuously held horse race.

★ The first Kentucky Fried Chicken owned and operated by Colonel Sanders is in Corbin.

★ Kentucky produced the first Miss America in 1918, Miss Heather Renee French.

★ Mammoth Cave National Park is the world's longest cave.

★ Fort Knox, where America's gold is stored, is an actual modern-day fort.

© 2001 McGraw-Hill. All Rights Reserved.

The Fifty States

Kentucky: The Bluegrass State

Look at an atlas or map of Kentucky. Add the names of the following places to the map below.

★ the home of the Kentucky Derby

★ the capital of Kentucky

★ the location of the gold reserve

★ the river which flows along the northern border of Kentucky

★ the river which forms a part of the western boundary of Kentucky

★ the longest cave in the world

★ the home of the Corvette plant

★ the seven states that border Kentucky

Size: 40,410 square miles
Population: 3,864,000

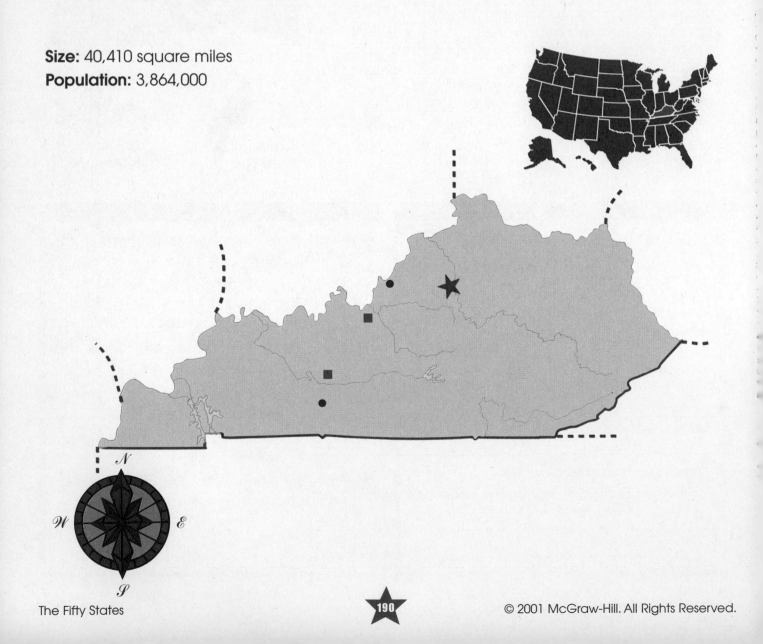

    © 2001 McGraw-Hill. All Rights Reserved.

Kentucky: The Bluegrass State

Answer the questions to learn the Kentucky state motto.

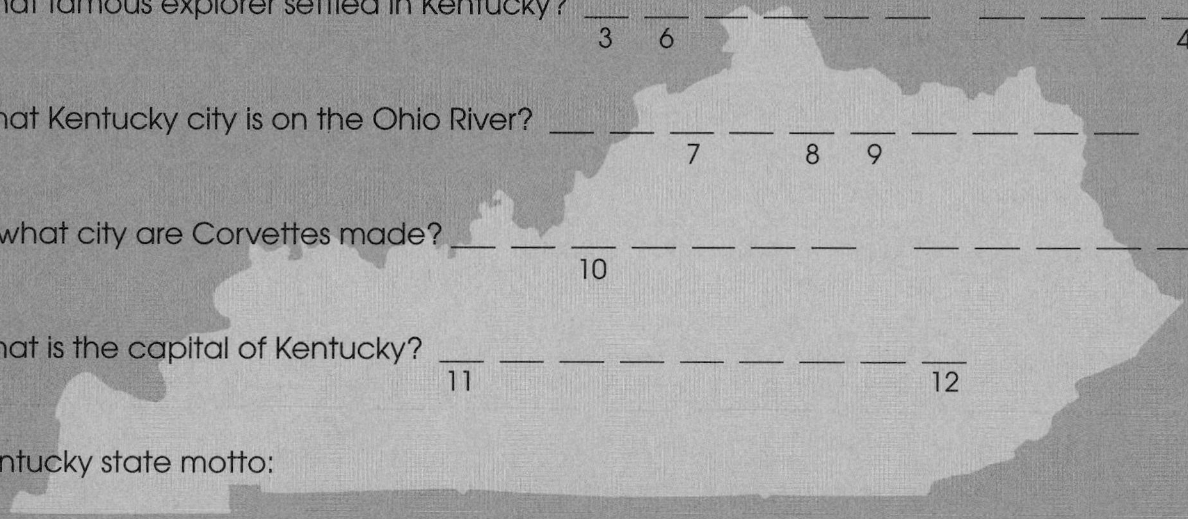

Who was the sixteenth president? __ __ __ __ __ __ __
                 1   5

What famous explorer settled in Kentucky? __ __ __ __ __ __ __ __ __ __ __ __
                      3 6   4 2

What Kentucky city is on the Ohio River? __ __ __ __ __ __ __ __ __
                  7   8 9

In what city are Corvettes made? __ __ __ __ __ __ __ __ __ __
              10

What is the capital of Kentucky? __ __ __ __ __ __ __ __ __ __
         11   12

Kentucky state motto:

"__ __ __ __ __ __ __ __ __ __ __ __ ;
  7 4 5 12 2 3   10 2   8 12 6 4 3

__ __ __ __ __ __ __ __ __ __ __ __ __ . "
3 5 9 5 3 2 3   10 2   11 6 1 1

Why is Kentucky called the "Bluegrass State"?

_____

_____

_____

_____

© 2001 McGraw-Hill. All Rights Reserved.

The Fifty States

Welcome to Louisiana

⭐ HOW LOUISIANA BECAME A STATE

In 1541, Spain's Hernando de Soto crossed the Mississippi River into Louisiana and claimed the land for Spain. At this time, the land was home to the Native American tribes of the Caddo, Houma, Tunica, Attakapa and Chitimacha. Then, in 1682, French explorer, Robert Cavelier sieur de La Salle, traveled down the Mississippi to the Gulf of Mexico and claimed the land for France. La Salle named it after France's king, Louis XIV. By the early 1700s, the French began to settle Louisiana and Jean Baptiste le Moyne founded New Orleans.

By the late 1700s, much of the land east of the Mississippi belonged to the United States. American trappers, traders and settlers started to cross the river. In 1800, Spain handed much of Louisiana over to France, and in 1803, the United States bought Louisiana from the French. Louisiana became the eighteenth state in April of 1812.

State Flag

UNION, JUSTICE & CONFIDENCE

Brown Pelican
State Bird

Magnolia
State Flower

FAMOUS LOUISIANANS

★ Pincey Pinchback was the country's first African-American state governor.

★ New Orleans was the birthplace of famous American author and playwright, Truman Capote.

★ Gospel legend, Mahalia Jackson, was born in New Orleans.

★ Football player and Fox TV Sports announcer, Terry Bradshaw, was born in Shreveport.

★ 1950s rocker, Antoine "Fats" Domino, was born in New Orleans.

★ Jazz legend, Louis Armstrong, also called "Satchmo," was born and raised in New Orleans.

★ Jerry Lee Lewis, one of the first rock-and-roll stars, is from Ferriday.

STATE GREATS

★ Zydeco, a mix of French and blues music, began in southwest Louisiana.

★ The McIlhenny family on Avery "Island" invented Tabasco sauce.

★ The Second Lake Pontchartrain Causeway is the longest bridge of its type in the world.

★ The Mardi Gras Festival in New Orleans is the country's most famous festival.

★ The tallest state capitol building in the U.S. is in Baton Rouge. The building is 32 stories high.

★ The Louisiana Superdome in New Orleans is the world's biggest indoor stadium.

★ The Mississippi, the longest river in the U.S., meets the ocean in New Orleans.

 © 2001 McGraw-Hill. All Rights Reserved.

Louisiana: The Pelican State

Look at an atlas or map of Louisiana. Add the names of the following places to the map below.

★ the river that creates the border between Texas and Louisiana

★ Tensas River National Wildlife Refuge

★ hometown of Jerry Lee Lewis

★ home of the tallest capitol building in the country

★ Chandeleur Island archipelago

★ Terry Bradshaw's birthplace

★ Bayou La Fourche

★ Lake Pontchartrain

★ Oil City

★ New Orleans

★ the longest river in the U.S.

★ Barataria Bay

Size: 47,472 square miles
Population: 4,389,000

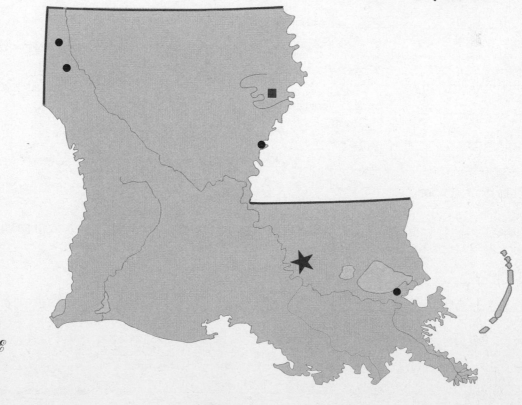

© 2001 McGraw-Hill. All Rights Reserved.

The Fifty States

Louisiana: **The Pelican State**

Find and circle the seven words about Louisiana hidden in the word search below. Then, fill in the sentences below with the words found in the word search.

```
R E S C A R T E C A D D O C
M L J S A T C H M O G A M A
M A C C K N O T H J Y O U P
P B R L A S A L L E I N S O
C E F C H J B A Y E O X O T
S A L A C L U W P O U N C E
C H R I M A G N O L I A E X
T A L R C U R T G O Y S D P
Y E L E J A M A R Z B H Y E
P J F D N B N P S A L E Z L
```

_____ was the nickname given to the jazz legend from New Orleans.

_____, the playwright and author, was born in New Orleans.

The _____ is the state flower of Louisiana.

_____ music was created in southwest Louisiana.

The _____ earned Louisiana its nickname.

The _____ Indians were among the first peoples of Louisiana.

The French explorer, _____, named Louisiana after King Louis XIV.

Imagine that you are trying to attract visitors to Louisiana. Design a travel poster that will persuade tourists to come. Write a slogan for the state.

_____

_____

_____

_____

© 2001 McGraw-Hill. All Rights Reserved.

Welcome to Maine

HOW MAINE BECAME A STATE

When navigator John Cabot explored Maine in 1498, many Algonquin tribes lived in the rugged wilderness. Later, Europeans began settling Maine in the 1600s. But life in the new land was not peaceful. For many years, France and Britain fought for control of the land. Native Americans were also involved in the fighting. Britain eventually gained control, and Maine became an important source of lobster, timber and fish.

Massachusetts claimed Maine as part of its colony in 1652. In 1691, Maine formally joined Massachusetts and stayed that way for more than 100 years. Maine applied for statehood in 1819. At the time, the United States had 22 states—11 were slave states and 11 were free states. Because of the Missouri Compromise, Maine was allowed to join the United States in 1820 as a free state. Maine was the twenty-third state to join the Union with Augusta as its capital.

State Flag

Chickadee
State Bird

**White Pine
Cone and Tassel
State Flower**

FAMOUS MAINERS

★ Henry Wadsworth Longfellow wrote the poem "Paul Revere's Ride."

★ Margaret Chase Smith was the first woman to serve in both houses of Congress.

★ Hannibal Hamlin was Abraham Lincoln's vice president.

★ Edna St. Vincent-Millay was the first woman poet to win the Pulitzer Prize.

★ Edmund Muskie was an important senator.

★ Stephen King lives in Bangor and writes horror novels.

★ Leon Leonwood "L.L." Bean started the L.L. Bean Company in Freeport.

STATE GREATS

★ Maine is the only state to share a border with only one other state—New Hampshire. Canada forms the other land borders.

★ The first naval battle of the Revolutionary War took place near Machias.

★ Nearly 90 percent of all lobster caught in the United States is caught off the coast of Maine. Many fishermen dock their boats in Rockland.

★ Maine's nickname is the "Pine Tree State." Almost 90 percent of the state is covered by forests.

© 2001 McGraw-Hill. All Rights Reserved.

The Fifty States

Maine: The Pine Tree State

Look at an atlas or map of Maine. Add the names of the following places to the map below.

★ the capital of Maine

★ the place where many lobster boats dock

★ the country that borders Maine

★ the one state that borders Maine

★ the site where the L.L. Bean Company is located

★ the town where Stephen King lives

★ the coastal town that was closest to the first Revolutionary War naval battle

★ the name of the body of water off the southern coast of Maine

★ Penobscot River

★ the Longfellow Mountains

Size: 33,265 square miles
Population: 1,245,000

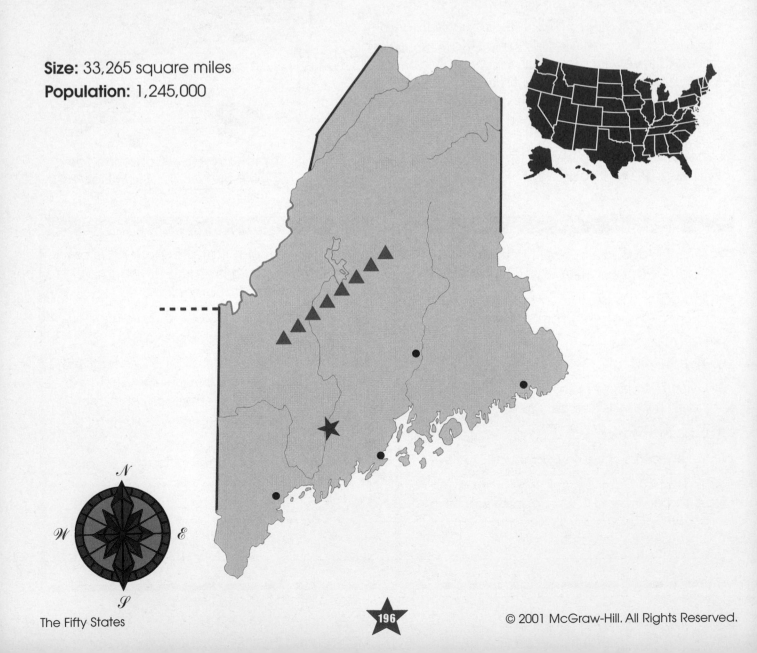

© 2001 McGraw-Hill. All Rights Reserved.

Maine: The Pine Tree State

Read the clues. Unscramble the words about Maine.

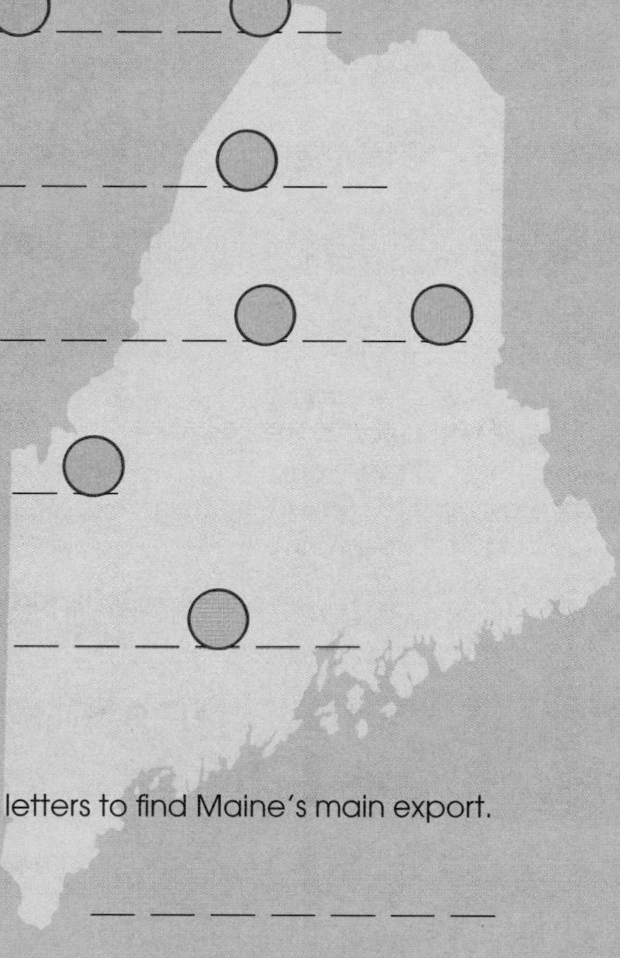

Stephen King's home ⚪__ __ __⚪__   O N B R A G

capital city of Maine __ __ __ __⚪__ __   U S A G U A T

St. Vincet-Millay's prize __ __ __ __⚪__ __⚪   Z R P I E L T U

nickname tree __ __ __⚪   E P N I

Lincoln's vice president __ __ __⚪__ __   A N H I L M

Unscramble the circled letters to find Maine's main export.

__ __ __ __ __ __ __ __

Maine is called the "Pine Tree State." Explain why trees are important and what they can be used for.

_____

_____

_____

_____

© 2001 McGraw-Hill. All Rights Reserved.

The Fifty States

Welcome to Maryland

HOW MARYLAND BECAME A STATE

When British settlers arrived in Maryland in 1633, they were led by a nobleman named Lord Baltimore. Baltimore started a new colony that was named Mariland, after Queen Henrietta Maria of England. The name of the colony was later changed to Maryland. The colonists settled along the Chesapeake Bay because it gave them a place to moor their boats. Maryland is an unusual state. The Chesapeake Bay splits Maryland almost in half.

The settlers built two main cities: Baltimore, named after Lord Baltimore, and Annapolis, which became the state's capital. In 1788, Maryland became the seventh state. Three years later, part of Maryland alongside the Potomac River was used to make Washington, D.C., the nation's capital. Today, the Chesapeake Bay is very polluted. Marylanders are working hard to clean the Bay and save it.

State Flag

Baltimore Oriole State Bird

Black-Eyed Susan State Flower

FAMOUS MARYLANDERS

★ Frederick Douglass, born a slave, escaped from his master. He started a newspaper called *North Star*.

★ John Wilkes Booth was an actor and the man who assassinated Abraham Lincoln.

★ Babe Ruth was perhaps the greatest baseball player ever.

★ Harriet Tubman escaped from slavery and helped free more than 300 slaves through the Underground Railroad.

★ Thurgood Marshall was the first African-American Supreme Court justice.

★ Billie Holiday was a popular jazz singer in the 1920s.

STATE GREATS

★ In 1784, the very first hot air balloon lifted off from Maryland.

★ The Baltimore and Ohio Railroad Company built the first passenger train in the United States.

★ Maryland's northern border is the Mason-Dixon line, which was drawn to separate the North from the South during the Civil War.

★ Francis Scott Key, a lawyer from Maryland, saw a Revolutionary War battle at Fort McHenry and wrote the "Star Spangled Banner."

★ The U.S. Naval Academy, in Annapolis, trains students to become officers in the Navy.

 © 2001 McGraw-Hill. All Rights Reserved.

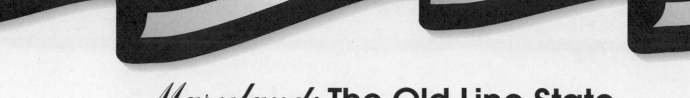

Maryland: The Old Line State

Look at an atlas or map of Maryland. Add the names of the following places to the map below.

- ★ a city named after a lord
- ★ this state is west of Maryland
- ★ the state capital
- ★ this waterway was a reason settlers came to Maryland
- ★ the line that separated the North from the South
- ★ the nation's capital

- ★ this state is south and west of Maryland
- ★ this state is on the other side of the Mason-Dixon line
- ★ this river drains into the Chesapeake Bay from Pennsylvania
- ★ this river cuts through Washington, D.C. and forms Maryland's western border
- ★ this state is east of Maryland

Size: 10,460 square miles
Population: 5,105,000

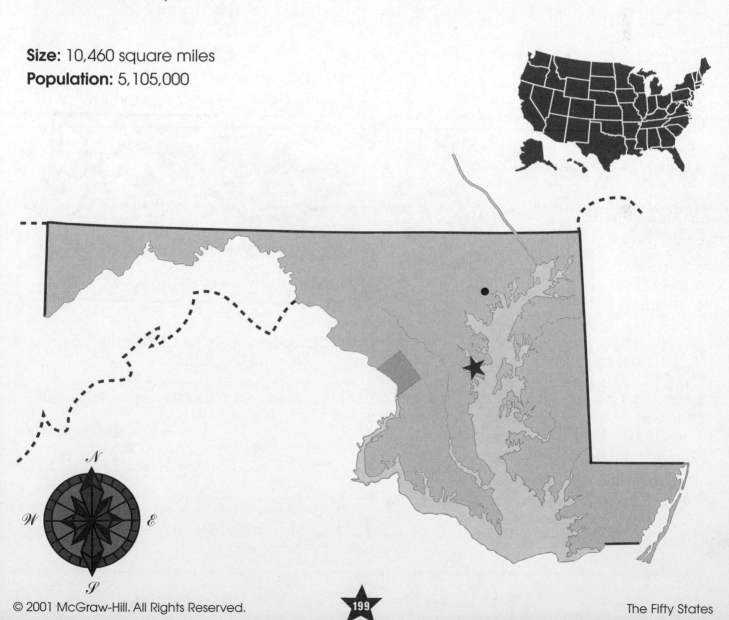

© 2001 McGraw-Hill. All Rights Reserved.

The Fifty States

Maryland: The Old Line State

Write the letter from column B next to the matching phrase in column A.

 A

1. _____ from here to the Navy

2. _____ passes by Washington, D.C.

3. _____ has a large natural harbor

4. _____ cuts through Maryland

5. _____ across the Potomac from Maryland

6. _____ east of Maryland

 B

A Delaware

B Potomac River

C Annapolis

D Chesapeake Bay

E Virginia

F Baltimore

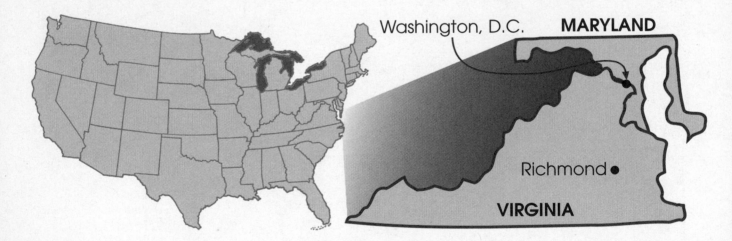

Maryland is south of the Mason-Dixon line but joined the Union during the Civil War. Richmond, Virginia was the Confederate capital. Washington, D.C. was the Union capital.

What might have happened to Washington, D.C. if Maryland had joined the South during the Civil War?

_____

_____

_____

_____

 © 2001 McGraw-Hill. All Rights Reserved.

Welcome to Massachusetts

★ ## HOW MASSACHUSETTS BECAME A STATE

Plymouth, Massachusetts is the place where the Pilgrims landed in 1620. The early settlers learned about living on the new land from the Wampanoag, a Native American tribe. The Wampanoag and the Pilgrims celebrated the first Thanksgiving in 1621. Unfortunately, the new settlers and the Native Americans did not always get along. A conflict called King Philip's War took place in 1675 when several tribes tried to stop the spread of English settlement.

Massachusetts still grew quickly. Many people left their homes in England. By 1760, nearly 250,000 people lived in the Massachusetts colony. Many of these residents were unhappy with the British laws. Massachusetts played a major part in America's fight for freedom. The American Revolution started fighting in the towns of Lexington and Concord. Massachusetts became the sixth state in February 1788.

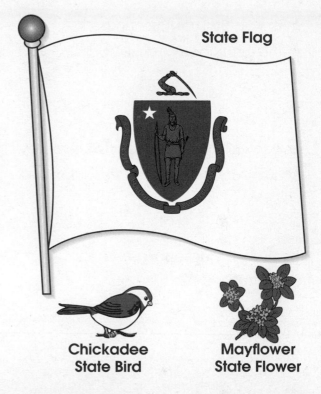

State Flag

**Chickadee
State Bird**

**Mayflower
State Flower**

FAMOUS BAY STATERS

★ John Adams and John Quincy Adams were presidents.

★ Paul Revere rode from Charlestown to Lexington on April 18, 1775, warning patriots of the arrival of British troops.

★ Clara Barton founded the American Red Cross.

★ Emily Dickinson wrote poetry in her Amherst home.

★ Ralph Waldo Emerson was a poet and essayist.

★ Bette Davis starred in films throughout the 1930s, 40s and 50s.

★ Barbara Walters is a television commentator.

STATE GREATS

★ Harvard University in Cambridge is the oldest college in the country.

★ Francis Cabot Lowell opened several manufacturing mills in the early 1800s. The town of East Chelmsford was renamed Lowell in his honor.

★ In 1891, James Naismith invented the game of basketball in Springfield.

★ Boston, Massachusetts' capital, is home to Boston Harbor—the site of the Boston Tea Party where colonists dumped tea into the water to protest the tax on tea.

★ Cape Cod and the islands off the coast of Massachusetts are popular vacation spots.

© 2001 McGraw-Hill. All Rights Reserved.

The Fifty States

Massachusetts: The Bay State

Look at an atlas or map of Massachusetts. Add the names of the following places to the map below.

★ the capital of Massachusetts

★ the birthplace of basketball

★ Cape Cod

★ the city with the oldest university in the United States

★ a town named for Francis Cabot Lowell

★ the place where the Pilgrims landed

★ the town where Emily Dickinson wrote her poems

★ the two sites where the first fighting of the Revolutionary War took place

★ the Berkshires

★ the place where Paul Revere began his ride

★ Martha's Vineyard

Size: 8,284 square miles
Population: 6,062,000

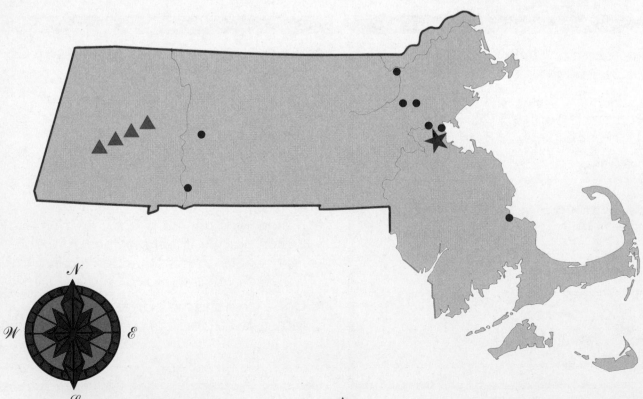

© 2001 McGraw-Hill. All Rights Reserved.

Massachusetts: **The Bay State**

Write the letter from column B next to the matching phrase in column A.

 A

 B

1. _____ capital city

2. _____ inventor of basketball

3. _____ founded the Red Cross

4. _____ oldest university in the country

5. _____ site where Pilgrims landed

6. _____ a Native American tribe

A Plymouth

B Harvard

C Naismith

D Boston

E Barton

F Wampanoag

Samuel Adams was a famous patriot from Massachusetts. Explain why he was important.

_____

_____

_____

_____

© 2001 McGraw-Hill. All Rights Reserved.

Welcome to Michigan

HOW MICHIGAN BECAME A STATE

*I*n the 1600s, Michigan was part of a wilderness called New France. Several Native American tribes, including the Ojibwa, the Miami, the Ottawa and the Huron, lived there along with a few French fur traders. The fur traders came down from what is now Canada and built settlements. The first was a mission started by Father Jacques Marquette at Sault Ste. Marie on the Upper Peninsula.

In 1763, the British took over and won a battle against the Native Americans led by the famous Chief Pontiac. After the Revolutionary War, when the United States won its independence from Britain, Michigan became part of the new United States. But it was not yet a state. The British tried to take over again in 1812, but they were beaten in battles on Lake Erie led by Oliver Hazard Perry. In the 1830s, settlers came flooding in because they could get good farmland cheaply. Michigan became the twenty-sixth state in 1837.

State Flag

Robin
State Bird

Apple Blossom
State Flower

FAMOUS MICHIGANDERS

★ Ralph Bunche was the first African-American to win the Nobel Peace Prize.

★ Charles Lindbergh was first to fly solo across the Atlantic Ocean.

★ Harriet Quimby was the first licensed American woman pilot.

★ Chief Pontiac was leader of the Ottawa.

★ Henry Ford created the modern automobile industry.

★ Gerald Ford became thirty-eighth president of the United States.

★ Della Reese is an actress and singer.

★ Edna Ferber is a novelist.

STATE GREATS

★ Michigan is the only state made up of two peninsulas. They are called the Upper Peninsula and the Lower Peninsula.

★ Corn flakes cereal was invented at Battle Creek.

★ More cars and trucks are made in Michigan than any other state. The city of Detroit is the center of the automobile industry.

★ The University of Michigan, a leading university, is located at Ann Arbor.

★ The Henry Ford Museum and Greenfield Village are in Dearborn. Thomas Edison's laboratory where he invented the light bulb was moved here from New Jersey. It also features some of the first cars made by Henry Ford.

 © 2001 McGraw-Hill. All Rights Reserved.

Michigan: **The Wolverine State**

Look at an atlas or map of Michigan. Add the names of the following places to the map below.

★ a city named after Chief Pontiac

★ the location of the University of Michigan

★ the place where corn flakes were invented

★ the Upper Peninsula

★ the Lower Peninsula

★ the lake where Oliver Hazard Perry fought the British

★ the other Great Lakes that border Michigan

★ Mackinac Island

★ the capital of Michigan

★ the center of the automobile industry

★ the place where Father Jacques Marquette started his mission

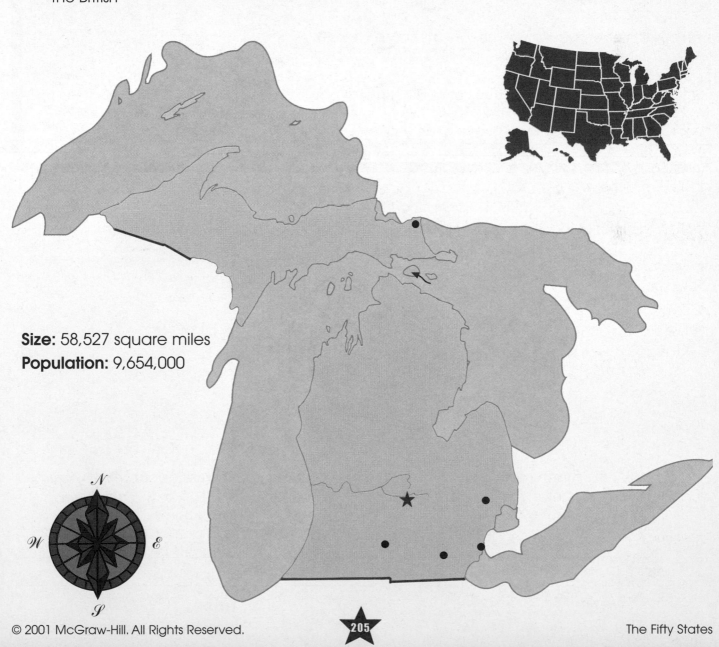

Size: 58,527 square miles
Population: 9,654,000

© 2001 McGraw-Hill. All Rights Reserved.

The Fifty States

Michigan: The Wolverine State

Read the clues. Unscramble the words about Michigan.

★ President Ford's first name   D Ⓐ R Ⓖ L E   _ _ _ _ _ _

★ light bulb man   Ⓢ I D O Ⓝ E   _ _ _ _ _ _

★ Chief   Ⓝ O P I A C T   _ _ _ _ _ _ _

★ automotive center   R O Ⓘ T T E D   _ _ _ _ _ _ _

★ Perry's place   K A Ⓛ E Ⓘ E R   _ _ _ _ _ _ _ _ _

★ Unscramble the circled letters to find Michigan's capital.

_ _ _ _ _ _ _

Look at the seal of the State of Michigan. The motto at the top reads: *E pluribus unum.*

Find out what this motto means. What language does it come from? Write about what it means and why it is important.

_____

_____

_____

 © 2001 McGraw-Hill. All Rights Reserved.

★ HOW MINNESOTA BECAME A STATE

*I*n the 1600s, Native Americans lived in northeastern Minnesota. The Dakota and Ojibwa hunted elk, deer and buffalo. French fur traders arrived around 1660. The fur traders traded cloth and weapons with the Native Americans for furs. The traders traveled south from Canada and built settlements. In 1679, Daniel Greysolon, sieur Duluth, came to Minnesota and claimed the land for France. In 1680, Father Louis Hennepin traveled the Mississippi River. At a site near present-day Minneapolis, he named a waterfall St. Anthony's Falls. More explorers and traders followed. Some were looking for a water route to the Pacific Ocean.

In 1763, England gained part of northeastern Minnesota from France. In 1783, the 13 colonies won their independence from England. However, it was not until the Louisiana Purchase of 1803, that the United States bought the land from France. In 1858, Minnesota became the thirty-second state.

State Flag

**Common Loon
State Bird**

**Pink and White
Lady's Slipper
State Flower**

FAMOUS MINNESOTANS

★ Charles A. Lindbergh was the first aviator to fly solo, nonstop, across the Atlantic Ocean.

★ Charlie Bender, an Ojibwa baseball pitcher, was elected to the Baseball Hall of Fame in 1951.

★ F. Scott Fitzgerald, a fiction writer, was born in St. Paul.

★ Judy Garland, an actress who played "Dorothy" in *The Wizard of Oz*, was born in Grand Rapids.

★ Hubert H. Humphrey became vice president of the United States.

★ Charles Schultz created the *Peanuts* comic strip.

★ Bob Dylan, singer songwriter, was born in Duluth.

STATE GREATS

★ Minnesota has the northernmost point of the continental United States.

★ Minnesota's capital, St. Paul, is part of a Twin City system with Minneapolis.

★ The Port of Duluth-Superior is the busiest port on the Great Lakes.

★ Fort Snelling was built at the fork of the Mississippi and Minnesota rivers in the 1820s.

★ The Mayo Clinic is in Rochester. The Mayo Clinic is famous throughout the world.

© 2001 McGraw-Hill. All Rights Reserved.

The Fifty States

Minnesota: The Gopher State

Look at an atlas or map of Minnesota. Add the names of the following places to the map below.

★ the place where Fort Snelling stands

★ the location of the Mayo Clinic

★ the lake that borders northeastern Minnesota

★ the city near St. Anthony's Falls

★ the city where Bob Dylan was born

★ the northernmost point of the continental United States

★ the city of Judy Garland's childhood home

★ the capital of Minnesota

Size: 84,402 square miles
Population: 4,642,000

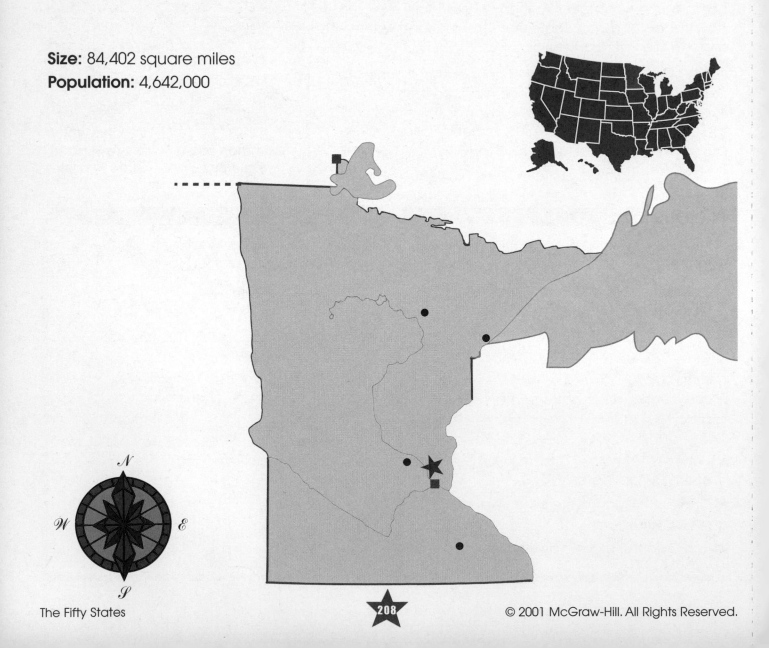

          © 2001 McGraw-Hill. All Rights Reserved.

Minnesota: **The Gopher State**

Read the clues. Unscramble the words about Minnesota.

Lake __ __ __ __ __ __ __ __   P S U E O I R R

Vice President Humphrey's first name __ __ __ __ __ __   R E H B T U

Fort __ __ __ __ __ __ __ __   N L E G S I N L

Lindbergh flew
nonstop across this ocean __ __ __ __ __ __ __ __   T T L A A I C N

Minnesota's capital __ __ __   __ __ __ __   P U A T S L

Minnesota's Native Americans __ __ __ __ __ __   A J O B I W

On a sunny afternoon in 1876, the James/Younger gang headed toward Northfield, Minnesota. The gang, which included Jesse James and Frank James, planned a daring deed.

Find out what happened in Northfield, Minnesota, on September 7, 1876. Write about what happened.

_____

_____

_____

_____

_____

_____

_____

© 2001 McGraw-Hill. All Rights Reserved.

The Fifty States

Welcome to Mississippi

HOW MISSISSIPPI BECAME A STATE

The Natchez, Chickasaw and Choctaw tribes lived in Mississippi when the first Europeans arrived in the 1540s. They traded and helped the French settlers at first, but when the settlers took their land, the Natchez turned against them. Today, the city of Natchez is named after the Natchez tribe. In fact, at one time, it was Mississippi's capital. In 1817, Mississippi became the twentieth state— but soon it would be ravaged by war. In the 1830s, the Army forced the Chickasaw and Choctaw tribes from their land. Thousands of people died. This forced march is called the "Trail of Tears."

During the Civil War, Mississippi fought on the side of the southern states. One of the biggest battles of the war was the Siege of Vicksburg. There, the Union army bombed Confederate troops for more than a month. After the war, the people of Mississippi had to rebuild their state. Mississippi rebuilt itself with strong industries in fishing, papermaking, cotton and even oil.

State Flag

Mockingbird State Bird

Magnolia State Flower

FAMOUS MISSISSIPPIANS

★ Charles and Medgar Evers were civil rights leaders. Medgar was murdered in 1963 and Charles served as mayor of Fayette.

★ Author William Faulkner won a Nobel Prize and two Pulitzer Prizes.

★ Oprah Winfrey has her own talk show and starred in *The Color Purple*.

★ Richard Wright wrote stories of his youth in the South.

★ Walter Payton was a football player for the Chicago Bears.

★ John Lee Hooker is one of the greatest blues singers and guitarists.

★ Elvis Presley became one of the most loved musicians in the world.

STATE GREATS

★ More upholstered, or padded, furniture comes from Mississippi than from any other state.

★ Every April, people from all over the world come to Belzoni to attend the World Catfish Festival.

★ Coca-Cola, invented in Georgia, was first bottled in Vicksburg, Mississippi.

★ The Tennessee-Tombigbee Waterway was built to connect two rivers and make transportation easier.

★ The Mississippi River is the longest river system in North America and the third longest in the world.

© 2001 McGraw-Hill. All Rights Reserved.

Mississippi: The Magnolia State

Look at an atlas or map of Mississippi. Add the names of the following places to the map below.

★ this river is one of the most important in the whole country

★ this state is south of Mississippi

★ the capital of Mississippi

★ the Mississippi flows into this body of water

★ this connects two rivers

★ this state is to the north

★ an important battle was fought here

★ go east to get to this state

★ this city is named after the Native Americans who lived there

★ a city on the Gulf of Mexico

★ this state is to the northwest of Mississippi

Size: 47,689 square miles
Population: 2,676,000

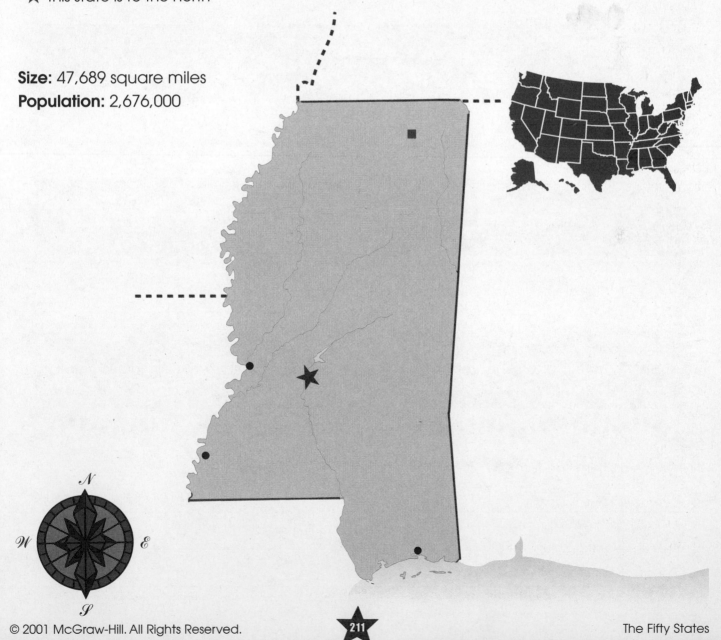

© 2001 McGraw-Hill. All Rights Reserved.

Mississippi: The Magnolia State

Next to each sentence write a T if the statement is true or an F if the statement is false.

_____ Mississippi is bordered by five states.

_____ The Mississippi River drains into the Pacific Ocean.

_____ The fishing industry helped rebuild the state.

_____ Coca-Cola was invented in Mississippi.

_____ The Natchez tribe turned against the French settlers.

_____ Biloxi has always been Mississippi's capital.

_____ The "Trail of Tears" refers to the march many Native Americans were forced to take.

Why do you think the forced march was called the "Trail of Tears?"

_____

_____

 © 2001 McGraw-Hill. All Rights Reserved.

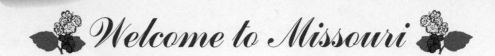

Welcome to Missouri

State Flag

Before it became a state, Missouri belonged to three nations. La Salle claimed the territory for France in 1682, and France gave it to Spain in 1764. Spain, in a secret treaty, gave the territory back to France in 1802. Napoleon Bonaparte wanted to get rid of the land and sold it to the United States as part of the Louisiana Purchase in 1803.

St. Louis soon became a gateway to the West—Lewis and Clark used it as a starting point for their famous expedition. The Missouri and Mississippi rivers were important routes for steamboat traffic. Missouri became a territory in 1812. The Missouri Compromise admitted Missouri as a slave state and Maine as a free state. Although admitted as a slave state, Missouri remained with the Union throughout the Civil War and gave men to both armies. Missouri became the twenty-fourth state in 1821. Missouri was named after a tribe called the Missouri, which means "town of the large canoes."

Bluebird
State Bird

Hawthorn
State Flower

FAMOUS MISSOURIANS

★ Harry S. Truman was president of the United States. His home and library are located in Independence.

★ Christopher Carson, later known as Kit Carson, grew up in Missouri and became a famous guide.

★ Samuel Clemens, known as Mark Twain, had his boyhood home in Hannibal.

★ George Washington Carver became one of America's greatest scientists.

★ Daniel Boone moved to Missouri in 1799 and became governor of the Spanish territory called Missouri.

★ Langston Hughes was one of America's most famous African-American poets.

STATE GREATS

★ Bagnell Dam across from the Osage River in the Ozarks is one of the largest man-made lakes in the world. It covers 65,000 acres.

★ In 1860, the Pony Express was started at St. Joseph, Missouri.

★ Jefferson City, a small riverboat town, was chosen as the capital in 1821. The town was laid out by Daniel M. Boone, son of the famous Daniel Boone.

★ After World War II, Missouri became the country's second largest manufacturer of automobiles.

★ Missouri is the home of the St. Louis Rams and the Kansas City Chiefs football teams.

© 2001 McGraw-Hill. All Rights Reserved.

The Fifty States

Missouri: **The Show-Me State**

Look at an atlas or map of Missouri. Add the names of the following places to the map below.

★ the lake where Bagnell Dam is located

★ the capital of Missouri

★ the mighty river on which many steamboats traveled

★ the mountains in Missouri

★ the place where the Pony Express started

★ the city that has the same name as Kansas

★ the river that borders Missouri on the west

★ the states that border Missouri

★ the location of the Harry S. Truman home and library

★ the boyhood home of Mark Twain

Size: 69,697 square miles
Population: 5,309,000

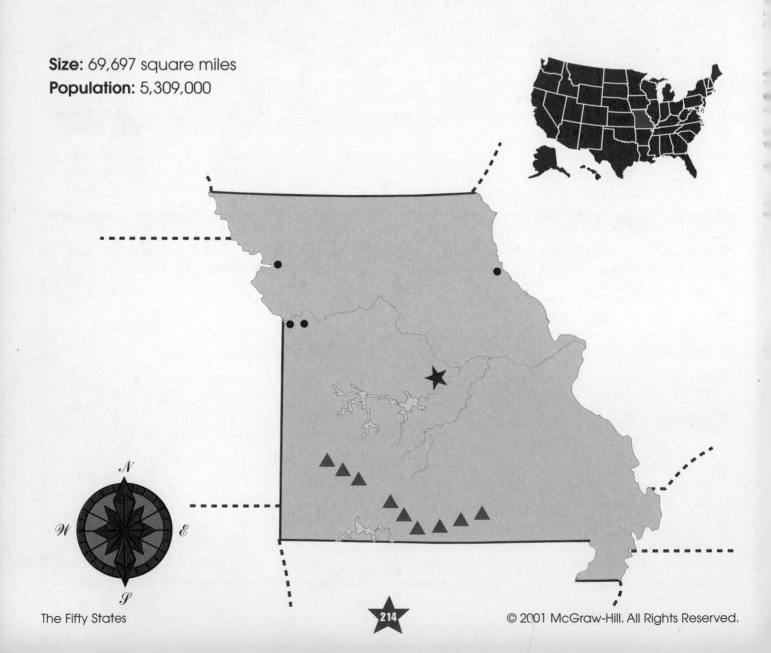

© 2001 McGraw-Hill. All Rights Reserved.

Missouri: **The Show-Me State**

Read the clues. Unscramble the words about Missouri.

a famous guide __ __ __ __ __ __   R O N S A C

a president of the U. S. __ __ __ __ __ __   M U N R A T

one of America's greatest scientists __ __ __ __ __ __   R E V A R C

Mark Twain's boyhood home __ __ __ __ __ __ __ __   N A H I N L A B

admitted as a free state
by the Missouri Compromise __ __ __ __ __   N E M I A

a large dam __ __ __ __ __ __ __ __   G L B N E A L

In Latin, the motto of Missouri reads: *Salus populi suprema lex esto.*

Find the meaning of this motto in a dictionary or encyclopedia. Write about what it means and why this idea is important to Missourians.

_____

_____

_____

_____

© 2001 McGraw-Hill. All Rights Reserved.   215

Welcome to Montana

State Flag

Western Meadowlark State Bird

Bitterroot State Flower

HOW MONTANA BECAME A STATE

The Native American tribes of the Crow and Blackfeet roamed Montana long before European explorers. These tribes lived mainly by hunting buffalo. In 1742, the French brothers Francois and Louis de La Vérendrye were the first Europeans to arrive. In 1803, the land in the east became part of the United States through the Louisiana Purchase. Soon, Lewis and Clark charted the new territory.

In 1842, Father Pierre-Jean DeSmet founded a mission. Stevensville, the first town, grew nearby. In 1862, when miners found gold in Bannack, a gold rush started. A year later, Bill Fairweather discovered gold at Alder Gulch. That gulch is now Main Street in Virginia City. Montana became a territory in 1864. A third rush of people arrived in Montana when silver was found in Butte in 1875. Soon, the Northern Pacific Railway crossed Montana to bring settlers and supplies. Montana became the forty-first state on November 8, 1889.

FAMOUS MONTANANS

★ Robert Yellowtail was the first Native American hired by the United States government to lead a reservation.

★ Plenty Coups was a Crow leader who represented the Indian nations at a ceremony for the Tomb of the Unknown Soldier.

★ Lester Carl Thurow, born in Livingston, was an economist and author.

★ Harold Clayton Urey grew up in Montana and won the Nobel Prize for chemistry.

★ Politician Jeannette Rankin was from Missoula. She was the only person to vote against both World Wars.

STATE GREATS

★ Fort Peck Dam is one of the biggest dams in the world.

★ In 1876, Lt. Col. George Armstrong Custer was defeated at the famous battle of Little Big Horn.

★ Visitors can see snow year round at Glacier National Park.

★ Pictograph Cave State Historic Site near Billings has cave drawings that are more than 5,000 years old.

★ Giant Springs is one of the largest fresh water springs—338 million gallons of water flow through it each day.

© 2001 McGraw-Hill. All Rights Reserved.

Montana: **The Treasure State**

Look at an atlas or map of Montana. Add the names of the following places to the map below.

★ mountain range in the western part of the state

★ the line that divides the continent

★ the country to the north of the state

★ the capital of Montana

★ one of the biggest dams in the world

★ the river where Lt. Col. Custer was defeated

★ the National Park with year-round snow

★ the city near the site of 5,000 year old cave drawings

★ the place near where Jeannette Rankin was born

★ where silver was discovered

★ the city where gold was discovered in a gulch

Size: 147,046 square miles
Population: 863,000

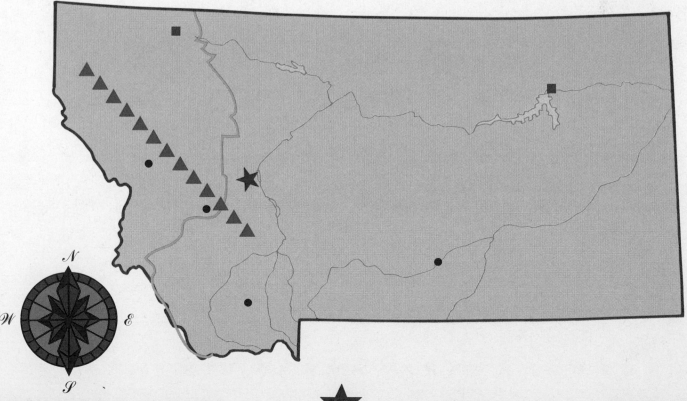

© 2001 McGraw-Hill. All Rights Reserved.

The Fifty States

Montana: **The Treasure State**

Read the clues. Circle each hidden word and draw a line to the phrase it answers.

the metal that started a "rush" to the area

U S T E V E N S V I L L E A

drawings found in caves

Y U R E Y O

last name of famous chemist

F F G O L D B

the first town

L P I C T O G R A P H S B

an animal hunted by Crow and Blackfeet Indians

F F B U F F A L O X

★★★★★★★★★★★★★★★★★★★★★★★★★★★★★★★★★★★★

Montana is called the "Treasure State." Write about what treasures you could find in Montana.

_____

_____

_____

★★★★★★★★★★★★★★★★★★★★★★★★★★★★★★★★★★★★

 © 2001 McGraw-Hill. All Rights Reserved.

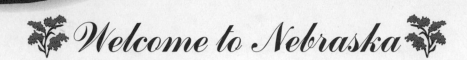

Welcome to Nebraska

★ HOW NEBRASKA BECAME A STATE

*N*ebraska is part of the Great Plains area in the central United States. Crossing through the Great Plains is a river that French explorers thought was flat. They called it the Platte River. Other rivers in Nebraska include the Niobrara and Missouri. Another area of Nebraska, called the Till Plains, is also flat. However, the Till Plains are more fertile than the Great Plains.

The first American traders arrived in 1807. Because Nebraska had so few trees, some settlers built houses out of grass and mud near what is now Omaha. At this time, Native American tribes also lived in Nebraska. However, life was not peaceful—the Sioux and Cheyenne fought to keep the settlers away. But in 1867, Nebraska became the thirty-seventh state. At first, the railroad companies owned much of Nebraska, but later they sold the land to farmers. In the 1930s, a drought forced many farmers to leave Nebraska. The corn farmers eventually returned. Now, most Nebraskans live in the cities of Omaha and the capital, Lincoln.

State Flag

Western Meadowlark State Bird

Goldenrod State Flower

FAMOUS NEBRASKANS

★ Malcolm Little was born in Omaha. He changed his name to Malcolm X and became a civil rights leader.

★ Marlon Brando is best known for his acting in *The Godfather*.

★ Actor Henry Fonda is the father of actors Jane Fonda and Peter Fonda and grandfather of actor Bridget Fonda.

★ Fred Astaire was a dancer who appeared in more than 30 film musicals.

★ Crazy Horse was a Native American who fought against U.S. settlers to reclaim land for his people.

★ Bob Gibson twice won the Cy Young award, baseball's top award for pitchers.

STATE GREATS

★ Nebraska held the world's first rodeo in 1882. It starred Buffalo Bill Cody.

★ The first fossil of a woolly mammoth was found in Nebraska. It's more than 13 feet high.

★ The largest planted forest in the country is the Nebraska National Forest. It covers 22,000 acres.

★ Millions of buffalo used to roam through Nebraska. They were hunted nearly to extinction but are now protected.

★ The first frozen dinners came from Omaha, Nebraska.

★ Despite the Nebraska National Forest, only 2 percent of the state is forest.

© 2001 McGraw-Hill. All Rights Reserved.

The Fifty States

Nebraska: The Cornhusker State

Look at an atlas or map of Nebraska. Add the names of the following places to the map below.

★ the N. Platte river flows from this state

★ Omaha is on this river

★ this state is to the east of Nebraska

★ the capital of Nebraska

★ this state shares Nebraska's northern border

★ this area makes up most of Nebraska

★ this state cuts into southwest Nebraska

★ Nebraska shares this area with Iowa

★ this river passes by Grand Island and flows into the Missouri River

★ this state is due south of Nebraska

★ Malcom X's birthplace

Size: 77,355 square miles
Population: 1,649,000

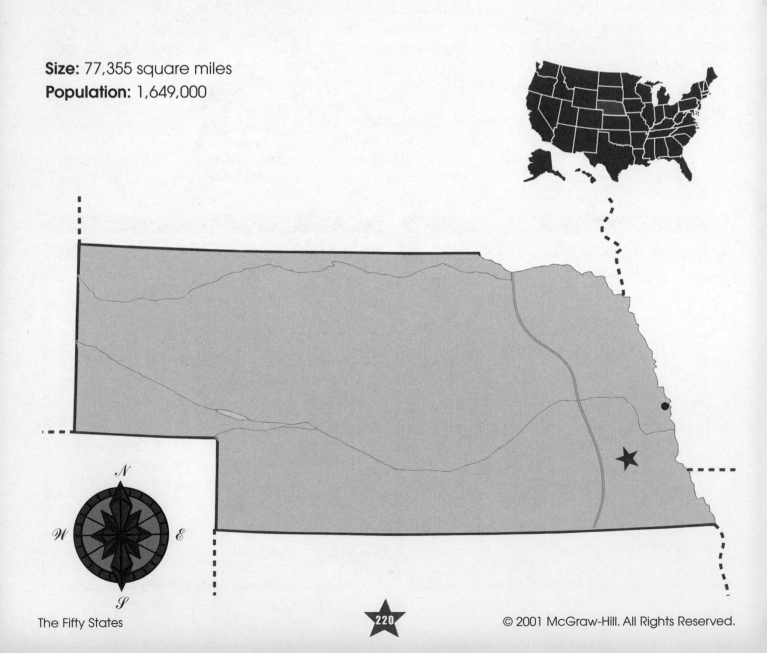

N

W   E

S

 © 2001 McGraw-Hill. All Rights Reserved.

Nebraska: The Cornhusker State

Next to each sentence write a T if the statement is true or an F if the statement is false.

_____ The Till Plains are more fertile than the Great Plains.

_____ Omaha is closer to Colorado than it is to Iowa.

_____ The city of Lincoln is in the Till Plains.

_____ The first frozen dinners were made in Lincoln.

_____ There are few trees in Nebraska.

_____ Now, most people in Nebraska live in cities.

_____ To get into Iowa, northern Nebraskans would have to cross the Platte River.

What do the images on the Nebraska state flag tell about Nebraska?

_____

_____

© 2001 McGraw-Hill. All Rights Reserved. The Fifty States

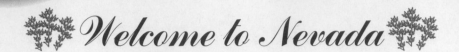
Welcome to Nevada

★ HOW NEVADA BECAME A STATE

*I*n 1859, the Paiute, Washoe and Shoshone tribes lived in Nevada. Fewer than 1,000 settlers lived in Nevada at this time. But soon, miners found gold and silver in the Comstock Lode, near Virginia City. Two years later, more than 20,000 people had settled in Nevada. So much gold and silver was discovered that the Carson City Mint was opened. Carson City became Nevada's capital. In 1864, Nevada became the thirty-sixth state. By then, mining had been replaced by ranching or raising cattle.

In 1905, the town of Las Vegas was built. It eventually grew into a big gambling city. Las Vegas is surrounded by the Mojave Desert. Because the state gets so little rainfall, the Hoover Dam was built to provide both power and water to Nevada. However, Nevada is not all desert. There are also mountains covered in snow, such as Nevada's tallest peak, Boundary Peak. Nevada is also home to beautiful Lake Tahoe, the biggest mountain lake in the country.

State Flag

Mountain Bluebird
State Bird

Sagebrush
State Flower

FAMOUS NEVADANS

★ Andre Agassi is a tennis player who won the U.S. Open in 1994.

★ Edna Purviance was born in Paradise Valley. She starred in more than 30 of Charlie Chaplin's movies.

★ Sarah Winnemucca Hopkins was a Native American who fought for Native Americans' rights.

★ Anne Martin was born in Empire City. She fought for the woman's right to vote.

★ Jack Kramer was born in Las Vegas. He won the U.S. Open in 1946 and 1947.

★ Waddie Mitchell, born in Elko, is a cowboy poet.

STATE GREATS

★ Any adult can adopt a wild horse or burro in Nevada. The cost is $125 per horse and $75 per burro.

★ There is a town in Nevada named Adaven. That is Nevada spelled backwards.

★ The largest cutthroat trout ever caught weighed 41 pounds. It was fished from Pyramid Lake in 1925.

★ Nevada has both the country's highest marriage rate and the country's highest divorce rate.

★ Nevada is the country's driest state. Less rain falls there than in any other state.

★ Hoover Dam is the tallest concrete dam in the country.

 © 2001 McGraw-Hill. All Rights Reserved.

Nevada: The Silver State

Look at an atlas or map of Nevada. Add the names of the following places to the map below.

★ the capital of Nevada

★ a very large dam

★ this town is Nevada spelled backwards

★ Waddie Mitchell was born here

★ this is Nevada's tallest mountain

★ this river forms a small part of Nevada's border with Arizona

★ odds are you can find gamblers in this southern city

★ this lake is near the Hoover Dam

★ this state shares Nevada's eastern border

★ this is the biggest mountain lake

★ this desert is in southeastern Nevada

Size: 110,561 square miles
Population: 1,206,000

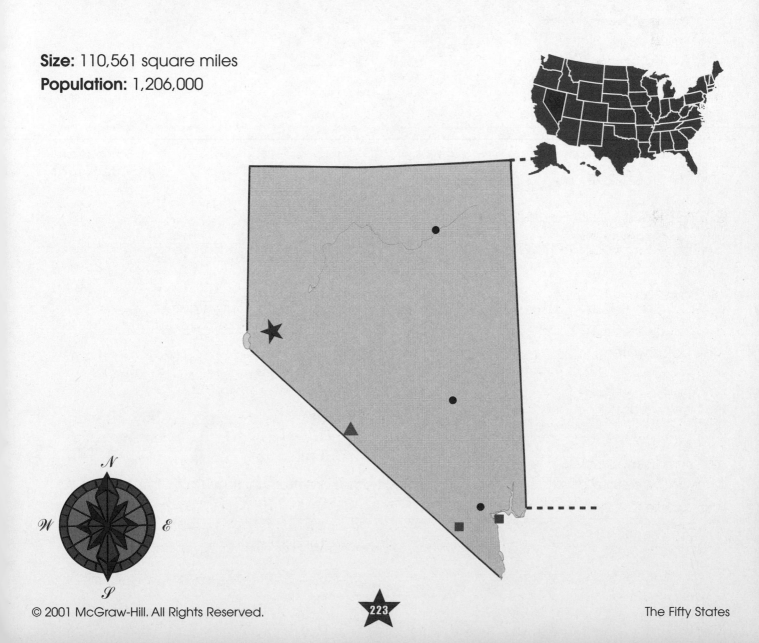

© 2001 McGraw-Hill. All Rights Reserved.

The Fifty States

Nevada: The Silver State

Use the code below to learn about some interesting people, places and events in Nevada.

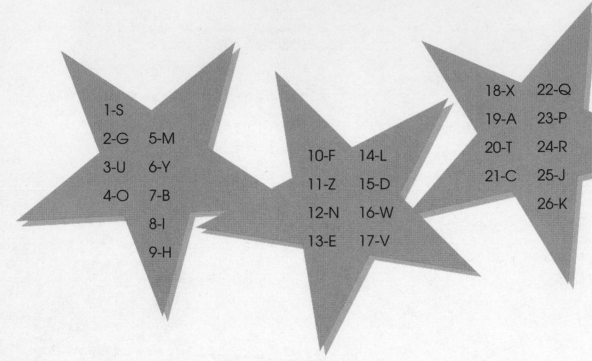

1-S

2-G   5-M

3-U   6-Y

4-O   7-B

     8-I

     9-H

10-F   14-L

11-Z   15-D

12-N   16-W

13-E   17-V

18-X   22-Q

19-A   23-P

20-T   24-R

21-C   25-J

       26-K

first a railroad town, now, a gambling town __ __ __ __ __ __ __ __
                                                14 19 1   17 13 2 19 1

Nevada's nickname __ __ __ __ __ __ __ __ __ __ __ __ __ __
                   20 9 13   1 8 14 17 13 24   1 20 19 20 13

a Cowboy poet __ __ __ __ __ __ __ __ __ __ __ __ __ __
               16 19 15 15 8 13   5 8 20 21 9 13 14 14

this holds water __ __ __ __ __ __ __ __ __
                9 4 4 17 13 24   15 19 5

a backwards name for a town __ __ __ __ __ __
                                  19 15 19 17 13 12

Nevada is a state of extremes. What kinds of extremes are there in Nevada?

_____

_____

_____

 © 2001 McGraw-Hill. All Rights Reserved.

Welcome to New Hampshire

HOW NEW HAMPSHIRE BECAME A STATE

The first settlers of New Hampshire were the Abnaki and Algonquin tribes. Many places in the state still have Algonquin names, including Nashua, Ossipee and Winnipesaukee. New Hampshire's coast was settled by Europeans in the 1620s. King James I of England gave a large area of land to Captain John Mason who named it. Until 1679, New Hampshire was a part of Massachusetts. At one time, New Hampshire even included parts of Vermont.

The people of New Hampshire were among the first to support American independence. In 1774, New Hampshire declared its independence from England. In honor of this, the people of New Hampshire were the first to vote for the Declaration of Independence on July 4, 1776. New Hampshire then became the ninth state on June 21, 1788. New Hampshire's approval of the Constitution officially created the United States.

State Flag

Purple Finch
State Bird

Purple Lilac
State Flower

FAMOUS NEW HAMPSHIRITES

★ Franklin Pierce was the fourteenth president of the United States.

★ Daniel Webster was a famous lawyer, speaker and statesman born in Franklin.

★ Horace Greely was the founder and publisher of the *New York Tribune*.

★ Sarah Josepha Hale wrote "Mary Had a Little Lamb."

★ Poet Robert Frost was born in California but considered Derry, New Hampshire, his home. He won the Pulitzer Prize four times.

★ Edward A. and Marian Nevins MacDowell founded the MacDowell Colony for artists in Peterborough.

★ Alan B. Shepard, Jr., was the first American astronaut in space.

STATE GREATS

★ Franconia is home to "The Old Man of the Mountain." The "Old Man" is a stone ledge that looks like the side view of a face.

★ The treaty ending the Russo-Japanese War was signed in Portsmouth in 1905.

★ Every 4 years, New Hampshire holds the country's first presidential primary.

★ The fastest winds in the world were recorded atop Mt. Washington in 1934. The winds were recorded at 231 miles per hour.

★ New Hampshire has the largest House of Representatives of any state in the country.

© 2001 McGraw-Hill. All Rights Reserved.

The Fifty States

New Hampshire: **The Granite State**

Look at an atlas or map of New Hampshire. Add the names of the following places to the map below.

★ the site where the treaty of the Russo-Japanese war was signed

★ the capital of New Hampshire

★ the location of the Old Man of the Mountain

★ the place where the fastest winds were recorded

★ Lake Winnipesaukee

★ the town where the MacDowell Colony is located

★ the state that once claimed New Hampshire

★ the birthplace of Daniel Webster

★ the home of Robert Frost

★ the Connecticut River

Size: 9,279 square miles
Population: 1,114,000

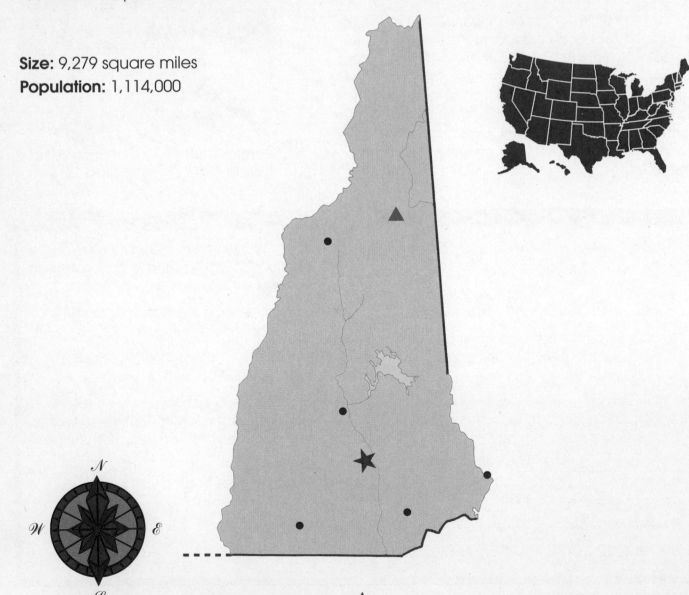

© 2001 McGraw-Hill. All Rights Reserved.

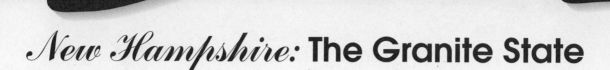

New Hampshire: **The Granite State**

Complete the crossword puzzle below.

Across

3 New Hampshire delegates were the first to vote on the _____ of Independence.

5 Sarah Josepha _____ wrote "Mary Had a Little Lamb."

6 New Hampshire is called the _____ State.

Down

1 Captain John _____ named New Hampshire.

2 The world's fastest winds were recorded on Mt. _____ .

4 The state's capital is _____.

7 In 1788, New Hampshire became the _____ state.

New Hampshire's motto is "Live Free or Die." Write about what you think this means and why you think New Hampshire chose this motto.

_____

_____

_____

_____

_____

© 2001 McGraw-Hill. All Rights Reserved.

The Fifty States

Welcome to New Jersey

HOW NEW JERSEY BECAME A STATE

The English explorer, John Cabot, saw the coast of New Jersey in 1498, but he did not set foot on land. Later, Henry Hudson explored the area in 1609. Dutch settlers soon built Fort Nassau and Jersey City. In 1638, the Dutch claimed the areas of New Jersey and New York as the colony of New Netherland. However, England never recognized the Dutch claims. In 1664, the Dutch surrendered New Netherland to the English. The area west of the Hudson River was named New Jersey, after the Isle of Jersey in the English Channel.

New Jersey was heavily involved in the fight for independence. Approximately 100 battles were fought within the state. Many of these battles were led by General George Washington. In June 1780, the British were beaten in the Battle of Springfield. New Jersey became the third state on December 18, 1787, with Trenton as its capital. Newark is now the largest city in New Jersey.

State Flag

Eastern Goldfinch
State Bird

Purple Violet
State Flower

FAMOUS NEW JERSEYANS

★ Frank Sinatra, a famous singer and actor, was born in Hoboken.

★ Aaron Burr was vice president of the United States under Thomas Jefferson.

★ James Fenimore Cooper wrote novels about western expansion.

★ Walt Whitman was a famous poet and writer.

★ Grover Cleveland was the twenty-second and twenty-fourth president of the United States.

★ Bruce Springsteen is a well-known musician and singer.

STATE GREATS

★ The science of studying dinosaur fossils began in 1858. Scientists discovered the first, nearly complete, skeleton of a dinosaur in Haddonfield.

★ Patterson was the first planned industrial city in America.

★ Princeton University is one of America's most respected universities. Albert Einstein did some of his research there.

★ Thomas Edison invented the electric light in his laboratory at Menlo Park.

★ Samuel Morse invented the telegraph near his home in Morristown.

★ Hoboken was the site of the first pro baseball game in 1846.

© 2001 McGraw-Hill. All Rights Reserved.

New Jersey: The Garden State

Look at an atlas or map of New Jersey. Add the names of the following places to the map below.

- ★ the state capital
- ★ the river that flows between New Jersey and Pennsylvania
- ★ the southernmost point of New Jersey
- ★ the location of one of America's leading universities
- ★ the largest city in New Jersey

- ★ the states that border New Jersey
- ★ the mountains in northern New Jersey
- ★ the city on the coast that shares its name with an ocean
- ★ the ocean bordering eastern New Jersey
- ★ the place where Samuel Morse invented the telegraph

Size: 7,787 square miles
Population: 7,878,000

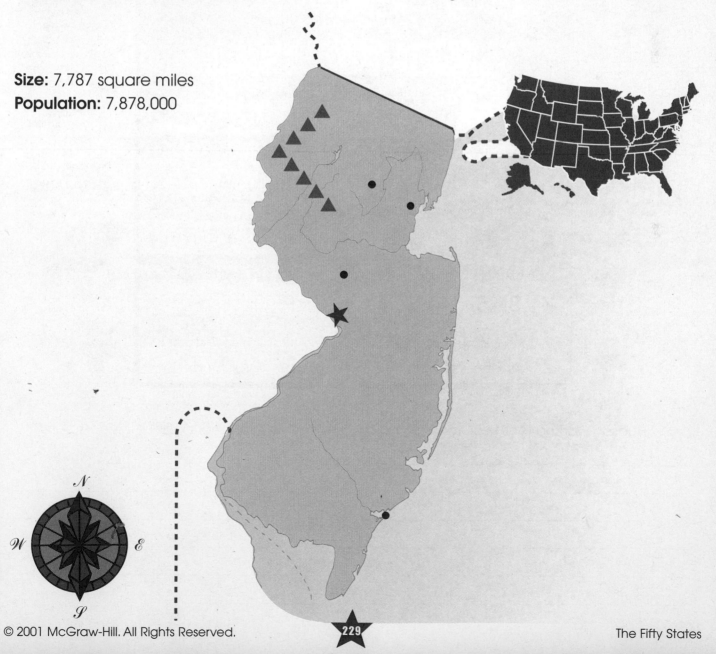

© 2001 McGraw-Hill. All Rights Reserved.

The Fifty States

New Jersey: The Garden State

Use the words in the Word Bank to find and circle the words about New Jersey in the word search below.

Word Bank   Cleveland   Hoboken   Princeton   Trenton   Morse

Hudson   Cooper   Sinatra   Washington   Edison

```
P I J E Y Y E K W D K N I
Y C A I C E T N A N J O W
C L Z A S L I G S A R S Q
M O B M T D G F H L N D A
D O O C Z A K S I E Y U X
T B N P K R E M N V S H P
I R R M E B S R G E S I E
H G E R H R R J T L W R L
E D I S O N O M O C T S U
R O C N V C M D N S O B W
N O T E C N I R P N Z W J
K S S N O T N E R T D Y U
Y X Y H H A N E K O B O H
Z N M B I D S I N A T R A
```

Henry Hudson worked for the Dutch East India Company. Find out more about this company.

_____

_____

_____

_____

_____

_____

© 2001 McGraw-Hill. All Rights Reserved.

Welcome to New Mexico

HOW NEW MEXICO BECAME A STATE

When Spanish explorers came to the land that would become New Mexico, they found the Navajo, Apache and Pueblo tribes living there. In 1610, Pedro de Peralta founded Santa Fe, which later became the capital of New Mexico. But in 1680, Popé, a Pueblo medicine man, took control of the city and drove the Spanish out. Twelve years later, the Spanish returned and recaptured Santa Fe. In 1706, Francisco Cuero y Valdes founded the city of Albuquerque. This strengthened the Spanish hold on the land.

When Mexico gained independence from Spain in 1821, Spain's power weakened. In 1846, General Kearny claimed New Mexico for the United States. However, Mexico did not accept this claim and began the Mexican-American War with the United States. After the war, most of New Mexico became a United States territory. The United States bought the rest of the land in 1853. It was not until January 6, 1912, that New Mexico became the forty-seventh state.

State Flag

Roadrunner
State Bird

Yucca Flower
State Flower

FAMOUS NEW MEXICANS

★ Dionisio Chavez was the first Mexican-American senator.

★ Georgia O'Keefe painted the New Mexican landscape and lived on a ranch near Taos.

★ Maria Martinez, born in San Ildefonso, created traditional Pueblo Indian pottery.

★ Charles Bent was the first governor of New Mexico.

★ Elizabeth Garrett wrote the state song in English in 1917.

★ Amadeo Lucero wrote the state song in Spanish in 1971.

★ Buffalo Bill started his first western road show from Cimarro.

STATE GREATS

★ Scientists developed the nuclear bomb in Los Alamos and tested it at the White Sands Missile Range.

★ Visitors can walk a 3 mile underground trail at Carlsbad Caverns National Park.

★ The international UFO Museum and Research Center is in Roswell.

★ At Taos Pueblo, outside the city of Taos, Pueblo Indians still live in adobe dwellings.

★ Capulin Volcano National Monument has a 1,000 foot volcano. The volcano is no longer active and is now a monument.

★ The Rio Grande (river) is one of the longest rivers in North America.

© 2001 McGraw-Hill. All Rights Reserved.

The Fifty States

New Mexico: The Land of Enchantment

Look at an atlas or map of New Mexico. Add the names of the following places to the map below.

★ the capital of New Mexico

★ the city started by Francisco Cuero y Valdes

★ the river whose name means "Big" or "Grand" river in Spanish

★ the river that shares its name with the city of San Francisco

★ the city where the first atomic bomb was developed

★ the place where the atomic bomb was tested

★ the country to the south of New Mexico

★ the place where you can walk a 3 mile underground trail

★ you might see UFOs here

★ the city near Taos Pueblo

★ the place where Maria Martinez grew up

Size: 121,593 square miles
Population: 1,685,000

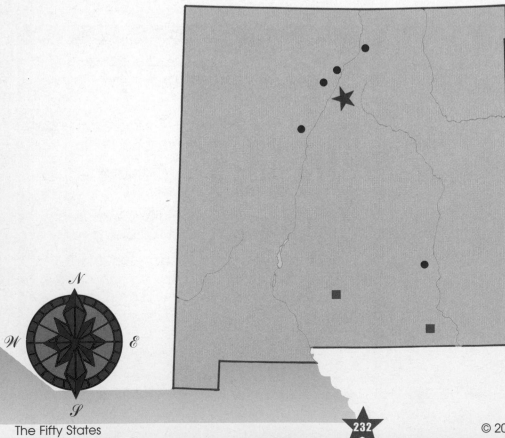

© 2001 McGraw-Hill. All Rights Reserved.

Welcome to New York

State Flag

EXCELSIOR

Bluebird
State Bird

Rose
State Flower

HOW NEW YORK BECAME A STATE

The first people living in the land that became New York were the Native American tribes, including the Iroquois and Algonquin. The first European explorer to visit New York was Giovanni da Verrazano in 1524. In 1609, the land was explored by Henry Hudson of the Netherlands and Samuel de Champlain of France. The Netherlands claimed the area for their own, but they did not settle it. In 1624, the Dutch built the first town, Fort Orange. This town would later become Albany. The next year, New Amsterdam was built.

In 1664, England took control of the land and renamed New Amsterdam, New York City. The French returned and joined forces with the Native Americans. The French attacked the English at Schenectady in 1690. England finally defeated the French in 1763. Despite the English victory, many people did not want to be part of England. In 1776, the United States declared its independence from England. New York became the eleventh state on July 26, 1788.

FAMOUS NEW YORKERS

★ Hiawatha was an Iroquois leader and peacemaker, who helped set up the Iroquois Federation.

★ Franklin D. Roosevelt was born in Hyde Park and became the thirty-second president of the United States.

★ James Baldwin wrote books about African-Americans and lived in New York City.

★ Woody Allen directs and acts in many movies about New York.

★ George Gershwin wrote music for orchestras.

★ Elizabeth Ann Seton was a saint and founded the Sisters of Charity.

★ Herman Melville is famous for writing the book *Moby Dick*.

STATE GREATS

★ From 1892 to 1954, millions of people came to America through Ellis Island. It is now a museum.

★ More than 500,000 gallons of water flow over Niagara Falls every second. It is one of the largest, most famous falls in the world. It is in both Canada and the U.S.

★ The first American women's rights convention was held in Seneca Falls.

★ The Kodak camera was invented by George Eastman in Rochester.

★ New York City has the country's largest art museum, the Metropolitan Museum of Art.

★ New York City was the first capital city of the United States.

 © 2001 McGraw-Hill. All Rights Reserved.

New Mexico: The Land of Enchantment

Read the clues. Unscramble the words about New Mexico.

a city founded
in 1706 __ __ __ __ __ __ __ __ __ __ __   Q U Q U E E R A L B U

the capital __ __ __ __ __ __   __ __   E F T A S A N

last name of an artist
who painted New Mexico __ __ __ __ __ __ __   E E E F K O

the big river
__ __ __ __   __ __ __ __   __ __ __ __ __ __ __   E H T   I R O   A R N E G D

Write the first letter of each word in the puzzle.

__ __ __ __

Unscramble the letters to find the name of a city in New Mexico.

__ __ __ __ __

New Mexico has a hot air balloon festival called "Albuquerque's International Balloon Fiesta" in October each year. Describe what people might see if they rode in a hot air balloon. Draw a picture to illustrate your description.

_____

_____

_____

_____

© 2001 McGraw-Hill. All Rights Reserved.

★ 233

New York: The Empire State

Look at an atlas or map of New York. Add the names of the following places to the map below.

★ the capital of New York

★ the city that used to be called New Amsterdam

★ the two Great Lakes that border the state

★ the island where people entered the U.S. from 1892 to 1954

★ the river named for the explorer, Henry Hudson

★ the largest waterfall in the United States

★ the city attacked in the French and Indian War

★ the city where the Kodak camera was invented

★ Franklin Roosevelt's birthplace

★ the site of the first women's rights convention

★ the ocean that borders New York

Size: 49,108 square miles
Population: 18,044,000

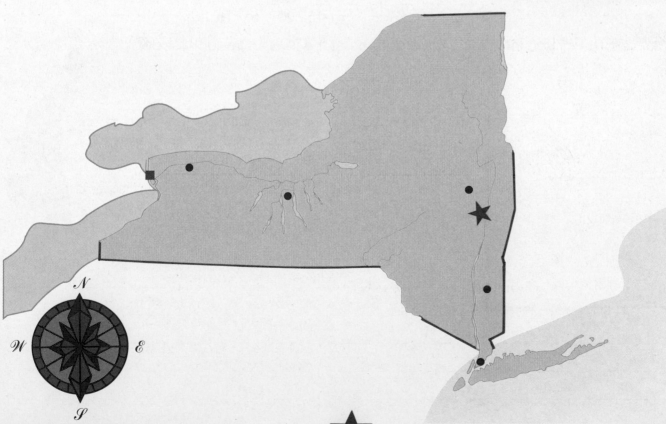

© 2001 McGraw-Hill. All Rights Reserved.

New York: The Empire State

Read each clue. Use the code to find the answers.

1-A	5-E	9-I	13-X	17-K	21-U	25-Y
2-G	6-J	10-P	14-D	18-R	22-V	26-F
3-C	7-B	11-M	15-O	19-Z	23-W	
4-N	8-H	12-L	16-S	20-T	24-Q	

first name of New York's famous actor and director

__ __ __ __ __
23 15 15 14 25

a river named for an explorer

__ __ __ __ __ __
8 21 14 16 15 4

first name of first explorer

__ __ __ __ __ __ __ __
2 9 15 22 1 4 4 9

used to be called Fort Orange

__ __ __ __ __ __
1 12 7 1 4 25

home of George Eastman

__ __ __ __ __ __ __ __ __
18 15 3 8 5 16 20 5 18

Unscramble the circled letters to write the name of the famous Iroquois leader.

__ __ __ __ __ __ __ __

The Statue of Liberty was the first thing many immigrants saw when they came to Ellis Island and entered New York Harbor. The Statue of Liberty stands for freedom.

If you built a new statue to welcome people to New York, what would it look like? Draw a picture of your statue and write about what it stands for.

_____

_____

_____

_____

_____

_____

 © 2001 McGraw-Hill. All Rights Reserved.

Welcome to North Carolina

HOW NORTH CAROLINA BECAME A STATE

In 1585, the first European settlers arrived in North Carolina. At the time, the Powhatan tribe, lead by Chief Powhatan, lived in the area. Sir Walter Raleigh sent a colony to settle Roanoke Island. But the settlers suffered great hardships in the new land. They were not prepared for the harsh weather on the island. Soon, they returned to England. Raleigh sent another colony to settle Roanoke Island in 1587. This colony became known as the "Lost Colony." When English ships returned in 1590, the people were gone. No one knows what happened to them.

During the American Revolution, North Carolinians removed the royal governor and his council. They replaced them with a new colonial government. The colonists defeated the British and the Loyalists at Moore's Creek Bridge in 1776. On November 21, 1789, North Carolina became the twelfth state to enter the Union, with Raleigh as its capital. Charlotte is now North Carolina's largest city.

State Flag

Cardinal State Bird

Dogwood State Flower

FAMOUS NORTH CAROLINIANS

★ James K. Polk was the eleventh president of the United States.

★ Andrew Johnson was the seventeenth president of the United States.

★ Levi Coffin was a leader of the Underground Railroad.

★ Dolley Madison was famous for entertaining as first lady.

★ Hiram Revels was the first African-American to serve in the United States Senate.

★ Michael Jordan is one of the greatest players in the history of the NBA.

★ Thelonious Monk is a famous jazz musician.

★ The Wright Brothers tested their invention, the airplane, at Kitty Hawk.

STATE GREATS

★ North Carolina is the nation's leading producer of tobacco.

★ The world's largest mill for weaving denim is at Greensboro.

★ The highest eastern American peak is Mt. Mitchell.

★ North Carolina is the home of the Charlotte Hornets and the Carolina Panthers.

★ North Carolina is a major producer of furniture.

★ The University of North Carolina at Chapel Hill is the oldest state-supported university in the country.

★ A lighthouse was installed at Cape Hatteras because of the great number of shipwrecks there.

© 2001 McGraw-Hill. All Rights Reserved.

The Fifty States

North Carolina: **The Tar Heel State**

Look at an atlas or map of North Carolina. Add the names of the following places to the map below.

★ the Wright Brothers Monument

★ the state capital

★ the Great Smoky Mountains

★ Pamlico Sound

★ Fayetteville, on the Cape Fear River

★ the world's largest mill for weaving denim

★ eastern America's highest peak

★ the largest city and home to the Hornets

★ the ocean to the east

★ the states around North Carolina

★ the site of many shipwrecks

Size: 52,699 square miles
Population: 6,658,000

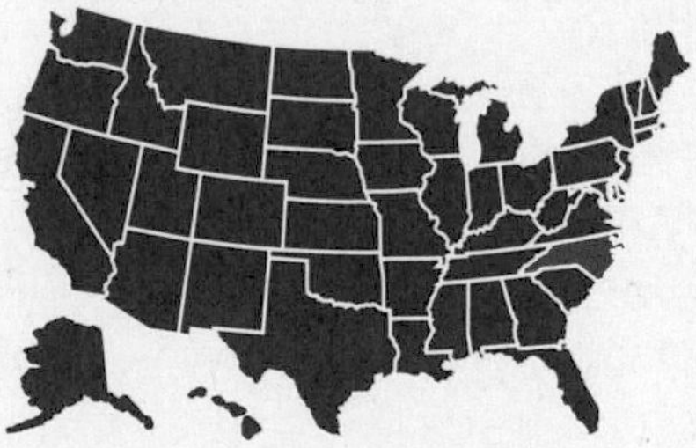

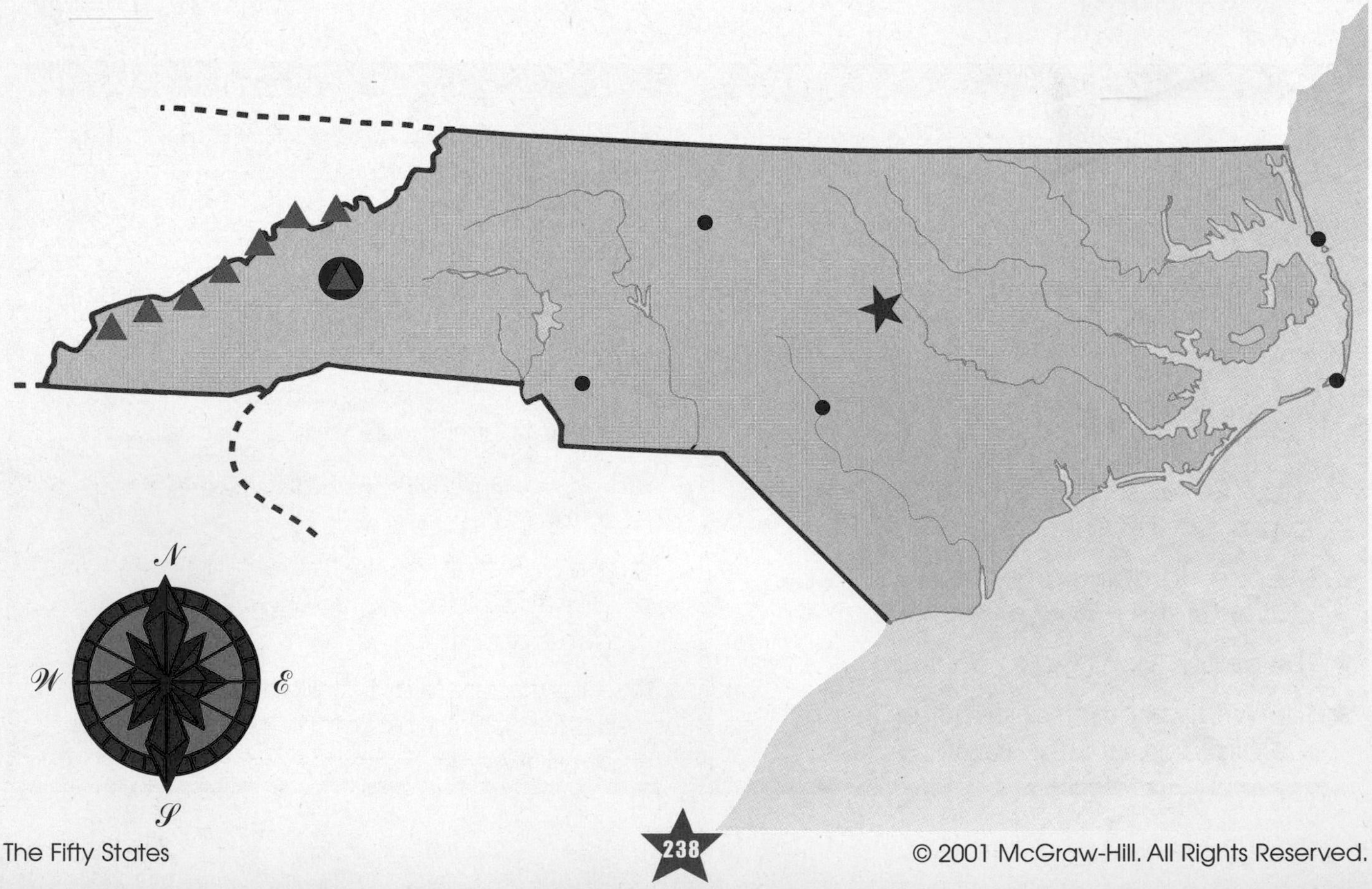

238

© 2001 McGraw-Hill. All Rights Reserved.

North Carolina: The Tar Heel State

Read the clues. Unscramble the words about North Carolina.

she was known for entertaining ___ ___ ___ ___ ___ ___ ___   N M D I O S A

first flyers ___ ___ ___ ___ ___ ___   G T W R H I

a famous jazz musician ___ ___ ___ ___   K M N O

a great slam dunker ___ ___ ___ ___ ___ ___   J N D O A R

the first African-American
to serve in the Senate ___ ___ ___ ___ ___ ___   V S E R E L

Unscramble the letters to find North Carolina's missing settlers.

S L T O Y L O C N O

___ ___ ___ ___ ___   ___ ___ ___ ___ ___ ___

Consider the state nickname: The Tar Heel State. Find out what this nickname means. What does it tell us about North Carolina?

_____

_____

_____

© 2001 McGraw-Hill. All Rights Reserved.

The Fifty States

Welcome to North Dakota

★ HOW NORTH DAKOTA BECAME A STATE

State Flag

Western Meadowlark State Bird

Wild Prairie Rose State Flower

Native Americans, including the Arikara, Cheyenne, Hidatsa and Mandan, were the first farmers of North Dakota. In the 1600s, Sioux also moved to the territory. The French explorer, sieur de La Salle, claimed the land for France in 1682. France then gave part of the land to England, even though neither country had visited the land. The first explorer, sieur de La Vérendrye, came in 1738. In 1762, France gave the land to Spain, then took it back in 1800. The United States bought the land in 1803 as part of the Louisiana Purchase. Lewis and Clark visited in 1804, lead by Sacajawea, a Native American guide. They built Fort Mandan, which later became Mandan.

The first European settlement was built in 1812, in Pembina. Slowly, settlers came to the area. In 1861, the United States formed the Dakota Territory. However, Sitting Bull and the Sioux began a war with the settlers. The Sioux did not surrender until 1881. In 1889, North Dakota split from South Dakota to become the thirty-ninth state.

FAMOUS NORTH DAKOTANS

★ Sitting Bull was the leader of the Sioux.

★ Lawrence Welk was a singer and musician.

★ Peggy Lee was a singer.

★ Angie Dickinson acted in popular movies and television shows.

★ Running Antelope was pictured on one of the earlier versions of the five-dollar bill.

★ D.H. Houston invented the roll film for photography.

★ Konrad Elias discovered a treatment for the skin disease, erysipelas.

STATE GREATS

★ North Dakota has two United States Strategic Air Commands, one at Grand Forks and one at Minot.

★ White Butte is 3,506 feet above sea level. It is the highest point in North Dakota.

★ The Theodore Roosevelt National Memorial Park is named for President Roosevelt.

★ Visitors can see ancient Native American petroglyphs at the Writing Rock near Crosby.

★ History buffs can celebrate at the "Pioneer Days at Bonanzaville" each year in West Fargo.

 © 2001 McGraw-Hill. All Rights Reserved.

North Dakota: The Flickertail State

Look at an atlas or map of North Dakota. Add the names of the following places to the map below.

★ the capital

★ the river that shares a name with a state

★ the country to the north

★ the city where Lewis and Clark built a fort

★ the first European settlement

★ the cities with the two United States Strategic Air Commands

★ the National Park to honor Theodore Roosevelt

★ the city near Writing Rock

★ the town that hosts "Pioneer Days at Bonanzaville"

★ the lake named for Lewis and Clark's guide

★ the state to the south that was once part of the Dakota Territory

Size: 70,702 square miles
Population: 641,000

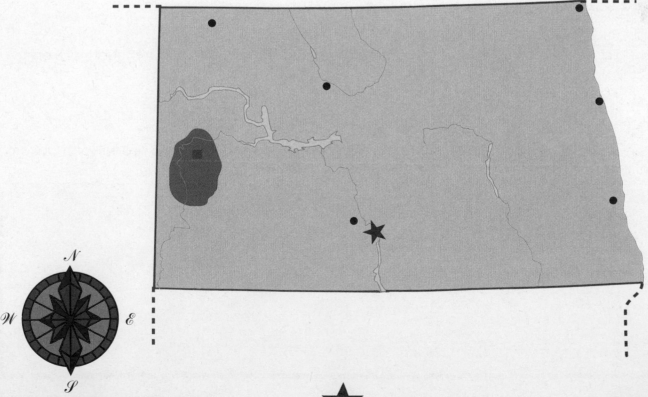

© 2001 McGraw-Hill. All Rights Reserved.

North Dakota: **The Flickertail State**

Anna wrote a report about her summer trip to North Dakota. Fill in the letters that she left out.

★ ★

My Summer trip to _____orth Dakota

_____orth Dak_____ta is a big state. My family and I didn't see everything, but here are the things I liked best.

We visited the _____ndian _____etroglyphs at Writing _____ock near _____rosby. It was fun to imagine the Native Amer_____cans who made these drawings. I can't believe how old the drawings are!

We also saw the United Stat_____s Strategic _____ir _____ommand at Grand _____orks. They have a lot of neat planes!

For natural beauty, the _____ eodore _____oosevelt National Memorial Park was the best. We went on a long hike.

I think you'd love North Dakota.

Anna Turner

Unscramble the letters you have written to find the name of the railroad that brought settlers to North Dakota.

_____ _____ _____ _____ _____ _____ _____ _____ _____ _____ _____ _____ _____ _____ _____

Anna enjoyed visiting North Dakota. What things might other travelers like to see in North Dakota? Design a travel brochure that shows visitors 3 things to see in North Dakota.

© 2001 McGraw-Hill. All Rights Reserved.

Welcome to Ohio

★ HOW OHIO BECAME A STATE

*M*any Native American tribes, including the Iroquois, Shawnee, Miami and Wyandot lived in Ohio before settlers arrived. "Ohio" comes from an Iroquois word meaning "beautiful." John D. Rockefeller built his oil empire in Cleveland. Akron was home to rubber factories that once made more tires than anywhere else in the world. All the while, corn and other crops grew on Ohio's farms.

Ohio became the seventeenth state in 1803. It was easy to travel and to ship goods on the Ohio waterways of Lake Erie and the Ohio River. Soon, Cleveland became a major port on the lake, while Cincinnati prospered on the Ohio River. Columbus, in the center of the state, was the perfect location for the capital. In the 1970s, Ohio became polluted by its factories. But now, Ohio has cleaned up the environment and people are returning. Although Ohio is not a large state, it has a large population.

State Flag

**Cardinal
State Bird**

**Scarlet Carnation
State Flower**

FAMOUS OHIOANS

★ John Glenn was the first American to orbit Earth. He also returned to space when he was 77.

★ Presidents Ulysses S. Grant, Rutherford B. Hayes, James A. Garfield, Benjamin Harrison, William McKinley, William H. Taft and Warren G. Harding came from Ohio.

★ Steven Spielberg made movies, such as *E.T., Raiders of the Lost Ark* and *Schindler's List*.

★ Neil Armstrong was the first person to walk on the Moon.

★ Maya Lin sculpted the Vietnam Veterans Memorial in Washington, D.C.

STATE GREATS

★ The Cincinnati Red Stockings, now the Reds, became the first professional baseball team.

★ Akron was once known as the "Rubber Capital of the World."

★ The Rock 'n' Roll Hall of Fame is located in Cleveland.

★ The Pro Football Hall of Fame is located in Canton.

★ The Cuyahoga River, near Lake Erie, was once so polluted that it caught fire. Today, it is a clean river.

★ Oberlin College was the first to educate men and women together.

© 2001 McGraw-Hill. All Rights Reserved.

The Fifty States

Ohio: The Buckeye State

Look at an atlas or map of Ohio. Add the names of the following places to the map below.

- ★ state to the north
- ★ this river empties into Lake Erie
- ★ buy some tires here
- ★ this city celebrates famous music and musicians
- ★ the city that boasts the birth of pro baseball

- ★ state to the west
- ★ Ohio's capital
- ★ this river forms much of the Ohio border
- ★ the major city in the northwest
- ★ state to the east
- ★ on one side of this lake is Ohio, on the other is Canada

Size: 41,330 square miles
Population: 10,887,000

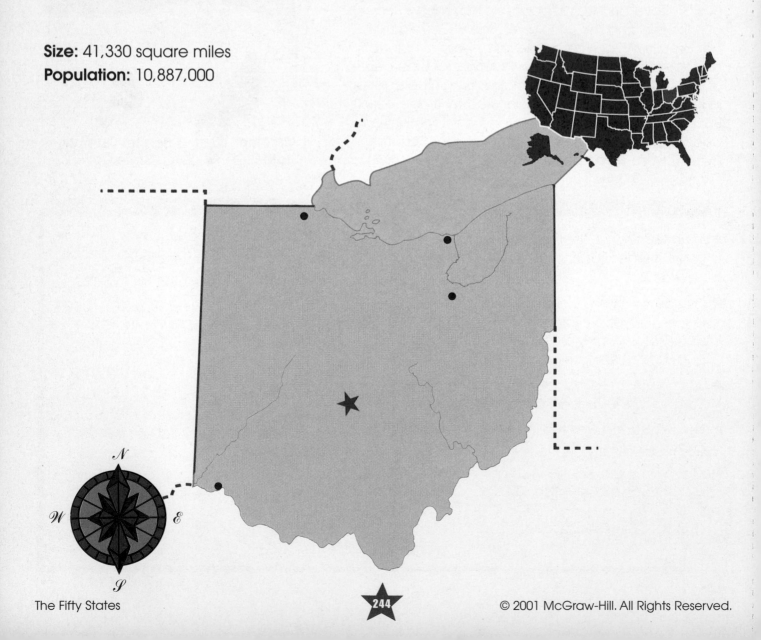

© 2001 McGraw-Hill. All Rights Reserved.

Ohio: **The Buckeye State**

Next to each sentence write a T if the statement is true or an F if the statement is false.

_____ The Ohio River forms the northern border of Ohio.

_____ The three largest cities in Ohio all start with "C."

_____ The Ohio River once caught fire.

_____ Toledo was known as an important producer of rubber.

_____ The Rock 'n' Roll Hall of Fame is located in Cleveland.

_____ The first professional baseball team is now known as the Cincinnati Reds.

What industries helped make Ohio an important state?

_____

_____

_____

© 2001 McGraw-Hill. All Rights Reserved.

 Welcome to Oklahoma

State Flag

Scissor-tailed Flycatcher State Bird

Mistletoe State Flower

The Spanish explorer Coronado first visited Oklahoma in 1541. After the War of 1812, the U. S. government moved the Native Americans west of the Mississippi River. Among the Native Americans forced to move were the Choctaw, Chickasaw, Creek, Seminole and Cherokee. Many people died during this long hard journey called the "Trail of Tears." In the 1830s, part of Oklahoma was made into a reservation called the Indian Territory.

1880s, the settlers wanted part of the Indian Territory for settlement. In 1889, Congress gave 2 million acres of the Indian Territory to settlers. On April 22, 1889, 50,000 people gathered at the border and on foot, on horses and in wagons, raced for a plot of land. People who snuck in early were called "Sooners." By 1906, the lands of western Oklahoma had been settled. The settlers called it the Oklahoma Territory. In 1907, Congress decided that the Indian Territory and Oklahoma Territory should be joined. Oklahoma became the forty-sixth state in 1907.

FAMOUS OKLAHOMANS

★ Will Rogers was a famous comedian and entertainer.

★ Mickey Mantle was a star baseball player for the New York Yankees.

★ Woody Guthrie was a folk singer, guitarist and composer.

★ Ralph Ellison was a well-known African-American writer and author of *The Invisible Man.*

★ Alice Mary Robertson was the first woman from Oklahoma to be elected to the U. S. House of Representatives.

★ Maria Tallchief is a classical dancer and prima ballerina for the New York City Ballet.

STATE GREATS

★ Oklahoma City is the only capital that has an operating oil well on its grounds.

★ U.S. Highway 69 follows Texas Road, one of the earliest routes through Indian Territory to Texas.

★ Barite rose rock is found only in Oklahoma. Cherokee legend says the rocks stand for the blood of the braves and the tears of the maidens who made the "Trail of Tears" journey.

★ Oklahoma's constitution allows citizens to write and submit their own laws to a direct vote.

★ The University of Oklahoma is in Norman, and Oklahoma State University is in Stillwater.

 © 2001 McGraw-Hill. All Rights Reserved.

Oklahoma: **The Sooner State**

Look at an atlas or map of Oklahoma. Add the names of the following places to the map below.

★ the states that border Oklahoma

★ the river that separates Texas and Oklahoma

★ three rivers that run through the state

★ the capital of Oklahoma

★ the area called the Panhandle

★ Tulsa, the second largest city

★ the location of the University of Oklahoma

★ a city in the Panhandle

★ a city north of Tulsa

★ the location of Oklahoma State University

Size: 69,919 square miles
Population: 3,158,000

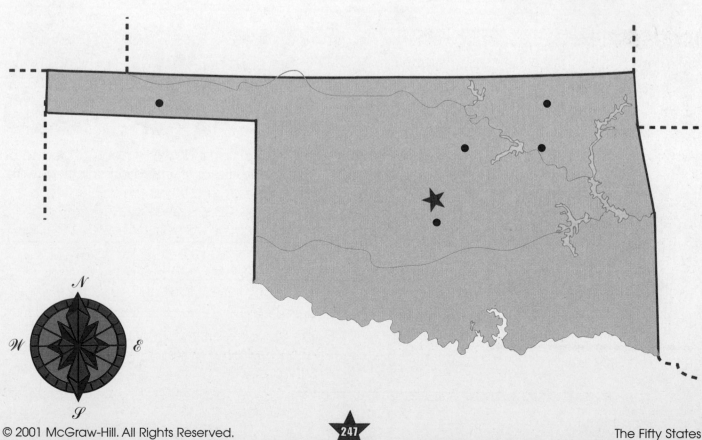

© 2001 McGraw-Hill. All Rights Reserved.

The Fifty States

Oklahoma: The Sooner State

Read the clues. Unscramble the words about Oklahoma.

This city has an oil well

_ _ _ _ _ _ _ _ _ _   _ _ _ _ _

AKI MLHOATOCY

This rock is only found in Oklahoma

_ _ _ _ _ _ _ _ _   _ _ _ _ _

RBITEOASER

A Native American tribe that lived in Oklahoma

_ _ _ _ _ _ _ _ _

HCACKASIW

The Spanish explorer who came to Oklahoma

_ _ _ _ _ _ _ _

DRONOCOA

The terrible journey of the Native Americans

_ _ _ _ _ _   _ _ _   _ _ _ _ _ _ _

FERALTOIRSAT

Look at the state flag of Oklahoma. Find two symbols of peace on the flag. Write about what they are and why you think they were included as a part of the flag.

_____

_____

_____

_____

 © 2001 McGraw-Hill. All Rights Reserved.

Welcome to Oregon

HOW OREGON BECAME A STATE

State Flag

Western Meadowlark State Bird

Oregon Grape State Flower

The Cascade Mountain Range runs from north to south across Oregon, creating a green forested coastline to the west and dry plateaus to the east. Before the first Europeans arrived, both areas were inhabited by Native Americans. The territory was home to over 100 different tribes, including the Nez Percé, Chinook, Cayuse and Yakima. Once Captain Robert Gray sailed up the mighty Columbia River in 1792, explorers and fur traders soon followed.

In 1805, the famous explorers Lewis and Clark traveled overland from the east and traveled along the Columbia River. Not realizing how close they were to the ocean, they built a shelter and spent a terrible winter at Fort Clatsop. By 1834, the first groups of settlers were arriving in the fertile Willamette River valley. Within 9 years, large wagon trains of people were following the Oregon Trail west, in hopes of finding land and wealth. Oregon became the thirty-third state in 1859.

FAMOUS OREGONIANS

★ Barbara Roberts was Oregon's first female governor.

★ Raymond Carver was an author and poet.

★ Chief Joseph was a great Nez Percé leader.

★ Phil Knight founded Nike, Inc.

★ Gary Payton is a professional basketball player.

★ Mark O. Hatfield was a governor and state senator.

★ Linus Pauling won Nobel prizes for chemistry and peace.

★ Beverly Cleary won the Newbery Medal for children's literature.

STATE GREATS

★ A volcanic explosion of Mt. Mazama created Crater Lake. Crater Lake is 1,932 feet deep, the deepest lake in the United States.

★ Oregon Dunes National Recreation Area contains miles of seaside sand dunes for family enjoyment.

★ Hells Canyon on the Snake River is 7,900 feet deep—deeper than the Grand Canyon.

★ Ashland is home to an annual Shakespearean Festival.

★ 75 percent of birds migrating along the Pacific "Flyway" stop in the national wildlife refuges near Upper Klamath Lake.

© 2001 McGraw-Hill. All Rights Reserved.

The Fifty States

Oregon: The Beaver State

Look at an atlas or map of Oregon. Add the names of the following places to the map below.

★ Portland, the largest city and a port on the Columbia River

★ a lake created when a volcano blew its top

★ the deepest canyon in the United States

★ the river found by Captain Robert Gray

★ the state capital

★ the location of Lewis and Clark's 1805–1806 winter camp

★ the city that hosts a Shakespearean festival

★ a family recreation area of beach sand dunes

★ the mountain range that divides the state

★ this river's valley was home to the first settlers

Size: 97,073 square miles
Population: 2,854,000

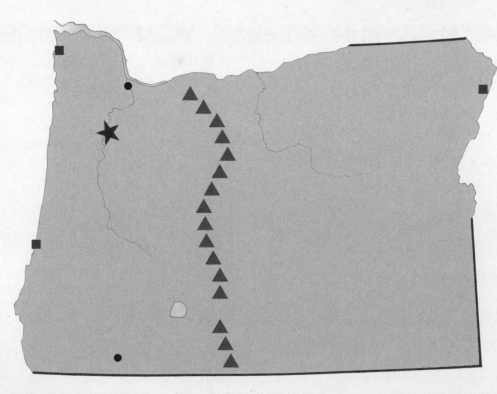

© 2001 McGraw-Hill. All Rights Reserved.

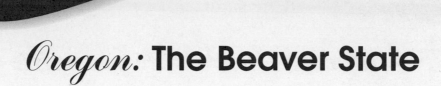

Oregon: **The Beaver State**

Read the clues. Complete the words about Oregon.

an explorer's fort   __ __ __ __ __ O __

a children's author   __ __ __ __ R __

Chief Joseph's tribe   __ __ __   __ E __ __ __

he explored the Columbia River   G __ __ __

Pauling won two of these prizes   __ O __ __ __

a shoe man   __ N __ __ __ __

The Oregon state flag is the only American flag with two different sides. The front shows a heart shaped shield to stand for early Oregon. The back shows a beaver. On a sheet of paper, design a new Oregon flag. What would you use to stand for Oregon?

_____

_____

_____

_____

© 2001 McGraw-Hill. All Rights Reserved.

The Fifty States

Welcome to Pennsylvania

HOW PENNSYLVANIA BECAME A STATE

The first people living in Pennsylvania were the Algonquin and Iroquoi tribes. In 1609, the explorer, Henry Hudson arrived in the land now called Pennsylvania. In 1615, Cornelius Henrickson, the Dutch explorer, also explored the land. However, it was almost 30 years later when Johan Printz, from Sweden, founded the first settlement in 1643. The site is now Philadelphia. Pennsylvania was ruled by many different countries—the Netherlands in 1655 and England in 1664. However, in 1681, King Charles II gave the land to William Penn. Penn was eager to live in the new land. Penn landed in America at Chester in 1682. Many Quaker settlers followed.

But the Native Americans fought against the English settlers. It was not until 1763 that the Ottawa chief, Pontiac, was defeated at Bushy Run. In 1774, the first Continental Congress was held in Philadelphia. The Revolutionary War that followed freed Pennsylvania from England. In 1787, Pennsylvania was the second state to join the Union.

State Flag

Ruffed Grouse State Bird

Mountain Laurel State Flower

FAMOUS PENNSYLVANIANS

★ James Buchanan was the fifteenth president.

★ General George Marshall, born in Uniontown, created the "Marshall Plan."

★ Louisa May Alcott, born in Germantown, wrote *Little Women*.

★ Mary Cassatt, from Allegheny City, was a modern painter.

★ Thomas Eakins, born in Philadelphia, was an oil painter.

★ Margaret Mead was an anthropologist and writer.

★ Bill Cosby, another Philadelphian, is an actor and comic.

STATE GREATS

★ Little League baseball started in Williamsport in 1939.

★ The world's largest chocolate factory is in Hershey.

★ When coal was discovered near Pittsburgh, the state became a leading coal producer.

★ Lincoln gave his famous Gettysburg address in Gettysburg in 1863.

★ In 1794, Pennsylvania built the country's first turnpike. This road connected Philadelphia and Lancaster.

★ Philadelphia was the nation's capital city after New York and before Washington, D.C.

© 2001 McGraw-Hill. All Rights Reserved.

Pennsylvania: **The Keystone State**

Look at an atlas or map of Pennsylvania. Add the names of the following places to the map below.

★ the great lake that borders northwest Pennsylvania

★ the river that separates Pennsylvania and New Jersey

★ the capital

★ the town that founded Little League baseball

★ the city where the Continental Congress met

★ the town where William Penn landed

★ coal was discovered near this city

★ the city where Lincoln gave his famous speech

★ General Marshall's hometown

★ the city named after the Duke of York

★ the site of the largest chocolate factory

Size: 45,308 square miles
Population: 12,000,000

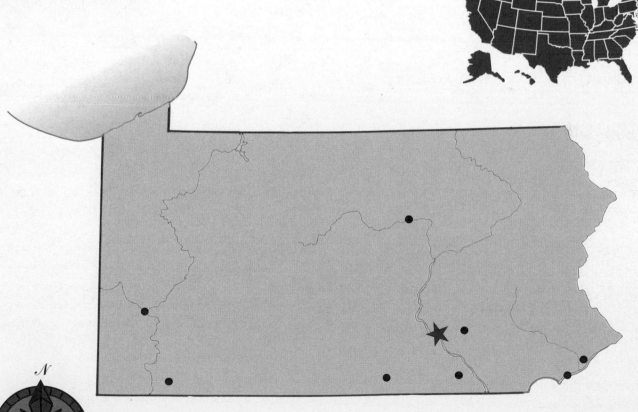

© 2001 McGraw-Hill. All Rights Reserved.

The Fifty States

Pennsylvania: The Keystone State

Read the clues about Pennsylvania. Use the code to find the answers.

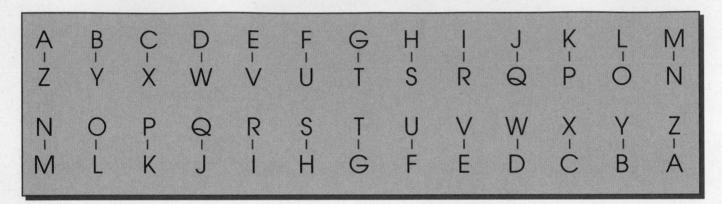

one of the first people living in Pennsylvania __ __ __ ◯ ◯ __ __ __
R I L J F L R H

an English ruler who gave the land to William Penn ◯ __ __ __ __ __ __ __ ◯ __ ◯ __
P R M T X S Z I O V H

an Ottawa chief who fought England __ __ __ __ ◯ __
K L M G R Z X

a comic and actor born in Philadelphia __ __ ◯ __ __
X L H Y B

Unscramble the circled letters. Find the name of the settlers who followed William Penn to Pennsylvania.

__ __ __ __ __ __ __

Religious freedom was very important to William Penn and the Quakers who settled in Pennsylvania. Freedom from England was important to the signers of the Declaration of Independence in Philadelphia. What kind of freedom is important to you? Write a few sentences telling why freedom is important to you.

_____

_____

_____

_____

 © 2001 McGraw-Hill. All Rights Reserved.

Welcome to Rhode Island

State Flag

Rhode Island Red
State Bird

Violet
State Flower

*M*any of the first European settlers of Rhode Island came from Massachusetts. Roger Williams is considered to be the founder of Rhode Island. He was banished from Massachusetts for his religious beliefs. He traveled to Rhode Island, and in 1636, Williams started a new settlement in Providence. From then on, people of all religions were welcome in Rhode Island. However, Rhode Island was the site of conflict between the European settlers and Native Americans, such as the Algonquins.

Rhode Island also took part in the Revolutionary War. Perhaps the earliest action against England took place on July 9, 1764, in Newport. Here, the Newporters clashed with sailors on a British ship called *H.M.S. Squirrel.* However, Rhode Island did not rush to join the Union after the Revolutionary War. They feared that the new government would change their way of life. Rhode Island was the last of the 13 original colonies to accept the Constitution. Rhode Island joined the United States on May 29, 1790.

FAMOUS RHODE ISLANDERS

★ Nathanael Greene was a general during the American Revolution.

★ Oliver Hazard Perry was a hero and U.S. Naval officer in the War of 1812.

★ Matthew Calbraith Perry opened up Japanese ports to western trade.

★ Anne Hutchinson protested against the religious leaders of Massachusetts.

★ Gilbert Stuart painted a famous portrait of George Washington.

★ Ida Lewis was a lighthouse keeper who saved many lives.

★ Napoleon "Nap" Lajoie was the first player named to the Baseball Hall of Fame.

STATE GREATS

★ Although Rhode Island is the smallest state, it has the longest name, "State of Rhode Island and Providence Plantations."

★ Slater Mill, America's first cotton mill, opened in Pawtucket in 1790.

★ Rhode Island is considered the birthplace of the American jewelry industry. Nehemia Dodge developed a way to cover metal with a thin layer of gold or silver. Before his discovery, jewelry was made out of pure gold or silver and only the rich could afford to buy it.

★ During the mid-nineteenth century, many wealthy families built mansions and vacationed in Newport.

★ Today, Block Island is a favorite vacation spot.

© 2001 McGraw-Hill. All Rights Reserved.

The Fifty States

Rhode Island: Little Rhody

Look at an atlas or map of Rhode Island. Add the names of the following places to the map below.

★ the site of America's first cotton mill

★ the capital of Rhode Island

★ Narragansett Bay

★ many wealthy families built mansions here

★ Block Island

★ Warwick, one of Rhode Island's first towns

★ the state that borders Rhode Island on the west

★ Block Island Sound

★ the ocean to the east

★ Pawtuxet River

★ Blackstone River

Size: 1,212 square miles
Population: 1,006,000

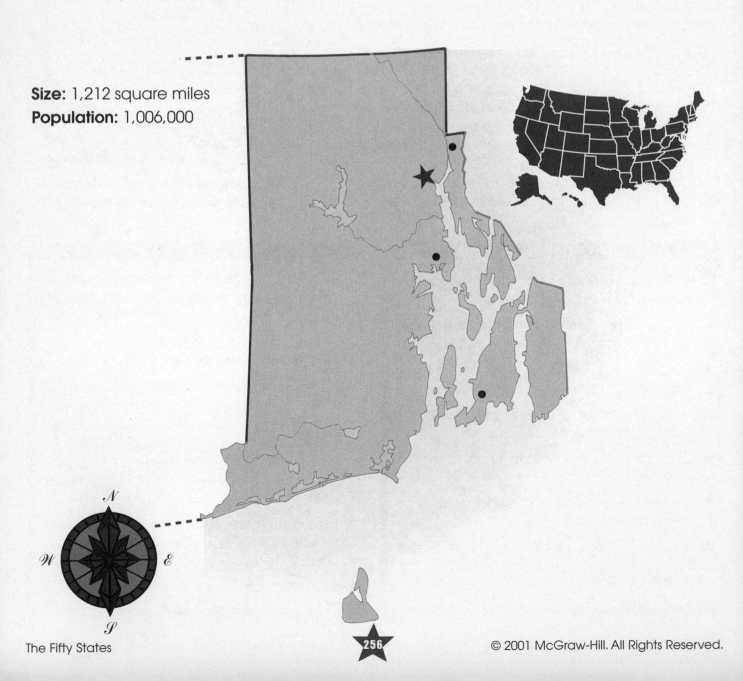

© 2001 McGraw-Hill. All Rights Reserved.

Rhode Island: **Little Rhody**

Write the letter from column B next to the matching phrase in column A.

 A

1. _____ founder of Rhode Island

2. _____ capital city

3. _____ U.S. general during Revolutionary War

4. _____ site of America's first cotton mill

5. _____ George Washington portrait painter

 B

A Nathanael Greene

B Pawtucket

C Providence

D Gilbert Stuart

E Roger Williams

"Good things come in small packages" is a famous saying. Explain why this might be true of Rhode Island.

_____

_____

_____

_____

© 2001 McGraw-Hill. All Rights Reserved.

The Fifty States

Welcome to South Carolina

HOW SOUTH CAROLINA BECAME A STATE

When English explorers came to South Carolina, they found the Cherokee, Catawba and Muskogee tribes living there. The English lived among these tribes and set up the city of Charleston in 1680. Charleston was named after an English king, Charles II. When the 13 colonies declared independence from Britain, several Revolutionary War battles were fought in South Carolina. Battles were also fought in South Carolina during the Civil War. South Carolina became the eighth state in 1788.

Today, South Carolina's beaches are popular tourist locations. Vacationers like to visit Hilton Head Island and Myrtle Beach. Industry and agriculture are important, too. South Carolina ships products all over the world. Dams on some of its rivers have created large lakes, such as Lake Marion. Although South Carolina's cities are not large by New York standards, many people live and work in the state capital, Columbia.

State Flag

Carolina Wren State Bird

Jessamine State Flower

FAMOUS SOUTH CAROLINIANS

★ Jesse Jackson is a civil rights leader.

★ James "Strom" Thurmond was governor of South Carolina and is currently a U.S. senator.

★ Larry Doby became the second African-American in Major League Baseball.

★ Pat Conroy wrote novels based on his childhood in South Carolina.

★ John Birks "Dizzy" Gillespie was a trumpet player who helped create the "bebop" style of jazz.

★ Althea Gibson was an African-American tennis player who dominated the sport in 1957 and 1958.

STATE GREATS

★ South Carolina was the eighth state to sign the Declaration of Independence.

★ In 1861, South Carolina became the first state to leave the United States of America during the Civil War.

★ The first shots of the Civil War were fired at Fort Sumter.

★ The Fireproof Building is the first fireproof building in the nation.

★ The world's first department store is located in the seaside town of Charleston.

★ Greenville is a large business district in the northwest.

 © 2001 McGraw-Hill. All Rights Reserved.

South Carolina: The Palmetto State

Look at an atlas or map of South Carolina. Add the names of the following places to the map below.

★ this is a popular seaside spot

★ the ocean to the east of South Carolina

★ this large city is in the northwestern part of the state

★ an island near the southern border

★ a big city on the ocean

★ the capital of South Carolina

★ a large lake between Columbia and Charleston

★ historic shots were fired here

★ the state south and west of South Carolina

★ the state to the north

Size: 31,113 square miles
Population: 3,506,000

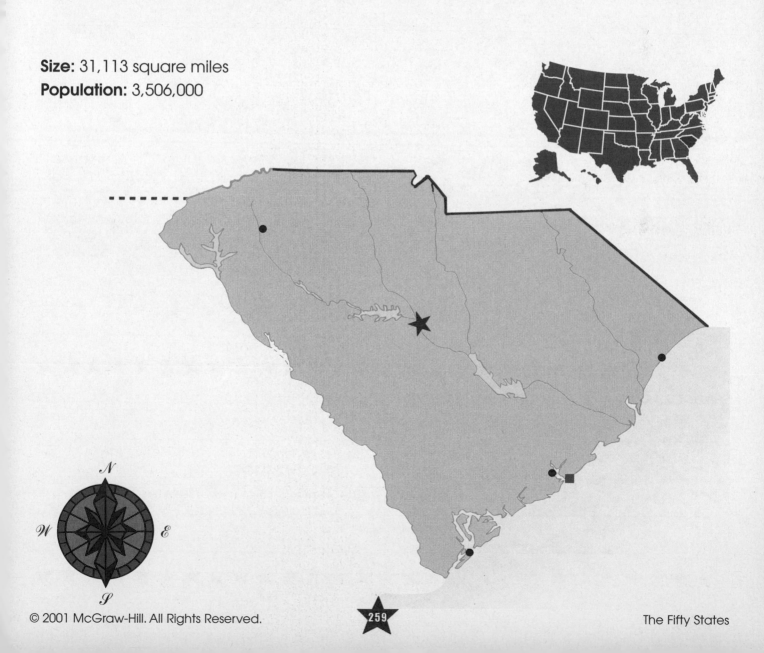

© 2001 McGraw-Hill. All Rights Reserved.

The Fifty States

South Carolina: The Palmetto State

Read the clues. Then, unscramble the words about South Carolina.

one of the first British settlements

— — — — — — — — — — —   LCHESATORN

a popular vacation beach

— — — — — — — — — — — — —   TMLRYE ECBAH

a state bordering South Carolina

— — — — — — — —   OEGGARI

where the Civil War started

— — — — — — — — — —   TRFO RUEMST

a vacation spot and an island

— — — — — — — — — — — —
— — — — — — —   OHTILN ADEH SNILDA

where the governor works

— — — — — — — — —   ACMLUBOI

★★★★★★★★★★★★★★★★★★★★★★★★★★★★★★★

What is it about South Carolina that attracts tourists in summertime?

_____

_____

_____

_____

★★★★★★★★★★★★★★★★★★★★★★★★★★★★★★★

 © 2001 McGraw-Hill. All Rights Reserved.

Welcome to South Dakota

★ HOW SOUTH DAKOTA BECAME A STATE

In 1743, Francois and Joseph La Vérendrye set off to find a new water route to the Pacific Ocean. They found the Missouri River and South Dakota. This land was home to the Arikara and the Cheyenne tribes. The Sioux came later in the mid-1700s. Fur trading soon followed.

In the 1850s, the Sioux sold part of their land to the United States. When gold was found in Montana, the United States tried to build roads through Sioux territory. In 1866, the Sioux, led by Chief Red Cloud, attacked. A treaty promising the Black Hills to the Sioux ended the fighting. However, in 1874, the discovery of gold in the Black Hills led to another war. The Sioux leaders, Sitting Bull, Crazy Horse and Gall, defended their land and won at Little Bighorn in 1876. But, by 1889, the United States had moved most Sioux onto reservations and South Dakota became a state. In 1890, soldiers shot and killed 300 Sioux at Wounded Knee Creek.

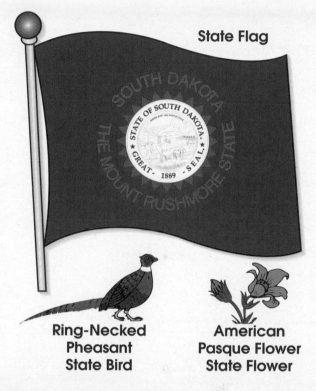

State Flag

Ring-Necked Pheasant State Bird

American Pasque Flower State Flower

FAMOUS SOUTH DAKOTANS

★ Sitting Bull was a Sioux warrior.

★ Zitkala-Sa was a Sioux author who lived on the Yankton Reservation.

★ Harvey Dunn painted pictures of World War I and life in South Dakota.

★ Allen Neuharth, of Eureka, is the founder of the newspaper *U.S.A. Today.*

★ Tom Brokaw, a national news anchorman, was born in Webster.

★ Sparky Anderson, from Bridgewater, is one of baseball's greatest managers.

★ Hubert Humphrey, of Wallace, was vice president and founder of the Peace Corps.

STATE GREATS

★ Wall Drug, the world's largest drugstore, is in Wall.

★ Citibank, the largest credit card company, has its headquarters in Sioux Falls.

★ Badlands National Park's colorful hills and canyons stretch for 400 square miles.

★ Mount Rushmore Memorial graces the hills of South Dakota.

★ The Jewel and Wind Caves of the Black Hills are two of the longest caves in the world.

★ The Crazy Horse Monument near Mt. Rushmore will be the largest sculpture in the world when completed.

© 2001 McGraw-Hill. All Rights Reserved.

The Fifty States

South Dakota: **The Mount Rushmore State**

Look at an atlas or map of South Dakota. Add the names of the following places to the map below.

★ Citibank headquarters is here

★ two of the world's longest caves

★ home of Allen Neuharth

★ Yankton Indian Reservation

★ Badlands National Park

★ the world's largest drugstore is here

★ Devil's Gulch, a 20-foot wide canyon

★ hometown of Hubert Humphrey

★ South Dakota's capital

★ Wounded Knee Creek

★ Waubay Lake

Size: 77,116 square miles
Population: 732,000

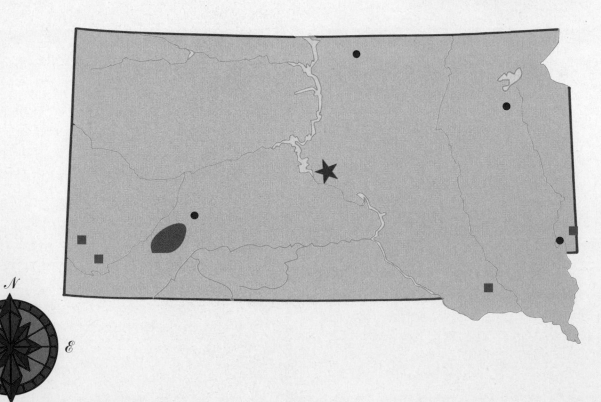

The Fifty States

262

© 2001 McGraw-Hill. All Rights Reserved.

South Dakota: **The Mount Rushmore State**

Draw a line to match the dates on the left with the events on the right.

1889 ★   ★ The La Vérendrye brothers find Missouri River.

1743 ★   ★ Massacre at Wounded Knee Creek kills 300 Sioux.

1876 ★   ★ South Dakota becomes a state and Sioux are moved onto reservations.

1874 ★   ★ Crazy Horse, Sitting Bull and Gall attack at Little Bighorn.

1890 ★   ★ Gold is found in the Black Hills.

Imagine that you are a Sioux child. What was it like to be a Sioux child before the Europeans arrived? Write a journal entry about your customs, culture and beliefs.

© 2001 McGraw-Hill. All Rights Reserved.

The Fifty States

Welcome to Tennessee

★ HOW TENNESSEE BECAME A STATE

*I*n 1540, Spanish explorer Hernando de Soto found that Tennessee was home to the Chickasaw, Creek, Shawnee and Cherokee tribes. In fact, Tennessee comes from the name of a Cherokee village, Tanasi. In the seventeenth century, the French settled on a site now called Memphis. Soon after, English traders moved in and competed with the French for control of the territory. After a series of wars that ended with the French and Indian War of 1754, the French surrendered and gave England control of all the land east of the Mississippi River.

At the time of the American Revolution, eastern Tennessee was a part of North Carolina. When North Carolina gave up the rights to the land, the people attempted to become a state named Franklin. Congress denied their request. Under the new constitution, the land became the Territory South of the River Ohio in 1789. In 1796, Tennessee became the sixteenth state, the first territory to become a state.

State Flag

Mockingbird State Bird

Iris State Flower

FAMOUS TENNESSEANS

★ Davy Crockett was the legendary "coonskin cap" frontiersman and politician.

★ Actor Gary Cooper won an Oscar for his portrayal of World War I hero, Alvin York.

★ Sequoyah, a Cherokee silversmith, developed an alphabet for the Cherokee language.

★ Albert Gore, Jr., served as vice president to President Clinton.

★ Author Alex Haley wrote historical books.

★ Elvis Presley, who lived in Memphis, was the King of Rock and Roll.

★ Actress Oprah Winfrey, a Nashville native, hosts a talk show.

★ James Polk was the eleventh president.

STATE GREATS

★ The Tennessee Aquarium in Chattanooga is the largest freshwater aquarium in the country.

★ The National Civil Rights Museum in Memphis at the Lorraine Motel is in honor of Martin Luther King, Jr. He was killed in the motel.

★ Bristol is the birthplace of "Country Music."

★ The Grand Ole Opry radio program has run continuously since 1925.

★ More people visit the Great Smoky Mountains National Park than any other national park in the United States. It is named for the bluish haze that covers the mountains.

The Fifty States 264 © 2001 McGraw-Hill. All Rights Reserved.

Tennessee: The Volunteer State

Look at an atlas or map of Tennessee. Add the names of the following places to the map below.

★ the capital of Tennessee

★ the easternmost and largest city in Tennessee

★ the city which is home to the Tennessee Aquarium

★ Elvis Presley's home

★ the river which creates Tennessee's western border

★ the river which flows through Nashville

★ the river which flows through Knoxville

★ the eight states that border Tennessee

Size: 42,144 square miles
Population: 4,897,000

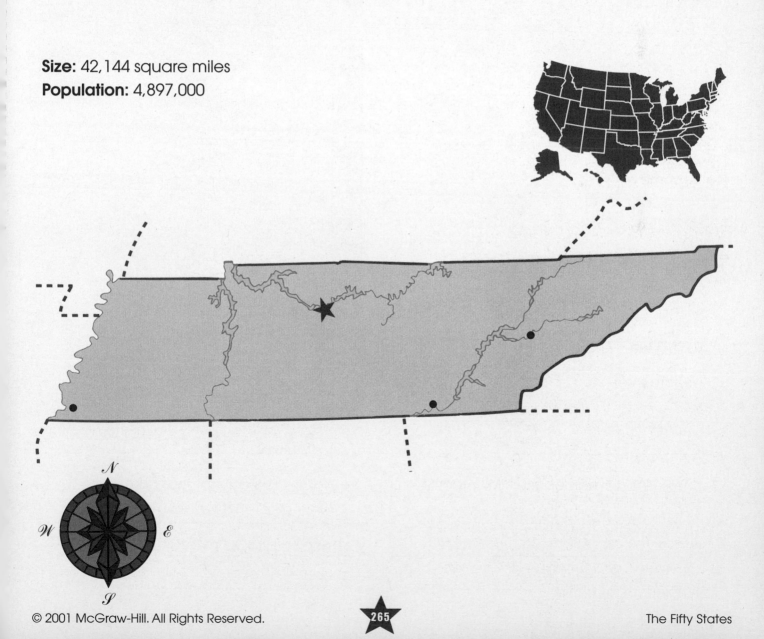

© 2001 McGraw-Hill. All Rights Reserved.

The Fifty States

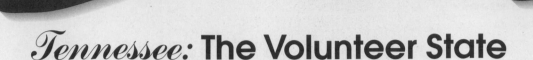

Tennessee: **The Volunteer State**

Read the clues. Write the answers on the lines. Then, read the boxed letters to find out where the Grand Ole Opry is.

1. What national park is found in Tennessee?
2. Who developed an alphabet?
3. What entertainer is known as the King of Rock and Roll?
4. Who wrote historical novels?
5. What is the name of the war hero Gary Cooper portrayed?

6. On what Cherokee word is the name Tennessee based?
7. What was the first name suggested for Tennessee?
8. Who was the eleventh president of the United States?
9. Who was the "coonskin cap" frontiersman?

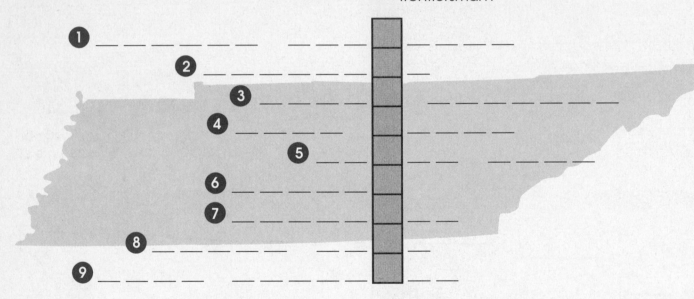

Where is the Grand Ole Opry Radio Show? _____

There are three stars on the flag of Tennessee. Find out what each represents.

_____

_____

Tennessee is nicknamed the "Volunteer State." Find out how the state got that name.

_____

_____

_____

© 2001 McGraw-Hill. All Rights Reserved.

Welcome to Texas

HOW TEXAS BECAME A STATE

In the early 1500s, when the first Spanish explorers arrived in the area, 30,000 Native Americans were living in Texas, including the Caddo, Apache and Comanche. In their search for the fabled Seven Cities of Gold, many Spanish explorers passed through Texas. In 1682, Spain claimed ownership of Texas by building two missions near what is now El Paso. In 1685, French explorer sieur de La Salle set up a colony near the coast. It only lasted 2 years. In 1821, Mexico gained its independence from Spain and allowed the first colony of Americans to settle in Texas.

In 1835, Texas declared its independence and the revolution against Mexico began. A year later, Texas became the Republic of Texas, a country in its own right. Later, Texas asked to join the United States. In 1845, Texas became the twenty-eighth state, with Austin as its capital. During the Civil War, Texas joined the Confederate States of America. Texas rejoined the Union in 1870.

State Flag

Mockingbird State Bird

Bluebonnet State Flower

FAMOUS TEXANS

★ Sam Houston led the Texans against Mexico and became the first president of the Republic of Texas.

★ Lieutenant Audie Murphy was the most decorated soldier in World War II.

★ Dwight D. Eisenhower was the thirty-fourth president of the United States.

★ Lyndon B. Johnson was the thirty-sixth president of the United States.

★ Vicki Carr is a singer and recording artist.

★ Mary Martin, a singer and actress, is the mother of actor Larry Hagman.

★ Dan Rather is a national news anchor.

STATE GREATS

★ Texas, the second largest state, is 220 times larger than Rhode Island.

★ 200 Texans died defending the Alamo, a mission in San Antonio.

★ The Lyndon Johnson Space Center in Houston is the headquarters for all manned spacecraft projects.

★ The Texas Rangers Hall of Fame in Waco honors the Texas Rangers.

★ The Rio Grande River is the largest in Texas and forms the boundary with Mexico.

★ Texas equals Alaska in producing the most petroleum in the United States.

★ President John F. Kennedy was killed while visiting Dallas.

© 2001 McGraw-Hill. All Rights Reserved.

The Fifty States

Texas: The Lone Star State

Look at an atlas or map of Texas. Add the names of the following places to the map below.

★ the city where the Alamo is located

★ the city where the first two missions were built

★ the location of the Texas Rangers Hall of Fame

★ the capital of Texas

★ the city where John F. Kennedy was assassinated

★ the location of the Lyndon B. Johnson Space Center

★ the country to the south

★ the state to the north

★ the Rio Grande River

★ the Gulf of Mexico

Size: 266,807 square miles
Population: 17,060,000

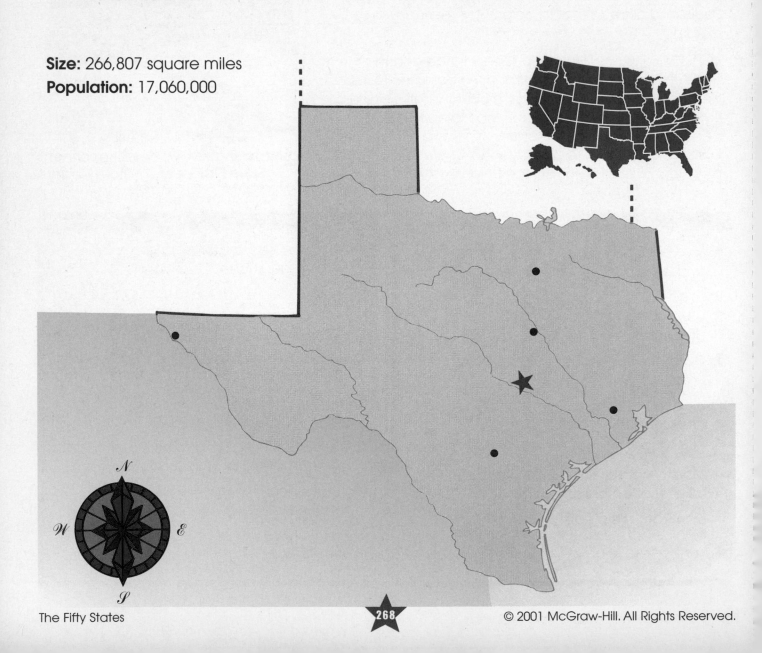

© 2001 McGraw-Hill. All Rights Reserved.

Texas: The Lone Star State

Complete the crossword puzzle below.

Across

3 The area south of Texas

6 The coast of Texas is on this body of water

7 A famous battle occurred here

9 Where astronauts report

10 John F. Kennedy was assassinated here

Down

1 This river is the boundary between Texas and Mexico

2 Texas Rangers Hall of Fame is here

4 You could find historical missions here

5 The Spanish built these when they claimed Texas

8 The president of Texas when it was a country

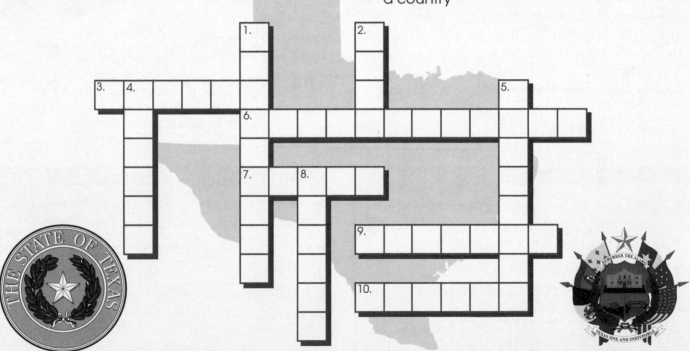

The state seal, adopted in 1961, has a star on the front and six flags on the back. Tell why there is one star on the seal and six flags on the back.

_____

_____

_____

_____

_____

© 2001 McGraw-Hill. All Rights Reserved.

The Fifty States

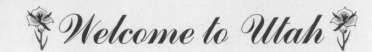

Welcome to Utah

★ HOW UTAH BECAME A STATE

Utah is a beautiful state. It is filled with hot, arid deserts and snow-capped mountains. And even though its American history did not start until the mid-1800s, ancient dinosaurs once roamed the state. Utah was settled by a man named Brigham Young. He was a member of the Mormon church. The Mormons first lived in New York but soon moved west. Finally, in 1847, about 170 Mormons arrived in Utah. They settled Salt Lake City, Utah's capital, near the Great Salt Lake.

A group of Native Americans, the Utes, were not happy with the arrival of the new settlers. During the 1850s, the Utes fought with the settlers for their land. Finally, in 1896, Utah became the forty-fifth state. Many Westerns are set in Utah's Monument Valley. Visitors come to swim in the Great Salt Lake, which is so salty that people can easily float in it. Of course, Utah has freshwater lakes too, like Utah Lake, just below the Great Salt Lake.

State Flag

Sea Gull
State Bird

Sego Lily
State Flower

FAMOUS UTAHNS

★ Butch Cassidy was born George LeRoy Parker. He robbed trains and banks, giving some of the money to people in need.

★ John Marriott was born near Ogden and grew up on a sheep ranch. He founded the Marriott hotel chain.

★ Donny and Marie Osmond are a brother and sister team who had several hit television shows.

★ Merlin Olsen, born in Logan, was a star quarterback for the Los Angeles Rams.

★ Steve Young, born in Salt Lake City, won the Super Bowl with the San Francisco 49ers.

★ Country singer and actress, Loretta Young, won an Academy Award.

STATE GREATS

★ The country's first traffic light was invented and installed in Salt Lake City in 1912.

★ The world's deepest open pit copper mine is near Salt Lake City.

★ In 1896, Martha Hughes Cannon became the first woman to serve as a state senator. The opposing candidate was her husband.

★ Lee Ann Roberts was the first woman racing driver to travel at more than 300 mph. She set the record on the Bonneville Salt Flats.

★ Utah is one of the states that makes up "Four Corners," where four states touch.

★ So many dinosaur bones have been discovered near the Dinosaur National Monument in northeastern Utah that it is nicknamed "Dinosaurland."

© 2001 McGraw-Hill. All Rights Reserved.

Utah: The Beehive State

Look at an atlas or map of Utah. Add the names of the following places to the map below.

★ Merlin Olsen is from here

★ the other states making the "four corners"

★ Utah's capital

★ a freshwater lake

★ where racecar records are set

★ a town near Utah Lake

★ many Western movies are filmed here

★ you can float in this lake

★ see dinosaur bones here

Size: 84,899 square miles
Population: 1,728,000

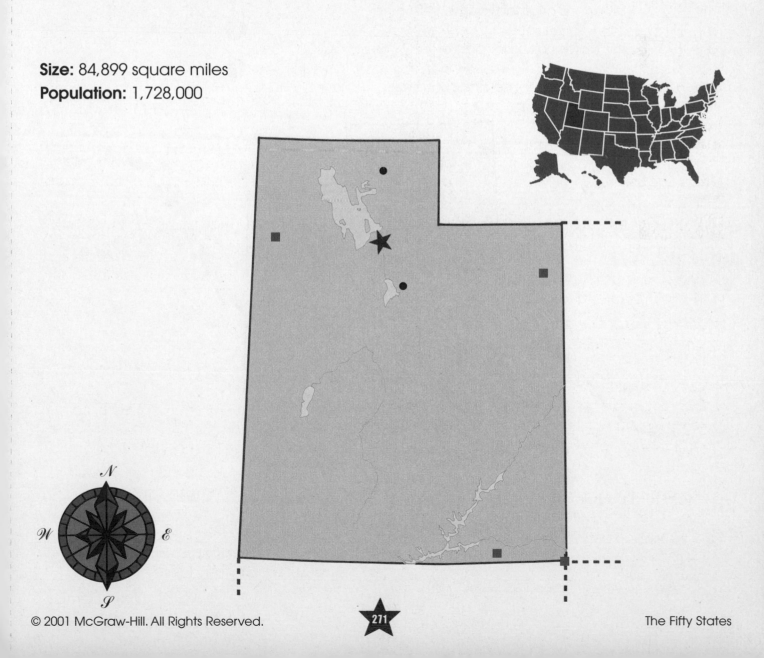

© 2001 McGraw-Hill. All Rights Reserved.

The Fifty States

Utah: The Beehive State

Write the letter from column B next to the matching phrase in column A.

 A

 B

1. _____ he led Mormons to Utah

2. _____ this lake has water you can drink

3. _____ these people were unhappy when the Mormons came

4. _____ Mormons originally came from here

5. _____ this state is another part of the "four corners"

6. _____ you can find these kinds of bones

A the Utes

B New York

C Bringham Young

D Colorado

E Utah Lake

F dinosaur

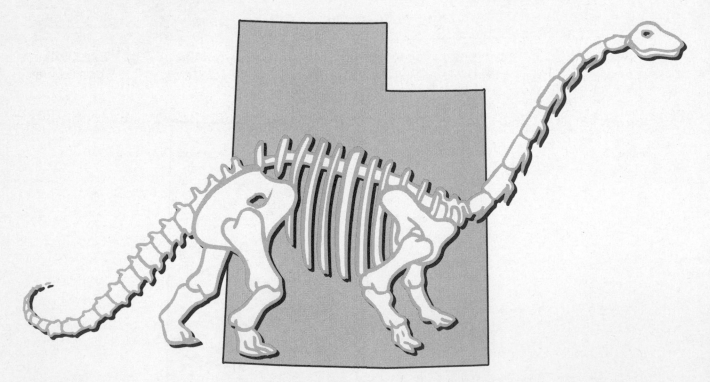

It is said that people swimming in the Great Salt Lake can float like corks. Why is this so?

_____

_____

 © 2001 McGraw-Hill. All Rights Reserved.

Welcome to Vermont

★ HOW VERMONT BECAME A STATE

*F*rench explorer, Samuel de Champlain journeyed from Canada to Vermont in 1609. He discovered the lake that now bears his name. At the time, Vermont was a popular hunting ground for the Algonquin and Iroquois tribes. In 1724, the first English settlement was set up near present day Brattleboro. In 1765, after the French and Indian War, the British took control of Vermont. The English kept the state's name, which comes from two French words: vert meaning "green" and mont "mountain."

For several years, New Hampshire and New York claimed Vermont. Ethan Allen formed the Green Mountain Boys in 1770 to force New Yorkers out. The group, which met in Bennington, went on to help the American cause against the British during the War of Independence. The Boys helped capture the British fort at Ticonderoga. But Vermont did not immediately join the United States. From 1777 until 1791, it was an independent country with its own government. Vermont became the fourteenth state on March 4, 1791.

State Flag

**Hermit Thrush
State Bird**

**Red Clover
State Flower**

FAMOUS VERMONTERS

★ Chester A. Arthur, born in Fairfield, became the twenty-first president of the United States.

★ George Dewey was a hero of the Spanish American War and an admiral in the Navy.

★ John Dewey was a philosopher and an educator.

★ Stephen Douglas was a senator and ran for president against Abraham Lincoln.

★ Rudy Vallee was a band leader and singer.

★ Orson Bean starred in the television show *Dr. Quinn, Medicine Woman*.

★ Billy Kidd won an Olympic skiing medal in 1964.

STATE GREATS

★ Vermont is the leading producer of maple syrup.

★ Montpelier is the least populated state capital in the nation.

★ Vermont was the first state to adopt a constitution that abolished slavery and gave all adult men the right to vote.

★ Marble from quarries located in Danby was used in many famous buildings including the Supreme Court Building in Washington, D.C.

★ The granite quarries near Barre are the largest in the country.

★ Burlington is the state's largest city and is called the "Queen City."

© 2001 McGraw-Hill. All Rights Reserved.

The Fifty States

Vermont: The Green Mountain State

Look at an atlas or map of Vermont. Add the names of the following places to the map below.

★ a lake named after an explorer

★ the capital of Vermont

★ a place near the first English settlement

★ a site where granite is quarried

★ the Green Mountains

★ the state which once claimed Vermont and now borders it to the east

★ the place where the Green Mountain Boys met

★ the state's largest city

★ the river that forms the border between New Hampshire and Vermont

★ Mount Mansfield

★ the birthplace of Chester Arthur

Size: 9,614 square miles
Population: 565,000

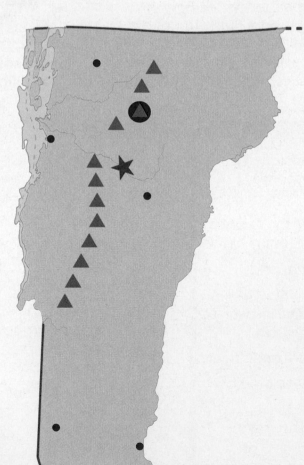

 © 2001 McGraw-Hill. All Rights Reserved.

Vermont: The Green Mountain State

Use the words in the Word Bank to complete each sentence.

Word Bank   Arthur   Montpelier   Ethan   Lake   Bennington   Rudy

_____ is the state capital.

_____ was a United States president from Vermont.

_____ Vallee was the name of a band leader.

_____ was the place where the Green Mountain Boys met.

_____ Champlain is the body of water named for Samuel de Champlain.

_____ was the first name of the Green Mountain Boys founder.

Write the first letter in each answer below to find out what was quarried in Danby.

__ __ __ __ __ __

Many people visit Vermont throughout the year. Find out why they visit and what they see. Write about why tourists travel to Vermont.

_____

_____

© 2001 McGraw-Hill. All Rights Reserved.

The Fifty States

Welcome to Virginia

HOW VIRGINIA BECAME A STATE

The first permanent English colony in America was set up in Virginia. In 1607, Captain John Smith set up the fort on Powhatan land. It was later called Jamestown. But colonial life was not easy. The settlers struggled with the harsh weather in the new land and their food supplies soon ran out. Luckily, they knew how to farm and the tobacco crop saved the colony. The settlers were able to trade tobacco for supplies from the Powhatan.

Two Virginians were important figures during this time—Thomas Jefferson and George Washington. The British and Loyalist armies were forced to surrender at Yorktown on October 19, 1781. Virginia became the tenth state to join the Union in 1788 but left 73 years later during the Civil War. Virginia was also the site of the surrender of the Confederacy by General Robert E. Lee at the town called Appomattox Court House in 1865. Virginia rejoined the Union in 1870.

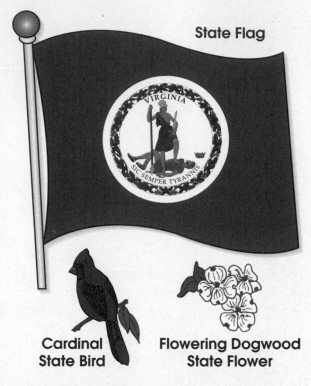

State Flag

Cardinal
State Bird

Flowering Dogwood
State Flower

FAMOUS VIRIGINIANS

★ Patrick Henry was the first governor of Virginia. He once said, "Give me liberty or give me death."

★ John Mercer Langston was the first African-American representative to Congress from Virginia.

★ Stonewall Jackson was a Confederate general during the Civil War.

★ Edgar Allan Poe was famous for writing short stories and poetry.

★ Meriwether Lewis and William Clark led an expedition to the Pacific Ocean.

★ Richard E. Byrd was the first man to fly over the North and South Poles.

STATE GREATS

★ The surrender that ended the American Revolution took place at Yorktown.

★ The surrender that ended the Civil War took place at Appomattox.

★ Virginia is called the "Mother of Presidents." Eight presidents were born in Virginia.

★ Tobacco was once Virginia's only economic crop.

★ The Chesapeake Bay Bridge-Tunnel is the longest bridge-tunnel in the world.

★ Government employment is now Virginia's number one industry.

 © 2001 McGraw-Hill. All Rights Reserved.

Virginia: Old Dominion

Look at an atlas or map of Virginia. Add the names of the following places to the map below.

- ★ the capital of Virginia
- ★ the site of the Civil War surrender
- ★ Thomas Jefferson's home, Monticello
- ★ George Washington's home, Mount Vernon
- ★ the site of the first permanent English colony

- ★ Arlington National Cemetery
- ★ the site of the British surrender
- ★ the Chesapeake Bay Bridge-Tunnel
- ★ the five states that border Virginia
- ★ the ocean to the east

Size: 40,767 square miles
Population: 6,217,000

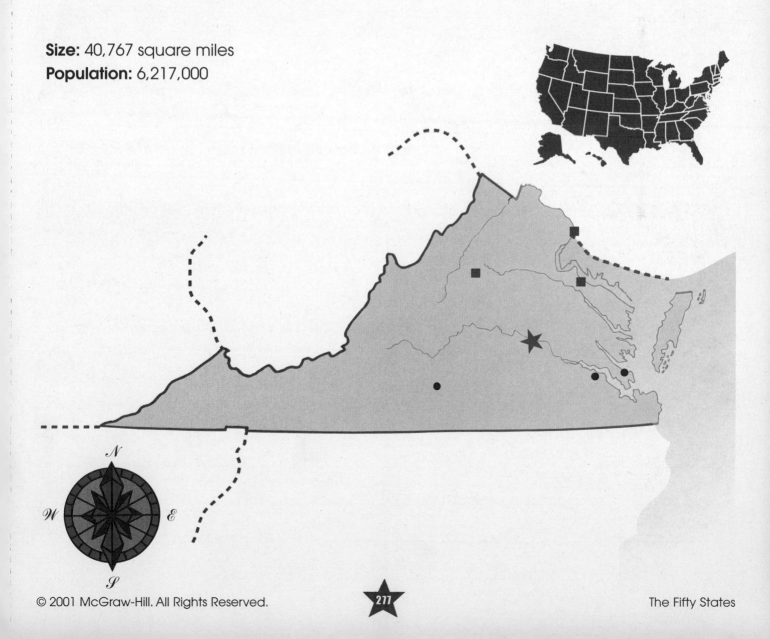

© 2001 McGraw-Hill. All Rights Reserved.

The Fifty States

Virginia: Old Dominion

Use the words in the Word Bank to complete the sentences.

Word Bank

Jamestown

Mount Vernon

Thomas Jefferson

Arlington

Appomattox

Monticello

Patrick Henry

_____ was Thomas Jefferson's home.

_____ was George Washington's home.

_____ was the site of the Confederate surrender by General Lee.

_____ was the first permanent English settlement in America.

_____ was the author of the Declaration of Independence.

_____ is the site of the National Cemetery.

_____ once said, "Give me liberty or give me death."

Consider the nickname: Old Dominion. Find out what this nickname means. What does it tell you about Virginia? Why is it important enough to identify the state?

_____

_____

_____

_____

 © 2001 McGraw-Hill. All Rights Reserved.

Welcome to Washington

★ HOW WASHINGTON BECAME A STATE

Before the arrival of the Europeans, many Native American tribes lived in Washington, including the Nez Percé, Walla Walla, Spokane, Yakima, Makah and Nooksak. In 1792, British naval officer, George Vancouver, mapped Puget Sound, and an American ship explored the Columbia River. By the early 1800s, Washington's rich wildlife and natural resources attracted British and American fur traders. The Columbia River offered easy access from the sea to the territory. The fur traders built their forts along the Columbia River. The Americans built Fort Okanogan, while the Canadians set up Spokane House. By 1825, the British Hudson Bay Company had established Fort Vancouver.

Soon, the first missionaries began arriving. Marcus Whitman founded a missionary settlement at Walla Walla in 1836. By 1846, the border with Canada was agreed upon. Within 2 years, hundreds of settlers came by way of the Oregon Trail. Washington became the forty-second state in 1889.

State Flag

Willow Goldfinch
State Bird

Coast Rhododendron
State Flower

FAMOUS WASHINGTONIANS

★ Bing Crosby was a well-known singer and actor.

★ Bill Gates founded Microsoft, a computer software company.

★ Edward R. Murrow was a reporter and television news pioneer.

★ Richard Hugo was an award-winning poet.

★ Gary Larson created "The Far Side" ™ cartoons.

★ Henry M. Jackson was an important state senator.

★ Judy Collins is a singer and songwriter.

STATE GREATS

★ The Boeing 747 airplane plant in Everett is the largest building in the United States. It covers 47 acres.

★ Olympic National Park protects the North American seashore and temperate rainforest.

★ Mount St. Helens, a volcano, erupted in 1980.

★ Microsoft's headquarters near Seattle has made Washington a leading state in computer software technology.

★ Mount Rainier has more glaciers than any other single peak in the United States. It is Washington's highest mountain.

★ The trees are an important resource. Timber from Washington is shipped all over the country.

© 2001 McGraw-Hill. All Rights Reserved.

The Fifty States

Washington: The Evergreen State

Look at an atlas or map of Washington. Add the names of the following places to the map below.

★ a software company's headquarters is near this city

★ a National Park that includes seashore and rainforests

★ a volcano that erupted in 1980

★ a large river that creates much of the border with Oregon

★ the capital of Washington

★ a tall glacier-covered mountain

★ a city, named for a Native American tribe, that began as a Canadian trading post

★ a city named after a British officer and a Hudson Bay fort

★ the settlement set up by missionary Marcus Whitman

★ the city where 747 aircraft are built

★ the bay mapped by George Vancouver

Size: 68,139 square miles
Population: 4,888,000

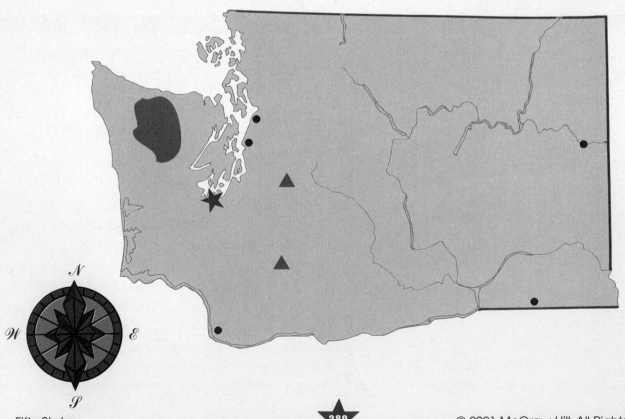

© 2001 McGraw-Hill. All Rights Reserved.

Washington: The Evergreen State

Complete the crossword puzzle below.

Across

1 the capital city

3 an American fort

6 the name of a British explorer and a modern city

8 a famous cartoonist

9 a television pioneer

Down

2 the name of a Native American tribe

4 the Hudson Bay Company and the Americans wanted this

5 Mount St. Helens is one, so is Mount Rainier

7 an important forest resource

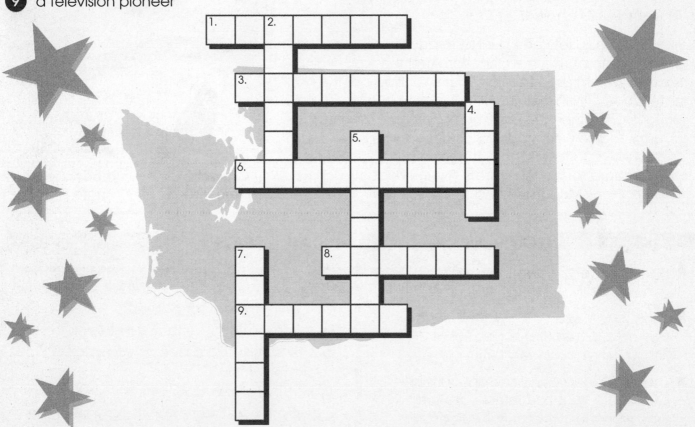

How many of Washington's major cities were built along the Columbia River? Write about why you think settlers chose to live along the river.

_____

_____

_____

_____

© 2001 McGraw-Hill. All Rights Reserved.

The Fifty States

Welcome to West Virginia

★ HOW WEST VIRGINIA BECAME A STATE

West Virginia used to be part of the original Virginian colony. But as time passed, the western part and the eastern part of the colony began to differ. People in the west wanted to abolish slavery. However, slavery was important to the east. When Virginia decided to leave the Union, people in western Virginia decided to stay and start their own state. West Virginia was created in 1863. It was the thirty-fifth state with Wheeling as its capital.

West Virginia is between the North and South, but it was a Union state during the Civil War. After the war, Virginia wanted West Virginia to rejoin, but the citizens of the new state did not. With the arrival of railroads, the need grew for coal to fuel them. So coal mining became an important industry. Today, West Virginia has a few large cities, such as the new capital in Charleston and Huntington. Many tourists come to see the state's natural beauty, such as the Allegheny Mountains and the Ohio River.

State Flag

**Cardinal
State Bird**

**Rhododendron
State Flower**

FAMOUS WEST VIRGINIANS

★ Mary Lou Retton won the gold medal in gymnastics in 1984.

★ John Brown was an abolitionist who led a raid on a United States arsenal at Harper's Ferry and was hanged for it.

★ Thomas "Stonewall" Jackson, born in Clarksburg, was a Confederate general who won the Battle of Bull Run against great odds. Afterwards, he was accidentally killed by one of his own men.

★ Chuck Yeager was the first pilot to break the sound barrier.

★ Don Knotts starred in many popular TV shows.

STATE GREATS

★ West Virginia is the third leading producer of coal. Its coal is some of the best because it burns the cleanest.

★ Smoke Hole Caverns are caves once used by Native Americans to smoke and store meat.

★ In central West Virginia, the National Radio Astronomy Observatory has some of the world's largest radio telescopes.

★ White Sulphur Springs is a mineral spring health spa where several presidents have vacationed.

★ The Blenko Glass Company in Milton made the windows of the National Cathedral in Washington, D.C., and the Cathedral of St. John the Divine in New York City.

 © 2001 McGraw-Hill. All Rights Reserved.

West Virginia: **The Mountain State**

Look at an atlas or map of West Virginia. Add the names of the following places to the map below.

- ★ a one time capital of West Virginia
- ★ the state to the north and west of West Virginia
- ★ West Virginia used to be a part of this state
- ★ beautiful mountains in the east
- ★ city near Kentucky
- ★ the capital of West Virginia

- ★ the state to the north and east
- ★ this river forms a border between West Virginia and Ohio
- ★ a one time confederate state to the south and west
- ★ John Brown raided this place

Size: 24,232 square miles
Population: 1,802,000

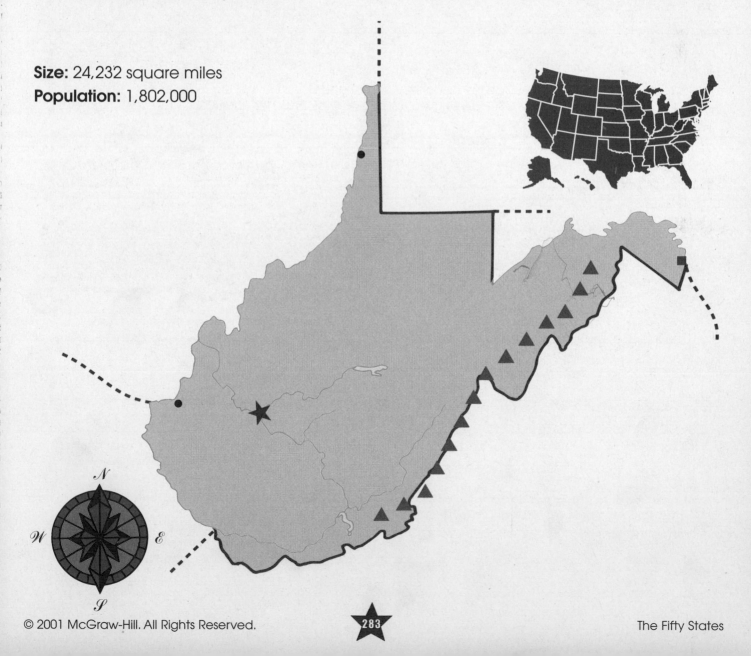

© 2001 McGraw-Hill. All Rights Reserved.

The Fifty States

West Virginia: **The Mountain State**

Complete the sentences using facts about West Virginia.

An abolitionist named _____ _____ raided a United States arsenal at Harpers Ferry.

The city of _____ was the capital before Charleston.

West Virginia's _____ is considered the best because it burns cleanly.

_____ wanted West Virginia to rejoin after the Civil War.

The _____ _____ forms much of West Virginia's northwestern border.

The building of the _____ created a huge demand for coal.

How did the state of West Virginia come about? Find out more about what made the people of western Virginia split from Virginia.

_____

_____

_____

_____

_____

_____

 © 2001 McGraw-Hill. All Rights Reserved.

Welcome to Wisconsin

State Flag

Robin
State Bird

Wood Violet
State Flower

*I*f you had to pick one state that could best represent the whole country, you might pick Wisconsin. Its large cities, rich farmland, high immigrant population and strong industries are typically American. Wisconsin was originally home to the Winnebago, Dakota and Menominee, and later the Sauk, Fox, Kickapoo and Potawatomi tribes. Wisconsin joined the United States in 1848 as the thirtieth state. Lumberjacks cleared forests to be used as farmland. Cities, such as Green Bay and Milwaukee, were founded, and people from Germany, Britain and Scandinavia settled in and around them.

For Wisconsin, the water is especially important. Lake Superior and Lake Michigan supply drinking water. The waterways also make it easy for farmers and industries to ship their goods to other parts of the world. The inland lake of Lake Winnebago links the Great Lakes to the Mississippi River. Many of Wisconsin's cities are by water. But Madison, the state capital, is inland.

FAMOUS WISCONSINITES

★ Gene Wilder was born Jerome (Jerry) Silberman and is an actor.

★ Vince Lombardi coached the Green Bay Packers to victory in the first two Super Bowls. The Super Bowl trophy is named after him.

★ Wladziu Valentino Liberace was a flashy classical pianist known commonly by his last name.

★ Joseph McCarthy was a U.S. senator who investigated many people whom he suspected of being unpatriotic communists.

★ Oshkosh was a Menominee who lobbied the federal government to grant his people a reservation. The city of Oshkosh is named after him.

STATE GREATS

★ Facial tissues were invented by a Wisconsin paper company in 1917.

★ Wisconsin produces more milk than any other state. In fact, it produces enough to fill 11 Olympic-sized swimming pools a day.

★ Wisconsinites were given the nickname "badgers" because early lead miners dug shelters underground.

★ On Oct. 8, 1871, the same night of the famous Chicago fires, a fire swept through Peshtigo, killing about 1,200 people.

★ The first kindergarten in the United States was set up in Watertown in 1856.

© 2001 McGraw-Hill. All Rights Reserved.

The Fifty States

Wisconsin: **The Badger State**

Look at an atlas or map of Wisconsin. Add the names of the following places to the map below.

- ★ this is a "super" Great Lake
- ★ the capital of Wisconsin
- ★ this bay feeds into Lake Michigan
- ★ this state is between Wisconsin and Canada
- ★ this state is to the south
- ★ this city is home to a pro football team

- ★ a large lake in Wisconsin
- ★ this river makes up the southwestern border
- ★ a large city on the banks of Lake Michigan
- ★ part of this state is wedged between the Great Lakes and Wisconsin
- ★ the only Great Lake to be entirely in the United States

Size: 56,153 square miles
Population: 4,907,000

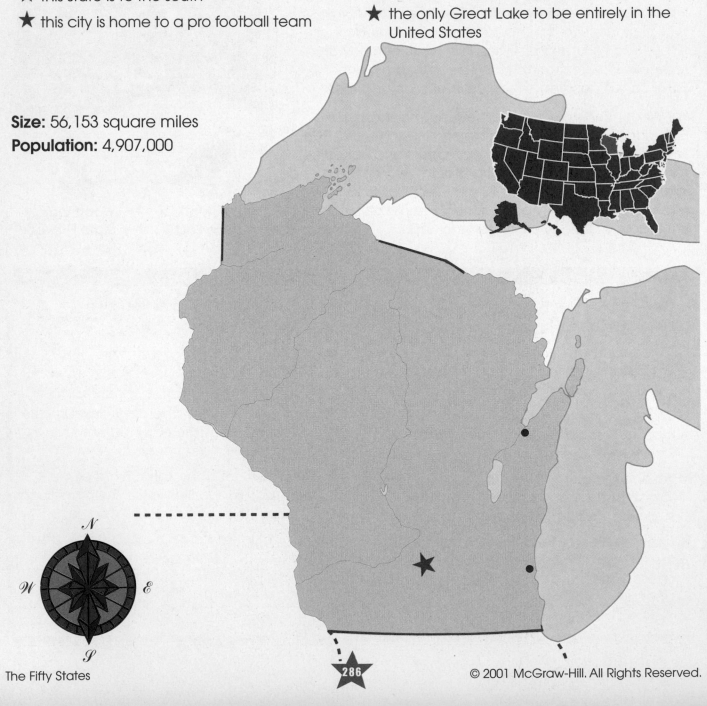

© 2001 McGraw-Hill. All Rights Reserved.

Wisconsin: The Badger State

Complete the crossword puzzle below.

Across

2. not a "great" lake

5. visit this city near Lake Michigan

6. a nickname for Wisconsinites

7. not just a city, a body of water, too

Down

1. it's the only Great Lake entirely in the United States

3. this city has a different-colored bay

4. an inland city

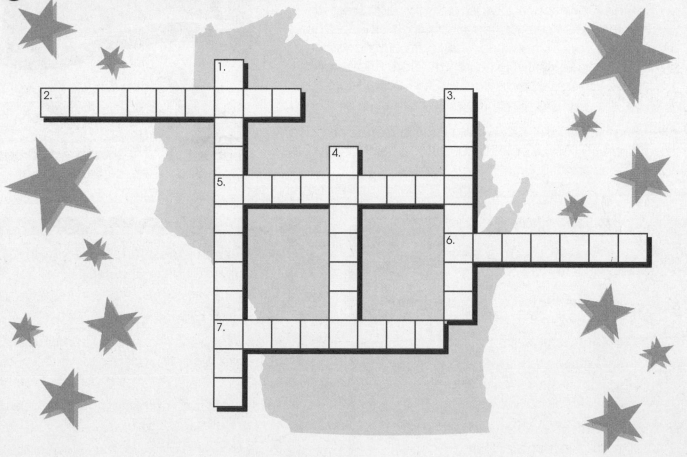

Why do you think Wisconsin is called America's Dairyland?

_____

_____

_____

© 2001 McGraw-Hill. All Rights Reserved.

The Fifty States

❧ Welcome to Wyoming ❧

★ HOW WYOMING BECAME A STATE

Wyoming is the least populated state in the country. Many settlers passed through Wyoming on their way to the gold fields of California. But some people decided to stay and set up farms or ranches. The Native American tribes, including the Cheyenne, Arapaho, Lakota and Sioux, fought the settlers. But in 1890, Wyoming became the forty-fourth state.

Wyoming is a beautiful state. The Rocky Mountains, part of the Continental Divide, pass through western Wyoming. Yellowstone National Park is also there—the first national park in the world. Just south of Yellowstone are the Grand Teton Mountains. The North Platte and the Snake Rivers also pass through the state. More than 5 million visitors travel to Wyoming every year.

Wyoming's capital, Cheyenne, and Casper each have fewer than 60,000 people. Laramie, the third largest city, has fewer than 30,000.

State Flag

**Meadowlark
State Bird**

**Indian Paintbrush
State Flower**

FAMOUS WYOMINGITES

★ Jackson Pollack, born near Cody, was an artist.

★ Joe Alexander was a world champion rodeo star elected to the ProRodeo Hall of Fame in 1979.

★ Curt Gowdy was a sportscaster whose television show, *American Sportsman*, ran for about 20 years.

★ Nancy Curtis started Wyoming's first book publishing company called High Plains Press.

★ In 1870, Esther Hobart Morris became the first female judge in the United States.

★ Patricia MacLachlan won the Newbery Medal for her children's book, *Sarah, Plain and Tall*.

STATE GREATS

★ Old Faithful is the most famous geyser in the United States.

★ Yellowstone National Park was established in 1872.

★ A ton of coal per second is dug at Black Thunder, the biggest coal mine in the Americas.

★ Wyoming elected the nation's first female governor, Nellie Ross, in 1924.

★ There are fewer people in Wyoming than in any other state.

★ Wyoming has about a half-million residents, but more than 5 million tourists come to visit every year.

© 2001 McGraw-Hill. All Rights Reserved.

Wyoming: **The Equality State**

Look at an atlas or map of Wyoming. Add the names of the following places to the map below.

★ this city is just east of central Wyoming

★ the capital of Wyoming

★ a city in northwest Wyoming

★ this river passes through the Grand Teton National Park

★ the first national park

★ these beautiful mountains are in their own national park

★ this river passes by Casper

★ a city near Cheyenne

★ this state is to the west and borders Montana

★ this mountain range divides North America

★ this state is to the east and borders Colorado

★ the Continental Divide

Size: 97,809 square miles
Population: 456,000

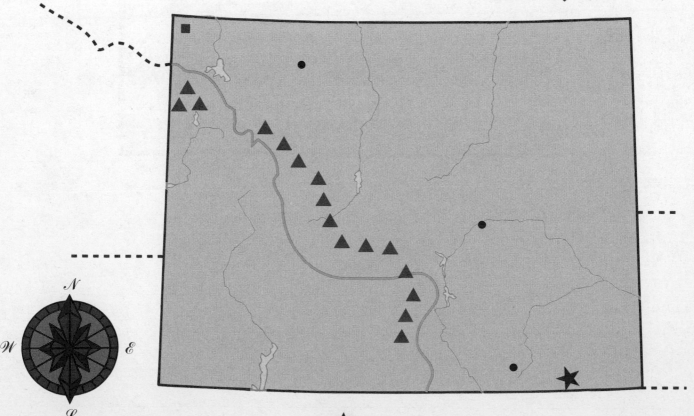

© 2001 McGraw-Hill. All Rights Reserved.

The Fifty States

Wyoming: **The Equality State**

Use these clues to find words about Wyoming in the word search below.

★ the first National Park

★ the capital of Wyoming

★ the name of an artist

★ the state nickname

★ these mountains are "grand"

★ a woman was elected to this position in 1924

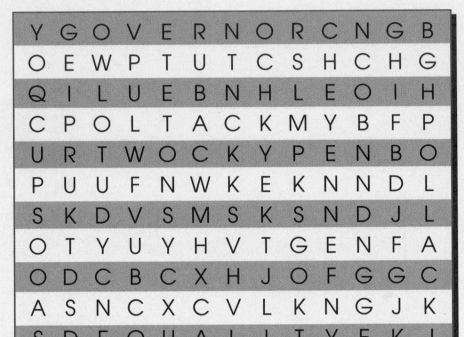

Y	G	O	V	E	R	N	O	R	C	N	G	B
O	E	W	P	T	U	T	C	S	H	C	H	G
Q	I	L	U	E	B	N	H	L	E	O	I	H
C	P	O	L	T	A	C	K	M	Y	B	F	P
U	R	T	W	O	C	K	Y	P	E	N	B	O
P	U	U	F	N	W	K	E	K	N	N	D	L
S	K	D	V	S	M	S	K	S	N	D	J	L
O	T	Y	U	Y	H	V	T	G	E	N	F	A
O	D	C	B	C	X	H	J	O	F	G	G	C
A	S	N	C	X	C	V	L	K	N	G	J	K
S	D	E	Q	U	A	L	I	T	Y	E	K	J

Why do so many people visit Wyoming? List five things to see in Wyoming.

_____

_____

_____

_____

 © 2001 McGraw-Hill. All Rights Reserved.

Welcome to Washington, D.C.

HOW WASHINGTON, D.C. BECAME THE CAPITAL

The Revolutionary War ended in 1783. The new United States of America named New York, then Philadelphia, as its capital. However, many people thought the capital should not belong to one state. In 1790, Congress said they would build a Federal City in the wilderness. It would lie between Maryland and Virginia. They called the land the District of Columbia, or "D.C."

President George Washington chose Pierre Charles L'Enfant to plan the city in 1790. Congress held a contest to design the Capitol building and the President's House, later called the White House. Andrew Thornton had the best plan for the Capitol. James Hoban had the best plan for the President's House. However, planning the capital was not easy. People disagreed about how the city should be laid out. L'Enfant quit halfway through the project. Andrew Ellicott took over to finish the job in 1793. In 1800, the Federal City was named the Capital. In 1801, it was renamed Washington in honor of George Washington.

Official Flag

**Wood Thrush
Official Bird**

**American
Beauty Rose
Official Flower**

FAMOUS WASHINGTONIANS

★ Edward Albee won three Pulitzer Prizes for his plays.

★ Duke Ellington was a famous jazz and blues musician.

★ John Foster Dulles was a secretary of state.

★ Edward Brooke was the first African-American senator elected by popular vote.

★ J. Edgar Hoover directed the Federal Bureau of Investigation (FBI).

★ John Philip Sousa was a bandmaster and composer who was famous for his marches.

CAPITAL GREATS

★ The Mall is a grassy area between the Capitol and the Potomac River. Most of the national museums and many of the monuments are on the Mall.

★ The Washington Monument is a hollow tower that stands 555 feet and 6 inches tall.

★ The Lincoln Memorial contains a large statue of President Lincoln created by Daniel French.

★ George Washington University is a leading university in D.C.

★ The Theodore Roosevelt Memorial is the only D.C. memorial on an island. The island is in the Potomac River.

© 2001 McGraw-Hill. All Rights Reserved.

The Fifty States

Washington, D.C.: The Nation's Capital

Look at an atlas or map of Washington, D.C. Add the names of the following places to the map below.

★ the house built for the president

★ the state to the southwest

★ the state to the northeast

★ the government building designed by Andrew Thornton

★ the river that divides D.C. from Virginia

★ the grassy area filled with national museums

★ a leading university

★ the monument that honors George Washington

★ the memorial that honors Abraham Lincoln

★ the memorial on an island

Size: 67 square miles
Population: 585,000

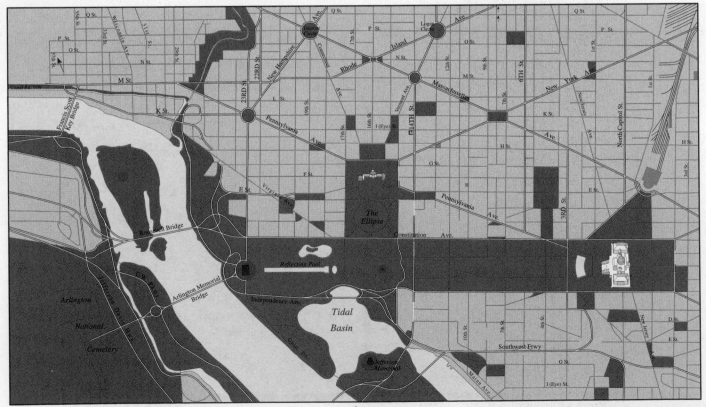

© 2001 McGraw-Hill. All Rights Reserved.

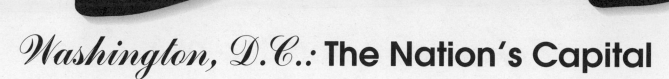

Washington, D.C.: The Nation's Capital

Andrew wants to work for the FBI one day. He wants to use codes to protect government secrets. This is Andrew's list of the best things to see in D.C. Use his code to find out what he likes best about D.C.

What to See in D.C.:

the tall, 555-foot tower _____ _____

the road that connects the Capitol and the White House _____ _____

the monument honoring Lincoln _____ _____

the rectangular body of water _____ _____

To find Andrew's favorite area of the city, follow these decoding steps.

1 Write the first letter of each answer on the line. _____

2 Cross out the W, M, P, R and P. Write the remaining letters on the line. _____

3 Rewrite the remaining letters on the line. Add an L. _____

4 Unscramble to the letters to find Andrew's favorite place in D.C. _____

If Washington, D.C. were to become a state, it would need a new state flag. What would it look like? Design your own flag to honor D.C. Explain your design.

_____
_____
_____
_____
_____

© 2001 McGraw-Hill. All Rights Reserved.

Riddles Across the USA

Riddles are so much fun to try to solve! Read the riddles below based on the information you have already learned about the states. Then, decide which state solves each riddle.

1 I am a "gem" of a state. My potatoes are found all over the U.S.A. Hells Canyon and Shoshone Falls can be visited in me. Which state am I? _____

2 Montgomery is my capital. I was once a one-crop (cotton) state. My state flower is the camellia. Which state am I? _____

3 Less rain falls in me than in any other state. I am home to Hoover Dam and Carson City. I'm not gold, but I am silver. Which state am I? _____

4 I was the first state to secede from the Union. My Fort Sumter was the place where the Civil War began. I am the Palmetto State. Which state am I? _____

5 My Jamestown was the site of the first permanent English settlement in America. Patrick Henry gave his famous speech in my Appomattox Court House. Which state am I? _____

6 I am the 42nd state. The Cascade Mountains divide me. The Grand Coulee Dam can be found in me. Which state am I? _____

7 I am the "Land of Lincoln." I contain the world's busiest airport. I lead the country in soybean and corn production. Which state am I? _____

8 My people are "Hoosiers." I am the 19th state. The University of Notre Dame is located in me. Which state am I? _____

9 I am the Old Line State. I'm separated into two parts by the Chesapeake Bay. Annapolis is my capital. Which state am I? _____

© 2001 McGraw-Hill. All Rights Reserved.

Riddles Across the USA

10 I was born during the Civil War as a result of the Civil War. Charleston is my capital. The site of John Brown's raid is in me. Which state am I? _____

11 My name means "mountainous." I'm a real "treasure." Many of the mountains in my Glacier National Park have never been climbed. Which state am I ?

_____

12 Gerald Ford was born in me. I contain the only national forest planted by foresters. Lincoln is my capital. Which state am I? _____

13 My name means "swift wind." I am located in the center of the original 48 states. You can see sunflowers growing in me. Which state am I? _____

14 Abraham Lincoln was born in me. A famous derby is held in me. The nation's gold vault is in my Fort Knox. Which state am I? _____

15 You can find lots of "sunshine" in me. My St. Augustine is the oldest European city in the U.S. Rockets launch out of my Kennedy Space Center. Which state am I?

_____

16 I lead the nation in tobacco farming. More wooden furniture and cloth is made in me than any other state. Which state am I? _____

17 I am big—220 times the size of Rhode Island! I have the most farms, farmland, cattle, horses and sheep in the nation. Which state am I? _____

18 I believe in "equality." My capital and largest city has only 50,000 people. Half of my land is federally owned and controlled. Which state am I? _____

19 I am the highest state in the nation. The highest road in the U.S. is in me. The Rocky Mountains are a big part of me. Which state am I? _____

© 2001 McGraw-Hill. All Rights Reserved.

The Fifty States

Riddles Across the USA

20 ★ I am often called the Great Lakes State because I touch four of the five. My Battle Creek is the largest producer of breakfast cereal. Which state am I?

_____

21 ★ My Mt. Washington is New England's highest peak. I am the Granite State. Concord is my capital. Which state am I?

_____

22 ★ I got my name from the Indians. Bismarck is my capital. I am the Flickertail State. Which state am I? _____

23 ★ I was the home of 7 U.S. presidents. The Pro Football Hall of Fame is located in my Canton. Which state am I? _____

24 ★ My Mount Rushmore attracts a lot of people. I am a "Land of Infinite Variety." Which state am I? _____

25 ★ I am the "Land of Opportunity." Bill Clinton was born in me. Little Rock is my capital. Which state am I? _____

26 ★ I have the largest population. Ribbon Falls, the highest waterfall in North America, is located in me. I am the "Golden" State. Which state am I? _____

27 ★ Tourists flock to my Nantucket. The Freedom Trail is located in my capital. I was the sixth state to join the Union. Which state am I? _____

28 ★ Brigham Young led Mormon settlers into my Salt Lake Valley. The sea gull is my bird. I am the Beehive State. Which state am I? _____

29 ★ I was the first state to join the newly formed U.S. in 1791 after the original 13 colonies. Ethan Allen and his Green Mountain Boys captured my Fort Ticonderoga. Which state am I? _____

30 ★ I am known as "America's Dairyland." I am a good example of the many different peoples in the U.S. Which state am I? _____

 © 2001 McGraw-Hill. All Rights Reserved.

Riddles Across the USA

31 I am the biggest state. The highest peak in the U.S., Mt. McKinley, is located in me. Which state am I? _____

32 I contain the Grand Canyon. Phoenix is my capital. Without irrigation, half of me would be desert. Which state am I? _____

33 I am the Garden State. My Atlantic City offers lots of exciting things for visitors to do. The purple violet is my flower. Which state am I? _____

34 I am the First State. I was named for Lord De La Warr. I was the first state to ratify the new constitution in 1787. Which state am I? _____

35 I am the first state in the U.S. to greet the sun each day. I lead the nation with my lobster catch. Ninety percent of my land is covered by woods. Which state am I?

_____

36 In 1610, I was founded by the Spanish. I am the "Land of Enchantment." My Santa Fe is the oldest seat of government in the nation. Which state am I?

_____

37 My Hartford is known as "Insurance City." The first constitution in the New World was adopted in me in 1639. Which state am I? _____

38 I can "show" you a lot. Jefferson City is my capital. In the summer of 1993, much of my land flooded. Which state am I? _____

39 I lead the nation in banking and wholesale trade. I contain the nation's largest city. I am the Empire State. Which state am I? _____

40 I am "the land where tall corn grows." I lead the nation in literacy. Des Moines is my capital. Which state am I? _____

© 2001 McGraw-Hill. All Rights Reserved.

The Fifty States

Riddles Across the USA

41 Portland is my largest city. My Columbia River Gorge attracts many tourists. There is year-round skiing at my Mount Hood. Which state am I? _____

42 I am the Gopher State. My Mesabi Range contains much iron ore. St. Paul is my capital. Which state am I? _____

43 I am the tiniest state. Roger Williams founded me in 1636. I produce the most costume jewelry in the world. Which state am I? _____

44 My name is an Indian word meaning "red people." The Five Civilized Tribes wanted me to become the state of Sequoyah in 1905. Instead, I am the Sooner State. Which state am I? _____

45 La Salle claimed my area for France in 1682. The U.S. bought me from France in 1803. I am the 18th state. Which state am I? _____

46 Elvis Presley was born in my Tupelo. I am the Magnolia State. Jackson is my capital and largest city. Which state am I? _____

47 You probably love my peaches. My most famous peanut farmer is Jimmy Carter. I am the Empire State of the South. Which state am I? _____

48 I was the second state to ratify the Constitution. I was the center, or "keystone," of the original 13 colonies. Which state am I? _____

49 I am the 50th state. My Pearl Harbor is very famous. Diamond Head is one of my most famous extinct volcanoes. Which state am I? _____

50 I have an east, a middle and a west. My state capital is the home of country music. I am the Volunteer State. Which state am I? _____

© 2001 McGraw-Hill. All Rights Reserved.

Abbreviate Those States!

When you mail something to someone, the state in the address is always abbreviated using two letters. See how many postal abbreviations you know!

_____ Alabama	_____ Louisiana	_____ North Dakota
_____ Alaska	_____ Maine	_____ Ohio
_____ Arizona	_____ Maryland	_____ Oklahoma
_____ Arkansas	_____ Massachusetts	_____ Oregon
_____ California	_____ Michigan	_____ Pennsylvania
_____ Colorado	_____ Minnesota	_____ Rhode Island
_____ Connecticut	_____ Mississippi	_____ South Carolina
_____ Delaware	_____ Missouri	_____ South Dakota
_____ Florida	_____ Montana	_____ Tennessee
_____ Georgia	_____ Nebraska	_____ Texas
_____ Hawaii	_____ Nevada	_____ Utah
_____ Idaho	_____ New Hampshire	_____ Vermont
_____ Illinois	_____ New Jersey	_____ Virginia
_____ Indiana	_____ New Mexico	_____ Washington
_____ Iowa	_____ New York	_____ West Virginia
_____ Kansas	_____ North Carolina	_____ Wisconsin
_____ Kentucky		_____ Wyoming

© 2001 McGraw-Hill. All Rights Reserved.

The Fifty States

Going Crossword Crazy!

See if you can solve the crossword puzzle on page 301 using the clues below. Hint: All answers are state names.

Across

4 You can eat lots of lobster in this state. Its only bordering state is New Hampshire.

5 The largest concrete dam in the U.S. is here. Water is one of this state's most important resources.

7 Brigham Young loved this state.

10 This state consists of a group of 132 islands formed from volcanic mountains.

11 This state is the Heart of Dixie.

13 This gem of a state leads the nation in its production of silver and lead.

14 This big state contains the cattle capital and the Manned Space Flight Center.

15 The "Sooner" you visit this state, the better.

16 The world's highest suspension bridge for vehicles can be found in this "high" state.

Down

1 A history of Mexican and Indian influence is very evident in this warm, dry state.

2 This state is a leading producer of peaches, peanuts and tobacco.

3 In the Hawkeye State, much corn, soybeans, beef cattle, hogs and dairy products are produced.

4 This state was the sixth state to join the Union and is the sixth smallest in size.

6 First in size but second to last in population accurately describes this state.

8 This state has the largest population, the most goods produced, the highest agriculture output, the tallest and oldest living things, and the largest city.

9 The Chesapeake Bay separates this state into two parts.

12 Although Lewis and Clark explored the area of this state in 1805, it was the discovery of gold that brought the first settlers to this "treasure" state.

The Fifty States

300

© 2001 McGraw-Hill. All Rights Reserved.

Going Crossword Crazy!

© 2001 McGraw-Hill. All Rights Reserved.

The Fifty States

Another Crazy Crossword

Now solve the crossword puzzle on page 303 using the clues below.

Across

5 California national park

7 Iowa's crop

9 Maryland's abbr.

10 Arizona desert

12 Alaska's abbr.

13 Minnesota's abbr.

14 South Carolina's abbr.

15 why many rushed to California in 1849

16 Arizona's abbr.

17 the 50th state's big island

18 what Roger Williams of Rhode Island was

20 Maine's abbr.

21 Indiana's abbr.

22 Alabama's abbr.

23 New Hampshire born president

25 Washington's capital

28 Mississippi's abbr.

Down

1 bridge now found in Arizona

2 river that borders Arkansas

3 founder of Pennsylvania

4 Missouri's abbr.

6 Florida national park

7 across New York's northern border

8 falls between Lakes Erie and Ontario

11 Texas' river border with Mexico

19 city in Nevada

23 Florida tree

24 California's abbr.

26 Louisiana's abbr.

27 Pennsylvania's abbr.

 © 2001 McGraw-Hill. All Rights Reserved.

Going Crossword Crazy!

The Northeast

Label the states in the Northeast region. Draw and label the Hudson River. Answer the questions below the map.

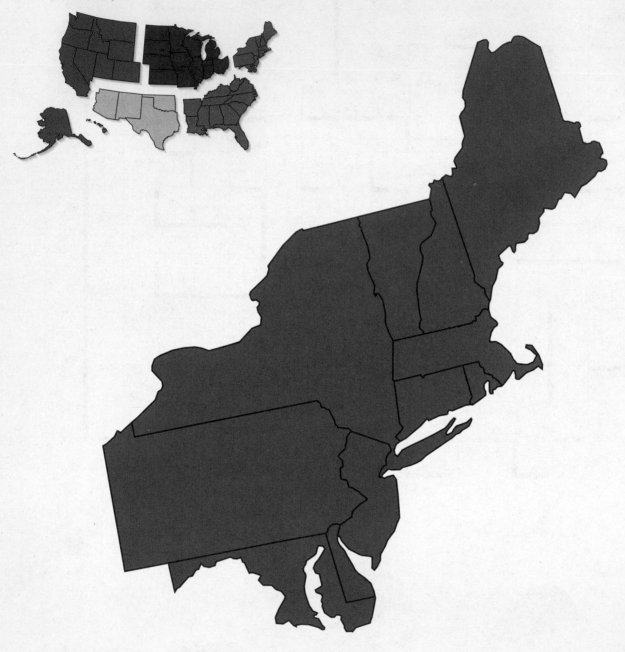

Which state in the Northeast has the largest population? _____

Which state in the Northeast has the largest area? _____

© 2001 McGraw-Hill. All Rights Reserved.

The Southeast

Label the states in the Southeast region. Draw and label the Tennessee and Savannah Rivers. Answer the questions below the map.

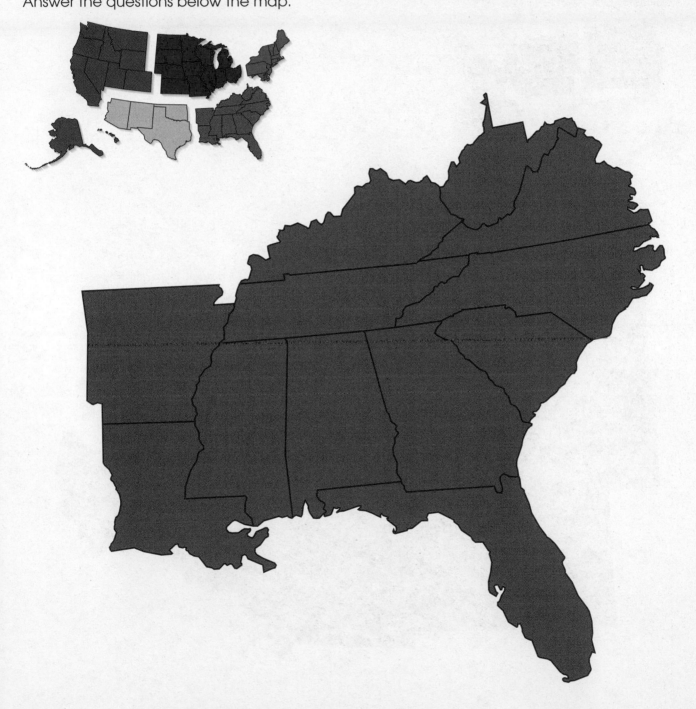

Which state in the Southeast has the largest population? _____

Which state in the Southeast has the largest area? _____

© 2001 McGraw-Hill. All Rights Reserved. The Fifty States

The Midwest

Label the states in the Midwest region. Draw and label the Missouri and Mississippi Rivers. Answer the questions below the map.

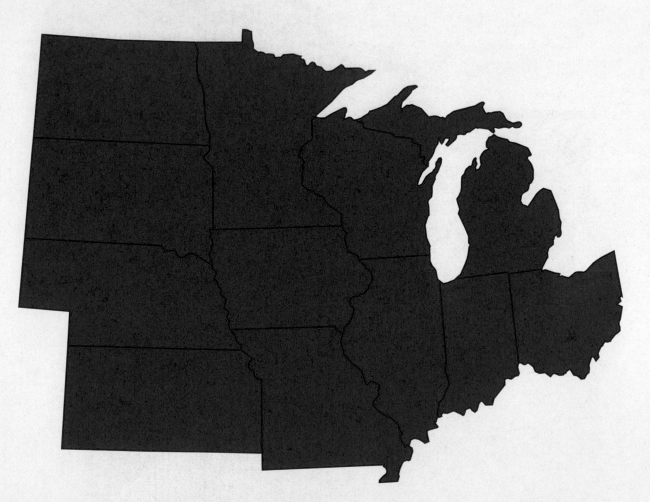

Which state in the Midwest has the largest population? _____

Which state in the Midwest has the largest area? _____

 © 2001 McGraw-Hill. All Rights Reserved.

The Southwest

Label the states in the Southwest region. Draw and label the Rio Grande River. Answer the questions below the map.

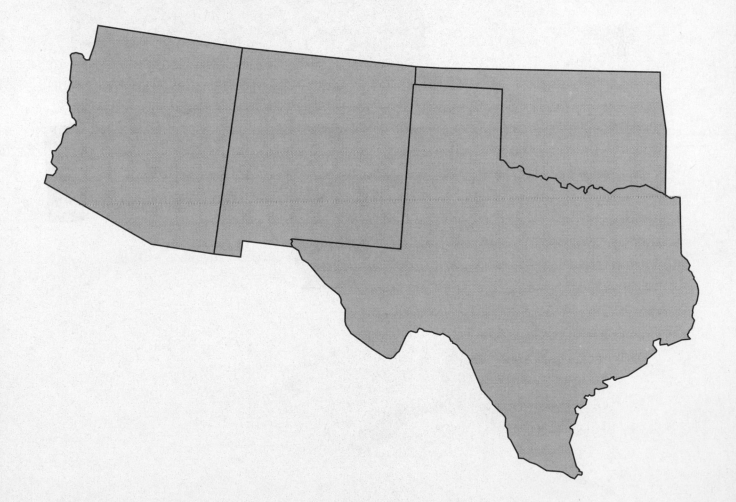

Which state in the Southwest has the largest population? _____

Which state in the Southwest has the largest area? _____

© 2001 McGraw-Hill. All Rights Reserved.

The Fifty States

The West

Label the states in the Western region. Draw and label the Colorado and Columbia Rivers. Answer the questions below the map.

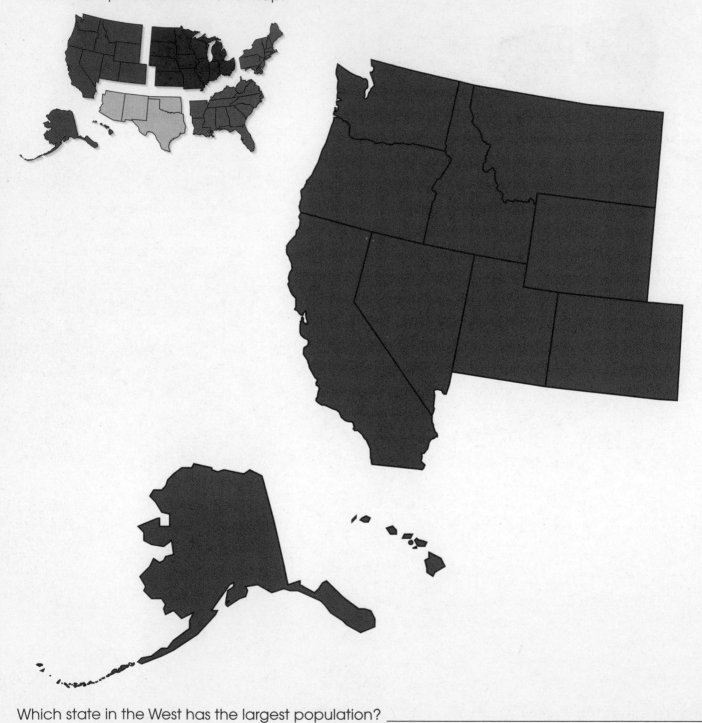

Which state in the West has the largest population? _____

Which state in the West has the largest area? _____

 © 2001 McGraw-Hill. All Rights Reserved.

Appendix

Bibliography

States

America the Beautiful (series). Various authors. New York: Children's Press, Grolier, Inc., 1987–2001. 144 pp. A very appealing series illustrated with color photographs, drawings and maps. Includes information on the history, environment, cities and citizens of each state. "Fast Facts" appendices include state symbols, demographics, annual events, and more. Bibliography. Index.

Celebrate the States (series). Various authors. New York: Benchmark Books, Matthew Cavendish Corp., 1997–1999. 144 pp. Readable series with colorful photographs, maps, charts and reproductions. Appendices include state songs, annual events and fun facts. Bibliography. Index.

Portrait of America (series). Various authors. Austin, TX: Raintree Steck-Vaughn, 1996–1998. 48 pp. These short but colorful overviews of the states include sections on history, economy, culture and the future. Famous citizens and events are featured in sidebars. Appendices include historical and annual events and state symbols. Index.

First Ladies

Abigail Adams: Women's Rights Advocate. Angela Osborne. American Women of Achievement Series. New York: Chelsea House Publishers, 1989. 111 pp. Examines the life of Abigail Adams within the international context of her time. Illustrated with black and white reproductions of period art, portraits and documents. Bibliography. Chronology. Index. (The reading level on this book is sixth grade and up, but it is very thorough and informative.)

Abigail Adams: Girl of Colonial Days. Jean Brown Wagoner. Childhood of Famous Americans Series. New York: Aladdin Paperbacks, 1992. 192 pp. Readable and interesting to young people, this book examines Adams' life with a focus on her childhood. Other titles in this series include *Martha Washington, George Washington, Thomas Jefferson, Theodore Roosevelt, John F. Kennedy* and *Abraham Lincoln.*

Encyclopedia of First Ladies (series). Various authors. New York: Children's Press, Grolier, Inc., 1997–2000. 112 pp. Series includes, among others: Jacqueline Bouvier Kennedy Onassis, Mary Todd Lincoln, Dolley Payne Todd Madison, Anna Eleanor Roosevelt and Martha Dandridge Custis Washington.

Eleanor Roosevelt: A Life of Discovery. Russell Freedman. New York: Clarion Books, 1993. 198 pp. This excellent biography for young readers is a Newbery Honor Book.

First Families (series). New York: Crestwood House, Macmillan Publishing Company, 1992. 48 pp. This series of books is about first families, including the Adamses, Bushes, Carters, Eisenhowers, Jacksons, Jeffersons, Johnsons, Kennedys, Lincolns, Madisons, Monroes, Nixons, Reagans, F. Roosevelts, T. Roosevelts, Tafts, Trumans and Wilsons. Each title offers a personal look at the life of a president, first lady and the family, including accounts of the childhood of the presidents and first ladies. Illustrated with black and white photographs. Bibliography. Index.

 © 2001 McGraw-Hill. All Rights Reserved.

★ Constitution

Creating the Constitution, 1787. Christopher Collier and James Lincoln Collier. Drama of American History (series). New York: Benchmark Books, Marshall Cavendish Corp., 1998. 96 pp. This basic book has a straightforward approach. Illustrated with color and black and white reproductions. Bibliography. Index. Other titles in this series include *Andrew Jackson's America 1824–1850* and *The Jeffersonian Republicans, 1800–1823: The Louisiana Purchase and the War of 1812.*

The Fight for the Women's Right to Vote in American History. Carol Rust Nash. An American History (series). Springfield, NJ: Enslow Publishers, Inc., 1998. 128 pp. Clearly written account illustrated with black and white photographs and reproductions. Time lines. Bibliography. Index.

First Constitution Books (series). Various authors. New York: Franklin Watts, Inc., 1986. 71 pp. Constitution series includes *Censorship, James Madison, The Right to Bear Arms, Separation of Church and State, States' Rights, Your Right to Privacy, George Washington, . . . the Constitution.*

The Constitution. Richard B. Morris. Illustrated by Leonard Everett Fisher. American History Topics Books. Minneapolis, MN: Lerner Publications Company, 1985. 69 pp. This older book (first published as *The First Book of the Constitution*) holds up well, with a straightforward narrative examining the history and context in which the Constitution came to be. Black and white illustrations. Includes simplified outline of the Constitution and Bill of Rights. Index.

★ The Presidents

There are numerous biographies on the presidents. The books listed below represent a selection of recent, recommended titles.

The Assassination of Abraham Lincoln. Brendan January. Cornerstones of Freedom (series). New York: Children's Press, Grolier, Inc., 1999. 32 pp. Solid and simply written, this book is a valuable resource, with archival illustrations. Time lines. Glossary. Index. Another title in this series is *Mount Vernon.*

Lives of the Presidents: Fame, Shame (and What the Neighbors Thought). Kathleen Krull. Illustrated by Kathryn Hewitt. New York: Harcourt Brace and Co., 1998. 96 pp. Entertaining accounts which bring these famous men down to earth, while maintaining a sense of respect for each individual. Bibliography. Index.

Presidents. Dorling Kindersley. Eyewitness Book, in association with The Smithsonian Institution. New York: DK Publishing, Inc., 2000. 64 pp. Packed with photographs of people, events and memorabilia, this eye-catching book includes information on the presidency and individual presidents. Index.

What's the Deal? Jefferson, Napoleon, and the Louisiana Purchase. Rhoda Blumberg. Washington, D.C. : National Geographic Society, 1998. 144 pp. This book is very appealing, lavishly illustrated with reproductions and maps. A clearly told account of the Louisiana Purchase, with a focus on the motivations of the key players. Bibliography. Index.

Young People's Letters to the President. Judith E. Greenberg. In Their Own Voices (series). New York: Franklin Watts, Inc., 1998. 96 pp. Illustrated with black and white photographs. Bibliography. Index.

© 2001 McGraw-Hill. All Rights Reserved.   Appendix

★ CD-ROMs

American Heritage for Young People. New Jersey: Simon and Schuster, 1997.

Chronicle Encyclopedia of History. New York: DK Multimedia, 1997. Newspaper-style articles with videos, animations, audio clips, music and biographies.

History of the World 2.0. New York: DK Multimedia, 1998. Includes interactive maps to link people, events and places.

USA Explorer. New York: DK Multimedia, 1999. Tour of the states with illustrated maps. Includes activities, games and information pop-outs. Ages 5–9 but may have broader appeal.

★ Videos

A&E Biographies. *Presidents and First Ladies* in this series includes George Bush, Jimmy Carter, Bill Clinton, Hillary Rodham Clinton, Dwight D. Eisenhower, Andrew Jackson, Thomas Jefferson, Lyndon Johnson, John F. Kennedy, Jacqueline Kennedy Onassis, Abraham Lincoln, Richard Nixon, Ronald Reagan, Nancy Reagan, Franklin Delano Roosevelt, Theodore Roosevelt, Harry Truman and Woodrow Wilson. Series also includes John Wilkes Booth.

Alabama to Wyoming: Flags of the United States. (1994) VHS. NR. Color.

Just the Facts: United States Constitution and the Bill of Rights. (1999) VHS. NR. Color, two tapes.

Portraits of American Presidents. (1992) VHS. NR. Color, three tapes.

"This Is America, Charlie Brown," v. 6: *The Birth of the Constitution.* (1989) VHS. NR. Color, closed-captioned, animated, HiFi, digital sound.

United States Constitution. (1995) VHS. NR. Color, closed-captioned.

United States: Railway Journeys Around the World. (1999) VHS. NR. Color.

★ Web Sites

Smithsonian Magazine for Ages 8–16: www.kidscastle.si.edu

Surfnet Kids: www.surfnetkids.com Posts newsletter for educational sites. Includes links to Constitution, 19th Amendment, major presidents (tours of homes, biographies, politics, works) and a chance to send messages to the president and other public officials.

White House for Kids: www.whitehouse.gov/WH/kids

www.state(add two-letter abbreviation for state of your choice).US./: The states maintain kids' pages that have state facts, weather info, contests and games, homework helpers, information on state government and other links.

 © 2001 McGraw-Hill. All Rights Reserved.

Glossary

abridge To abridge the rights of a person or group is to lessen, reduce or cut off those rights.

Alamo This Spanish Catholic mission became the site of a battle between Texans and the Mexican troops of General Santa Anna. The Texans held the fort until the last man had been killed. "Remember the Alamo!" became a famous battle cry.

ambassador An ambassador is one country's official messenger to another country. In the U.S., the president appoints ambassadors for special and usually temporary assignments.

amendment To change something for the better is to amend it. An amendment to our Constitution is a correction or addition to its original text that makes things better for all Americans.

Annapolis Convention Delegates from five of the 13 colonies met in the Maryland capital to discuss a more permanent governing document. Their ideas led to the formation of the Constitutional Convention.

apprentice A person bound by a contract in order to learn a trade or profession is known as an apprentice. In the new American colonies, becoming an apprentice was often the easiest way to advance without being born rich or gaining a higher education.

article Our Constitution contains many separate, numbered sections, known as articles, that make it easier to read and reference.

Articles of Confederation This was our nation's first constitution. The Articles were written in 1777 during the Second Continental Congress and were in force from 1781 to 1788.

assassination Assassination is sudden, unexpected murder by treachery. Three of our country's presidents—Lincoln, McKinley and Kennedy—were assassinated.

Battle of Tippecanoe This battle helped the United States win control of the Northwest Territory. One thousand U.S. troops fought 6,000 Shawnee under the command of William Henry Harrison. His fame from the victory helped win him the office of president.

bill When Congress wishes to make a new law, a rough version, or draft, of that law is presented before the House of Representatives or the Senate. It is known as a bill.

Bill of Rights The first 10 articles of our Constitution are known as the Bill of Rights. They outline those rights that our Founding Fathers believed all citizens should have.

Boston Tea Party In 1773, a new British government gave English merchants an unfair advantage in selling its tea cheaply. Angry Bostonians disguised as Native Americans dumped chests full of the tea into Boston Harbor, joking that it was a "Boston Tea Party."

Boxer Rebellion In 1900, Chinese nationalists began attacking foreigners living in Beijing. President McKinley sent in 5,000 American troops to stop this uprising.

branch Our government is divided into three distinct parts, or branches, known as legislative, executive and judicial.

cabinet The body of advisers who serve the president, including the secretary of state, the attorney general and secretary of defense.

capital A city that serves as the seat of a government, be it state or federal.

cash crop Any crop that is grown not for use, but for its market value, is known as a cash crop. In the United States, these crops included tobacco, corn and cotton.

census Our Constitution requires that a count of all citizens, called the census, be taken every 10 years. This helps the government allow the right number of representatives for each state.

checks and balances The delegates who drafted our Constitution wanted to make sure that power could not be taken unfairly by a king, emperor or general. They made sure that each of our three branches of government could check the power of the other two so that balances of power could exist.

Chief Justice Head of the nine justices of the Supreme Court.

© 2001 McGraw-Hill. All Rights Reserved.

Appendix

Chisholm Trail The Chisholm Trail was used by American pioneers in the 1860s to move and trade cattle. It stretched from San Antonio, Texas, to Abilene, Kansas.

citizen A person who owes allegiance to a government is called a citizen. Under our Constitution, all citizens have equal rights under the law.

Civil Rights These are rights of personal freedom guaranteed to all U.S. citizens by the 13th and 14th Constitutional amendments.

Civil War Also known as The War Between the States. This conflict of 1861–1865 began when Southern states left the Union because they did not wish to abolish slavery.

committee In the U.S. Congress, legislators form groups to study legislative matters. For example, the House Budget Committee is a group of representatives who carefully examine and analyze the U.S. budget.

compromise Any settlement of differences can be called a compromise. Sometimes a compromise is reached through mutual consent and, sometimes, through a third party.

confederacy The eleven Southern states that seceded from the U.S. Union in 1860 called themselves a confederacy. This means a group united by a common purpose.

Confederate States of America After the Southern states left the Union, they formed a separate nation called the Confederate States of America, with Jefferson Davis as president.

Congress Congress is our government's legislative, or law-making, branch. The Constitution specifies that Congress consist of two bodies, the House of Representatives and the Senate.

congressperson A delegate elected by citizens of an individual state to represent them in Congress, usually in the House of Representatives.

conservation Carefully protecting and preserving something. Conservation of our Constitution means reading and interpreting it carefully so its original wording is honored.

Constitution Our Constitution is really three things. First, it is a written document that shows our rules. Second, it is a statement of the basic principles and laws of our country that guarantee certain rights for our citizens. Third, it is the way in which our society operates.

Constitutional Convention During the summer of 1787, delegates from 12 states met to write a new governing document for the United States of America. The Constitution they wrote embodies the idea of two legislative bodies and was approved in 1788.

copyright The exclusive legal right to sell, publish and reproduce a literary, artistic or musical work.

corruption In government, corruption often means that an official has been influenced by a bribe of money or gifts to do something illegal.

cotton gin Invented in 1793 by Eli Whitney, this machine made the process of separating cotton fiber from its seeds much faster and less expensive.

counterfeiting Making illegal and fake money on purpose to deceive a person or agency.

Cumberland Gap A natural pass through the mountains connecting Kentucky, Tennessee and Virginia. Daniel Boone marked the Wilderness Road here in 1775. The Gap was important during the Civil War and changed hands often during that conflict.

dark horse Lengthy voting procedures can result in a stalemate. This has led to an American political phenomenon known as the "dark horse" candidate, an individual who gains the nomination in spite of having had little or no formal support before the convention opens. President James Polk is the most famous Democratic dark horse candidate.

Declaration of Independence At the Second Continental Congress, a committee of five men drafted a document stating that the 13 colonies were officially its own country, free from English laws. All people have rights that no one should take away. A version written mostly by Thomas Jefferson was accepted on July 4, 1776.

delegate A representative to a convention or a conference, such as the Constitutional Convention.

 © 2001 McGraw-Hill. All Rights Reserved.

Democratic-Republican Party An early political party in the U.S., led by Thomas Jefferson and James Madison in opposition to Alexander Hamilton's Federalist Party. It was the forerunner of today's Democratic Party, favoring states' rights, for example.

Democratic Party During the presidential campaign of 1828, one faction of the Democratic-Republican party split off to become the Democratic party, still active today.

diplomat Someone who is skilled in negotiating between nations without making any of the nations angry.

duel In the eighteenth century, disputes might be resolved through a formal fight with weapons (pistols or swords) conducted in front of witnesses. Aaron Burr, the third vice president, killed his political rival Alexander Hamilton in this type of fight.

Dust Bowl This area of the southern Great Plains was heavily settled by homesteaders in the late nineteenth century. In the early 1930s, severe drought ruined farming conditions and many settlers were forced to move, accept government assistance or starve.

elevation The highest point in North America, Mount McKinley, or Denali (6,194 m/20,320 ft), is situated in the Alaska Range. The lowest point (86 m/282 ft below sea level) is in Death Valley, California—part of the Great Basin.

Emancipation Proclamation Issued by President Abraham Lincoln on January 1, 1863, this speech freed all slaves in the states "in rebellion."

Equal Rights Wording that would give women equal rights with men under the law was first introduced as a possible amendment in 1923. Although the Equal Rights Amendment (ERA) has still not become part of the Constitution, it is now in sixteen states' constitutions.

executive Someone who controls or directs an organization or group is its executive. In the United States, the head of the executive branch is the president.

Fair Deal President Harry S. Truman wanted the government to ensure that the nation's growing post-World War II economy provided increased opportunities for all Americans, particularly those with low incomes.

federal In our country, the government that joins all the states together as a nation (a kind of federation) is called the federal government. Our federal government is located in Washington, D.C.

Founding Fathers Because they established the basis of American government, the delegates to the Constitutional Convention are called our "Founding Fathers."

French and Indian War From 1754 to 1763, this was the last of four wars between the British and the French in North America. It established British dominance of the continent.

frontier As the United States expanded west, south and north, new settlements grew along each new limit of civilization. These frontiers were usually hard places to live. Weather, geography and unknown conditions made life rough and sometimes impossible.

Gettysburg Address President Abraham Lincoln delivered this brief, moving speech on November 1, 1863, at the Gettysburg Battlefield. He honored the dead by expressing the democratic spirit of the American Republic.

Gold Standard Act Passed by Congress in 1900, President William McKinley's gold money standard remained in place until President Franklin D. Roosevelt brought a silver standard for money back during his New Deal program.

Great Depression It began in the U.S. in 1929 and lasted until the 1940s. During the Great Depression, businesses and banks closed their doors; people lost their jobs, homes and savings; and many depended on charity to survive.

Great Plains This huge plateau (rise of level land) in North America extends from northwestern Canada down to Texas.

Great Society President Lyndon Baines Johnson proposed this program in a speech on May 22, 1964. The policy was his attempt to end poverty and racial injustice in the U.S.

© 2001 McGraw-Hill. All Rights Reserved.

Appendix

grievance The formal expression of a charge of injustice against a person or persons.

impeachment Impeachment refers to an accusation against a government official. It also refers to the trial of that official. The Senate has the power to try impeachment cases for all officials except for its own members.

inauguration The act of inducting into public office. At Inauguration, U.S. presidents take an Oath of Office to "preserve, protect and defend the Constitution of the United States." Presidential inaugurations always take place on January 20 following an election year.

income tax The 16th Amendment to the Constitution states that every U.S. citizen who earns or receives money must give a certain amount of that money to the Federal government. With this money, the government runs programs.

integration The act of bringing members of a group into full membership in a society. In the 1950s, the U.S. began a long and painful process of integrating African-Americans into their rightful place as full citizens.

Journey of Discovery A journey undertaken by Lewis and Clark with their team of 48 civilian hunters, soldiers and French boatmen from their base camp outside of St. Louis.

judicial The branch of government that tries cases and decides if laws are constitutional. It is led by the Supreme Court.

justice One of nine members of the Supreme Court.

Know-Nothing Party The Know-Nothings were a nineteenth-century political group who disliked and feared the influence of recent immigrants, especially those who were Roman Catholic.

lame duck An elected official who is serving out the time between an election and the inauguration of a replacement.

landslide An election won by a large majority of the votes cast.

League of Nations This international alliance for peace lasted from 1920 to 1946. It was founded by President Woodrow Wilson after the First World War. The United Nations took its place on April 8, 1946.

legislative The branch of our government that has the power to draft laws. The Legislative Branch also makes financial decisions for the government, including taxes. It is led by Congress.

levy A levy is a tax on goods or services.

Lewis and Clark Meriwether Lewis and William Clark were army colleagues and friends who undertook a mission from President Thomas Jefferson in 1803. Jefferson had recently completed the Louisiana Purchase and wanted to find the Northwest Passage that would easily connect the eastern and western portions of the continent.

lobbyist Someone who tries to influence the passage of a bill. Lobbyists often try to develop special relationships with members of Congress and the Administration.

Louisiana Purchase In 1803, the U.S., under President Thomas Jefferson, purchased the interior of the North American continent from the French. The U.S. paid $15 million for land stretching from the Missouri River to the Rocky Mountains.

margin The measure or degree of difficulty in passing a bill. "The new tax bill passed by a wide margin."

Marshall Plan After World War II, Secretary of State George C. Marshall made a plan to help the European countries that were suffering from wartime damages. President Harry S. Truman approved the plan as a means of keeping these countries as allies.

Mexican War This war lasted from 1846 to 1848. The U.S. victory meant Mexico had to give over half of its territory to the States. This marked the rise of the U.S. as a global power.

militia The whole body of able-bodied citizens declared by law as subject to military service. In the U.S., this has historically meant white male citizens.

Monroe Doctrine President James Monroe stated this doctrine in a speech, his annual address to Congress in 1823. It was taken at that time as justification for the U.S. involvement in Central and South America.

 © 2001 McGraw-Hill. All Rights Reserved.

NATO The North Atlantic Treaty Organization (NATO) is an alliance of countries that began in 1949. The members of the alliance agree to protect and defend each other from attack by other nations. Members include nations of Europe and the United States.

naturalization The process by which a person born in one country becomes a citizen of another.

New Deal A program begun by President Franklin D. Roosevelt during the Great Depression. To counter the economic and social ills of the Depression, the administration opened a wide spectrum of programs and agencies to help our nation back on its feet.

New York City This city in New York State was our nation's first capital. President and Mrs. Washington lived there before the nation's capital was moved to Philadelphia.

Nobel Peace Prize An award to recognize someone in the world who has done something to promote peace between countries.

nomination The process of appointing a candidate to office.

pardon A pardon is an official action that frees a guilty person from further punishment.

Peace Corps An organization of volunteers who go to underdeveloped countries to teach farming, engineering, education and other skills. The U.S. Peace Corps was begun by President John F. Kennedy in 1961.

petition A formal request for action. The Thirteen Colonies petitioned the British government several times for more independence.

Philadelphia Its name means "love of brotherhood," which fits a city founded by peace-loving members of the Quaker religion. Philadelphia was our nation's second capital and the site of the Constitutional Convention.

preamble An introductory statement that states the reasons for and intent of the law. The Preamble of the U.S. Constitution is one of the most famous pieces of writing in history.

press The group of journalists from different kinds of media, including newspapers, television and radio, who cover a government's activities, among other things.

Prohibition The era during the 1920s and 30s when laws passed by Congress forbade the sale, serving and manufacture of alcoholic beverages anywhere in the United States. Some individual states still have prohibition laws.

pueblos Communal dwellings of Native American tribes in the Southwest region. These buildings are made of adobe clay or stone and often have flat roofs.

Pulitzer Prize The highest prize in journalism in the United States.

ratification The process by which a government document, such as the Constitution, is approved.

redress A formal process to correct an injustice.

representation The system by which officials for all three branches of the U.S. government may be chosen by a vote of the people.

Republican Party Founded in 1854, this is the second of the two great modern political parties. The party was started by Democrats in the North who were dissatisfied with conciliatory attitudes towards slavery in other parties.

Revolutionary War In 1776, the Thirteen Colonies formally declared their independence from British rule. Hostilities had already begun the previous year at Lexington, Concord and Bunker Hill. The British surrendered to the new United States in 1781.

Rhodes Scholarship This famous scholarship allows young college graduates from around the world to attend Oxford University in England. President William Jefferson Clinton received a Rhodes Scholarship in 1973.

segregation The act of keeping a person or a group separate from mainstream society. Segregation involves suppressing a group's civil rights.

senator A member of the Senate, one of the two law-making bodies in the U.S. Congress. Two senators of different parties are elected from each state, no matter how large or small the state's population.

© 2001 McGraw-Hill. All Rights Reserved.

slavery The practice of keeping slaves, or people who are not given any rights. Slaves are regarded as possessions of their owners. Until the end of the Civil War, the U.S. had states that practiced slavery of Africans.

Spanish-American War A brief war of four months in 1898. The Spanish naval forces were defeated badly by the U.S. Navy. The war marked the rise of the U.S. as a global military power.

Speaker of the House The speaker is the head of the House of Representatives. The Speaker of the House is selected by the majority party in power.

speech A public address, usually delivered to a large group of people.

Stamp Act After the First Continental Congress, the British government tried to stop the Thirteen Colonies from acting for independence. One tax that was put in place was the Stamp Act, which required a fee be paid to the British for any legal or business document written.

Supreme Court The highest court in our nation consists of nine justices, one of whom acts as Chief Justice. The Supreme Court heads the judicial branch of the federal government.

Teapot Dome In 1921, President Warren G. Harding gave the Department of the Interior the power over two government-owned oil production sites. The Interior secretary committed fraud by leasing these sites out for profit. The scandal opened many people's eyes to the need for openness and honesty in government.

treaty A contract in writing between political groups, such as states or countries. Treaties are formally signed, usually in the presence of many witnesses.

Treaty of Ghent Signed on December 24, 1814, this treaty concluded the War of 1812 between the United States and Great Britain.

Treaty of Guadalupe Hidalgo An agreement, signed on February 2, 1848, between the United States and Mexico that marked the end of the Mexican War (1846–1848). The treaty established the boundary between Mexico and Texas at the Rio Grande.

Treaty of Paris The Treaty of Paris signed on September 3, 1783, by Great Britain and the United States concluded the American Revolution. By its terms, Great Britain recognized its former 13 colonies as the free and sovereign United States of America.

U.S. Capitol A capitol is a building where a government meets. Our federal capitol building with its striking rotunda, or dome, is located in Washington, D.C.

U.S. Constitution This system of laws was drawn up by 55 delegates to the Constitutional Convention in 1787. It establishes our three branches of government and outlines the rights and freedoms of all U.S. citizens.

U.S. House of Representatives One of two law-making bodies in the U.S. Congress. The House of Representatives (or "House") includes representation based on state population. The more people in a state, the more congresspersons that state is allowed.

U.S. Senate One of two law-making bodies in the legislative branch of the U.S. Government. The Senate includes equal representation from each state regardless of the state's population. There are two Senators per state.

union A political unit formed from two or more units (such as states) that agree to operate under a single system (such as our Constitution).

veto A power given to the chief executive, or president. The president can temporarily or permanently stop a bill from becoming law.

Watergate Close to the Potomac River in Washington, D.C., is a large luxury apartment complex called The Watergate. It was here in the early 1970s that members of the Republican Party spied on the Democratic National Headquarters.

Whig Party The Whig Party was one of the two dominant political parties in the U.S from the mid-1830s to the mid-1850s. It was formed by those opposed to the policies of President Andrew Jackson and the Democratic party.

 © 2001 McGraw-Hill. All Rights Reserved.

Answer Key

George Washington

Born: February 22, 1732
Birthplace: Pope's Creek, Westmoreland County, Virginia
Political Party: Federalist
State Represented: Virginia
Term: April 30, 1789–March 3, 1797
Died: December 14, 1799
Vice President: John Adams (F)

George Washington was a leader long before he became our first president. In 1755, at the age of 23, Washington led the Virginian forces to victory in the French and Indian War. However, Washington and the other colonists soon grew tired of British rule. By 1775, Washington became the commander of the Continental Army. His army defeated the British in 1783. George Washington also helped write our new Constitution, making sure the states had a strong role in the government. By 1789, Washington was the most popular man in the United States. He was also tired after serving our country for many years. Still, he knew a new nation needed strong leadership. When George Washington agreed to run for president, everyone voted for him. Washington served two terms as president of the United States. He died two years after his retirement, at his farm in Virginia.

★ **SHOW WHAT YOU KNOW**

Write in the missing words on the lines below.
Washington led British troops in the French and Indian **W A R**.
　　　　　　　　　　　　　　　　　　　　　　　　　　　　　　1　2　3

Then, he led the **C O N T I N E N T A L   A R M Y** against
　　　　　　　　　7　　　　　　　　　　　　　　6
the **B R I T I S H**.
　　　10　　　　　　9

Washington **S E R V E D** his **N A T I O N** in many ways.
　　　　　　　　　4　12　5　14　　　　　　　8　　13

He was then elected **P R E S I D E N T**
　　　　　　　　　　　4　12　5　14　　8　　13

Match the letters to the numbers under each line. Write the letters on the lines below to learn what people said about George Washington.
"First in **W A R**, first in **P E A C E**, and first in the **H E A R T S** of
　　　　　1　2　3　　　　　4　5　6　7　8　　　　　　　9　10　11　12　13　14
his countrymen."

★ **FIND OUT MORE**

Who was the king of Britain when the
United States won its freedom from British rule? **King George III**

26

John Adams

Born: October 30, 1735
Birthplace: Braintree, Massachusetts
Political Party: Federalist
State Represented: Massachusetts
Term: March 4, 1797–March 3, 1801
Died: July 4, 1826
Vice President: Thomas Jefferson

John Adams began his long career as a lawyer in the colony of Massachusetts. A fiery speaker, Adams strongly opposed the unfair taxes that Britain forced on the colonists. He also tried to convince Britain to give the colonies more freedom. He did not succeed. Instead, Adams asked George Washington to organize the Continental Army to fight the British. In 1776, Adams helped write the Declaration of Independence. In 1783, he helped write the Treaty of Paris. This treaty ended the Revolutionary War and created the United States. When Washington became president of the United States in 1789, Adams became the first vice president. However, Adams was not pleased with the office or the appointment. He called the vice presidency "the most insignificant office" ever created. He was elected president in 1797. During his service to his country, John Adams's wife, Abigail, gave birth to a son, John Quincy. Abigail was not only a president's wife but became the mother of a future president.

★ **SHOW WHAT YOU KNOW**

Answer each of the following questions, then circle the answers in the word search.

Adams was George Washington's **vice** president.

Adams helped write the Treaty of **Paris**, which ended the Revolutionary War.

Adams's wife was named **Abigail**.

They had a **son** who was also elected president.

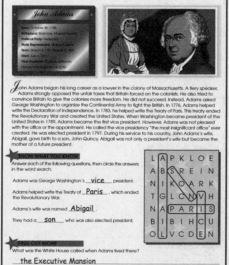

```
L  A  P  K  L  O  E
A  B  S  R  E  I  N
N  I  K  O  A  R  K
T  G  L  C  N  V  H
N  A  P  A  R  I  S
B  I  B  I  H  C  U
O  L  V  C  D  E  N
```

★ **FIND OUT MORE**

What was the White House called when Adams lived there?
the Executive Mansion

27

Thomas Jefferson

Born: April 13, 1743
Birthplace: Goochland, Virginia
Political Party: Democratic-Republican
State Represented: Virginia
Term: March 4, 1801–March 3, 1809
Died: July 4, 1826
Vice President: (1) Aaron Burr (DR) (2) George Clinton (DR)

Thomas Jefferson led the colonies' fight for freedom, but he was not a soldier. Jefferson was the main author of the two documents that helped form our nation—the Declaration of Independence and the Bill of Rights. Jefferson strongly believed that the states should have a strong role in the new government of the United States. The main political party of that time, the Federalists, disagreed. So Jefferson formed a new political party, the Democratic-Republicans. Before becoming president, Jefferson was the U.S. ambassador to France. As president, he bought the Louisiana Territory for $15 million, doubling the size of the United States. He then sent the explorers, Lewis and Clark, to explore this large unknown area. Jefferson was a politician, an educator, an architect, an inventor, a pioneer in scientific farming, a musician and a writer. Before and after becoming president, Jefferson contributed to the new nation in lasting ways.

★ **SHOW WHAT YOU KNOW**

Write the answer to each clue on the lines below.

Jefferson was the ambassador to **France**.

Jefferson sent **Lewis** and **Clark** to explore the unknown territory.

Jefferson helped write the Bill of **Rights**.

Jefferson called his home **Monticello**.

Jefferson had no interest in becoming a **soldier**.

★ **FIND OUT MORE**

What is the Louisiana Territory?
It's a vast area extending from the Mississippi River to the Rocky Mountains and from the Gulf of Mexico to the Canadian border.

28

© 2001 McGraw-Hill. All Rights Reserved.

Appendix

James Madison

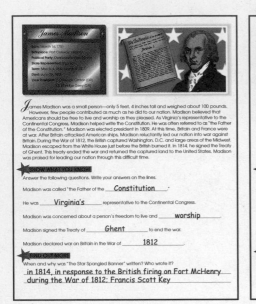

Born: March 16, 1751
Birthplace: Port Conway, Virginia
Political Party: Democratic-Republican
State Represented: Virginia
Term: March 4, 1809–March 4, 1817
Died: June 28, 1836
Vice President: George Clinton (D6)
Elbridge Gerry (D6)

James Madison was a small person—only 5 feet, 4 inches tall and weighed about 100 pounds. However, few people contributed as much as he did to our nation. Madison believed that Americans should be free to live and worship as they pleased. As Virginia's representative to the Continental Congress, Madison helped write the Constitution. He was often referred to as "the Father of the Constitution." Madison was elected president in 1809. At this time, Britain and France were at war. After Britain attacked American ships, Madison reluctantly led our nation into war against Britain. During the War of 1812, the British captured Washington, D.C. and large areas of the Midwest. Madison escaped from the White House just before the British burned it. In 1814, he signed the Treaty of Ghent. This treaty ended the war and returned the captured land to the United States. Madison was praised for leading our nation through this difficult time.

SHOW WHAT YOU KNOW

Answer the following questions. Write your answers on the lines.

Madison was called "the Father of the ___Constitution___."

He was ___Virginia's___ representative to the Continental Congress.

Madison was concerned about a person's freedom to live and ___worship___.

Madison signed the Treaty of ___Ghent___ to end the war.

Madison declared war on Britain in the War of ___1812___.

FIND OUT MORE

When and why was "The Star Spangled Banner" written? Who wrote it?

___in 1814, in response to the British firing on Fort McHenry during the War of 1812; Francis Scott Key___

29

James Monroe

Born: April 28, 1758
Birthplace: Westmoreland County, Virginia
Political Party: Democratic-Republican
State Represented: Virginia
Term: March 4, 1817–March 3, 1825
Died: July 4, 1831
Vice President: Daniel Tompkins (DR)

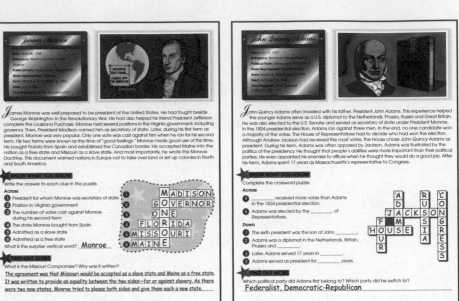

James Monroe was well prepared to be president of the United States. He had fought beside George Washington in the Revolutionary War. He had also helped his friend President Jefferson complete the Louisiana Purchase. Monroe held several positions in the Virginia government, including governor. Then, President Madison named him as secretary of state. Later, during his first term as president, Monroe was very popular. Only one vote was cast against him when he ran for his second term. His two terms were known as the time of "good feelings." Monroe made good use of this time. He bought Florida from Spain and established the Canadian border. He accepted Maine into the nation as a free state and Missouri as a slave state. And most importantly, he wrote the Monroe Doctrine. This document warned nations in Europe not to take over land or set up colonies in North and South America.

SHOW WHAT YOU KNOW

Write the answer to each clue in the puzzle.

Across
1. President for whom Monroe was secretary of state
2. Position in Virginia government
3. The number of votes cast against Monroe during his second term
4. The state Monroe bought from Spain
5. Admitted as a slave state
6. Admitted as a free state

What is the surprise vertical word? ___Monroe___

1. MADISON
2. GOVERNOR
3. ONE
4. FLORIDA
5. MISSOURI
6. MAINE

FIND OUT MORE

What is the Missouri Compromise? Why was it written?

___The agreement was that Missouri would be accepted as a slave state and Maine as a free state. It was written to provide an equality between the two sides—or against slavery. As there were two new states, Monroe tried to please both sides and give them each a new state.___

30

John Quincy Adams

Born: July 11, 1767
Birthplace: Braintree, Massachusetts
Political Party: Democratic-Republican
State Represented: Massachusetts
Term: March 4, 1825–March 4, 1829
Died: February 23, 1848
Vice President: John C. Calhoun (DR)

John Quincy Adams often traveled with his father, President John Adams. This experience helped the younger Adams serve as a U.S. diplomat to the Netherlands, Prussia, Russia and Great Britain. He was also elected to the U.S. Senate and served as secretary of state under President Monroe. In the 1824 presidential election, Adams ran against three men. In the end, no one candidate won a majority of the votes. The House of Representatives had to decide who had won the election. Although Andrew Jackson had received the most votes, the House chose John Quincy Adams as president. During his term, Adams was often opposed by Jackson. Adams was frustrated by the politics of the presidency. He thought that people's abilities were more important than their political parties. He even appointed his enemies to offices when he thought they would do a good job. After his term, Adams spent 17 years as Massachusetts's representative to Congress.

SHOW WHAT YOU KNOW

Complete the crossword puzzle.

Across
4. ___ received more votes than Adams in the 1824 presidential election.
6. Adams was elected by the ___ of Representatives.

Down
1. The sixth president was the son of John ___.
2. Adams was a diplomat in the Netherlands, Britain, Prussia and ___.
3. Later, Adams served 17 years in ___.
5. Adams served as president for ___ years.

FIND OUT MORE

Which political party did Adams first belong to? Which party did he switch to?

___Federalist, Democratic-Republican___

31

Andrew Jackson

Born: March 15, 1767
Birthplace: Waxhaw District, South Carolina
Political Party: Democratic
State Represented: Tennessee
Term: March 4, 1829–March 4, 1837
Died: June 8, 1845
Vice President: John C. Calhoun (D)
Martin Van Buren (D)

Andrew Jackson was a new kind of president. He was born to a poor mother in a log cabin on the South Carolina frontier. His father had already died. As a young man, Jackson fought in the Revolutionary War and later became a lawyer. He was elected to the U.S. House of Representatives and later became a senator for Tennessee. In the War of 1812, Jackson led an army that defeated the British in the Battle of New Orleans. Then, Jackson moved the Native American tribes—the Cherokee, Choctaw, Creek and Chickasaw—from their homes in the eastern United States to the area now called Oklahoma. He also fought the Seminole tribe in Florida. Jackson was elected president due to his reputation as an "Indian fighter." He was also known for upholding the rights of "ordinary Americans."

SHOW WHAT YOU KNOW

Find the letters that spell the four Native American groups that Jackson moved. Cross out the letters as you write the names below.

___Creek___
___Cherokee___
___Choctaw___
___Chickasaw___

Find the letters that spell the Native American group that Jackson did not move. Write their name on the line below.

___Seminoles___

FIND OUT MORE

In which state did the Cherokee live before Jackson moved them?

___Georgia___

32

Martin Van Buren

Born: December 5, 1782
Birthplace: Kinderhook, New York
Political Party: Democratic
State Represented: New York
Term: March 4, 1837–March 4, 1841
Died: July 24, 1862
Vice President: Richard Johnson (D)

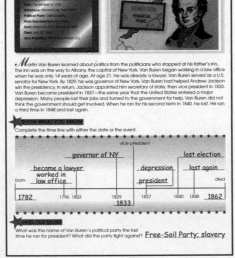

Martin Van Buren learned about politics from the politicians who stopped at his father's inn. The inn was on the way to Albany, the capital of New York. Van Buren began working in a law office when he was only 14 years of age. At age 21, he was already a lawyer. Van Buren served as a U.S. senator for New York. By 1829, he was governor of New York. Van Buren had helped Andrew Jackson win the presidency. In return, Jackson appointed him secretary of state, then vice president in 1833. Van Buren became president in 1837—the same year that the United States entered a major depression. Many people lost their jobs and turned to the government for help. Van Buren did not think the government should get involved. When he ran for his second term in 1840, he lost. He ran a third time in 1848 and lost again.

SHOW WHAT YOU KNOW

Complete the time line with either the date or the event.

vice president

governor of NY

lost election

became a lawyer
worked in
law office

depression

president

lost again

born   died

1782   1796   1803   1829   1837   1840   1848   1862
                                    1833

FIND OUT MORE

What was the name of Van Buren's political party the last time he ran for president? What did the party fight against? ___Free-Soil Party; slavery___

33

William H. Harrison

Born: February 9, 1773
Birthplace: Charles City County, Virginia
Political Party: Whig
State Represented: Ohio
Term: March 4, 1841–April 4, 1841
Died: April 4, 1841
Vice President: John Tyler (W)

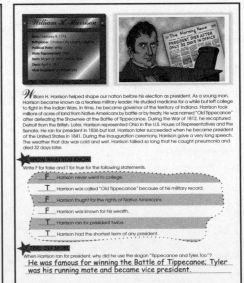

William H. Harrison helped shape our nation before his election as president. As a young man, Harrison became known as a fearless military leader. He studied medicine for a while but left college to fight in the Indian Wars. In time, he became governor of the territory of Indiana. Harrison took millions of acres of land from Native Americans by battle or by treaty. He was named "Old Tippecanoe" after defeating the Shawnee at the Battle of Tippecanoe. During the War of 1812, he recaptured Detroit from the British. Later, Harrison represented Ohio in the U.S. House of Representatives and the Senate. He ran for president in 1836 but lost. Harrison later succeeded when he became president of the United States in 1841. During the inauguration ceremony, Harrison gave a very long speech. The weather that day was cold and wet. Harrison talked so long that he caught pneumonia and died 32 days later.

SHOW WHAT YOU KNOW

Write F for false and T for true for the following statements.

___F___ Harrison never went to college.

___T___ Harrison was called "Old Tippecanoe" because of his military record.

___T___ Harrison fought for the rights of Native Americans.

___F___ Harrison was known for his wealth.

___T___ Harrison ran for president twice.

___T___ Harrison had the shortest term of any president.

FIND OUT MORE

When Harrison ran for president, why did he use the slogan "Tippecanoe and Tyler, Too"?

___He was famous for winning the Battle of Tippecanoe; Tyler was his running mate and became vice president.___

34

Appendix

320

© 2001 McGraw-Hill. All Rights Reserved.

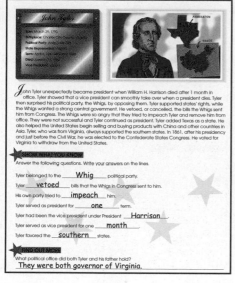

John Tyler

John Tyler unexpectedly became president when William H. Harrison died after 1 month in office. Tyler showed that a vice president can smoothly take over when a president dies. Tyler then surprised his political party, the Whigs, by opposing them. Tyler supported states' rights, while the Whigs wanted a strong central government. He vetoed, or cancelled, the bills the Whigs sent him from Congress. The Whigs were so angry that they tried to impeach Tyler and remove him from office. They were not successful and Tyler continued as president. Tyler added Texas as a state. He also helped the United States begin selling and buying products with China and other countries in Asia. Tyler, who was from Virginia, always supported the southern states. In 1861, after his presidency and just before the Civil War, he was elected to the Confederate States Congress. He voted for Virginia to withdraw from the United States.

SHOW WHAT YOU KNOW

Answer the following questions. Write your answers on the lines.

Tyler belonged to the **Whig** political party.

Tyler **vetoed** bills that the Whigs in Congress sent to him.

His own party tried to **impeach** him.

Tyler served as president for **one** term.

Tyler had been the vice president under President **Harrison**.

Tyler served as vice president for one **month**.

Tyler favored the **southern** states.

FIND OUT MORE

What political office did both Tyler and his father hold?
They were both governor of Virginia.

35

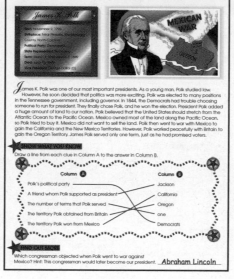

James K. Polk

James K. Polk was one of our most important presidents. As a young man, Polk studied law. However, he soon decided that politics was more exciting. Polk was elected to many positions in the Tennessee government, including governor. In 1844, the Democrats had trouble choosing someone to run for president. They finally chose Polk, and he won the election. President Polk added a huge amount of land to our nation. Polk believed that the United States should stretch from the Atlantic Ocean to the Pacific Ocean. Mexico owned most of the land along the Pacific Ocean, so Polk tried to buy it. Mexico did not want to sell the land. Polk then went to war with Mexico to gain the California and the New Mexico Territories. However, Polk worked peacefully with Britain to gain the Oregon Territory. James Polk served only one term, just as he had promised voters.

SHOW WHAT YOU KNOW

Draw a line from each clue in Column A to the answer in Column B.

Column A	Column B
Polk's political party	Jackson
A friend whom Polk supported as president	California
The number of terms that Polk served	Oregon
The territory Polk obtained from Britain	one
The territory Polk won from Mexico	Democrats

FIND OUT MORE

Which congressman objected when Polk went to war against Mexico? Hint: This congressman would later become our president. **Abraham Lincoln**

36

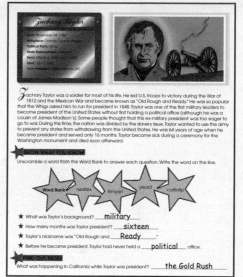

Zachary Taylor

Zachary Taylor was a soldier for most of his life. He led U.S. troops to victory during the War of 1812 and the Mexican War and became known as "Old Rough and Ready." He was so popular that the Whigs asked him to run for president in 1848. Taylor was one of the first military leaders to become president of the United States without first holding a public office (although he was a cousin of James Madison's). Some people thought that this ex-military president was too eager to go to war. During this time, the nation was divided by the slavery issue. Taylor wanted to use the army to prevent any states from withdrawing from the United States. He was 64 years of age when he became president and served only 16 months. Taylor became sick during a ceremony for the Washington monument and died soon afterward.

SHOW WHAT YOU KNOW

Unscramble a word from the Word Bank to answer each question. Write the word on the line.

Word Bank nestfex itimyari yearid catilolp

★ What was Taylor's background? **military**

★ How many months was Taylor president? **sixteen**

★ Taylor's nickname was "Old Rough and **Ready**."

★ Before he became president, Taylor had never held a **political** office.

FIND OUT MORE

What was happening in California while Taylor was president? **the Gold Rush**

37

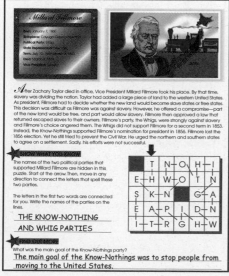

Millard Fillmore

After Zachary Taylor died in office, Vice President Millard Fillmore took his place. By that time, slavery was dividing the nation. Taylor had added a large piece of land to the western United States. As president, Fillmore had to decide whether the new land would become slave states or free states. This decision was difficult as Fillmore was against slavery. However, he offered a compromise—part of the new land would be free, and part would allow slavery. Fillmore then approved a law that returned escaped slaves to their owners. Fillmore's party, the Whigs, were strongly against slavery and Fillmore's choice angered them. The Whigs did not support Fillmore for a second term in 1853. Instead, the Know-Nothings supported Fillmore's nomination for president in 1856. Fillmore lost the 1856 election. Yet he still tried to prevent the Civil War. He urged the northern and southern states to agree on a settlement. Sadly, his efforts were not successful.

SHOW WHAT YOU KNOW

The names of the two political parties that supported Millard Fillmore are hidden in this puzzle. Start at the arrow. Then, move in any direction to connect the letters that spell these two parties.

The letters in the first two words are connected for you. Write the names of the parties on the lines.

T	N	O	H	I
E	H	W	O	T	N
S	K	N		G	A
I	A	P	I	D	N
I	T	R	G	H	W

THE KNOW-NOTHING
AND WHIG PARTIES

FIND OUT MORE

What was the main goal of the Know-Nothings party?
The main goal of the Know-Nothings was to stop people from
moving to the United States.

38

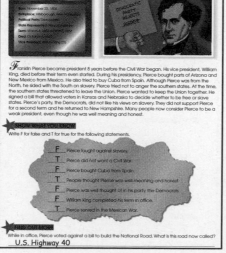

Franklin Pierce

Franklin Pierce became president 8 years before the Civil War began. His vice president, William King, died before their term even started. During his presidency, Pierce bought parts of Arizona and New Mexico from Mexico. He also tried to buy Cuba from Spain. Although Pierce was from the North, he sided with the South on slavery. Pierce tried not to anger the southern states. At the time, the southern states threatened to leave the Union. Pierce wanted to keep the Union together. He signed a bill that allowed voters in Kansas and Nebraska to decide whether to be free or slave states. Pierce's party, the Democrats, did not like his views on slavery. They did not support Pierce for a second term and he returned to New Hampshire. Many people now consider Pierce to be a weak president, even though he was well meaning and honest.

SHOW WHAT YOU KNOW

Write F for false and T for true for the following statements.

F Pierce fought against slavery.

T Pierce did not want a Civil War.

F Pierce bought Cuba from Spain.

T People thought Pierce was well meaning and honest.

F Pierce was well thought of in his party, the Democrats.

F William King completed his term in office.

T Pierce served in the Mexican War.

FIND OUT MORE

While in office, Pierce voted against a bill to build the National Road. What is this road now called?
U.S. Highway 40

39

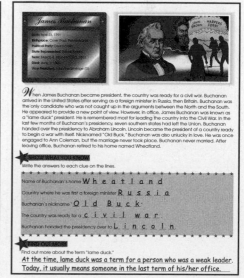

James Buchanan

When James Buchanan became president, the country was ready for a civil war. Buchanan arrived in the United States after serving as a foreign minister in Russia, then Britain. Buchanan was the only candidate who was not caught up in the arguments between the North and the South. He appeared to provide a new point of view. However, in office, James Buchanan was known as a "lame duck" president. He is remembered most for leading the country into the Civil War. In the last few months of Buchanan's presidency, seven southern states had left the Union. Buchanan handed over the presidency to Abraham Lincoln. Lincoln became the president of a country ready to begin a war with itself. Nicknamed "Old Buck," Buchanan was also unlucky in love. He was once engaged to Ann Coleman, but the marriage never took place. Buchanan never married. After leaving office, Buchanan retired to his home named Wheatland.

SHOW WHAT YOU KNOW

Write the answers to each clue on the lines.

Name of Buchanan's home **Wheatland**

Country where he was first a foreign minister **Russia**

Buchanan's nickname "**Old Buck**"

The country is ready for a **civil war**

Buchanan handed the presidency over to **Lincoln**

FIND OUT MORE

Find out more about the term "lame duck."
At the time, lame duck was a term for a person who was a weak leader.
Today, it usually means someone in the last term of his/her office.

40

© 2001 McGraw-Hill. All Rights Reserved.

Appendix

41

Abraham Lincoln

Born: February 12, 1809
Birthplace: Hardin County, Kentucky
Political Party: Republican
State Represented: Illinois
Term: March 4, 1861–April 15, 1865
Died: April 15, 1865
Vice President: (1) Hannibal Hamlin (1) (2) Andrew Johnson (1)

Abraham Lincoln is remembered as the greatest president of the United States. As a young man, Lincoln worked in many different jobs, including cutting wood and serving in the military. Even before he became president, Lincoln knew that the country must stay united to become a powerful nation. However, Lincoln's ideas were not shared and he was not a popular candidate. The South viewed Lincoln as an enemy who did not care about their issues. Despite these problems, Lincoln was elected president. Shortly after his inauguration in 1861, the Civil War began. Lincoln guided the country through the Civil War. His Gettysburg Address inspired the weary North to continue fighting for freedom. He also declared freedom for the slaves in the Emancipation Proclamation. Lincoln lived to see the end of the Civil War with General Robert E. Lee's surrender in 1865. However, Lincoln was assassinated 5 days later at a performance of *Our American Cousin* at Ford's Theatre in Washington, D.C.

SHOW WHAT YOU KNOW

Answer the following questions. Write your answers on the lines.

What are two jobs Lincoln held as a young man? **woodcutter and soldier**

Why was the Gettysburg Address important? **It inspired the weary North to continue fighting for freedom.**

When did the Civil War begin? **1861**

What is a famous statement of Lincoln's? What was it about? **"A house divided against itself cannot stand." He meant that the Civil War would hurt both sides (no matter who won).**

Who surrendered and ended the Civil War? **General Robert E. Lee**

FIND OUT MORE

How did people communicate with each other over long distances during Lincoln's time as president? **People communicated by telegraph and by mail or messenger.**

42

Andrew Johnson

Born: December 29, 1808
Birthplace: Raleigh, North Carolina
Political Party: Democratic
State Represented: Tennessee
Term: April 15, 1865–March 4, 1869
Died: July 31, 1875
Vice President: (none)

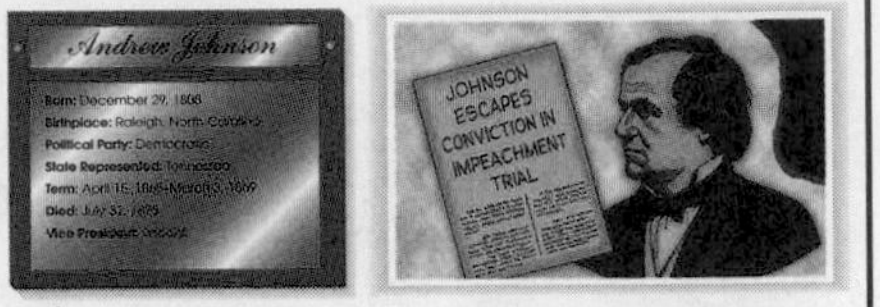

Andrew Johnson was born to a poor family in Raleigh, North Carolina in 1808. Johnson did not have a formal education. Instead, he became an apprentice tailor. His wife, Eliza, later taught him to read and write. As a young man, Johnson became interested in politics. Johnson supported the States' Rights position and believed that government should not interfere in people's private lives. His pro-South views helped balance Abraham Lincoln's pro-North views, and Johnson became Lincoln's vice president. After Lincoln's assassination in 1865, Johnson became president. He had a difficult time as president. Johnson struggled with Congress and fought against new laws that would protect the rights of ex-slaves. Johnson was later tried by Congress for "high crimes and misdemeanors," and was impeached. The Senate found him not guilty by only one vote. His main accomplishment was the purchase of Alaska, known as "Seward's Folly." Johnson returned to politics in 1874 to serve in the Senate.

SHOW WHAT YOU KNOW

Write F for false and T for true for the following statements.

F Johnson was impeached and convicted by one vote.
T Johnson was an apprentice tailor.
T Eliza taught Johnson to write.
T The purchase of Alaska was called "Seward's Folly."
T Johnson felt that the government should not interfere with people's private lives.
F Johnson served as president before Lincoln.
T Lincoln was Johnson's vice president.
F Secretary of State Stanton was fired by Johnson.

FIND OUT MORE

Why was Alaska's purchase called "Seward's Folly"? **The purchase was named after Secretary of State William Seward who arranged for the United States to buy what is now Alaska from Russia. The purchase was regarded as a folly because the land was thought to be worthless.**

43

Ulysses S. Grant

Born: April 27, 1822
Birthplace: Point Pleasant, Ohio
Political Party: Republican
State Represented: Illinois
Term: March 4, 1869–March 3, 1877
Died: July 23, 1885
Vice President: (1) Schuyler Colfax (1) (2) Henry Wilson (1)

Born Hiram Ulysses Grant, an error in his enrollment at West Point listed his name as Ulysses Simpson Grant. Grant liked the new name and he kept it. As a young man, Ulysses S. Grant thrived during his service in the Mexican War. After the war, Grant struggled to make a living, taking jobs as a farmer, real estate salesman and finally a clerk in his father's leathergoods store in Galena, Illinois. The Civil War brought a new opportunity for Grant, and he impressed President Lincoln with his courage and leadership. Grant was promoted to general in chief of all the federal armies. On April 9, 1865, General Robert E. Lee surrendered the Confederacy to Grant at the town called Appomattox Court House. Grant became known as the "Hero of Appomattox." After the Civil War, Grant served briefly as secretary of war. Grant's Civil War fame made him a popular choice for president. Off the battlefield, however, Grant was not the greatest leader. His presidency was known for corruption and scandal.

SHOW WHAT YOU KNOW

Write the answer to each clue on the lines below.

Grant's nickname **Hero of Appomattox**

Grant fought in this war before the Civil War **Mexican**

Grant went to this college **West Point**

Grant worked as a clerk in this town **Galena**

Grant's administration had corruption and **scandal**

FIND OUT MORE

What major event involving transportation happened during Grant's first year as president? **the completion of the Transcontinental Railroad**

44

Rutherford B. Hayes

Born: October 4, 1822
Birthplace: Delaware, Ohio
Political Party: Republican
State Represented: Ohio
Term: March 4, 1877–March 3, 1881
Died: January 17, 1893
Vice President: William Wheeler (1)

Rutherford B. Hayes set serious goals for himself when he was young. One of his goals was to "…acquire a character distinguished for energy (and) firmness…." He even once decided to stop laughing so he could be more serious. He did not stop laughing, but he did grow up to be a serious president who fought for voting rights for African-Americans and against fraud in government. Hayes was a "dark horse" nominee at the Republican Convention of 1876. No one expected him to be the candidate that year, but he was the only one acceptable to everyone. The election itself was very close—many people thought Samuel Tilden, his opponent, received more votes. In the end, Congress decided for Hayes. His most important accomplishment was ending Reconstruction— the period after the Civil War during which the southern states were reorganized and made part of the Union once again.

SHOW WHAT YOU KNOW

The motto by which Hayes lived is hidden in the puzzle to the right. Start in the box where the arrow is pointing. Move from left to right without jumping a letter. Write his motto on the lines below.

He serves his party best who serves his country best.

H	E	S	E	R	V	E	S
H	I	S	P	A	R	T	Y	B
E	S	T	W	H	O	S	E	R
V	E	S	H	I	S	C	O	U
N	T	R	Y	B	E	S	T

FIND OUT MORE

Explain the term "dark horse." **It is an unknown or surprise candidate.**

45

James A. Garfield

Born: November 19, 1831
Birthplace: Orange, Ohio
Political Party: Republican
State Represented: Ohio
Term: March 4, 1881–September 19, 1881
Died: September 19, 1881
Vice President: Chester A. Arthur (1)

James A. Garfield was the last president to be born in a log cabin. Despite growing up in a poor family, Garfield received an excellent education. He graduated from Williams College in 1856, then became principal of Hiram College. After 4 years at Hiram, Garfield said, "Teaching is not the work in which a man can live and grow." Garfield joined the Army and served bravely in the Civil War battles at Shiloh and Chickamauga. After the war, Garfield served nine terms in Congress. While running for president, Garfield was nicknamed a "dark horse" candidate. Once in office, bribery and political favors blackened Garfield's one year as president. On July 2, 1881, Garfield was shot by Charles J. Guiteau, a disappointed office seeker who had not been appointed to Garfield's cabinet. A bullet remained in Garfield's body, and he lived in great pain for 11 weeks before dying in Elberon, New Jersey.

SHOW WHAT YOU KNOW

Write F for false and T for true for the following statements.

F Garfield was born in a hospital.
T Garfield served nine terms in Congress.
T Garfield's reputation was blackened by bribes.
F Garfield did not serve in the Civil War.
T Garfield graduated from college.
T Garfield was from Ohio.
F Garfield died during his second term.

FIND OUT MORE

What might doctors use today to help find a bullet lodged in a person's body? **Doctors could use an x-ray machine to locate a bullet.**

46

Chester A. Arthur

Born: October 5, 1829
Birthplace: Fairfield, Vermont
Political Party: Republican
State Represented: New York
Term: September 20, 1881–March 3, 1885
Died: November 18, 1886
Vice President: (none)

Chester A. Arthur was a Civil War veteran and a defender of civil rights for slaves. He became president at a time when the public had lost respect for the office. Scandal and the "spoils system" had blackened the presidency of Garfield. The American public expected Arthur to follow Garfield's example and choose friends and political supporters for his cabinet members. As a Union College graduate and the son of a clergyman, Arthur brought values back to the presidency. Arthur acted honestly during his term as president. He passed the Pendleton Act, which helped to eliminate the corruption of political favors. Arthur was a private man who believed that the president's private life should be kept from the public. When his wife died, his sister took over the duties of the first lady. Arthur's main accomplishment was the modernization of the navy. He did not win the Republican Party's nomination for re-election in 1884.

SHOW WHAT YOU KNOW

Circle the hidden words in the puzzle using the clues below. Write the answers on the lines.

Name of act passed **Pendleton**

Wife's name **Ellen**

College name **Union**

Person who took over first lady's duties **sister**

Branch of the armed service he modernized **navy**

O	G	A	C	I	H	C	N	N
G	O	N	T	H	R	E	E	O
Y	T	R	H	A	U	N	D	T
E	L	L	E	N	A	V	Y	E
N	A	Y	T	H	E	D	L	
D	S	O	S	H	S	T	I	D
I	N	E	Y	A	V	I	K	N
K	C	O	C	N	A	H	S	E
E	V	I	T	I	G	U	F	P

FIND OUT MORE

How did Arthur modernize the navy? What does modernized mean? **He authorized the building of the first steel cruisers, or ships. Modernized means to update or adopt modern ways.**

© 2001 McGraw-Hill. All Rights Reserved.

Page 47 — Grover Cleveland

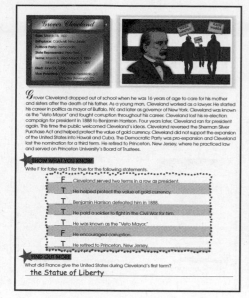

Grover Cleveland
Born: March 18, 1837
Birthplace: Caldwell, New Jersey
Political Party: Democratic
State Represented: New York
Terms: March 4, 1885–March 3, 1889; March 4, 1893–March 3, 1897
Died: June 24, 1908
Vice President: Thomas Hendricks (D); (1793) Adlai Stevenson (D)

Grover Cleveland dropped out of school when he was 16 years of age to care for his mother and sisters after the death of his father. As a young man, Cleveland worked as a lawyer. He started his career in politics as mayor of Buffalo, NY, and later as governor of New York. Cleveland was known as the "Veto Mayor" and fought corruption throughout his career. Cleveland lost his re-election campaign for president in 1888 to Benjamin Harrison. Four years later, Cleveland ran for president again. This time the public welcomed Cleveland's ideas. Cleveland reversed the Sherman Silver Purchase Act and helped protect the value of gold currency. Cleveland did not support the expansion of the United States into Hawaii and Cuba. The Democratic Party was pro-expansion and Cleveland lost the nomination for a third term. He retired to Princeton, New Jersey, where he practiced law and served on Princeton University's Board of Trustees.

SHOW WHAT YOU KNOW

Write F for false and T for true for the following statements.

F	Cleveland served two terms in a row as president.
T	He helped protect the value of gold currency.
T	Benjamin Harrison defeated him in 1888.
T	He paid a soldier to fight in the Civil War for him.
T	He was known as the "Veto Mayor."
F	He encouraged corruption.
T	He retired to Princeton, New Jersey.

FIND OUT MORE

What did France give the United States during Cleveland's first term?
the Statue of Liberty

47

Page 48 — Benjamin Harrison

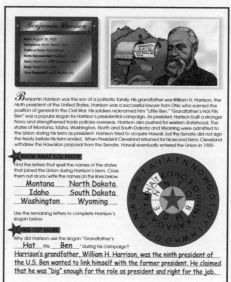

Benjamin Harrison
Born: August 20, 1833
Birthplace: North Bend, Ohio
Political Party: Republican
State Represented: Indiana
Term: March 4, 1889–March 3, 1893
Died: March 13, 1901
Vice President: Levi Morton (R)

Benjamin Harrison was the son of a patriotic family. His grandfather was William H. Harrison, the ninth president of the United States. Harrison was a successful lawyer from Ohio who earned the position of general in the Civil War. His soldiers nicknamed him "Little Ben." "Grandfather's Hat Fits Ben" was a popular slogan for Harrison's presidential campaign. As president, Harrison built a stronger Navy and strengthened trade policies overseas. Harrison also pushed for western statehood. The states of Montana, Idaho, Washington, North and South Dakota and Wyoming were admitted to the Union during his term as president. Harrison tried to acquire Hawaii, but the Senate did not sign the treaty before his term ended. When President Cleveland returned for his second term, Cleveland withdrew the Hawaiian proposal from the Senate. Hawaii eventually entered the Union in 1959.

SHOW WHAT YOU KNOW

Find the letters that spell the names of the states that joined the Union during Harrison's term. Cross them out as you write the names on the lines below.

Montana   North Dakota
Idaho   South Dakota
Washington   Wyoming

Use the remaining letters to complete Harrison's slogan below.

FIND OUT MORE

Why did Harrison use the slogan "Grandfather's
Hat Fits Ben " during his campaign?
Harrison's grandfather, William H. Harrison, was the ninth president of the U.S. Ben wanted to link himself with the former president. He claimed that he was "big" enough for the role as president and right for the job.

48

Page 49 — William McKinley

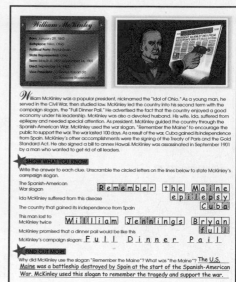

William McKinley
Born: January 29, 1843
Birthplace: Niles, Ohio
Political Party: Republican
State Represented: Ohio
Term: March 4, 1897–September 14, 1901
Died: September 14, 1901
Vice President: Garret Hobart (R); (1901) Theodore Roosevelt (R)

William McKinley was a popular president, nicknamed the "Idol of Ohio." As a young man, he served in the Civil War, then studied law. McKinley led the country into its second term with the campaign slogan, the "Full Dinner Pail." He advertised the fact that the country enjoyed a good economy under his leadership. McKinley was also a devoted husband. His wife, Ida, suffered from epilepsy and needed special attention. As president, McKinley guided the country through the Spanish-American War. McKinley used the war slogan, "Remember the Maine" to encourage the public to support the war. The war lasted 100 days. As a result of the war, Cuba gained its independence from Spain. McKinley's other accomplishments were the signing of the Treaty of Paris and the Gold Standard Act. He also signed a bill to annex Hawaii. McKinley was assassinated in September 1901 by a man who wanted to get rid of all leaders.

SHOW WHAT YOU KNOW

Write the answer to each clue. Unscramble the circled letters on the lines below to state McKinley's campaign slogan.

The Spanish-American
War slogan   Remember the Maine
Ida McKinley suffered from this disease   epilepsy
The country that gained its independence from Spain   Cuba
This man lost to
McKinley twice   William Jennings Bryan
McKinley promised that a dinner pail would be like this   full
McKinley's campaign slogan: Full Dinner Pail

FIND OUT MORE

Why did McKinley use the slogan "Remember the Maine"? What was "the Maine"? The U.S. Maine was a battleship destroyed by Spain at the start of the Spanish-American War. McKinley used this slogan to remember the tragedy and support the war.

49

Page 50 — Theodore Roosevelt

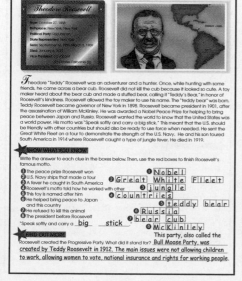

Theodore Roosevelt
Born: October 27, 1858
Birthplace: New York, New York
Political Party: Republican
State Represented: New York
Terms: September 14, 1901–March 3, 1909
Died: January 6, 1919
Vice President: Charles Fairbanks (R)

Theodore "Teddy" Roosevelt was an adventurer and a hunter. Once, while hunting with some friends, he came across a bear cub. Roosevelt did not kill the cub because it looked so cute. A toy maker heard about the bear cub and made a stuffed bear, calling it "Teddy's Bear." In honor of Roosevelt's kindness, Roosevelt allowed the toy maker to use his name. The "teddy bear" was born. Teddy Roosevelt became governor of New York in 1898. Roosevelt became president in 1901, after the assassination of William McKinley. He was awarded a Nobel Peace Prize for helping to bring peace between Japan and Russia. Roosevelt wanted the world to know that the United States was a world power. His motto was "Speak softly and carry a big stick." This meant that the U.S. should be friendly with other countries but should also be ready to use force when needed. He sent the Great White Fleet on a tour to demonstrate the strength of the U.S. Navy. He and his son toured South America in 1914 where Roosevelt caught a type of jungle fever. He died in 1919.

SHOW WHAT YOU KNOW

Write the answer to each clue in the boxes below. Then, use the red boxes to finish Roosevelt's famous motto.

1. The peace prize Roosevelt won — Nobel
2. U.S. Navy ships that made a tour — Great White Fleet
3. A fever he caught in South America — jungle
4. Roosevelt's motto told how he worked with other — countries
5. This toy is named after him — teddy bear
6. He helped bring peace to Japan and this country — Russia
7. He refused to kill this animal — bear cub
8. The president before Roosevelt — McKinley

"Speak softly and carry a _big_ _stick_."

FIND OUT MORE

Roosevelt created the Progressive Party. What did it stand for? Bull Moose Party, was created by Teddy Roosevelt in 1912. The main issues were not allowing children to work, allowing women to vote, national insurance and rights for working people.

50

Page 51 — William H. Taft

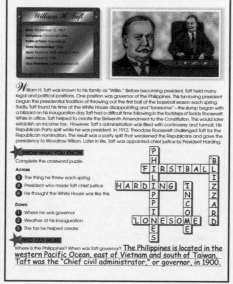

William H. Taft
Born: September 15, 1857
Birthplace: Cincinnati, Ohio
Political Party: Republican
State Represented: Ohio
Term: March 4, 1909–March 3, 1913
Died: March 8, 1930
Vice President: James Sherman (R)

William H. Taft was known to his family as "Willie." Before becoming president, Taft held many legal and political positions. One position was governor of the Philippines. This fun-loving president began the presidential tradition of throwing out the first ball of the baseball season each spring. Sadly, Taft found his time at the White House disappointing and "lonesome"—the slump began with a blizzard on his inauguration day. Taft had a difficult time following in the footsteps of Teddy Roosevelt. While in office, Taft helped to create the Sixteenth Amendment to the Constitution. This would later establish an income tax. However, Taft's administration was filled with controversy and turmoil. His Republican Party split while he was president. In 1912, Theodore Roosevelt challenged Taft for the Republican nomination. The result was a party split that weakened the Republicans and gave the presidency to Woodrow Wilson. Later in life, Taft was appointed chief justice by President Harding.

SHOW WHAT YOU KNOW

Complete the crossword puzzle.

Across
3. The thing he threw each spring
4. President who made Taft chief justice
6. He thought the White House was like this

Down
1. Where he was governor
2. Weather at his inauguration
5. The tax he helped create

(Crossword answers: FIRST BALL, HARDING, PHILIPPINES, BLIZZARD, INCOME, LONESOME)

FIND OUT MORE

Where is the Philippines? When was Taft governor? The Philippines is located in the western Pacific Ocean, east of Vietnam and south of Taiwan. Taft was the "Chief civil administrator," or governor, in 1900.

51

Page 52 — Woodrow Wilson

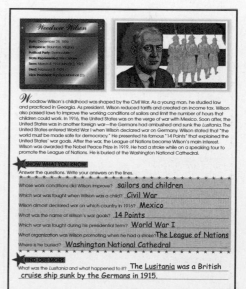

Woodrow Wilson
Born: December 28, 1856
Birthplace: Staunton, Virginia
Political Party: Democratic
State Represented: New Jersey
Term: March 4, 1913–March 3, 1921
Died: February 3, 1924
Vice President: Thomas Marshall (D)

Woodrow Wilson's childhood was shaped by the Civil War. As a young man, he studied law and practiced in Georgia. As president, Wilson reduced tariffs and created an income tax. Wilson also passed laws to improve the working conditions of sailors and limit the number of hours that children could work. In 1916, the United States was on the verge of war with Mexico. Soon after, the United States was in another foreign war—the Germans had ambushed and sunk the Lusitania. The United States entered World War I when Wilson declared war on Germany. Wilson stated that "the world must be made safe for democracy." He presented his famous "14 Points" that explained the United States' war goals. After the war, the League of Nations became Wilson's main interest. Wilson was awarded the Nobel Peace Prize in 1919. He had a stroke while on a speaking tour to promote the League of Nations. He is buried at the Washington National Cathedral.

SHOW WHAT YOU KNOW

Answer the questions. Write your answers on the lines.

Whose work conditions did Wilson improve? sailors and children
Which war was fought when Wilson was a child? Civil War
Wilson almost declared war on which country in 1916? Mexico
What was the name of Wilson's war goals? 14 Points
Which war was fought during his presidential term? World War I
What organization was Wilson promoting when he had a stroke? The League of Nations
Where is he buried? Washington National Cathedral

FIND OUT MORE

What was the Lusitania and what happened to it? The Lusitania was a British cruise ship sunk by the Germans in 1915.

52

© 2001 McGraw-Hill. All Rights Reserved.

Appendix

53

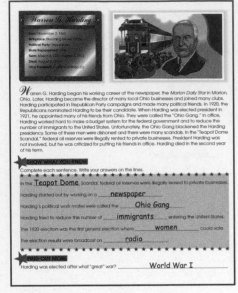

Warren G. Harding
Born: November 2, 1865
Birthplace: Blooming Grove, Ohio
Political Party: Republican
State Represented: Ohio
Term: March 4, 1921–August 2, 1923
Died: August 2, 1923
Vice President: Calvin Coolidge (R)

Warren G. Harding began his working career at the newspaper, the *Marion Daily Star* in Marion, Ohio. Later, Harding became the director of many local Ohio businesses and joined many clubs. Harding participated in Republican Party campaigns and made many political friends. In 1920, the Republicans nominated Harding to be their candidate. When Harding was elected president in 1921, he appointed many of his friends from Ohio. They were called the "Ohio Gang." In office, Harding worked hard to make a budget system for the federal government and to reduce the number of immigrants to the United States. Unfortunately, the Ohio Gang blackened the Harding presidency. Some of these men were dishonest and there were many scandals. In the "Teapot Dome Scandal," federal oil reserves were illegally rented to private businesses. President Harding was not involved, but he was criticized for putting his friends in office. Harding died in the second year of his term.

SHOW WHAT YOU KNOW
Complete each sentence. Write your answers on the lines.

In the **Teapot Dome** scandal, federal oil reserves were illegally leased to private businesses.

Harding started out by working on a **newspaper**.

Harding's political work mates were called the **Ohio Gang**.

Harding tried to reduce the number of **immigrants** entering the United States.

The 1920 election was the first general election where **women** could vote.

The election results were broadcast on **radio**.

FIND OUT MORE
Harding was elected after what "great" war? **World War I**

54

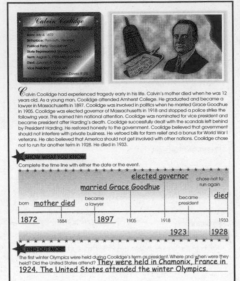

Calvin Coolidge
Born: July 4, 1872
Birthplace: Plymouth, Vermont
Political Party: Republican
State Represented: Massachusetts
Term: August 3, 1923–March 4, 1929
Died: January 5, 1933
Vice President: Charles Dawes (R)

Calvin Coolidge had experienced tragedy early in his life. Calvin's mother died when he was 12 years old. As a young man, Coolidge attended Amherst College. He graduated and became a lawyer in Massachusetts in 1897. Coolidge was involved in politics when he married Grace Goodhue in 1905. Coolidge was elected governor of Massachusetts in 1918 and stopped a police strike the following year. This earned him national attention. Coolidge was nominated for vice president and became president after Harding's death. Coolidge successfully dealt with the scandals left behind by President Harding. He restored honesty to the government. Coolidge believed that government should not interfere with private business. He vetoed bills for farm relief and a bonus for World War I veterans. He also believed that America should not get involved with other nations. Coolidge chose not to run for another term in 1928. He died in 1933.

SHOW WHAT YOU KNOW
Complete the time line with either the date or the event.

born	mother died	became a lawyer	married Grace Goodhue	elected governor	became president	chose not to run again	died
1872	1884	1897	1905	1918	1923	1928	1933

FIND OUT MORE
The first winter Olympics were held during Coolidge's term as president. Where and when were they held? Did the United States attend? **They were held in Chamonix, France in 1924. The United States attended the winter Olympics.**

55

Herbert C. Hoover
Born: August 10, 1874
Birthplace: West Branch, Iowa
Political Party: Republican
State Represented: California
Term: March 4, 1929–March 4, 1933
Died: October 20, 1964
Vice President: Charles Curtis (R)

Herbert C. Hoover was an orphan before he was 9 years old. Then, he was raised by several relatives. Hoover attended Stanford University and graduated as a mining engineer. After college, Hoover was known for his work as the head of the Allied Relief Program in Europe during World War I. Hoover then joined the political world and served under Presidents Wilson, Harding and Coolidge. In 1921, Hoover became secretary of commerce. In office, he worked to improve the standards of radio broadcasting, aviation, housing and highway safety. Hoover was elected president in 1929. Soon after his election, the stock market crashed. This caused the Great Depression. Many people lost their jobs. Some people became homeless. President Hoover felt that the government should not help the public. Instead, he believed that charities should help the poor. Under Hoover's leadership, the Depression got worse. Hoover lost the 1932 election by a landslide vote.

SHOW WHAT YOU KNOW
Answer the following questions, then circle the answers in the word search.

Where Hoover went to college **Stanford**

Hoover's wife's name (2 words) **Lou Henry**

The crash of the stock market caused this The Great **Depression**

Hoover was this by the age of nine **orphan**

Hoover felt that these groups should help the poor **charities**

```
D C H A R I T I E S D
I A M L B O N T L H I
L U K O R P H A N T V
N D A U B M E O C U I
Y F G H E R S P B D S
E J H E K F S C I O I
S T A N F O R D D E O
D E P R E S S I O N M
A Q R V I G J L P R S
```

FIND OUT MORE
What famous dam is named after President Hoover? Where is this dam located? **The Hoover Dam is located on the Colorado River between Nevada and Arizona.**

56

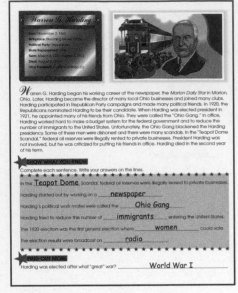

Franklin D. Roosevelt
Born: January 30, 1882
Birthplace: Hyde Park, New York
Political Party: Democratic
State Represented: New York
Term: March 4, 1933–April 12, 1945
Died: April 12, 1945
Vice President:
(1) John Garner (D) (2) Henry Wallace (D) (3) Harry Truman (D)

Franklin D. Roosevelt, or "FDR," was president during hard times. He was elected for four terms and became our longest serving president. In 1933, when Roosevelt first became president, the United States was suffering under the Great Depression. Many banks had failed, industries produced less than half of their normal production and more than 13 million people were out of work. FDR was determined to make things better. Roosevelt introduced a program called the "New Deal." It created work, built roads and provided electricity to rural areas. As time went on, the United States became involved in another great struggle—World War II. In 1941, the United States entered World War II and helped fight the Axis powers of Japan, Germany and Italy. Roosevelt led the United States during most of World War II. Roosevelt died while still in office in 1945.

SHOW WHAT YOU KNOW
A famous saying of FDR's is hidden in the puzzle. Start with the first box. Move from left to right. Write down every other letter. Then, start at the end and go backwards to the beginning. Write his saying on the lines below.

```
T F H L E E O S N T
L I Y R T A H E
I F N S G I W R
E A H E A F V O E T
```

THE ONLY THING WE HAVE TO FEAR IS FEAR ITSELF

FIND OUT MORE
Which twentieth-century president was Franklin D. Roosevelt's cousin? When was he president?
Theodore Roosevelt, 1901–1909

57

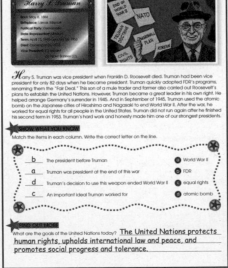

Harry S. Truman
Born: May 8, 1884
Birthplace: Lamar, Missouri
Political Party: Democratic
State Represented: Missouri
Term: April 12, 1945–January 20, 1953
Died: December 26, 1972
Vice President: (1) vacant (2) Alben Barkley (D)

Harry S. Truman was vice president when Franklin D. Roosevelt died. Truman had been vice president for only 82 days when he became president. Truman quickly adopted FDR's programs, renaming them the "Fair Deal." This son of a mule trader and farmer also carried out Roosevelt's plans to establish the United Nations. However, Truman became a great leader in his own right. He helped arrange Germany's surrender in 1945. And in September of 1945, Truman used the atomic bomb on the Japanese cities of Hiroshima and Nagasaki to end World War II. After the war, he worked for equal rights for all people in the United States. Truman did not run again after he finished his second term in 1953. Truman's hard work and honesty made him one of our strongest presidents.

SHOW WHAT YOU KNOW
Match the items in each column. Write the correct letter on the line.

b The president before Truman — World War II
a Truman was president at the end of this war — FDR
d Truman's decision to use this weapon ended World War II — equal rights
c An important ideal Truman worked for — atomic bomb

FIND OUT MORE
What are the goals of the United Nations today? **The United Nations protects human rights, upholds international law and peace, and promotes social progress and tolerance.**

58

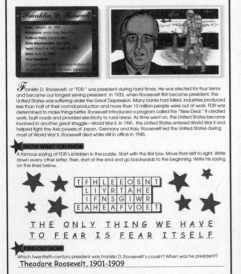

Dwight D. Eisenhower
Born: October 14, 1890
Birthplace: Denison, Texas
Political Party: Republican
State Represented: New York
Term: January 20, 1953–January 20, 1961
Died: March 28, 1969
Vice President: Richard Nixon (R)

As a young man, Dwight D. Eisenhower excelled in sports. Everyone called him "Ike." After high school, he attended the Military Academy at West Point. He fought in World War I and became a hero for helping to win World War II. When he ran for president in 1952, he used the slogan, "I like Ike." He won by more votes than anyone before him. As a soldier, he had fought to win a war. As president, he fought to keep the peace. In 1953, Eisenhower ended the Korean War. During Ike's term, Khrushchev, the leader of the Soviet Union, began to threaten world peace. This was the beginning of the Cold War, a time when countries fought with each other without firing shots or using deadly weapons. Ike had problems at home, too. Schools were being racially integrated, some for the first time. This meant that children of different races went to school together. Integration tried to promote unity. After his second term, Eisenhower retired to his farm in Pennsylvania.

SHOW WHAT YOU KNOW
Write the answer to each clue in the boxes. The circled letters spell out Eisenhower's first presidential slogan.

1. College Eisenhower attended — **West Point**
2. Eisenhower fought in this war — **World War II**
3. Wife's first name — **Mamie**
4. Name of Soviet leader — **Khrushchev**
5. Policy that tried to promote unity between people — **Integration**
6. Eisenhower ended America's conflict with this country — **Korea**

Eisenhower's first presidential slogan: **I Like Ike**

FIND OUT MORE
The "Space Race" was part of the Cold War with the Soviet Union. Find two interesting facts about our race into space with the Soviet Union. **Answers will vary. The Soviets were the first to put a satellite into space. The Americans were the first to put people on the Moon.**

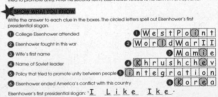

© 2001 McGraw-Hill. All Rights Reserved.

John F. Kennedy

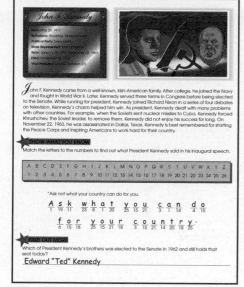

Born: May 29, 1917
Birthplace: Brookline, Massachusetts
Political Party: Democrat
State Represented: Massachusetts
Term: January 20, 1961–November 22, 1963
Died: November 22, 1963
Vice President: Lyndon B. Johnson (D)

John F. Kennedy came from a well-known, Irish-American family. After college, he joined the Navy and fought in World War II. Later, Kennedy served three terms in Congress before being elected to the Senate. While running for president, Kennedy joined Richard Nixon in a series of four debates on television. Kennedy's charm helped him win. As president, Kennedy dealt with many problems with other countries. For example, when the Soviets sent nuclear missiles to Cuba, Kennedy forced Khrushchev, the Soviet leader, to remove them. Kennedy did not enjoy his success for long. On November 22, 1963, he was assassinated in Dallas, Texas. Kennedy is best remembered for starting the Peace Corps and inspiring Americans to work hard for their country.

SHOW WHAT YOU KNOW

Match the letters to the numbers to find out what President Kennedy said in his inaugural speech.

A B C D E F G H I J K L M N O P Q R S T U V W X Y Z
1 2 3 4 5 6 7 8 9 10 11 12 13 14 15 16 17 18 19 20 21 22 23 24 25 26

"Ask not what your country can do for you.

A s k   w h a t   y o u   c a n   d o
1 19 11 23 8 1 20 25 15 21 3 1 14 4 15

f o r   y o u r   c o u n t r y .
6 15 18 25 15 21 18 3 15 21 14 20 18 25

FIND OUT MORE

Which of President Kennedy's brothers was elected to the Senate in 1962 and still holds that seat today?
Edward "Ted" Kennedy

59

Lyndon B. Johnson

Born: August 27, 1908
Birthplace: Stonewall, Texas
Political Party: Democrat
State Represented: Texas
Term: November 22, 1963–January 20, 1969
Died: January 22, 1973
Vice President: Hubert H. Humphrey (D)

Lyndon B. Johnson grew up in a three-room house in southwest Texas. As a young man, Johnson became interested in politics and went to work in Washington, D.C. Later, Johnson served as a member of both the House of Representatives and in the Senate for a total of 24 years. President Kennedy chose Johnson to be his running mate and he became vice president in 1961. Two years into his term as vice president, Johnson was sworn into office aboard the presidential jet, Air Force One, after Kennedy's assassination. Johnson tried to unite the nation after Kennedy's death. He passed Kennedy's bills on civil rights, poverty and conservation. Johnson then created a program called the "Great Society." The Great Society promoted equal rights for all, helped African-Americans with their right to vote and provided health insurance for the elderly. However, because of the turmoil of the Vietnam War, Johnson decided not to run for re-election in 1968. He retired to his ranch in Texas.

SHOW WHAT YOU KNOW

Complete each sentence. Write your answers on the lines.

Johnson's program was called the   Great Society
He worked in Washington, D.C. before becoming a member of the House of Representatives.
Johnson was Kennedy's   vice president
Johnson helped get   equal   rights for all.
The   Vietnam   War put the country in turmoil.

FIND OUT MORE

Robert Weaver became the first African-American to join a president's cabinet. What position did he hold? Robert Weaver became the head of a newly created Department of Housing and Urban Development.

60

Richard M. Nixon

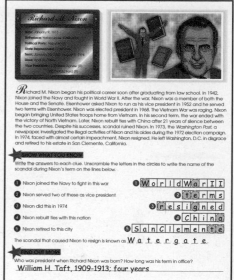

Born: January 9, 1913
Birthplace: Yorba Linda, California
Political Party: Republican
State Represented: California
Term: January 20, 1969–August 9, 1974
Died: April 22, 1994
Vice President: Spiro T. Agnew (R); Gerald R. Ford (R)

Richard M. Nixon began his political career soon after graduating from law school. In 1942, Nixon joined the Navy and fought in World War II. After the war, Nixon was a member of both the House and the Senate. Eisenhower asked Nixon to run as his vice president in 1952 and he served two terms with Eisenhower. Nixon was elected president in 1968. The Vietnam War was raging. Nixon began bringing United States troops home from Vietnam. In his second term, the war ended with the victory of North Vietnam. Later, Nixon rebuilt ties with China after 21 years of silence between the two countries. Despite his successes, scandal ruined Nixon. In 1973, the Washington Post, a newspaper, investigated the illegal activities of Nixon and his aides during the 1972 election campaign. In 1974, faced with almost certain impeachment, Nixon resigned. He left Washington, D.C. in disgrace and retired to his estate in San Clemente, California.

SHOW WHAT YOU KNOW

Write the answers to each clue. Unscramble the letters in the circles to write the name of the scandal during Nixon's term on the lines below.

1. Nixon joined the Navy to fight in this war   ① W o r l d W a r I I
2. Nixon served two of these as vice president   ② t e r m s
3. Nixon did this in 1974   ③ r e s i g n e d
4. Nixon rebuilt ties with this nation   ④ C h i n a
5. Nixon retired to this city   ⑤ S a n C l e m e n t e

The scandal that caused Nixon to resign is known as W a t e r g a t e

FIND OUT MORE

Who was president when Richard Nixon was born? How long was his term in office?
William H. Taft, 1909–1913; four years

61

Gerald Ford

Born: July 14, 1913
Birthplace: Omaha, Nebraska
Political Party: Republican
State Represented: Michigan
Term: August 9, 1974–January 20, 1977
Died:
Vice President: Nelson A. Rockefeller (R)

Young Gerald Ford was a good student. He studied hard and played football in high school and college. Ford then earned his law degree and joined the Navy during World War II. After the war, he ran for a seat in Congress and won. In 1973, after the resignation of Vice President Spiro T. Agnew, President Nixon asked Ford to be the new vice president. Ford became president in 1974 when Nixon resigned. Ford was the first vice president and president to take office without having been elected. As president, Ford gave Nixon a pardon "for all offenses against the United States." This act made him unpopular with many people. Ford, who was a Republican, had many differences with the Democratic-controlled Congress. He vetoed over 50 bills. Despite Ford's friendly manner and strong efforts to pull the nation together, he lost his bid for a second term in 1976.

SHOW WHAT YOU KNOW

Write the answer to each clue. The circled letters spell two important words.

1. Gerald Ford was this kind of student   ① g o o d
2. After college, he earned his law   ② d e g r e e
3. He joined this branch of the armed forces   ③ n a v y
4. Ford became vice president even though he wasn't this   ④ e l e c t e d
5. He played this in high school and college   ⑤ f o o t b a l l
6. He gave this to Nixon   ⑥ p a r d o n

Write the two words here: G e r a l d   F o r d

FIND OUT MORE

The Bicentennial was celebrated during Ford's term as president. What is a bicentennial? When was it celebrated in the United States? The celebration of the nation's 200th birthday. It was celebrated in 1976.

62

James E. Carter, Jr.

Born: October 1, 1924
Birthplace: Plains, Georgia
Political Party: Democrat
State Represented: Georgia
Term: January 20, 1977–January 20, 1981
Died:
Vice President: Walter F. Mondale (D)

James Earl Carter, Jr., better known as "Jimmy," is the son of a Georgia peanut farmer. He went to the U.S. Naval Academy at Annapolis and graduated in 1946. After serving in the Navy for 7 years, Carter resigned to run the family business. As a young man, Carter was active in defending civil rights. In 1962, he was elected state senator and later governor of Georgia. Carter ran for president in 1976. He presented himself as a man of the people and won the election. As president, Carter improved our ties with China and helped to write a peace treaty between Egypt and Israel. However, his success was to change. The economy was bad. In 1979, a group of Iranian students took the U.S. embassy staff hostage. Carter tried to get the hostages released, but he was unsuccessful. The public saw this as a weakness and Carter became very unpopular. Carter was defeated in the 1980 election. After his term as president, Carter was an unofficial diplomat to Nicaragua, Ethiopia, North Korea, Haiti and Serbia.

SHOW WHAT YOU KNOW

Answer the questions. Write your answers on the lines.

What was the family business? peanut farming

What two government posts did Carter hold in Georgia? state senator and governor

Between which two countries did Carter make peace while president? Egypt and Israel

Students in which country kidnapped the U.S. embassy staff? Iran

In which countries did Carter work as an unofficial diplomat? Nicaragua, Ethiopia, North Korea, Haiti and Serbia

FIND OUT MORE

How long did the Iran hostage crisis last? When were the hostages freed? It lasted 444 days, over 1 year. The hostages were freed in 1981.

63

Ronald Reagan

Born: February 6, 1911
Birthplace: Tampico, Illinois
Political Party: Republican
State Represented: California
Term: January 20, 1981–January 20, 1989
Died:
Vice President: George H.W. Bush (R)

Ronald Reagan went to school in Illinois where he studied economics and sociology. After college, he was a sportscaster in Chicago before beginning a long career as an actor. Reagan later became active in politics as a Democrat in 1948, but he became a Republican in 1962. His first public office was governor of California in 1966. In 1980, at the age of 69, Reagan won the Republican nomination for president. He promoted traditional American values and won a landslide victory over Jimmy Carter. Reagan then set out to strengthen military defense, stop inflation and improve business growth. During his second term, terrorism rose worldwide. In 1986, it was discovered that the Reagan administration had shipped guns to Iran in an effort to get American hostages released. Reagan was criticized from around the world. Reagan finished his second term in poor health.

SHOW WHAT YOU KNOW

Write the answer to each clue. The circled letters spell the name of a famous comet seen during Reagan's term.

1. Reagan was a sportscaster in this city   ① C h i c a g o
2. Besides politics, Reagan had a long career as this   ② a c t o r
3. He went to school in this state   ③ I l l i n o i s
4. Reagan studied this subject related to how people behave   ④ s o c i o l o g y
5. Reagan became this in 1962   ⑤ R e p u b l i c a n
6. When first inaugurated, he was this age   ⑥ s i x t y n i n e
7. He also studied this subject   ⑦ e c o n o m i c s

The name of the comet seen in 1986 is H a l l e y s.

FIND OUT MORE

In 1994, Reagan wrote a letter to the American people telling them about his ill health. What did the letter say? That Reagan had Alzheimer's disease which affects memory.

64

© 2001 McGraw-Hill. All Rights Reserved.

Appendix

George Bush

Born: June 12, 1924
Birthplace: Milton, Massachusetts
Political Party: Republican
State Represented: Texas
Term: January 20, 1989–January 20, 1993
Died:
Vice President: Dan Quayle (R)

George H. W. Bush was born into a successful New England family. Before finishing his degree in economics at Yale University, Bush spent over 2 years as a Navy pilot during World War II. After the war, Bush was awarded the Distinguished Flying Cross for his bravery. Bush began his political career when he represented Texas in the House of Representatives in 1966. Bush then served as the ambassador to the United Nations and head of the Central Intelligence Agency (CIA). In 1980, Bush became vice president under Reagan. Bush was later elected president in 1988. President Bush quickly made his mark upon the office. In 1989, Bush ordered an invasion of Panama to remove the country's leader, General Manuel Noriega. In 1990, Iraq invaded Kuwait. President Bush led the worldwide forces against Iraq in the Persian Gulf War. Bush earned much praise for his leadership during the Persian Gulf War.

SHOW WHAT YOU KNOW

Answer the questions. Write your answers on the lines.

What did Bush do during World War II? He was a Navy pilot.

What college did Bush attend? Yale

What award did Bush receive for his World War II service? Distinguished Flying Cross

When did Bush first enter politics? Where? 1966; he represented Texas in the House of Representatives.

Which country did Bush invade? Panama

What was the war in 1990 called? Persian Gulf War

FIND OUT MORE

The Bush family has a long political history. George Bush's father, Prescott S. Bush, was a United States senator from Connecticut. Find out two interesting facts about George Bush's son, George W. Bush. Answers will vary. George W. Bush was the governor of Texas; he was part owner of the Texas Rangers baseball team; he became President of the United States.

65

William Clinton

Born: August 19, 1946
Birthplace: Hope, Arkansas
Political Party: Democratic
State Represented: Arkansas
Term: January 20, 1993–January 20, 2001
Died:
Vice President: Al Gore (D)

William Clinton grew up in Arkansas. A well-educated young man, Clinton graduated from Georgetown University and Yale Law School. He also spent 2 years studying in England on a Rhodes scholarship. Clinton returned to Arkansas to become attorney general, then governor. Later, Clinton won the Democratic nomination in 1992 and was elected president. As president, Clinton successfully reduced the national debt and promoted trade between the United States, Canada and Mexico. In foreign policy, Clinton was successful in restoring the presidency of Haiti's Jean-Bertrand Aristide after he was forcefully removed from office. Clinton also sent peace keeping forces to the war-torn areas of Bosnia and Herzegovina. In 1999, Clinton supported NATO forces to end the Serbian occupation of Kosovo, Yugoslavia. Clinton was re-elected in 1996. During his second term, Clinton became involved in a scandal over court testimony and was impeached by the House of Representatives. Clinton was acquitted of the charges by the U.S. Senate.

SHOW WHAT YOU KNOW

Answer the questions. Write your answers on the lines.

Clinton was governor of which state? Arkansas

Which president inspired Clinton as a young man? President Kennedy

Where did Clinton attend university? Georgetown University, Yale Law School and Oxford

Clinton sent peace keeping forces to which areas? Bosnia and Herzegovina

What musical instrument does Clinton play? saxophone

How many other presidents have been impeached? one

FIND OUT MORE

What is a Rhodes scholarship? A Rhodes scholarship is an award that allows a student to attend the University of Oxford, England, for 2 to 3 years. It was created to promote unity among English-speaking nations.

66

George W. Bush

Born: July 6, 1946
Birthplace: New Haven, Connecticut
Political Party: Republican
State Represented: Texas
Term: January 20, 2001–
Died:
Vice President: Richard B. Cheney (R)

George Walker Bush was named after his father, the 41st President, George Herbert Walker Bush. George Walker grew up in Midland, Texas, graduated from Yale University in 1968, and served as a pilot in the Texas Air National Guard. After receiving a degree from Harvard Business School in 1975, he began working in the oil business. In the late 1980's, Bush helped manage his father's presidential campaign, and later became the managing general partner of the Texas Rangers baseball team. Elected governor of Texas in 1994 and reelected in 1998, Bush was the first Texas governor to be elected to consecutive four-year terms. While governor, he decided to run for president. The 2000 presidential election was one of the closest in U.S. history. Bush received a smaller number of popular votes than Democrat Al Gore, but won more votes in the Electoral College. The outcome of the election was in doubt until five weeks later, when a decision by the U.S. Supreme Court ended vote recounts in Florida, and Bush became the 43rd president. A "compassionate conservative," Bush's platform included limiting government, cutting taxes, and improving education.

SHOW WHAT YOU KNOW

Answer the questions. Write your answers on the lines.

What college did Bush attend? Yale University

What did he do in the Texas Air National Guard? served as a pilot

Bush was governor of what state? Texas

Bush was managing general partner of what baseball team? the Texas Rangers

Who won the most popular votes in the 2000 presidential election? Al Gore

FIND OUT MORE

Bush's election was the fourth in U.S. history in which the winner received fewer popular votes than his opponent. Who were the other three? John Quincy Adams in 1824, Rutherford B. Hayes in 1876, and Benjamin Harrison in 1888

67

Famous First Ladies

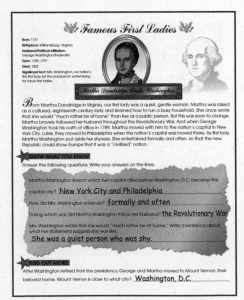

Born: 1731
Birthplace: Williamsburg, Virginia
Husband/Political Affiliation: George Washington/Federalist
Term: 1789–1797
Died: 1802
Significant fact: Mrs. Washington, our nation's first first lady, set the standard in entertaining for future first ladies.

Martha Dandridge Custis Washington

Born Martha Dandridge in Virginia, our first lady was a quiet, gentle woman. Martha was raised as a cultured, eighteenth century lady and learned how to run a busy household. She once wrote that she would "much rather be at home" than live as a public person. But this was soon to change. Martha bravely followed her husband throughout the Revolutionary War. And when George Washington took his oath of office in 1789, Martha moved with him to the nation's capital in New York City. Later, they moved to Philadelphia when the nation's capital was moved there. As first lady, Martha Washington put aside her shyness. She entertained formally and often, so that the new Republic could show Europe that it was a "civilized" nation.

SHOW WHAT YOU KNOW

Answer the following questions. Write your answers on the lines.

Martha Washington lived in which two capital cities before Washington, D.C. became the capital city? New York City and Philadelphia

How did Mrs. Washington entertain? formally and often

During which war did Martha Washington follow her husband? the Revolutionary War

Mrs. Washington wrote that she would "much rather be at home." Write a sentence about what her statement suggests she was like.
She was a quiet person who was shy.

FIND OUT MORE

After Washington retired from the presidency, George and Martha moved to Mount Vernon, their beloved home. Mount Vernon is close to what city? Washington, D.C.

68

Famous First Ladies

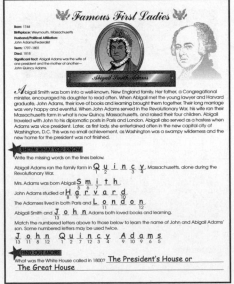

Born: 1744
Birthplace: Weymouth, Massachusetts
Husband/Political Affiliation: John Adams/Federalist
Term: 1797–1801
Died: 1818
Significant fact: Abigail Adams was the wife of one president and the mother of another—John Quincy Adams.

Abigail Smith Adams

Abigail Smith was born into a well-known, New England family. Her father, a Congregational minister, encouraged his daughter to read often. When Abigail met the young lawyer and Harvard graduate, John Adams, their love of books and learning brought them together. Their long marriage was very happy and eventful. When John Adams served in the Revolutionary War, his wife ran their Massachusetts farm in what is now Quincy, Massachusetts, and raised their four children. Abigail traveled with John to his diplomatic posts in Paris and London. Abigail also served as a hostess when Adams was vice president. Later, as first lady, she entertained often in the new capital city of Washington, D.C. This was no small achievement, as Washington was a swampy wilderness and the new home for the president was not finished.

SHOW WHAT YOU KNOW

Write the missing words on the lines below.

Abigail Adams ran the family farm in Q(1) u(2) i n c(3) y(4), Massachusetts, alone during the Revolutionary War.

Mrs. Adams was born Abigail S(5) m(6) i(7) t h.

John Adams studied at H(8) a(9) r v a r d(10).

The Adamses lived in both Paris and L o(11) n d o n(12).

Abigail Smith and J(13) o h n Adams both loved books and learning.

Match the numbered letters above to those below to learn the name of John and Abigail Adams' son. Some numbered letters may be used twice.

J(13) o(11) h(8) n(12) Q(1) u(2) i(7) n(12) c(3) y(4) A(9) d(10) a(9) m(6) s(5)

FIND OUT MORE

What was the White House called in 1800? The President's House or The Great House

69

Famous First Ladies

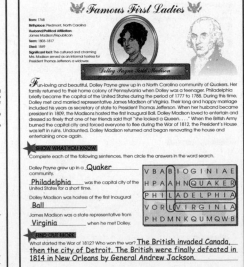

Born: 1768
Birthplace: Piedmont, North Carolina
Husband/Political Affiliation: James Madison/Republican
Term: 1809–1817
Died: 1849
Significant fact: The cultured and charming Mrs. Madison served as an informal hostess for President Thomas Jefferson, a widower.

Dolley Payne Todd Madison

Fun-loving and beautiful, Dolley Payne grew up in a North Carolina community of Quakers. Her family returned to their home colony of Pennsylvania when Dolley was a teenager. Philadelphia briefly became the capital of the United States during the period of 1777 to 1788. During this time, Dolley met and married representative James Madison of Virginia. Their long and happy marriage included his years as secretary of state to President Thomas Jefferson. When her husband became president in 1809, the Madisons hosted the first Inaugural Ball. Dolley Madison loved to entertain and dressed so finely that one of her friends said that "she looked a Queen. . . ." When the British Army burned the capital city and forced everyone to flee during the War of 1812, the President's House was left in ruins. Undaunted, Dolley Madison returned and began renovating the house and entertaining once again.

SHOW WHAT YOU KNOW

Complete each of the following sentences, then circle the answers in the word search.

Dolley Payne grew up in a Quaker community.

Philadelphia was the capital city of the United States for a short time.

Dolley Madison was hostess of the first Inaugural Ball.

James Madison was a state representative from Virginia when he met Dolley.

V	B	A	B	I	O	G	I	N	I	A	E
H	P	A	A	H	N	Q	U	A	K	E	R
P	H	I	L	A	D	E	L	P	H	I	A
V	O	R	L	V	I	R	G	I	N	I	A
P	H	D	M	N	K	Q	U	M	Q	W	B

FIND OUT MORE

What started the War of 1812? Who won the war? The British invaded Canada, then the city of Detroit. The British were finally defeated in 1814 in New Orleans by General Andrew Jackson.

70

© 2001 McGraw-Hill. All Rights Reserved.

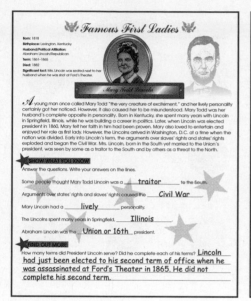

Famous First Ladies

Born: 1818
Birthplace: Lexington, Kentucky
Husband/Political Affiliation: Abraham Lincoln/Republican
Term: 1861–1865
Died: 1882
Significant fact: Mrs. Lincoln was seated next to her husband when he was shot at Ford's Theater.

Mary Todd Lincoln

A young man once called Mary Todd "the very creature of excitement," and her lively personality certainly got her noticed. However, it also caused her to be misunderstood. Mary Todd was her husband's complete opposite in personality. Born in Kentucky, she spent many years with Lincoln in Springfield, Illinois, while he was building a career in politics. Later, when Lincoln was elected president in 1860, Mary felt her faith in him had been proven. Mary also loved to entertain and enjoyed her role as first lady. However, the Lincolns arrived in Washington, D.C. at a time when the nation was divided. Early into Lincoln's term, the arguments over slaves' rights and states' rights exploded and began the Civil War. Mrs. Lincoln, born in the South yet married to the Union's president, was seen by some as a traitor to the South and by others as a threat to the North.

SHOW WHAT YOU KNOW
Answer the questions. Write your answers on the lines.

Some people thought Mary Todd Lincoln was a ___traitor___ to the South.

Arguments over states' rights and slaves' rights caused the ___Civil War___.

Mary Lincoln had a ___lively___ personality.

The Lincolns spent many years in Springfield, ___Illinois___.

Abraham Lincoln was the ___Union or 16th___ president.

FIND OUT MORE
How many terms did President Lincoln serve? Did he complete each of his terms? ___Lincoln had just been elected to his second term of office when he was assassinated at Ford's Theater in 1865. He did not complete his second term.___

71

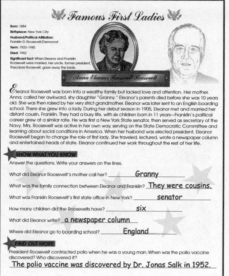

Famous First Ladies

Born: 1884
Birthplace: New York City
Husband/Political Affiliation: Franklin D. Roosevelt/Democrat
Term: 1933–1945
Died: 1962
Significant fact: When Eleanor and Franklin Roosevelt were married, her uncle, former president Theodore Roosevelt, gave away the bride.

Anna Eleanor Roosevelt Roosevelt

Eleanor Roosevelt was born into a wealthy family but lacked love and attention. Her mother, Anna, called her awkward, shy daughter "Granny." Eleanor's parents died before she was 10 years old. She was then raised by her very strict grandmother. Eleanor was later sent to an English boarding school. There she grew into a lady. During her debut season in 1905, Eleanor met and married her distant cousin, Franklin. They had a busy life, with six children born in 11 years—Franklin's political career grew at a similar rate. He was first a New York State senator, then served as secretary of the Navy. Mrs. Roosevelt was active in her own way, serving on the State Democratic Committee and learning about social conditions in America. When her husband was elected president, Eleanor Roosevelt began to change the role of first lady. She traveled, lectured, wrote a newspaper column and entertained heads of state. Eleanor continued her work throughout the rest of her life.

SHOW WHAT YOU KNOW
Answer the questions. Write your answers on the lines.

What did Eleanor Roosevelt's mother call her? ___Granny___

What was the family connection between Eleanor and Franklin? ___They were cousins.___

What was Franklin Roosevelt's first state office in New York? ___senator___

How many children did the Roosevelts have? ___six___

What did Eleanor write? ___a newspaper column___

Where did Eleanor go to boarding school? ___England___

FIND OUT MORE
President Roosevelt contracted polio when he was a young man. When was the polio vaccine discovered? Who discovered it? ___The polio vaccine was discovered by Dr. Jonas Salk in 1952.___

72

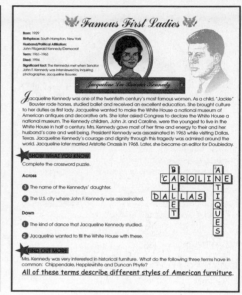

Famous First Ladies

Born: 1929
Birthplace: South Hampton, New York
Husband/Political Affiliation: John Fitzgerald Kennedy/Democrat
Term: 1961–1963
Died: 1994
Significant fact: The Kennedys met when Senator John F. Kennedy was interviewed by inquiring photographers, Jacqueline Bouvier.

Jacqueline Lee Bouvier Kennedy

Jacqueline Kennedy was one of the twentieth century's most famous women. As a child, "Jackie" Bouvier rode horses, studied ballet and received an excellent education. She brought culture to her duties as first lady. Jacqueline wanted to make the White House a national museum of American antiques and decorative arts. She later asked Congress to declare the White House a national museum. The Kennedy children, John Jr. and Caroline, were the youngest to live in the White House in half a century. Mrs. Kennedy gave most of her time and energy to their and her husband's care and well being. President Kennedy was assassinated in 1963 while visiting Dallas, Texas. Jacqueline Kennedy's courage and dignity through this tragedy was admired around the world. Jacqueline later married Aristotle Onassis in 1968. Later, she became an editor for Doubleday.

SHOW WHAT YOU KNOW
Complete the crossword puzzle.

Across
3 The name of the Kennedys' daughter.
4 The U.S. city where John F. Kennedy was assassinated.

Down
1 The kind of dance that Jacqueline Kennedy studied.
2 Jacqueline wanted to fill the White House with these.

(Crossword answers: CAROLINE, DALLAS, BALLET, ANTIQUES)

FIND OUT MORE
Mrs. Kennedy was very interested in historical furniture. What do the following three terms have in common: Chippendale, Hepplewhite and Duncan Phyfe? ___All of these terms describe different styles of American furniture.___

73

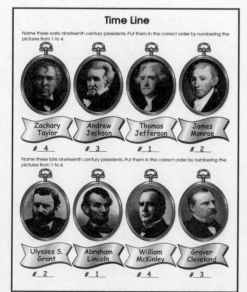

Time Line

Name these early nineteenth century presidents. Put them in the correct order by numbering the pictures from 1 to 4.

Zachary Taylor — # 4
Andrew Jackson — # 3
Thomas Jefferson — # 1
James Monroe — # 2

Name these late nineteenth century presidents. Put them in the correct order by numbering the pictures from 1 to 4.

Ulysses S. Grant — # 2
Abraham Lincoln — # 1
William McKinley — # 4
Grover Cleveland — # 3

74

Time Line

Name these early twentieth century presidents. Put them in the correct order by numbering the pictures from 1 to 4.

Theodore Roosevelt — # 1
Franklin D. Roosevelt — # 2
Woodrow Wilson — # 3
Herbert C. Hoover — # 4

Name these late twentieth century presidents. Put them in the correct order by numbering the pictures from 1 to 4.

Ronald Reagan — # 3
Richard Nixon — # 2
John F. Kennedy — # 1
William Clinton — # 4

75

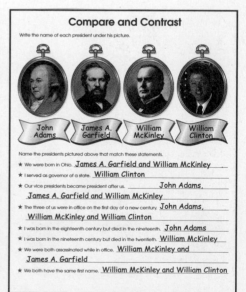

Compare and Contrast

Write the name of each president under his picture.

John Adams, James A. Garfield, William McKinley, William Clinton

Name the presidents pictured above that match these statements.

★ We were born in Ohio. ___James A. Garfield and William McKinley___

★ I served as governor of a state. ___William Clinton___

★ Our vice presidents became president after us. ___John Adams, James A. Garfield and William McKinley___

★ The three of us were in office on the first day of a new century. ___John Adams, William McKinley and William Clinton___

★ I was born in the eighteenth century but died in the nineteenth. ___John Adams___

★ I was born in the nineteenth century but died in the twentieth. ___William McKinley___

★ We were both assassinated while in office. ___William McKinley and James A. Garfield___

★ We both have the same first name. ___William McKinley and William Clinton___

76

© 2001 McGraw-Hill. All Rights Reserved.

Compare and Contrast

Write the name of each president under his picture.

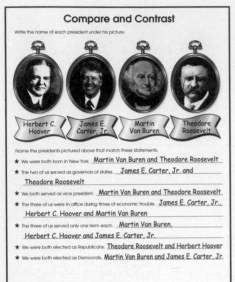

Herbert C. Hoover | James E. Carter, Jr. | Martin Van Buren | Theodore Roosevelt

Name the presidents pictured above that match these statements.

★ We were both born in New York. **Martin Van Buren and Theodore Roosevelt**

★ The two of us served as governors of states. **James E. Carter, Jr. and Theodore Roosevelt**

★ We both served as vice president. **Martin Van Buren and Theodore Roosevelt**

★ The three of us were in office during times of economic trouble. **James E. Carter, Jr., Herbert C. Hoover and Martin Van Buren**

★ The three of us served only one term each. **Martin Van Buren, Herbert C. Hoover and James E. Carter, Jr.**

★ We were both elected as Republicans. **Theodore Roosevelt and Herbert Hoover**

★ We were both elected as Democrats. **Martin Van Buren and James E. Carter, Jr.**

77

Presidents and Wars

Write the name of each president under his picture. Then, draw a line to the name of the war with which he is most closely associated.

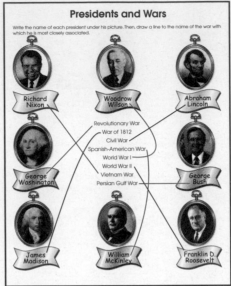

Richard Nixon | Woodrow Wilson | Abraham Lincoln

George Washington | George Bush

James Madison | William McKinley | Franklin D. Roosevelt

Revolutionary War
War of 1812
Civil War
Spanish-American War
World War I
World War II
Vietnam War
Persian Gulf War

78

Who's Who

Write the name of each president under his picture. Then, draw a line to another name by which each president was known.

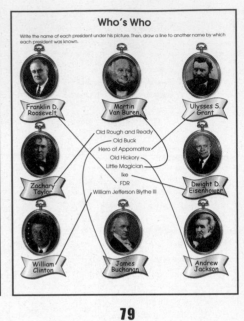

Franklin D. Roosevelt | Martin Van Buren | Ulysses S. Grant

Zachary Taylor | Dwight D. Eisenhower

William Clinton | James Buchanan | Andrew Jackson

Old Rough and Ready
Old Buck
Hero of Appomattox
Old Hickory
Little Magician
Ike
FDR
William Jefferson Blythe III

79

Slogans and Quotations

Write the name of each president under his picture. Then, draw a line to the slogan or quotation with which he is associated.

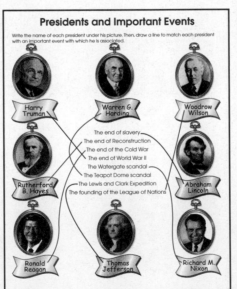

Woodrow Wilson | George Washington | John F. Kennedy

"He serves his party best who serves his country best."
"First in war, first in peace, first in the hearts of his countrymen."
"Remember the Maine."
"Ask not what your country can do for you — ask what you can do for your country."
"A house divided against itself cannot stand."
"...the world must be made safe for democracy."

William McKinley | Rutherford B. Hayes | Abraham Lincoln

80

Presidents and Important Events

Write the name of each president under his picture. Then, draw a line to match each president with an important event with which he is associated.

Harry Truman | Warren G. Harding | Woodrow Wilson

Rutherford B. Hayes | Abraham Lincoln

The end of slavery
The end of Reconstruction
The end of the Cold War
The end of World War II
The Watergate scandal
The Teapot Dome scandal
The Lewis and Clark Expedition
The founding of the League of Nations

Ronald Reagan | Thomas Jefferson | Richard M. Nixon

81

Presidents and Programs

Write the name of each president under his picture. Then, draw a line to match each president with an important program with which he is associated.

William McKinley | Woodrow Wilson | Harry S. Truman

14 Points
The New Deal
The Fair Deal
The Great Society
The Time of Good Feelings
The Full Dinner Pail

James Monroe | Franklin D. Roosevelt | Lyndon B. Johnson

82

© 2001 McGraw-Hill. All Rights Reserved.

Presidential Quiz

Which two presidents died on the same day? Thomas Jefferson and John Adams

What is interesting about the date? It was 50 years after both men helped write the Declaration of Independence.

Which three men served as president during 1841? Martin Van Buren, William H. Harrison and John Tyler

Which three men served as president during 1881? Rutherford B. Hayes, James A. Garfield and Chester A. Arthur

Name the two presidents who were father and son. John Adams and John Quincy Adams

Name the two presidents who were grandfather and grandson. William H. Harrison and Benjamin Harrison

Which man gave up the presidency? Richard M. Nixon

Which two presidents graduated from West Point? Ulysses S. Grant and Dwight D. Eisenhower

Name three successive presidents who were born in Ohio. Ulysses S. Grant, Rutherford B. Hayes and James A. Garfield

Which two presidents helped write the U.S. Constitution? George Washington and James Madison

Which man had the shortest presidency? William H. Harrison

Which man had the longest presidency? Franklin D. Roosevelt

Name two sets of presidents who were distant cousins. Theodore Roosevelt and Franklin D. Roosevelt; James Madison and Zachary Taylor

Which president is called "the Father of His Country"? George Washington

Which president is called "the Father of the Declaration of Independence"? Thomas Jefferson

Which president is called "the Father of the Constitution"? James Madison

83

The American Colonies Under British Rule

During America's first 150 years, most settlers came from Great Britain. These colonists built settlements up and down America's Atlantic coast. The settlements eventually became the states we now call the original Thirteen Colonies.

British settlers worked hard creating homes, farms and towns. Yet these places were not their own. They still lived under the rule of the King of England. Through their labors, the colonists eventually came to desire a larger role in making decisions about their land and lives.

The British tightened their control when they saw the colonists wanted independence. By the mid-1770s, King George III and the British government had imposed heavy taxes on everyday goods like tea. These taxes made it difficult for the colonists to afford their basic necessities.

On June 7, 1776, Richard Henry Lee, a delegate to the Second Continental Congress, presented a new idea. He proposed that the colonies should be free and independent of Great Britain. As a result of Lee's proposal, a committee was appointed to write the Declaration of Independence.

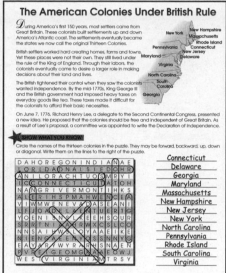

SHOW WHAT YOU KNOW

Circle the names of the thirteen colonies in the puzzle. They may be forward, backward, up, down or diagonal. Write them on the lines to the right of the puzzle.

Connecticut
Delaware
Georgia
Maryland
Massachusetts
New Hampshire
New Jersey
New York
North Carolina
Pennsylvania
Rhode Island
South Carolina
Virginia

85

Before the Declaration of Independence

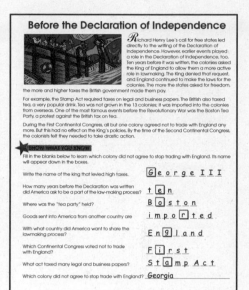

Richard Henry Lee's call for free states led directly to the writing of the Declaration of Independence. However, earlier events played a role in the Declaration of Independence, too. Ten years before it was written, the colonies asked the King of England to allow them a more active role in lawmaking. The King denied that request, and England continued to make the laws for the colonies. The more the states asked for freedom, the more and higher taxes the British government made them pay.

For example, the Stamp Act required taxes on legal and business papers. The British also taxed tea, a very popular drink. Tea was not grown in the 13 colonies; it was imported into the colonies from overseas. One of the most famous events before the Revolutionary War was the Boston Tea Party, a protest against the British tax on tea.

During the First Continental Congress, all but one colony agreed not to trade with England any more. By the time of the Second Continental Congress, the colonists felt they needed to take drastic action.

SHOW WHAT YOU KNOW

Fill in the blanks below to learn which colony did not agree to stop trading with England. Its name will appear down in the boxes.

Write the name of the king that levied high taxes. George III

How many years before the Declaration was written did America ask to be a part of the law-making process? ten

Where was the "tea party" held? Boston

Goods sent into America from another country are imported.

With what country did America want to share the lawmaking process? England

Which Continental Congress voted not to trade with England? First

What act taxed many legal and business papers? Stamp Act

Which colony did not agree to stop trade with England? Georgia

86

The Declaration of Independence

By the time the Second Continental Congress met to discuss stronger action for independence, tensions in the American colonies were very high. Colonists who did not wish to remain British subjects declared themselves Patriots; those who remained faithful to England called themselves Loyalists. The Revolutionary War broke out on April 19, 1775, at the Battle of Lexington and Concord.

The Second Continental Congress appointed a committee of five men to write a Declaration of Independence from British Rule. Those five men were Thomas Jefferson, John Adams, Benjamin Franklin, Robert Livingston and Roger Sherman. Jefferson wrote the first draft. The committee declared it to be almost perfect. After making a few corrections, the committee presented the document to the Congress. After a few more small changes, Thomas Jefferson's work was approved. Church bells rang out on July 4, 1776, the day the Declaration of Independence was adopted and our nation was officially born.

SHOW WHAT YOU KNOW

Find and circle the first and last names of the five men who created the Declaration of Independence.

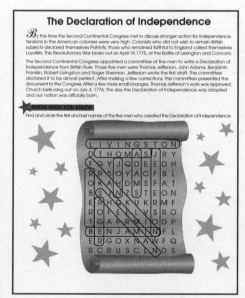

87

The Declaration of Independence, Part II

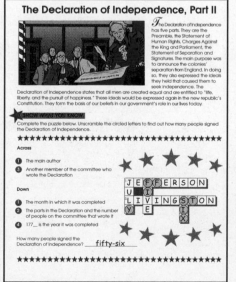

The Declaration of Independence has five parts. They are the Preamble, the Statement of Human Rights, Charges Against the King and Parliament, the Statement of Separation and Signatures. The main purpose was to announce the colonies' separation from England. In doing so, they also expressed the ideals they held that caused them to seek independence. The Declaration of Independence states that all men are created equal and are entitled to "life, liberty, and the pursuit of happiness." These ideals would be expressed again in the new republic's Constitution. They form the basis of our beliefs in our government's role in our lives today.

SHOW WHAT YOU KNOW

Complete the puzzle below. Unscramble the circled letters to find out how many people signed the Declaration of Independence.

Across

1 The main author
3 Another member of the committee who wrote the Declaration

Down

1 The month in which it was completed
2 The parts in the Declaration and the number of people on the committee that wrote it
4 177___ is the year it was completed

How many people signed the Declaration of Independence? fifty-six

88

The Articles of Confederation

During the Revolutionary War, the Continental Congress wrote the Articles of Confederation. These were meant to give the colonies some sense of a unified government. However, once the thirteen colonies became thirteen states, each one began to act alone in its own best interest. In order for these new states to act together, a new governing document was needed. In September 1786, delegates from Maryland, New York, New Jersey, Virginia, Pennsylvania and Delaware met in Annapolis, Maryland. At the Annapolis Convention, these delegates discussed states' rights. Recognizing the need for a stronger central government, they recommended that a convention be held with the purpose of changing the Articles of Confederation.

The Constitutional Convention of May 1787 was held in Philadelphia, Pennsylvania. Delegates from 12 of the 13 states were present. The state of Rhode Island refused to send a delegate because it was afraid of losing its states' rights. For 4 months, the delegates worked behind the closed doors of the statehouse to draft a new document, which would be known later as the Constitution.

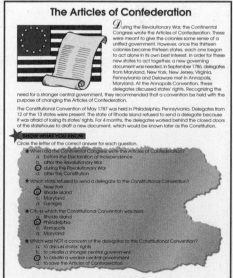

SHOW WHAT YOU KNOW

Circle the letter of the correct answer for each question.

★ When did the Continental Congress write the Articles of Confederation?
  a. before the Declaration of Independence
  b. after the Revolutionary War
  c. during the Revolutionary War
  d. after the Constitution

★ Which state refused to send a delegate to the Constitutional Convention?
  a. New York
  b. Rhode Island
  c. Maryland
  d. Georgia

★ City in which the Constitutional Convention was held.
  a. Rhode Island
  b. Philadelphia
  c. Annapolis
  d. Maryland

★ Which was NOT a concern of the delegates to the Constitutional Convention?
  a. to discuss states' rights
  b. to create a stronger central government
  c. to create a weaker central government
  d. to save the Articles of Confederation

89

© 2001 McGraw-Hill. All Rights Reserved.

Appendix

Writing the Constitution

As commander of the Continental Army, George Washington won the respect of his countrymen. Because of the high esteem in which they held him, Washington's fellow delegates elected him president of the Constitutional Convention. As President of the Convention, Washington's job was to keep the meetings orderly and effective. Considering the many different points of view among the delegates, this was no small task. When President Washington broke in to make a contribution, the delegates listened carefully.

Before the Convention began its work, a rules committee decided how the process would work. Each state was given only one vote, no matter how many delegates that state sent. If a state sent more than one delegate, they all had to come to an agreement about their state's one vote. Any delegate could voice an opinion, but all proceedings would be kept secret until the Convention presented a finished Constitution.

SHOW WHAT YOU KNOW

Complete the crossword puzzle.

Across
1. Washington commanded the army in this war
5. They elected Washington president of the convention
7. Where the convention took place.

Down
2. The means by which different laws are settled
3. The month the convention began
4. The meetings were held in _____.
6. The number of votes allowed per state

REVOLUTIONARY / DELEGATES / STATEHOUSE

90

The Great Compromise

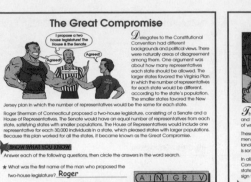

Delegates to the Constitutional Convention had different backgrounds and political views. There were naturally areas of disagreement among them. One argument was about how many representatives each state should be allowed. The larger states favored the Virginia Plan in which the number of representatives for each state would be different, according to the state's population. The smaller states favored the New Jersey plan in which the number of representatives would be the same for each state.

Roger Sherman of Connecticut proposed a two-house legislature, consisting of a Senate and a House of Representatives. The Senate would have an equal number of representatives from each state, satisfying states with smaller populations. The House of Representatives would include one representative for each 30,000 individuals in a state, which pleased states with larger populations. Because this plan worked for all the states, it became known as the Great Compromise.

SHOW WHAT YOU KNOW

Answer each of the following questions, then circle the answers in the word search.

★ What was the first name of the man who proposed the two-house legislature? **Roger**
★ What was the last name of the man who proposed the two-house legislature? **Sherman**
★ Which legislative body has an equal number of representatives from each state? **Senate**
★ Which states favored the Virginia Plan? **large**
★ Which states favored the New Jersey Plan? **small**
★ Which plan was based on equal representation? **New Jersey**
★ Which plan was based on population to determine representation? **Virginia**

```
A I N I G R I V
E S E D M U R L
N H W D R E L A
E E J N G A D O
T R E O M L P L
A M R S H W A I
N A S L L R I A
E N E M G P A T
S E Y E R S O N
```

91

Signing the Constitution

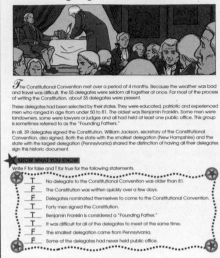

The Constitutional Convention met over a period of 4 months. Because the weather was bad and travel was difficult, the 55 delegates were seldom all together at once. For most of the process of writing the Constitution, about 35 delegates were present.

These delegates had been selected by their states. They were educated, patriotic and experienced men who ranged in age from under 50 to 81. The oldest was Benjamin Franklin. Some men were landowners, some were lawyers or judges and all had held at least one public office. This group is sometimes referred to as the "Founding Fathers."

In all, 39 delegates signed the Constitution. William Jackson, secretary of the Constitutional Convention, also signed. Both the state with the smallest delegation (New Hampshire) and the state with the largest delegation (Pennsylvania) shared the distinction of having all their delegates sign this historic document.

SHOW WHAT YOU KNOW

Write F for false and T for true for the following statements.

T No delegate to the Constitutional Convention was older than 81.
F The Constitution was written quickly over a few days.
F Delegates nominated themselves to come to the Constitutional Convention.
T Forty men signed the Constitution.
T Benjamin Franklin is considered a "Founding Father."
T It was difficult for all of the delegates to meet at the same time.
F The smallest delegation came from Pennsylvania.
F Some of the delegates had never held public office.

92

The Three Branches of Government

Delegates to the Constitutional Convention first designated which powers would be given to the federal government. They needed to decide how these powers would be divided, since they did not want them to all be controlled by one man or group alone. The delegates feared that if any small group was given too much power, the United States would once again be under the rule of another tyrant.

To avoid the threat of tyranny, the group divided the new government into three parts, or branches: the executive branch, the legislative branch and the judicial branch.

Legislative Branch: Headed by Congress, which consists of the House of Representatives and the Senate. The main task of these two bodies is to make the laws by which our government operates. Its powers include passing laws, originating spending bills (House), impeaching officials (Senate) and approving treaties (Senate).

Executive Branch: Headed by the president. The president carries out federal laws and recommends new ones, directs national defense and foreign policy, and performs ceremonial duties. Powers include administering government, commanding the Armed Forces, dealing with international powers, acting as chief law enforcement office and vetoing laws.

Judicial Branch: Headed by the Supreme Court. Its powers include interpreting the Constitution, reviewing laws and deciding cases involving states' rights.

SHOW WHAT YOU KNOW

Match the power with the branch that is responsible for it.

c Interprets the law
a Performs ceremonial duties
b Makes the laws
c Settles states' disputes
a Directs foreign policy

Ⓐ Executive Branch
Ⓑ Legislative Branch
Ⓒ Judicial Branch

93

Checks and Balances

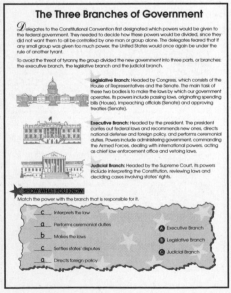

The delegates built a "check and balance" system into the Constitution, so that no one branch of our government could become too powerful. Each branch is controlled by the other two in several ways. For example, the president may veto a law passed by Congress. However, Congress can override that veto with a vote of two-thirds of both houses. Another example is that the Supreme Court may check Congress by declaring a law unconstitutional. This power is balanced by the fact that members of the Supreme Court are appointed by the president, but those appointments have to be approved by Congress.

SHOW WHAT YOU KNOW

Use the information here and on the previous page to complete the chart.

POWER	HOW IT CAN BE CHECKED
Congress passes a law.	The president may **sign a bill into law** OR the president may **veto a bill.** THEN, the Supreme Court may **declare a law unconstitutional or allow it to stand.**
The president vetoes a law passed by Congress.	Congress may **override the veto with 2/3 of members voting to do so.**
The president appoints a Supreme Court judge.	The Senate may **accept or reject the nomination by a majority vote.**
The president makes a treaty with another country.	The Senate may **accept or reject the treaty.**
The president enforces a law.	The Supreme Court may **declare the law unconstitutional or allow it to stand.**

94

The House of Representatives

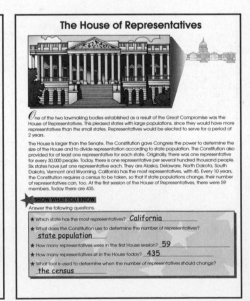

One of the two lawmaking bodies established as a result of the Great Compromise was the House of Representatives. This pleased states with large populations, since they would have more representatives than the small states. Representatives would be elected to serve for a period of 2 years.

The House is larger than the Senate. The Constitution gave Congress the power to determine the size of the House and to divide representation according to state population. The Constitution also provided for at least one representative for each state. Originally, there was one representative for every 30,000 people. Today, there is one representative per several hundred thousand people. Six states have just one representative each. They are Alaska, Delaware, North Dakota, South Dakota, Vermont and Wyoming. California has the most representatives, with 45. Every 10 years, the Constitution requires a census to be taken, so that if state populations change, their number of representatives can, too. At the first session of the House of Representatives, there were 59 members. Today there are 435.

SHOW WHAT YOU KNOW

Answer the following questions.

★ Which state has the most representatives? **California**
★ What does the Constitution use to determine the number of representatives? **state population**
★ How many representatives were in the first House session? **59**
★ How many representatives sit in the House today? **435**
★ What tool is used to determine when the number of representatives should change? **the census**

95

© 2001 McGraw-Hill. All Rights Reserved.

The Senate

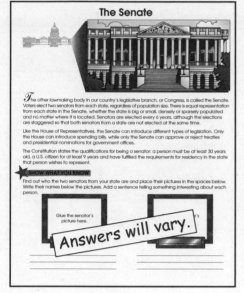

The other lawmaking body in our country's legislative branch, or Congress, is called the Senate. Voters elect two senators from each state, regardless of population size. There is equal representation from each state in the Senate, whether the state is big or small, densely or sparsely populated and no matter where it is located. Senators are elected every 6 years, although the elections are staggered so that both senators from a state are not elected at the same time.

Like the House of Representatives, the Senate can introduce different types of legislation. Only the House can introduce spending bills, while only the Senate can approve or reject treaties and presidential nominations for government offices.

The Constitution states the qualifications for being a senator: a person must be at least 30 years old, a U.S. citizen for at least 9 years and have fulfilled the requirements for residency in the state that person wishes to represent.

★ **SHOW WHAT YOU KNOW**

Find out who the two senators from your state are and place their pictures in the spaces below. Write their names below the pictures. Add a sentence telling something interesting about each person.

Glue the senator's picture here.

Answers will vary.

96

The Executive Branch—Presidency

New laws are first introduced as "bills" in the two bodies of Congress. A bill has to be approved by both the House and the Senate through a series of votes and debates. Once a bill has been approved by Congress, it is sent to the president, who heads the Executive Branch. The president has several options about what to do with a bill. He may sign it into law, send it back to Congress to be changed or veto the bill.

These presidential powers are designed to keep Congress from taking too much control. In Article II of the Constitution, the president's qualifications and powers are detailed: The president will be elected for a term of 4 years at a time. A vice president of the same political party will be elected for the same term. In order to be considered for the office, a presidential candidate must be at least 35 years old, a natural-born U.S. citizen and have at least 14 years of residence in the United States.

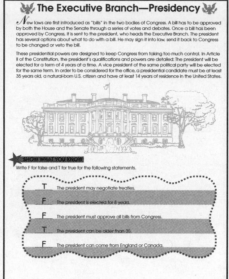

★ **SHOW WHAT YOU KNOW**

Write F for false and T for true for the following statements.

T The president may negotiate treaties.

F The president is elected for 8 years.

F The president must approve all bills from Congress.

T The president can be older than 35.

F The president can come from England or Canada.

97

Making Laws

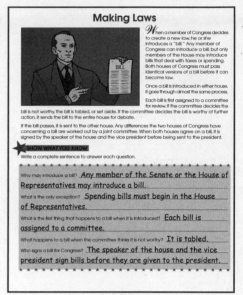

When a member of Congress decides to create a new law, he or she introduces a "bill." Any member of Congress can introduce a bill, but only members of the House may introduce bills that deal with taxes or spending. Both houses of Congress must pass identical versions of a bill before it can become law.

Once a bill is introduced in either house, it goes through almost the same process.

Each bill is first assigned to a committee for review. If the committee decides the bill is not worthy, the bill is tabled, or set aside. If the committee decides the bill is worthy of further action, it sends the bill to the entire house for debate.

If the bill passes, it is sent to the other house. Any differences the two houses of Congress have concerning a bill are worked out by a joint committee. When both houses agree on a bill, it is signed by the speaker of the house and the vice president before being sent to the president.

★ **SHOW WHAT YOU KNOW**

Write a complete sentence to answer each question.

Who may introduce a bill? *Any member of the Senate or the House of Representatives may introduce a bill.*

What is the only exception? *Spending bills must begin in the House of Representatives.*

What is the first thing that happens to a bill when it is introduced? *Each bill is assigned to a committee.*

What happens to a bill when the committee thinks it is not worthy? *It is tabled.*

Who signs a bill for Congress? *The speaker of the house and the vice president sign bills before they are given to the president.*

98

Impeachment

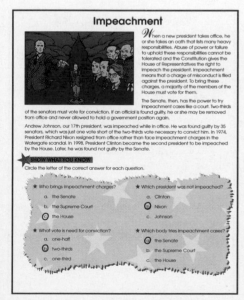

When a new president takes office, he or she takes an oath that lists many heavy responsibilities. Abuse of power or failure to uphold these responsibilities cannot be tolerated and the Constitution gives the House of Representatives the right to impeach the president. Impeachment means that a charge of misconduct is filed against the president. To bring these charges, a majority of the members of the House must vote for them.

The Senate, then, has the power to try impeachment cases like a court. Two-thirds of the senators must vote for conviction. If an official is found guilty, he or she may be removed from office and never allowed to hold a government position again.

Andrew Johnson, our 17th president, was impeached while in office. He was found guilty by 35 senators, which was just one vote short of the two-thirds vote necessary to convict him. In 1974, President Richard Nixon resigned from office rather than face impeachment charges in the Watergate scandal. In 1998, President Clinton became the second president to be impeached by the House. Later, he was found not guilty by the Senate.

★ **SHOW WHAT YOU KNOW**

Circle the letter of the correct answer for each question.

★ Who brings impeachment charges?
a. the Senate
b. the Supreme Court
c. the House

★ Which president was not impeached?
a. Clinton
b. Nixon
c. Johnson

★ What vote is need for conviction?
a. one-half
b. two-thirds
c. one-third

★ Which body tries impeachment cases?
a. the Senate
b. the Supreme Court
c. the House

99

The Judicial Branch

The Supreme Court heads the judicial branch of the United States government. It is the only court established by the Constitution. Decisions made by the Supreme Court are usually of national importance. Because the wording of the Constitution is complex, it must be studied and interpreted carefully. Interpreting the Constitution is one of the main duties of the justices who make up the Supreme Court.

Once the justices of the Supreme Court reach a decision, all other courts in the United States must follow that ruling. The Constitution also gives the Supreme Court the power to judge whether federal, state and local governments are acting within the law. The Supreme Court can also decide if a president's action is unconstitutional.

★ **SHOW WHAT YOU KNOW**

Answer the questions below. Write the letter above each number on its matching blank to find out who heads up the Supreme Court.

The Supreme Court usually only hears cases of n a t i o n a l Importance.
                                               1

What guides Supreme Court decisions?
t h e   C o n s t i t u t i o n
        2   3   4

What branch of the government does the Supreme Court head?
J u d i c i a l
5   6

Which other U.S. courts must follow Supreme Court decisions?
f e d e r a l s t a t e AND l o c a l
7   8   9   10

What is the title of a member of the Supreme Court? J u s t i c e
                                                      10 11 12

THE C h i e f J u s t i c e
     11 2 6 12 7   5 4 3 1 10 9 8

100

Powers of the Federal Government

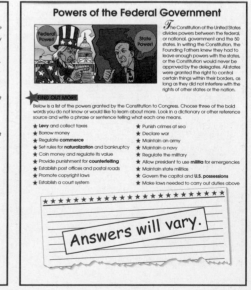

The Constitution of the United States divides powers between the federal, or national, government and the 50 states. In writing the Constitution, the Founding Fathers knew they had to leave enough powers with the states, or the Constitution would never be approved by the delegates. All states were granted the right to control certain things within their borders, as long as they did not interfere with the rights of other states or the nation.

★ **FIND OUT MORE**

Below is a list of the powers granted by the Constitution to Congress. Choose three of the bold words you do not know or would like to learn about more. Look in a dictionary or other reference source and write a phrase or sentence telling what each one means.

★ Levy and collect taxes
★ Borrow money
★ Regulate commerce
★ Set rules for naturalization and bankruptcy
★ Coin money and regulate its value
★ Provide punishment for counterfeiting
★ Establish post offices and postal roads
★ Promote copyright laws
★ Establish a court system

★ Punish crimes at sea
★ Declare war
★ Maintain an army
★ Maintain a navy
★ Regulate the military
★ Allow president to use militia for emergencies
★ Maintain state militias
★ Govern the capitol and U.S. possessions
★ Make laws needed to carry out duties above

Answers will vary.

101

© 2001 McGraw-Hill. All Rights Reserved.

Appendix

Ratifying the Constitution

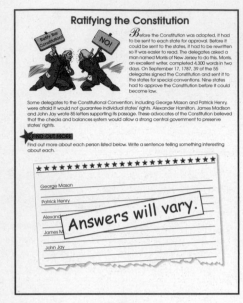

Before the Constitution was adopted, it had to be sent to each state for approval. Before it could be sent to the states, it had to be rewritten so it was easier to read. The delegates asked a man named Morris of New Jersey to do this. Morris, an excellent writer, completed 4,300 words in two days. On September 17, 1787, 39 of the 55 delegates signed the Constitution and sent it to the states for special conventions. Nine states had to approve the Constitution before it could become law.

Some delegates to the Constitutional Convention, including George Mason and Patrick Henry, were afraid it would not guarantee individual states' rights. Alexander Hamilton, James Madison and John Jay wrote 85 letters supporting its passage. These advocates of the Constitution believed that the checks and balances system would allow a strong central government to preserve states' rights.

★ **FIND OUT MORE**
Find out more about each person listed below. Write a sentence telling something interesting about each.

George Mason

Patrick Henry

Alexander

James M

John Jay

Answers will vary.

102

The Bill of Rights

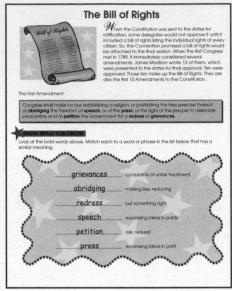

When the Constitution was sent to the states for ratification, some delegates would not approve it until it included a bill of rights listing the individual rights of every citizen. So, the Convention promised a bill of rights would be attached to the final version. When the first Congress met in 1789, it immediately considered several amendments. James Madison wrote 12 of them, which were presented to the states for final approval. Ten were approved. Those ten make up the Bill of Rights. They are also the first 10 Amendments to the Constitution.

The First Amendment:

Congress shall make no law establishing a religion, or prohibiting the free exercise thereof; or **abridging** the freedom of **speech**, or of the **press**; or the right of the people to assemble peaceably, and to **petition** the Government for a **redress** of **grievances**.

★ **SHOW WHAT YOU KNOW**
Look at the bold words above. Match each to a word or phrase in the list below that has a similar meaning.

grievances — complaints of unfair treatment
abridging — making less; reducing
redress — put something right
speech — expressing ideas in public
petition — ask; request
press — expressing ideas in print

103

More About the Bill of Rights

The authors of the Bill of Rights could not list every individual right, so they put in the Ninth and Tenth Amendments to cover all those not listed. For example, one right not specifically listed is privacy. Many people consider privacy to be covered under the Ninth and Tenth Amendments.

The Ninth Amendment:

The **enumeration** in the Constitution of certain rights shall not be **construed** to deny or **disparage** others **retained** by the people.

★ This amendment means that nothing written in the Constitution can be used to cancel amendments to it.

The Tenth Amendment:

The powers not **delegated** to the United States by the Constitution nor **prohibited** by states, are reserved to the states respectively or to the people.

★ This amendment means that anything the Constitution does not mention can be considered by states as part of their powers if they wish to do so.

★ **SHOW WHAT YOU KNOW**
Look at the bold words above. Match each to a word or phrase in the list below that has a similar meaning.

retained — kept
prohibited — made illegal
disparage — discourage
construed — interpreted
enumeration — listing
delegated — given

104

Amendments

Nothing is perfect, and very few things last long without change. The writers of the Constitution realized this when they provided for amendments to the Constitution. Amendments to the Constitution can be either additions or changes to the original text. It is not easy to change the Constitution. Over 9,000 amendments have been proposed since 1787, but only 27 have been approved.

Listed below are the rest of the Amendments that have been made so far to the Constitution. On the right are brief descriptions of what those Amendments are about, in scrambled order. Read a copy of the Amendment section of the Constitution. Use it to help you match the Amendment number with its definition.

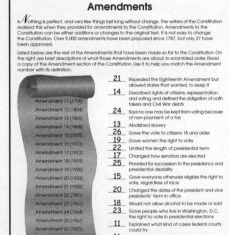

Amendment 11 (1798)
Amendment 12 (1804)
Amendment 13 (1865)
Amendment 14 (1868)
Amendment 15 (1870)
Amendment 16 (1913)
Amendment 17 (1913)
Amendment 18 (1919)
Amendment 19 (1920)
Amendment 20 (1933)
Amendment 21 (1933)
Amendment 22 (1951)
Amendment 23 (1961)
Amendment 24 (1964)
Amendment 25 (1967)
Amendment 26 (1971)
Amendment 27 (1992)

21 Repealed the Eighteenth Amendment but allowed states that wanted to, to keep it
14 Described rights of citizens, representation and voting, and defined the obligation of oath takers and Civil War debts
24 Says no one may be kept from voting because of non-payment of a tax
13 Abolished slavery
26 Gave the vote to citizens 18 and older
19 Gave women the right to vote
22 Limited the length of presidential term
17 Changed how senators are elected
25 Provided for succession to the presidency and presidential disability
15 Gave everyone otherwise eligible the right to vote, regardless of race
20 Changed the dates of the president and vice presidents' term in office
18 Would not allow alcohol to be made or sold
23 Gave people who live in Washington, D.C. the right to vote in presidential elections
11 Explained what kind of cases federal courts could try
16 Established the income tax
12 Changed how the Electoral College voted
27 Congressional members may not raise their own salaries

105

Know Your Constitution

Circle the correct answer to each of the following questions.

★ How many delegates signed the Constitution?
a. 50
b. 40
c. **39**
d. 55

★ What had to be done to ratify the Constitution?
a. A Bill of Rights had to be written
b. The delegates had to sign it
c. Eighty-five letters were written to support it
d. **Nine states had to approve it**

★ Who was not a delegate but signed the Constitution?
a. **William Jackson**
b. Benjamin Franklin
c. George Mason
d. Gouverneur Morris

★ Who was considered the author of the Declaration of Independence?
a. George Washington
b. James Madison
c. **Thomas Jefferson**
d. Roger Sherman

★ Which part of the Constitution has seven parts?
a. Bill of Rights
b. Amendments
c. **Articles**
d. Preamble

★ Who may introduce all kinds of bills?
a. The Supreme Court justices
b. **Members of the House of Representatives**
c. Members of the Senate
d. The vice president

★ Who can veto a bill?
a. A senator
b. A justice
c. A representative
d. **The president**

★ What document did the Constitution replace?
a. Declaration of Independence
b. **Articles of Confederation**
c. Bill of Rights
d. The Magna Carta

★ Who tries impeachment charges against a government official?
a. **The Senate**
b. The Supreme Court
c. The Executive Branch
d. The House of Representatives

106

Matching Constitutional Facts

Write the number of the item in the top box next to the phrase in the bottom box that tells more about it.

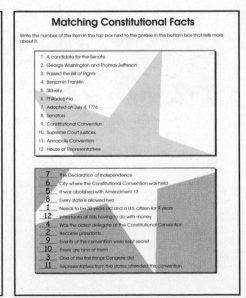

1. A candidate for the Senate
2. George Washington and Thomas Jefferson
3. Passed the Bill of Rights
4. Benjamin Franklin
5. Slavery
6. Philadelphia
7. Adopted on July 4, 1776
8. Senators
9. Constitutional Convention
10. Supreme Court justices
11. Annapolis Convention
12. House of Representatives

7 The Declaration of Independence
6 City where the Constitutional Convention was held
5 It was abolished with Amendment 13
1 Needs to be 30 years old and a U.S. citizen for 9 years
12 Introduces all bills having to do with money
4 Was the oldest delegate at the Constitutional Convention
2 Become presidents
9 Events of this convention were kept secret
10 There are nine of them
3 One of the first things Congress did
11 Representatives from five states attended this convention

107

© 2001 McGraw-Hill. All Rights Reserved.

Constitutional Vocabulary

Write the definitions for the following words as they relate to the Constitution of the United States.

abolish __cancel, remove__
amendment __an addition to the Constitution__
ballot __list of candidates__
bill __a proposed law__
census __an official count of the population__
chief justice __head justice of the Supreme Court__
civil rights __rights of people under the Constitution__
compromise __reaching an agreement or settlement__
delegate __an appointed representative__
due process __following a set procedure under the law__
elector __member of electoral college__
federal __the central government__
impeach __accuse an elected or appointed official of misconduct__
lame duck __office holder with little time left in office__
legislature __a law-making body__
majority __more than half__
petition __an appeal or request__
preamble __the introduction to the Constitution__
president pro tempore __leader of the Senate__
quorum __having enough of a group assembled to conduct business__
ratify __to agree with or approve__
reapportion __to change congressional seats due to population change__
seizure __to take by force__
treason __betraying one's country__
veto __presidential right to block a law__

108

Complete the Time Line

An important event in the making of our government occurred on each of the dates listed in the time line below. Write a phrase or sentence to complete the information for each date.

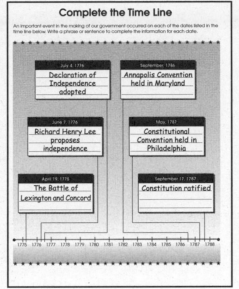

| July 4, 1776 | September, 1786 |
| Declaration of Independence adopted | Annapolis Convention held in Maryland |

| June 7, 1776 | May, 1787 |
| Richard Henry Lee proposes independence | Constitutional Convention held in Philadelphia |

| April 19, 1775 | September 17, 1787 |
| The Battle of Lexington and Concord | Constitution ratified |

1775 1776 1777 1778 1779 1780 1781 1782 1783 1784 1785 1786 1787 1788

109

Our Heritage

Written in the box below are names of some symbols of our heritage. Below the box are pictures of these symbols. Write the name for each symbol on the line under its picture. Color each picture as you are directed.

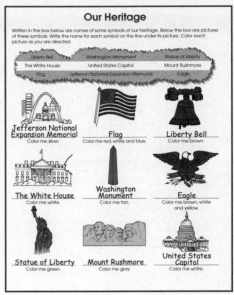

Liberty Bell   Washington Monument   Statue of Liberty
The White House   United States Capitol   Mount Rushmore
Flag   Jefferson National Expansion Memorial   Eagle

Jefferson National Expansion Memorial — Color me silver.
Flag — Color me red, white and blue.
Liberty Bell — Color me brown.
The White House — Color me white.
Washington Monument — Color me tan.
Eagle — Color me brown, white and yellow.
Statue of Liberty — Color me green.
Mount Rushmore — Color me gray.
United States Capitol — Color me white.

110

Alabama: The Heart of Dixie

Look at an atlas or map of Alabama. Add the names of the following places to the map below.

★ the capital of Alabama
★ the site of Rosa Parks' civil rights protest
★ the large body of water to the south of Alabama
★ the city that shares the name of the Tuskegee Institute
★ the city named after Andrew Jackson
★ the river named after the state
★ the cave where humans lived more than 9,000 years ago
★ the site of NASA's first headquarters
★ the first French settlement
★ the town named after a Choctaw chief

Size: 51,705 square miles
Population: 4,283,000

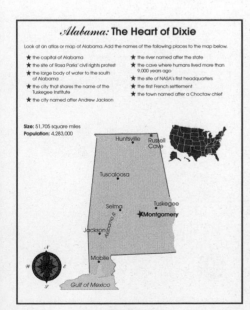

142

Alabama: The Heart of Dixie

Read the clues. Circle the answers in the word search below.

Across
★ the capital of Alabama
★ the name of the city near Russell Cave
★ this crop is grown in Alabama

Down
★ the state flower
★ General Jackson's first name
★ the city that had the first major civil rights protest

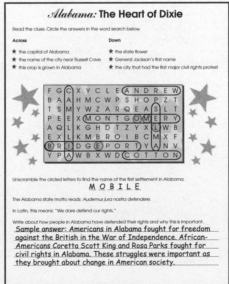

Unscramble the circled letters to find the name of the first settlement in Alabama.

__MOBILE__

The Alabama state motto reads: *Audemus jura nostra defendere.*

In Latin, this means: "We dare defend our rights."

Write about how people in Alabama have defended their rights and why this is important.
__Sample answer: Americans in Alabama fought for freedom against the British in the War of Independence. African-Americans Coretta Scott King and Rosa Parks fought for civil rights in Alabama. These struggles were important as they brought about change in American society.__

143

Alaska: The Last Frontier

Look at an atlas or map of Alaska. Add the names of the following places to the map below.

★ a chain of islands crossing into the eastern hemisphere
★ the highest mountain in North America
★ a gold rush town and Alaska's second largest city
★ the state capital where Chief Kowee first found gold
★ a narrow waterway between Alaska and Russia, named for a Danish scientist
★ the northern beginning of the Trans Alaska Pipeline
★ the northernmost point in the United States
★ the Trans Alaska Pipeline ends at Valdez and this large area of water
★ the island first settled by Russians
★ the city named after the man who purchased Alaska

Size: 591,004 square miles
Population: 551,947

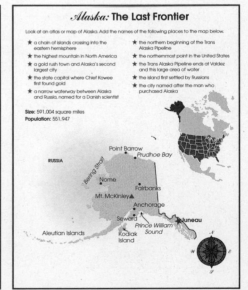

145

© 2001 McGraw-Hill. All Rights Reserved.

Alaska: The Last Frontier

Use the words in the Word Bank to find and circle words about Alaska in the word search below.

Word Bank: Bering Strait, Klondike, Aleut, Gold Rush, Seward's Folly, Inuit, oil

Alaska's state motto is: *North to the Future.*

Write about what the motto means. Then, design a new state seal with your own image of *North to the Future.*

Sample answer: Alaska was seen as the country of promise. It was full of natural resources such as gold, and people felt that going to the north was the future of the United States.

Student's images may include gold, snow, Native Americans, oil and fishing.

146

Arizona: The Grand Canyon State

Look at an atlas or map of Arizona. Add the names of the following places to the map below.

★ the river named for the state of Colorado
★ the country to the south that once owned Arizona
★ the town where Wyatt Earp was deputy U.S. Marshall
★ the river named after the poisonous lizard
★ the city named after a flag pole
★ the capital of Arizona
★ the largest canyon in the United States
★ the place where the corners of four states meet
★ the dam named after Herbert Hoover
★ the Indian reservation that has the oldest village
★ the city that is home to Arizona State University

Size: 114,000 square miles
Population: 3,677,985

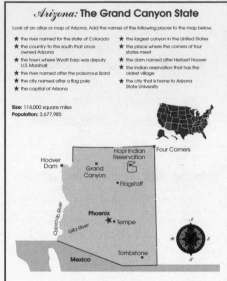

148

Arizona: The Grand Canyon State

Match the Arizona words with their definitions. Each time you make a match, your line should cross out a letter. You can cross out a letter more than once.

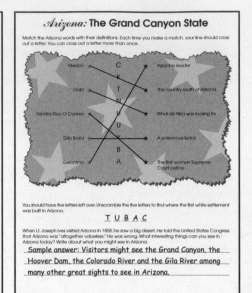

You should have five letters left over. Unscramble the five letters to find where the first white settlement was built in Arizona.

T U B A C

When Lt. Joseph Ives visited Arizona in 1858, he saw a big desert. He told the United States Congress that Arizona was "altogether valueless." He was wrong. What interesting things can you see in Arizona today? Write about what you might see in Arizona.

Sample answer: Visitors might see the Grand Canyon, the Hoover Dam, the Colorado River and the Gila River among many other great sights to see in Arizona.

149

Arkansas: The Land of Opportunity

Look at an atlas or map of Arkansas. Add the names of the following places to the map below.

★ the river that has the same name as the state
★ the nation's first national river
★ the river that runs down the east side of the state
★ the location of the University of Arkansas
★ the city on the border of Texas and Arkansas that takes its name from the two states
★ the capital of Arkansas
★ the tourist town named after its many natural hot springs
★ the town where the Ozark Folk Center was built
★ the birthplace of Maya Angelou
★ the town where surveyors began mapping the Louisiana territory
★ the town where President Clinton was born

Size: 53,187 square miles
Population: 2,473,000

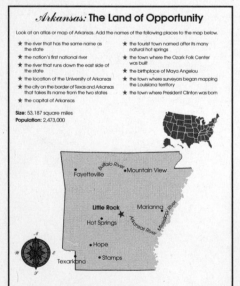

151

Arkansas: The Land of Opportunity

Read the clues and unscramble the words. Then, find and circle them in the word search below.

★ President Clinton's first name — LBIL — **B I L L**
★ A national river — FFULBOA — **B U F F A L O**
★ First explorer of Arkansas — LLLAASE — **L A S A L L E**
★ Founder of Arkansas Post — TINTO — **T O N T I**
★ President Clinton's home town — EOPH — **H O P E**
★ A writer who lives in Stamps — AAYM — **M A Y A**

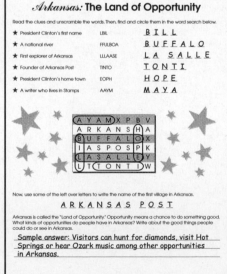

Now, use some of the left over letters to write the name of the first village in Arkansas.

A R K A N S A S P O S T

Arkansas is called the "Land of Opportunity." Opportunity means a chance to do something good. What kinds of opportunities do people have in Arkansas? Write about the good things people could do or see in Arkansas.

Sample answer: Visitors can hunt for diamonds, visit Hot Springs or hear Ozark music among other opportunities in Arkansas.

152

California: The Golden State

Look at an atlas or map of California. Add the names of the following places to the map below.

★ the capital city of California
★ the place near where the Gold Rush started
★ the city where Disneyland is located
★ the place where the first mission was built
★ the city where the Golden Gate Bridge is located
★ the location of Yosemite Falls
★ the highest mountain in the lower 48 states
★ the location of the giant sequoia trees
★ the lowest point in the Western Hemisphere
★ the country that owned California in 1821

Size: 158,706 square miles
Population: 29,839,250

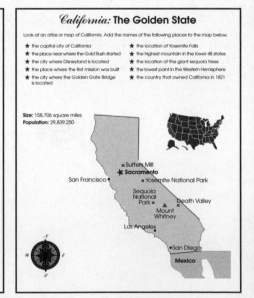

154

© 2001 McGraw-Hill. All Rights Reserved.

California: The Golden State

Read the clues. Unscramble the words about California.

★ the state flower — YPPOP — **POPPY**
★ the tallest mountain in California — TYHNIWE — **WHITNEY**
★ the lowest place in California — EATDH AYLLVE — **DEATH VALLEY**
★ a famous national park — OSMTYEIE — **YOSEMITE**
★ the Spanish built 21 of them — SISMNIOS — **MISSIONS**
★ the movie capital of the world — LLDOOHYOW — **HOLLYWOOD**
★ the state nickname — OGDLNE — **GOLDEN**

In the past, California was known as "The Bear Flag Republic." There is a grizzly bear on California's state seal and flag today. Draw a picture of the flag and write about why a grizzly bear might have been chosen.

Sample answer: At the time when California was a republic, there were many grizzly bears living in California. That is why the bear was chosen as the state symbol.

The state seal has the word "Eureka" on it which means "I have found it." Write about the things that were found in California.

Sample answer: In 1542, Spanish explorer Juan Cabrillo found new land and claimed it for Spain. Gold was found in California in 1848.

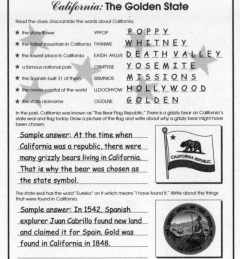

155

Colorado: The Centennial State

Look at an atlas or map of Colorado. Add the names of the following places to the map below.

★ an astronaut's hometown
★ the state capital
★ the Colorado River
★ the highest city in America
★ the site that inspired "America the Beautiful"
★ the home of the U.S. Air Force Academy

★ the national park that preserves the cliff dwellings
★ a ski community whose population grows by almost five times on winter weekends
★ the mining town of Pueblo
★ the Rio Grande
★ Dinosaur National Monument

Size: 104,091 square miles
Population: 3,307,912

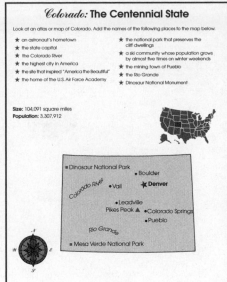

157

Colorado: The Centennial State

Use the words in the Word Bank to find and circle the words about Colorado in the word search below.

Word Bank: Bates, Dempsey, Denver, Pikes Peak, gold, Leadville, Mesa

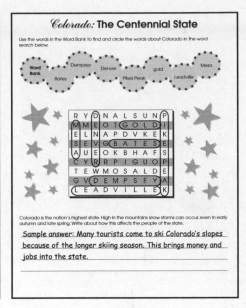

Colorado is the nation's highest state. High in the mountains snow storms can occur, even in early autumn and late spring. Write about how this affects the people of the state.

Sample answer: Many tourists come to ski Colorado's slopes because of the longer skiing season. This brings money and jobs into the state.

158

Connecticut: The Constitution State

Look at an atlas or map of Connecticut. Add the names of the following places to the map below.

★ the place where visitors can tour the U.S.S. Nautilus
★ the site of Yale University
★ the town where the first helicopter was developed
★ the state capital
★ Long Island Sound

★ the Connecticut River
★ the town known as "Park City"
★ a city that takes its name from London, England
★ Block Island Sound
★ the former fishing town of Norwalk
★ a popular vacation spot

Size: 5,018 square miles
Population: 3,296,000

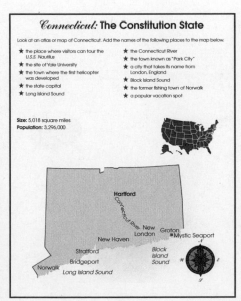

160

Connecticut: The Constitution State

Complete the crossword puzzle.

Across
1. The man who invented the cotton gin
4. A university located in New Haven
6. The town where the first helicopter was developed

Down
2. First name of author of *Uncle Tom's Cabin*
3. First nuclear-powered submarine
5. He discovered Connecticut

Hartford is called the "Insurance City." Explain why this is so.

The first insurance company in the United States is based in Hartford, Connecticut. Hartford is called the insurance city as it is the "birthplace" of American insurance.

161

Delaware: The First State

Look at an atlas or map of Delaware. Add the names of the following places to the map below.

★ the home of E.I. du Pont de Nemours and Company
★ the place where the Town Hall of Hoorn was built
★ the state capital
★ the river where three countries started settlements
★ Nanticoke River

★ the state that shares a rounded border with Delaware
★ the ocean that borders Delaware to the east
★ the two communities that are in both Delaware and Maryland
★ the bay that is named for Delaware
★ the town that was once called New Amstel

Size: 2,045 square miles
Population: 669,000

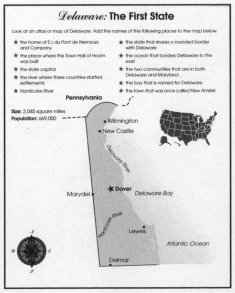

163

© 2001 McGraw-Hill. All Rights Reserved.

Delaware: The First State

Unscramble the words to complete the sentences.

★ Delaware was the **F I R S T** state to enter the Union. SRFIT

D O V E R is the state capital of Delaware. OREDV

★ There are two towns that are located on the border of Delaware and **M A R Y L A N D** YLNMAARD

★ Richard **A L L E N** created the African Methodist Episcopal Church. EANLL

Rearrange the circled letters to form the name of a Delaware hero.

R O D N E Y

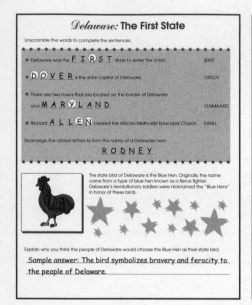

The state bird of Delaware is the Blue Hen. Originally, the name came from a type of blue hen known as a fierce fighter. Delaware's revolutionary soldiers were nicknamed the "Blue Hens" in honor of these birds.

Explain why you think the people of Delaware would choose the Blue Hen as their state bird.

Sample answer: The bird symbolizes bravery and ferocity to the people of Delaware.

164

Florida: The Sunshine State

Look at an atlas or map of Florida. Add the names of the following places to the map below.

★ the ocean that borders Florida
★ the space shuttle is launched from this spot
★ this is Florida's largest lake
★ the capital of Florida
★ a long bridge links these islands called the Florida Keys
★ the body of water Florida shares with Alabama

★ Gloria Estefan was in a group with this city's name
★ a city near where many baseball teams train
★ the first permanent Spanish settlement
★ Mickey Mouse lives here
★ this area is known for its alligators and crocodiles

Size: 58,664 square miles
Population: 13,003,362

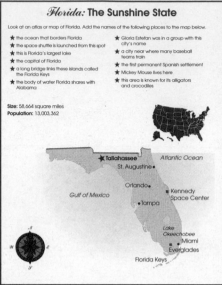

166

Florida: The Sunshine State

Complete the sentences about Florida.

★ Big reptiles live in the **E v e r g l a d e s**
★ The state flower is the **o r a n g e b l o s s o m**
★ Ponce de Leon was looking for a **f o u n t a i n** of youth when he arrived in Florida.
★ Lake **O k e e c h o b e e** is the largest lake in Florida.
★ Tallahassee is Florida's **c a p i t a l**
★ St. **A u g u s t i n e** was founded by the Spanish.

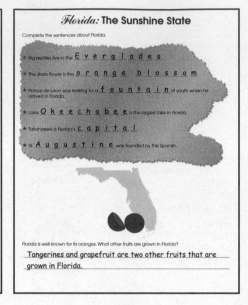

Florida is well known for its oranges. What other fruits are grown in Florida?

Tangerines and grapefruit are two other fruits that are grown in Florida.

167

Georgia: The Empire State of the South

Look at an atlas or map of Georgia. Add the names of the following places to the map below.

★ capital of Georgia
★ Girl Scouts were founded in this city
★ you can swim in this ocean
★ the state to the south of Georgia
★ Georgia shares these mountains with South Carolina

★ Georgia's eastern border is shared with this state
★ the big city in central Georgia
★ "Land of the Trembling Earth"
★ a city on the border with Alabama
★ you can see confederate heroes here

Size: 58,910 square miles
Population: 7,184,000

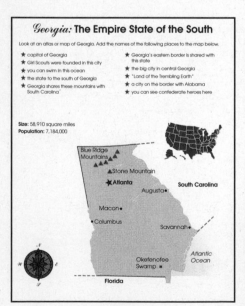

169

Georgia: The Empire State of the South

Complete the crossword puzzle.

Across
3 Home of Coca-Cola and CNN
5 Famous civil rights leader
6 Peanut farmer and former president

Down
1 Columbus is on the border with this state
2 The first English colony in Georgia
4 This city's name sounds like a summer month
6 One of the greatest baseball players

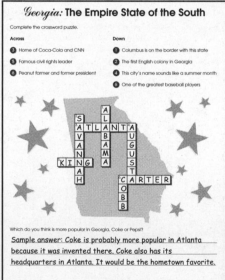

Which do you think is more popular in Georgia, Coke or Pepsi?

Sample answer: Coke is probably more popular in Atlanta because it was invented there. Coke also has its headquarters in Atlanta. It would be the hometown favorite.

170

Hawaii: The Aloha State

Look at an atlas or map of Hawaii. Add the names of the following places to the map below.

★ Honolulu, the capital city of the islands
★ Hawaii, the "big island"
★ the island of Maui
★ the "Garden Isle" where Waimea Canyon is located
★ the location of Volcanoes National Park

★ the island where the Polynesian Cultural center is located
★ Pearl Harbor
★ the "Pineapple Island" of Lanai
★ the "Friendly Island" of Molokai
★ the "Forbidden Island" of Niihau

Size: 6,471 square miles
Population: 1,243,000

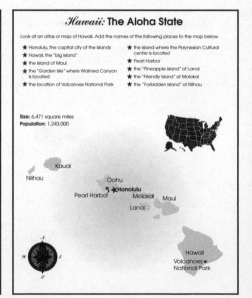

172

  © 2001 McGraw-Hill. All Rights Reserved.

Hawaii: The Aloha State

Use the words in the Word Bank to find and circle the words about Hawaii in the word search below.

Word Bank: aloha, Hawaii, pineapple, volcano, Polynesian, Pearl Harbor, hibiscus, nene, Oahu, Lanai, flag, Mauna Loa, island, canoes

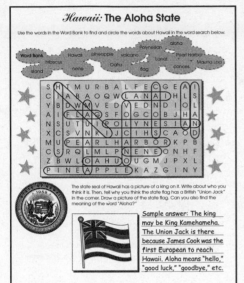

The state seal of Hawaii has a picture of a king on it. Write about who you think it is. Then, tell why you think the state flag has a British "Union Jack" in the corner. Draw a picture of the state flag. Can you also find the meaning of the word "Aloha?"

Sample answer: The king may be King Kamehameha. The Union Jack is there because James Cook was the first European to reach Hawaii. Aloha means "hello," "good luck," "goodbye," etc.

173

Idaho: The Gem State

Look at an atlas or map of Idaho. Add the names of the following places to the map below.

★ the city where Philo Farnsworth invented the television
★ the oldest town in Idaho
★ the capital of Idaho
★ site of the first trading post in Idaho
★ the site of the Bear River Massacre
★ Coeur d'Alene Lake
★ Craters of the Moon National Park
★ Birds of Prey Natural Area is on this river
★ Borah Peak, Idaho's tallest mountain
★ Hells Canyon National Park

Size: 83,564 square miles
Population: 1,164,000

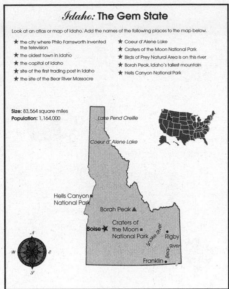

175

Idaho: The Gem State

Find five names related to the Gem State in the word puzzle below. Some letters are together, but others are mixed up. You will use each box only once. The first letters are already there for you.

EW	L	GL	H	O
L	D	J	I	EA
SA	B	M	O	K
I	U	A	AW	S
C	CA	A	R	R

Lewis _____   Clark _____
Idaho _____   Sacajawea _____   Borglum _____

The governor of Idaho is holding a contest to find a new nickname for the state of Idaho. Look for four things that Idaho is known for and write a new nickname.

Sample answer: Idaho is known for its potato production, garnet mining, lumber and silver mining. I would nickname Idaho the "Silver Mountain State" because it is part of the Rocky Mountain region and it is the second biggest mining state for silver.

176

Illinois: The Land of Lincoln

Look at an atlas or map of Illinois. Add the names of the following places to the map below.

★ this city has one of the world's tallest skyscrapers
★ this city sits on the Illinois river
★ one settler thought this city was opposite from China
★ this river links the Mississippi to the Illinois-Michigan Canal
★ this lake is the largest wholly within the United States
★ the capital of Illinois
★ where Native Americans built a large structure
★ this river forms the western border of Illinois
★ a large city in the north
★ Abraham Lincoln lived here as a boy
★ boats use this man-made waterway to reach Chicago

Size: 56,345 square miles
Population: 11,467,000

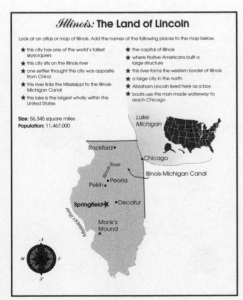

178

Illinois: The Land of Lincoln

Complete the clues. Then, use the clues to find words in the word search below.

★ Illinois is called the Land of **Lincoln**
★ A Native American who fought against settlers **Black Hawk**
★ The lake that borders Chicago **Michigan**
★ The northernmost city **Rockford**
★ An amusement ride invented in Illinois was the **Ferris** wheel.
★ The state bird of Illinois is the **Cardinal**

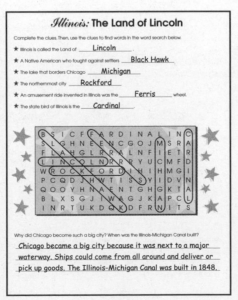

Why did Chicago become such a big city? When was the Illinois-Michigan Canal built?

Chicago became a big city because it was next to a major waterway. Ships could come from all around and deliver or pick up goods. The Illinois-Michigan Canal was built in 1848.

179

Indiana: The Hoosier State

Look at an atlas or map of Indiana. Add the names of the following places to the map below.

★ the capital of Indiana
★ the first permanent French settlement
★ the river that flows along the southern border of Indiana
★ the Studebaker automobile was built here
★ the Great Lake that borders Indiana
★ the location of the Indianapolis Motor Speedway
★ the city named for a Revolutionary War General
★ a city near the junction of the Wabash and Tippecanoe Rivers
★ the states which border Indiana

Size: 36,185 square miles
Population: 5,841,000

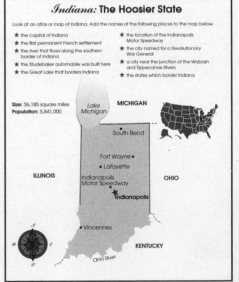

181

© 2001 McGraw-Hill. All Rights Reserved.

Appendix

Indiana: The Hoosier State

Read the clues and unscramble the words about Indiana.

Lincoln's first name	A B R A H A M	M A B A R A H
a car made in South Bend	S T U D E B A K E R	K R A T U S E B D E
Indianapolis's football team	C O L T S	S L O C T

Unscramble the boxed letters to find the name of the Indian chief who was defeated at the Battle of Tippecanoe.

T E C U M S E H

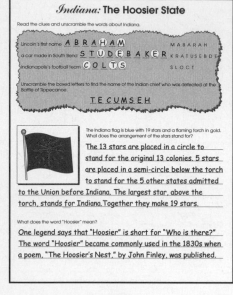

The Indiana flag is blue with 19 stars and a flaming torch in gold. What does the arrangement of the stars stand for?

The 13 stars are placed in a circle to stand for the original 13 colonies. 5 stars are placed in a semi-circle below the torch to stand for the 5 other states admitted to the Union before Indiana. The largest star, above the torch, stands for Indiana. Together they make 19 stars.

What does the word "Hoosier" mean?

One legend says that "Hoosier" is short for "Who is there?" The word "Hoosier" became commonly used in the 1830s when a poem, "The Hoosier's Nest," by John Finley, was published.

182

Iowa: The Hawkeye State

Look at an atlas or map of Iowa. Add the names of the following places to the map below.

★ this city is known for making popcorn
★ the capital of Iowa
★ mined lead could be sent down this eastern river
★ the state to the south of Iowa
★ the river that shares the same name as the capital
★ this town celebrates Capt. James T. Kirk's birthday each year
★ a city where early settlers came to mine lead
★ this river makes up Iowa's western border
★ an area in southern Iowa
★ the state to the north of Iowa

Size: 56,275 square miles
Population: 2,865,000

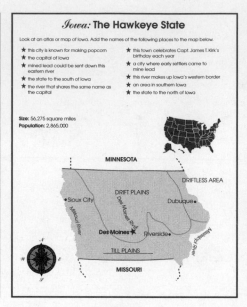

184

Iowa: The Hawkeye State

Read the clues. Unscramble the words about Iowa.

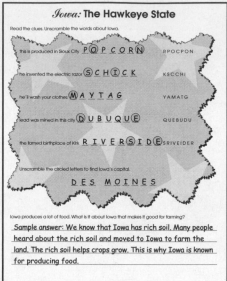

this is produced in Sioux City	P O P C O R N	R P O C P O N
he invented the electric razor	S C H I C K	K S C C H I
he'll wash your clothes	M A Y T A G	Y A M A T G
lead was mined in this city	D U B U Q U E	Q U E B U D U
the famed birthplace of Kirk	R I V E R S I D E	S R I V E I D E R

Unscramble the circled letters to find Iowa's capital.

D E S   M O I N E S

Iowa produces a lot of food. What is it about Iowa that makes it good for farming?

Sample answer: We know that Iowa has rich soil. Many people heard about the rich soil and moved to Iowa to farm the land. The rich soil helps crops grow. This is why Iowa is known for producing food.

185

Kansas: The Sunflower State

Look at an atlas or map of Kansas. Add the names of the following places to the map below.

★ the state capital
★ the city that has the same name as the state
★ the river that separates Kansas and Missouri
★ the place where salt was first produced
★ the birthplace of Melissa Etheridge
★ the states that border Kansas
★ the birthplace of Amelia Earhart
★ the city that was an important site in the Underground Railroad
★ the location of the Dwight D. Eisenhower Museum and Library
★ the city that produces small aircraft

Size: 82,277 square miles
Population: 2,591,000

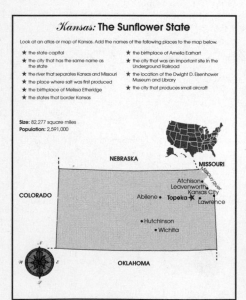

187

Kansas: The Sunflower State

The motto of Kansas is: Ad astra per aspera.

Unscramble the letters below to find out what the motto means.

O T   H E T   S R A S T   G H R O U H T
T O   T H E   S T A R S   T H R O U G H

F I C I D U T F I L E S
D I F F I C U L T I E S

Rewrite the motto in your own words. What do you think it means?

Sample answer: "Keep trying" or "Never be afraid to try for your goals, even if it is hard."

Think of a personal motto for yourself. Write it below.

Answers will vary.

★★★★★★★★★★★★★★★★★★★★★★★★

The Jayhawkers were a very important part of Kansas history. Today, the athletic teams at Kansas University are called Jayhawks. Find out who the original Jayhawkers were. Explain their importance.

Sample answer: The original Jayhawks were the first Kansas cavalry. Later, the Jayhawkers were an anti-slavery group that fought with the Missourians over slavery.

★★★★★★★★★★★★★★★★★★★★★★★★

188

Kentucky: The Bluegrass State

Look at an atlas or map of Kentucky. Add the names of the following places to the map below.

★ the home of the Kentucky Derby
★ the capital of Kentucky
★ the location of the gold reserve
★ the river which flows along the northern border of Kentucky
★ the river which forms a part of the western boundary of Kentucky
★ the longest cave in the world
★ the home of the Corvette plant
★ the seven states that border Kentucky

Size: 40,410 square miles
Population: 3,864,000

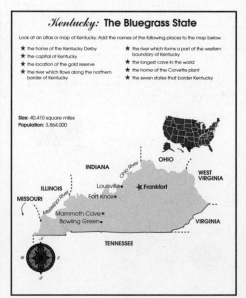

190

© 2001 McGraw-Hill. All Rights Reserved.

Kentucky: The Bluegrass State

Answer the questions to learn the Kentucky state motto.

Who was the sixteenth president? L I N C O L N
1 5

What famous explorer settled in Kentucky? D A N I E L B O O N E
3 6 4 2

What Kentucky city is on the Ohio River? L O U I S V I L L E
10

In what city are Corvettes made? B O W L I N G G R E E N
10

What is the capital of Kentucky? F R A N K F O R T
11 7 12

Kentucky state motto:

U N I T E D W E S T A N D
7 4 5 12 2 8 12 6 4 3

D I V I D E D W E F A L L
3 5 9 5 3 2 3 10 2 11 6 1

Why is Kentucky called the "Bluegrass State"?

Sample answer: The grass that covers the fields has buds
that make it look bluish-purple when seen from a distance.
Early traders asked for the seed of the "blue grass from
Kentucky." The name stuck and today Kentucky is known as
the "Bluegrass State."

191

Louisiana: The Pelican State

Look at an atlas or map of Louisiana. Add the names of the following places to the map below.

★ the river that creates the border between Texas and Louisiana
★ Tensas River National Wildlife Refuge
★ hometown of Jerry Lee Lewis
★ home of the tallest capitol building in the country
★ Chandeleur Island archipelago
★ Terry Bradshaw's birthplace
★ Bayou La Fourche
★ Lake Pontchartrain
★ Oil City
★ New Orleans
★ the longest river in the U.S.
★ Barataria Bay

Size: 47,472 square miles
Population: 4,389,000

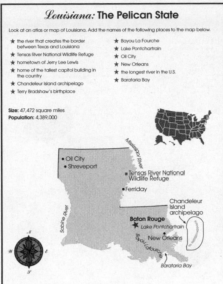

193

Louisiana: The Pelican State

Find and circle the seven words about Louisiana hidden in the word search below. Then, fill in the sentences below with the words found in the word search.

___Satchmo___ was the nickname given to the jazz legend from New Orleans.

___Capote___, the playwright and author, was born in New Orleans.

The ___magnolia___ is the state flower of Louisiana.

___Zydeco___ music was created in southwest Louisiana.

The ___pelican___ earned Louisiana its nickname.

The ___Caddo___ Indians were among the first peoples of Louisiana.

The French explorer, ___La Salle___, named Louisiana after King Louis XIV.

Imagine that you are trying to attract visitors to Louisiana. Design a travel poster that will persuade tourists to come. Write a slogan for the state.

Answers will vary. Students might draw
images of jazz instruments, Mardi Gras
masks, magnolias, etc. A sample slogan:
"Come to Louisiana, don't be 'blue
bayou'... we'll jazz up your life!"

194

Maine: The Pine Tree State

Look at an atlas or map of Maine. Add the names of the following places to the map below.

★ the capital of Maine
★ the place where many lobster boats dock
★ the country that borders Maine
★ the one state that borders Maine
★ the site where the L.L. Bean Company is located
★ the town where Stephen King lives
★ the coastal town that was closest to the first Revolutionary War naval battle
★ the name of the body of water off the southern coast of Maine
★ Penobscot River
★ the Longfellow Mountains

Size: 33,265 square miles
Population: 1,245,000

196

Maine: The Pine Tree State

Read the clues. Unscramble the words about Maine.

Stephen King's home B A N G O R   ONBRAG

capital city of Maine A U G U S T A   USAGUAT

St. Vincent-Millay's prize P U L I T Z E R   ZRPIELTU

nickname tree P I N E   EPNI

Lincoln's vice president H A M L I N   ANHILM

Unscramble the circled letters to find Maine's main export.

L O B S T E R

Maine is called the "Pine Tree State." Explain why trees are important and what they can be used for.

Sample answer: Trees provide many jobs. Trees are used
to make paper, packing crates, toothpicks and timber for
buildings.

197

Maryland: The Old Line State

Look at an atlas or map of Maryland. Add the names of the following places to the map below.

★ a city named after a lord
★ this state is west of Maryland
★ the state capital
★ this state is on the other side of the Mason-Dixon line
★ this state is south and west of Maryland
★ this waterway was a reason settlers came to Maryland
★ this river drains into the Chesapeake Bay from Pennsylvania
★ the line that separated the North from the South
★ this river cuts through Washington, D.C. and forms Maryland's western border
★ the nation's capital
★ this state is east of Maryland

Size: 10,460 square miles
Population: 5,105,000

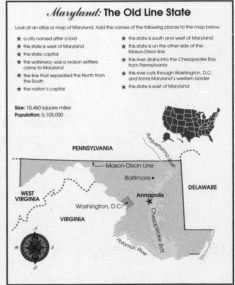

199

© 2001 McGraw-Hill. All Rights Reserved.

Appendix

Maryland: The Old Line State

Write the letter from column B next to the matching phrase in column A.

1. **C**   from here to the Navy
2. **B**   passes by Washington, D.C.
3. **F**   has a large natural harbor
4. **D**   cuts through Maryland
5. **E**   across the Potomac from Maryland
6. **A**   east of Maryland

- Ⓐ Delaware
- Ⓑ Potomac River
- Ⓒ Annapolis
- Ⓓ Chesapeake Bay
- Ⓔ Virginia
- Ⓕ Baltimore

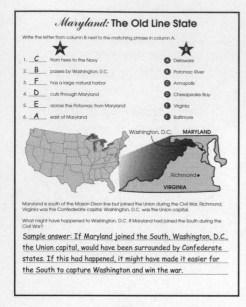

Maryland is south of the Mason-Dixon line but joined the Union during the Civil War. Richmond, Virginia was the Confederate capital. Washington, D.C. was the Union capital.

What might have happened to Washington, D.C. if Maryland had joined the South during the Civil War?

Sample answer: If Maryland joined the South, Washington, D.C., the Union capital, would have been surrounded by Confederate states. If this had happened, it might have made it easier for the South to capture Washington and win the war.

200

Massachusetts: The Bay State

Look at an atlas or map of Massachusetts. Add the names of the following places to the map below.

- ★ the capital of Massachusetts
- ★ the birthplace of basketball
- ★ Cape Cod
- ★ the city with the oldest university in the United States
- ★ a town named for Francis Cabot Lowell
- ★ the place where the Pilgrims landed
- ★ the town where Emily Dickinson wrote her poems
- ★ the two sites where the first fighting of the Revolutionary War took place
- ★ the Berkshires
- ★ the place where Paul Revere began his ride
- ★ Martha's Vineyard

Size: 8,284 square miles
Population: 6,062,000

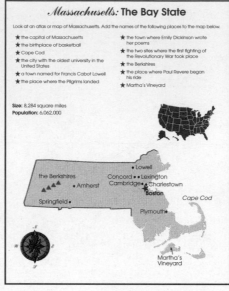

202

Massachusetts: The Bay State

Write the letter from column B next to the matching phrase in column A.

1. **D**   capital city
2. **C**   inventor of basketball
3. **E**   founded the Red Cross
4. **B**   oldest university in the country
5. **A**   site where Pilgrims landed
6. **F**   a Native American tribe

- Ⓐ Plymouth
- Ⓑ Harvard
- Ⓒ Naismith
- Ⓓ Boston
- Ⓔ Barton
- Ⓕ Wampanoag

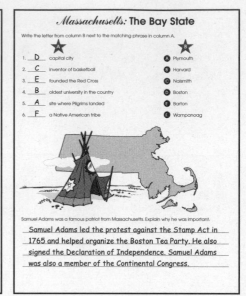

Samuel Adams was a famous patriot from Massachusetts. Explain why he was important.

Samuel Adams led the protest against the Stamp Act in 1765 and helped organize the Boston Tea Party. He also signed the Declaration of Independence. Samuel Adams was also a member of the Continental Congress.

203

Michigan: The Wolverine State

Look at an atlas or map of Michigan. Add the names of the following places to the map below.

- ★ a city named after Chief Pontiac
- ★ the location of the University of Michigan
- ★ the place where corn flakes were invented
- ★ the Upper Peninsula
- ★ the Lower Peninsula
- ★ the lake where Oliver Hazard Perry fought the British
- ★ the other Great Lakes that border Michigan
- ★ Mackinac Island
- ★ the capital of Michigan
- ★ the center of the automobile industry
- ★ the place where Father Jacques Marquette started his mission

Size: 58,527 square miles
Population: 9,654,000

205

Michigan: The Wolverine State

Read the clues. Unscramble the words about Michigan.

- ★ President Ford's first name   DARⒼLE   **G E R A L D**
- ★ light bulb man   SIDⓄNE   **E D I S O N**
- ★ Chief   ⓃOPIACT   **P O N T I A C**
- ★ automotive center   ROⓉTED   **D E T R O I T**
- ★ Perry's place   KAⓁEⓉEER   **L A K E   E R I E**

★ Unscramble the circled letters to find Michigan's capital.

L A N S I N G

Look at the seal of the State of Michigan. The motto at the top reads: *E pluribus unum.*

Find out what this motto means. What language did it come from? Write about what it means and why it is important.

Sample answer: The motto is in Latin. It means "From Many, One." It tells how the state is made up of many people that came together to make one state.

206

Minnesota: The Gopher State

Look at an atlas or map of Minnesota. Add the names of the following places to the map below.

- ★ the place where Fort Snelling stands
- ★ the location of the Mayo Clinic
- ★ the lake that borders northeastern Minnesota
- ★ the city near St. Anthony's Falls
- ★ the city where Bob Dylan was born
- ★ the northernmost point of the continental United States
- ★ the city of Judy Garland's childhood home
- ★ the capital of Minnesota

Size: 84,402 square miles
Population: 4,642,000

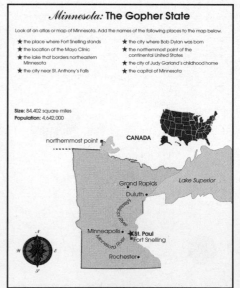

208

Appendix

★ 340 ★

© 2001 McGraw-Hill. All Rights Reserved.

Minnesota: The Gopher State

Read the clues. Unscramble the words about Minnesota.

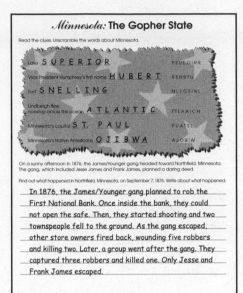

Lake **SUPERIOR** — PSUEOIRR

Vice President Humphrey's first name **HUBERT** — REHBTU

Fort **SNELLING** — NLEGSINL

Lindbergh flew nonstop across this ocean **ATLANTIC** — TTLAAICN

Minnesota's capital **ST. PAUL** — PUATSL

Minnesota's Native Americans **OJIBWA** — AJOBIW

On a sunny afternoon in 1876, the James/Younger gang headed toward Northfield, Minnesota. The gang, which included Jesse James and Frank James, planned a daring deed.

Find out what happened in Northfield, Minnesota, on September 7, 1876. Write about what happened.

In 1876, the James/Younger gang planned to rob the First National Bank. Once inside the bank, they could not open the safe. Then, they started shooting and two townspeople fell to the ground. As the gang escaped, other store owners fired back, wounding five robbers and killing two. Later, a group went after the gang. They captured three robbers and killed one. Only Jesse and Frank James escaped.

209

Mississippi: The Magnolia State

Look at an atlas or map of Mississippi. Add the names of the following places to the map below.

★ this river is one of the most important in the whole country
★ this state is south of Mississippi
★ the capital of Mississippi
★ the Mississippi flows into this body of water
★ this connects two rivers
★ this state is to the north
★ an important battle was fought here
★ go east to get to this state
★ this city is named after the Native Americans who lived there
★ a city on the Gulf of Mexico
★ this state is to the northwest of Mississippi

Size: 47,689 square miles
Population: 2,676,000

211

Mississippi: The Magnolia State

Next to each sentence write a T if the statement is true or an F if the statement is false.

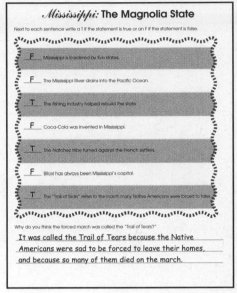

F — Mississippi is bordered by five states.

F — The Mississippi River drains into the Pacific Ocean.

T — The fishing industry helped rebuild the state.

F — Coca-Cola was invented in Mississippi.

T — The Natchez tribe turned against the French settlers.

F — Biloxi has always been Mississippi's capital.

T — The "Trail of Tears" refers to the march many Native Americans were forced to take.

Why do you think the forced march was called the "Trail of Tears?"

It was called the Trail of Tears because the Native Americans were sad to be forced to leave their homes, and because so many of them died on the march.

212

Missouri: The Show-Me State

Look at an atlas or map of Missouri. Add the names of the following places to the map below.

★ the lake where Bagnell Dam is located
★ the capital of Missouri
★ the mighty river on which many steamboats traveled
★ the mountains in Missouri
★ the place where the Pony Express started
★ the city that has the same name as Kansas
★ the river that borders Missouri on the west
★ the states that border Missouri
★ the location of the Harry S. Truman home and library
★ the boyhood home of Mark Twain

Size: 69,697 square miles
Population: 5,309,000

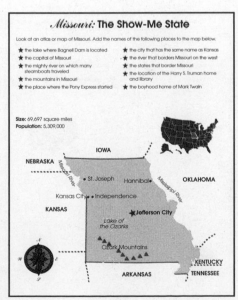

214

Missouri: The Show-Me State

Read the clues. Unscramble the words about Missouri.

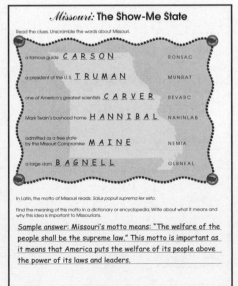

a famous guide **CARSON** — RONSAC

a president of the U.S. **TRUMAN** — MUNRAT

one of America's greatest scientists **CARVER** — REVARC

Mark Twain's boyhood home **HANNIBAL** — NAHINLAB

admitted as a free state by the Missouri Compromise **MAINE** — NEMIA

a large dam **BAGNELL** — GLBNEAL

In Latin, the motto of Missouri reads: *Salus populi suprema lex esto.*

Find the meaning of this motto in a dictionary or encyclopedia. Write about what it means and why this idea is important to Missourians.

Sample answer: Missouri's motto means: "The welfare of the people shall be the supreme law." This motto is important as it means that America puts the welfare of its people above the power of its laws and leaders.

215

Montana: The Treasure State

Look at an atlas or map of Montana. Add the names of the following places to the map below.

★ mountain range in the western part of the state
★ the line that divides the continent
★ the country to the north of the state
★ the capital of Montana
★ one of the biggest dams in the world
★ the river where Lt. Col. Custer was defeated
★ the National Park with year-round snow
★ the city near the site of 5,000 year old cave drawings
★ the place near where Jeannette Rankin was born
★ where silver was discovered
★ the city where gold was discovered in a gulch

Size: 147,046 square miles
Population: 863,000

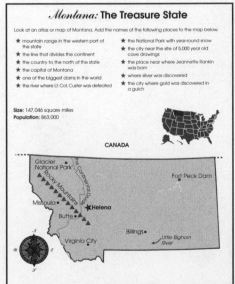

217

© 2001 McGraw-Hill. All Rights Reserved.

Appendix

Montana: The Treasure State

Read the clues. Circle each hidden word and draw a line to the phrase it answers.

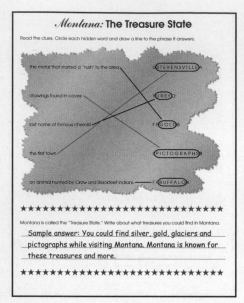

- the metal that started a "rush" to the area — STEVENSVILLE
- drawings found in caves — UREYO
- last name of famous chemist — GOLDB
- the first town — PICTOGRAPHSB
- an animal hunted by Crow and Blackfeet Indians — F BUFFALO K

★★★★★★★★★★★★★★★★★★★★★★★★★

Montana is called the "Treasure State." Write about what treasures you could find in Montana.

Sample answer: You could find silver, gold, glaciers and pictographs while visiting Montana. Montana is known for these treasures and more.

★★★★★★★★★★★★★★★★★★★★★★★★★

218

Nebraska: The Cornhusker State

Look at an atlas or map of Nebraska. Add the names of the following places to the map below.

- ★ the N. Platte river flows from this state
- ★ Omaha is on this river
- ★ this state is to the east of Nebraska
- ★ the capital of Nebraska
- ★ this state shares Nebraska's northern border
- ★ this area makes up most of Nebraska
- ★ this state cuts into southwest Nebraska
- ★ Nebraska shares this area with Iowa
- ★ this river passes by Grand Island and flows into the Missouri River
- ★ this state is due south of Nebraska
- ★ Malcom X's birthplace

Size: 77,355 square miles
Population: 1,649,000

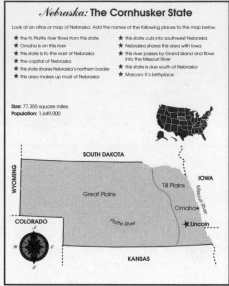

220

Nebraska: The Cornhusker State

Next to each sentence write a T if the statement is true or an F if the statement is false.

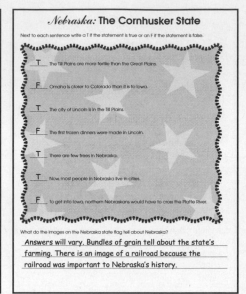

- T The Till Plains are more fertile than the Great Plains.
- F Omaha is closer to Colorado than it is to Iowa.
- T The city of Lincoln is in the Till Plains.
- F The first frozen dinners were made in Lincoln.
- T There are few trees in Nebraska.
- T Now, most people in Nebraska live in cities.
- F To get into Iowa, northern Nebraskans would have to cross the Platte River.

What do the images on the Nebraska state flag tell about Nebraska?

Answers will vary. Bundles of grain tell about the state's farming. There is an image of a railroad because the railroad was important to Nebraska's history.

221

Nevada: The Silver State

Look at an atlas or map of Nevada. Add the names of the following places to the map below.

- ★ the capital of Nevada
- ★ a very large dam
- ★ this town is Nevada spelled backwards
- ★ Waddie Mitchell was born here
- ★ this is Nevada's tallest mountain
- ★ this river forms a small part of Nevada's border with Arizona
- ★ odds are you can find gamblers in this southern city
- ★ this lake is near the Hoover Dam
- ★ this state shares Nevada's eastern border
- ★ this is the biggest mountain lake
- ★ this desert is in southeastern Nevada

Size: 110,561 square miles
Population: 1,206,000

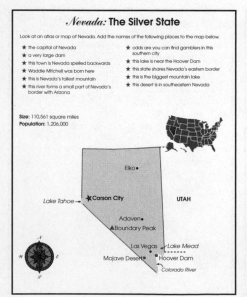

223

Nevada: The Silver State

Use the code below to learn about some interesting people, places and events in Nevada.

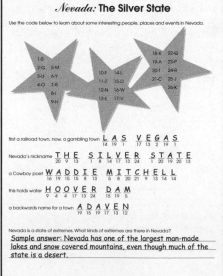

first a railroad town, now, a gambling town L A S   V E G A S
Nevada's nickname T H E   S I L V E R   S T A T E
a Cowboy poet W A D D I E   M I T C H E L L
this holds water H O O V E R   D A M
a backwards name for a town A D A V E N

Nevada is a state of extremes. What kinds of extremes are there in Nevada?

Sample answer: Nevada has one of the largest man-made lakes and snow covered mountains, even though much of the state is a desert.

224

New Hampshire: The Granite State

Look at an atlas or map of New Hampshire. Add the names of the following places to the map below.

- ★ the site where the treaty of the Russo-Japanese war was signed
- ★ the capital of New Hampshire
- ★ the location of the Old Man of the Mountain
- ★ the place where the fastest winds were recorded
- ★ Lake Winnipesaukee
- ★ the town where the MacDowell Colony is located
- ★ the state that once claimed New Hampshire
- ★ the birthplace of Daniel Webster
- ★ the home of Robert Frost
- ★ the Connecticut River

Size: 9,279 square miles
Population: 1,114,000

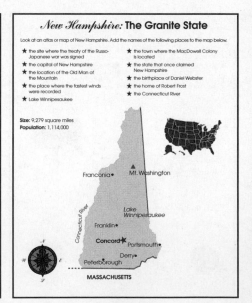

226

Appendix

★ **342**

© 2001 McGraw-Hill. All Rights Reserved.

New Hampshire: The Granite State

Complete the crossword puzzle below.

Across

3. New Hampshire delegates were the first to vote on the _____ of Independence.
5. Sarah Josepha _____ wrote "Mary Had a Little Lamb."
6. New Hampshire is called the _____ State.

Down

1. Captain John _____ named New Hampshire.
2. The world's fastest winds were recorded on Mt. _____.
4. The state's capital is _____.
7. In 1788, New Hampshire became the _____ state.

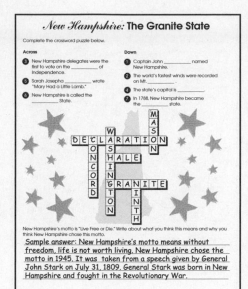

New Hampshire's motto is "Live Free or Die." Write about what you think this means and why you think New Hampshire chose this motto.

Sample answer: New Hampshire's motto means without freedom, life is not worth living. New Hampshire chose the motto in 1945. It was taken from a speech given by General John Stark on July 31, 1809. General Stark was born in New Hampshire and fought in the Revolutionary War.

227

New Jersey: The Garden State

Look at an atlas or map of New Jersey. Add the names of the following places to the map below.

★ the state capital
★ the river that flows between New Jersey and Pennsylvania
★ the southernmost point of New Jersey
★ the location of one of America's leading universities
★ the largest city in New Jersey
★ the states that border New Jersey
★ the mountains in northern New Jersey
★ the city on the coast that shares its name with an ocean
★ the ocean bordering eastern New Jersey
★ the place where Samuel Morse invented the telegraph

Size: 7,787 square miles
Population: 7,878,000

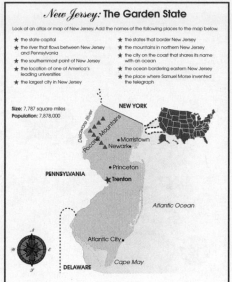

229

New Jersey: The Garden State

Use the words in the Word Bank to find and circle the words about New Jersey in the word search puzzle.

| Word Bank | Cleveland | Hoboken | Princeton | Trenton | Morse |
| | Hudson | Cooper | Sinatra | Washington | Edison |

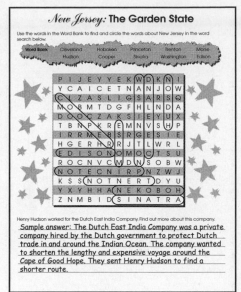

Henry Hudson worked for the Dutch East India Company. Find out more about this company.

Sample answer: The Dutch East India Company was a private company hired by the Dutch government to protect Dutch trade in and around the Indian Ocean. The company wanted to shorten the lengthy and expensive voyage around the Cape of Good Hope. They sent Henry Hudson to find a shorter route.

230

New Mexico: The Land of Enchantment

Look at an atlas or map of New Mexico. Add the names of the following places to the map below.

★ the capital of New Mexico
★ the city started by Francisco Cuero y Valdes
★ the river whose name means "Big" or "Grand" river in Spanish
★ the river that shares its name with the city of San Francisco
★ the city where the first atomic bomb was developed
★ the place where the atomic bomb was tested
★ the country to the south of New Mexico
★ the place where you can walk a 3 mile underground trail
★ you might see UFOs here
★ the city near Taos Pueblo
★ the place where Maria Martinez grew up

Size: 121,593 square miles
Population: 1,685,000

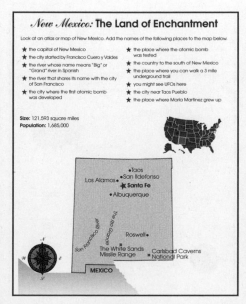

232

New Mexico: The Land of Enchantment

Read the clues. Unscramble the words about New Mexico.

a city founded in 1706 **ALBUQUERQUE** QUQUEERALBU

the capital **SANTE FE** EFTASAN

last name of an artist who painted New Mexico **OKEEFE** EEEFKO

the big river **THE RIO GRANDE** EHT IRO ARNEGD

Write the first letter of each word in the puzzle. **ASOT**

Unscramble the letters to find the name of a city in New Mexico. **TAOS**

New Mexico has a hot air balloon festival called "Albuquerque's International Balloon Fiesta" in October each year. Describe what people might see if they rode in a hot air balloon. Draw a picture to illustrate your description.

Pictures will vary.

Sample answer: We would see desert, a volcano, the Rio Grande snaking through the hot earth and we would see bison, cattle and horses running across the plains.

233

New York: The Empire State

Look at an atlas or map of New York. Add the names of the following places to the map below.

★ the capital of New York
★ the city that used to be called New Amsterdam
★ the two Great Lakes that border the state
★ the island where people entered the U.S. from 1892 to 1954
★ the river named for the explorer, Henry Hudson
★ the largest waterfall in the United States
★ the city attacked in the French and Indian War
★ the city where the Kodak camera was invented
★ Franklin Roosevelt's birthplace
★ the site of the first women's rights convention
★ the ocean that borders New York

Size: 49,108 square miles
Population: 18,044,000

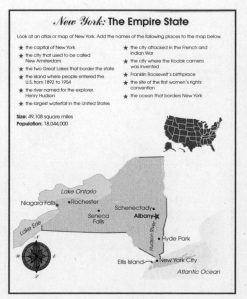

235

© 2001 McGraw-Hill. All Rights Reserved.

Appendix

New York: The Empire State

Read each clue. Use the code to find the answers.

1-A	5-E	9-I	13-X	17-K	21-U	25-Y
2-G	6-J	10-P	14-D	18-R	22-V	26-F
3-C	7-B	11-M	15-O	19-Z	23-W	
4-N	8-H	12-L	16-S	20-T	24-Q	

first name of New York's famous actor and director
W O O D Y
23 15 15 14 25

a river named for an explorer
H U D S O N
8 21 14 16 15 4

first name of first explorer
G I O V A N N I
2 9 15 22 1 4 4 9

used to be called Fort Orange
A L B A N Y
1 12 7 1 4 25

home of George Eastman
R O C H E S T E R
18 15 3 8 5 16 20 5 18

Unscramble the circled letters to write the name of the famous Iroquois leader.
H I A W A T H A

Pictures will vary.

The Statue of Liberty was the first thing many immigrants saw when they came to Ellis Island and entered New York Harbor. The Statue of Liberty stands for freedom.

If you built a new statue to welcome people to New York, what would it look like? Draw a picture of your statue and write about what it stands for.

Answers will vary. Children might draw a dollar bill, a dollar sign, a computer, a camera, a guitar, etc. Children might write, "A dollar bill or dollar sign stands for a country with good jobs." "A computer stands for America's use of the Internet." "A camera stands for America's inventors." "A guitar stands for America's music."

236

North Carolina: The Tar Heel State

Look at an atlas or map of North Carolina. Add the names of the following places to the map below.

★ the Wright Brothers Monument
★ the state capital
★ the Great Smoky Mountains
★ Pamlico Sound
★ Fayetteville, on the Cape Fear River
★ the world's largest mill for weaving denim

★ eastern America's highest peak
★ the largest city and home to the Hornets
★ the ocean to the east
★ the states around North Carolina
★ the site of many shipwrecks

Size: 52,699 square miles
Population: 6,658,000

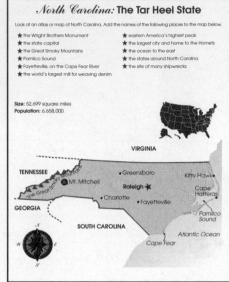

238

North Carolina: The Tar Heel State

Read the clues. Unscramble the words about North Carolina.

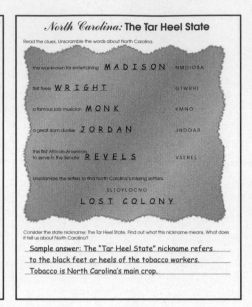

she was known for entertaining **M A D I S O N**   NMDIOSA

first flyers **W R I G H T**   GTWRHI

a famous jazz musician **M O N K**   KMNO

a great slam dunker **J O R D A N**   JNDOAR

the first African-American to serve in the Senate **R E V E L S**   VSEREL

Unscramble the letters to find North Carolina's missing settlers.
SLTOYLOCNO
L O S T   C O L O N Y

Consider the state nickname: The Tar Heel State. Find out what this nickname means. What does it tell us about North Carolina?

Sample answer: The "Tar Heel State" nickname refers to the black feet or heels of the tobacco workers. Tobacco is North Carolina's main crop.

239

North Dakota: The Flickertail State

Look at an atlas or map of North Dakota. Add the names of the following places to the map below.

★ the capital
★ the river that shares a name with a state
★ the country to the north
★ the city where Lewis and Clark built a fort
★ the first European settlement
★ the cities with the two United States Strategic Air Commands

★ the National Park to honor Theodore Roosevelt
★ the city near Writing Rock
★ the town that hosts "Pioneer Days" at Bonanzaville"
★ the lake named for Lewis and Clark's guide
★ the state to the south that was once part of the Dakota Territory

Size: 70,702 square miles
Population: 641,000

241

North Dakota: The Flickertail State

Anna wrote a report about her summer trip to North Dakota. Fill in the letters that she left out.

My Summer trip to **N**orth Dakota.

North Dak**O**ta is a big state. My family and I didn't see everything, but here are the things I liked best.

We visited the **I**ndian **P**etroglyphs at Writing **R**ock near C**R**osby. It was fun to imagine the Native Amer**I**cans who made these drawings. I can't believe how old the drawings are!

We also saw the United Stat**E**s Strategic **A**ir **C**ommand at Grand **F**orks. They have a lot of neat planes!

For natural beauty, the **TH**eodore **R**oosevelt National Memorial Park was the best! We went on a long hike.

I think you'd love North Dakota.

Anna Turner

Unscramble the letters you have written to find the name of the railroad that brought settlers to North Dakota.

N O R T H E R N   P A C I F I C

Anna enjoyed visiting North Dakota. What things might other travelers like to see in North Dakota? Design a travel brochure that shows visitors 3 things to see in North Dakota.

Answers will vary. Students might include images of petroglyphs, jet planes, Lake Sacajawea, pioneers, White Butte, a train or Sioux Indians.

242

Ohio: The Buckeye State

Look at an atlas or map of Ohio. Add the names of the following places to the map below.

★ state to the north
★ this river empties into Lake Erie
★ buy some tires here
★ this city celebrates famous music and musicians
★ the city that boasts the birth of pro baseball

★ state to the west
★ Ohio's capital
★ this river forms much of the Ohio border
★ the major city in the northwest
★ state to the east
★ on one side of this lake is Ohio, on the other is Canada

Size: 41,330 square miles
Population: 10,887,000

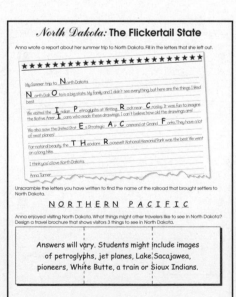

244

© 2001 McGraw-Hill. All Rights Reserved.

Ohio: The Buckeye State

Next to each sentence write a T if the statement is true or an F if the statement is false.

- **F** The Ohio River forms the northern border of Ohio.
- **T** The three largest cities in Ohio all start with "C."
- **F** The Ohio River once caught fire.
- **F** Toledo was known as an important producer of rubber.
- **T** The Rock 'n' Roll Hall of Fame is located in Cleveland.
- **T** The first professional baseball team is now known as the Cincinnati Reds.

What industries helped make Ohio an important state?

Sample answer: The oil, rubber, farming and steel industries all were important to Ohio and helped it grow.

245

Oklahoma: The Sooner State

Look at an atlas or map of Oklahoma. Add the names of the following places to the map below.

- ★ the states that border Oklahoma
- ★ the river that separates Texas and Oklahoma
- ★ three rivers that run through the state
- ★ the capital of Oklahoma
- ★ the area called the Panhandle
- ★ Tulsa, the second largest city
- ★ the location of the University of Oklahoma
- ★ a city in the Panhandle
- ★ a city north of Tulsa
- ★ the location of Oklahoma State University

Size: 69,919 square miles
Population: 3,158,000

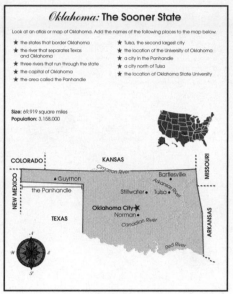

247

Oklahoma: The Sooner State

Read the clues. Unscramble the words about Oklahoma.

This city has an oil well
O K L A H O M A   C I T Y — AKIMLHOATOCY

This rock is only found in Oklahoma
B A R I T E   R O S E — RBITEOASER

A Native American tribe that lived in Oklahoma
C H I C K A S A W — HCACKASIW

The Spanish explorer who came to Oklahoma
C O R O N A D O — DRONOCOA

The terrible journey of the Native Americans
T R A I L   O F   T E A R S — EERALTOIREAT

Look at the state flag of Oklahoma. Find two symbols of peace on the flag. Write about what they are and why you think they were included as a part of the flag.

Sample answer: The olive branch is a symbol of peace for Europeans. The peace pipe is a symbol of peace to Native Americans. The two symbols together represent the coming together of Europeans and Native Americans in peace.

248

Oregon: The Beaver State

Look at an atlas or map of Oregon. Add the names of the following places to the map below.

- ★ Portland, the largest city and a port on the Columbia River
- ★ a lake created when a volcano blew its top
- ★ the deepest canyon in the United States
- ★ the river found by Captain Robert Gray
- ★ the state capital
- ★ the location of Lewis and Clark's 1805–1806 winter camp
- ★ the city that hosts a Shakespearean festival
- ★ a family recreation area of beach sand dunes
- ★ the mountain range that divides the state
- ★ this river's valley was home to the first settlers

Size: 97,073 square miles
Population: 2,854,000

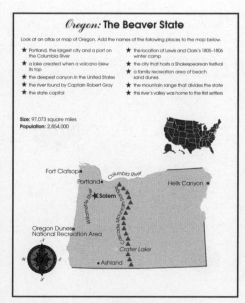

250

Oregon: The Beaver State

Read the clues. Complete the words about Oregon.

an explorer's fort **C L A T S o P**

a children's author **C L E A R Y**

Chief Joseph's tribe **N E Z   P e R C É**

he explored the Columbia River **G R A Y**

Pauling won two of these prizes **N o B E L**

a shoe man **K N I G H T**

The Oregon state flag is the only American flag with two different sides. The front shows a heart shaped shield to stand for early Oregon. The back shows a beaver. On a sheet of paper, design a new Oregon flag. What would you use to stand for Oregon?

Answers will vary. Students might draw a Douglas fir tree, Lewis and Clark, the rocky coastline of Oregon, a wagon train or a snow goose.

251

Pennsylvania: The Keystone State

Look at an atlas or map of Pennsylvania. Add the names of the following places to the map below.

- ★ the great lake that borders northwest Pennsylvania
- ★ the river that separates Pennsylvania and New Jersey
- ★ the capital
- ★ the town that founded Little League baseball
- ★ the city where the Continental Congress met
- ★ the town where William Penn landed
- ★ coal was discovered near this city
- ★ the city where Lincoln gave his famous speech
- ★ General Marshall's hometown
- ★ the city named after the Duke of York
- ★ the site of the largest chocolate factory

Size: 45,308 square miles
Population: 12,000,000

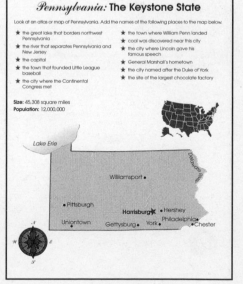

253

© 2001 McGraw-Hill. All Rights Reserved.

Appendix

Pennsylvania: The Keystone State

Read the clues about Pennsylvania. Use the code to find the answers.

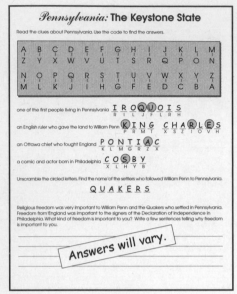

A	B	C	D	E	F	G	H	I	J	K	L	M
Z	Y	X	W	V	U	T	S	R	Q	P	O	N

N	O	P	Q	R	S	T	U	V	W	X	Y	Z
M	L	K	J	I	H	G	F	E	D	C	B	A

one of the first people living in Pennsylvania   I R O Q U O I S
R I L J F L R H

an English ruler who gave the land to William Penn   K I N G   C H A R L E S
P R M T   X S Z I O V H

an Ottawa chief who fought England   P O N T I A C
K L M G R Z X

a comic and actor born in Philadelphia   C O S B Y
X L H V B

Unscramble the circled letters. Find the name of the settlers who followed William Penn to Pennsylvania.

Q U A K E R S

Religious freedom was very important to William Penn and the Quakers who settled in Pennsylvania. Freedom from England was important to the signers of the Declaration of Independence in Philadelphia. What kind of freedom is important to you? Write a few sentences telling why freedom is important to you.

Answers will vary.

254

Rhode Island: Little Rhody

Look at an atlas or map of Rhode Island. Add the names of the following places to the map below.

★ the site of America's first cotton mill
★ the capital of Rhode Island
★ Narragansett Bay
★ many wealthy families built mansions here
★ Block Island
★ Warwick, one of Rhode Island's first towns

★ the state that borders Rhode Island on the west
★ Block Island Sound
★ the ocean to the east
★ Pawtuxet River
★ Blackstone River

Size: 1,212 square miles
Population: 1,006,000

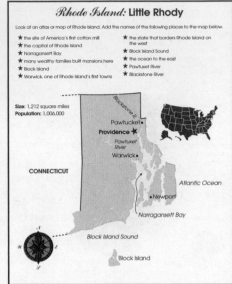

256

Rhode Island: Little Rhody

Write the letter from column B next to the matching phrase in column A.

1. E founder of Rhode Island
2. C capital city
3. A U.S. general during Revolutionary War
4. B site of America's first cotton mill
5. D George Washington portrait painter

Ⓐ Nathanael Greene
Ⓑ Pawtucket
Ⓒ Providence
Ⓓ Gilbert Stuart
Ⓔ Roger Williams

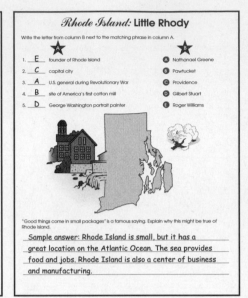

"Good things come in small packages" is a famous saying. Explain why this might be true of Rhode Island.

Sample answer: Rhode Island is small, but it has a great location on the Atlantic Ocean. The sea provides food and jobs. Rhode Island is also a center of business and manufacturing.

257

South Carolina: The Palmetto State

Look at an atlas or map of South Carolina. Add the names of the following places to the map below.

★ this is a popular seaside spot
★ the ocean to the east of South Carolina
★ this large city is in the northwestern part of the state
★ an island near the southern border
★ a big city on the ocean

★ the capital of South Carolina
★ a large lake between Columbia and Charleston
★ historic shots were fired here
★ the state south and west of South Carolina
★ the state to the north

Size: 31,113 square miles
Population: 3,506,000

NORTH CAROLINA

• Greenville

★ Columbia

Myrtle Beach •

Lake Marion

GEORGIA

Charleston • ★ Fort Sumter

Atlantic Ocean

• Hilton Head Island

259

South Carolina: The Palmetto State

Read the clues. Then, unscramble the words about South Carolina.

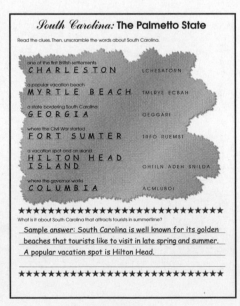

one of the first British settlements
C H A R L E S T O N   LCHESATORN

a popular vacation beach
M Y R T L E   B E A C H   TMLRYE ECBAH

a state bordering South Carolina
G E O R G I A   OEGGARI

where the Civil War started
F O R T   S U M T E R   TRFO RUEMST

a vacation spot and an island
H I L T O N   H E A D   I S L A N D   OHTILN ADEH SNILDA

where the governor works
C O L U M B I A   ACMLUBOI

★★★★★★★★★★★★★★★★★★★★★★★

What is it about South Carolina that attracts tourists in summertime?

Sample answer: South Carolina is well known for its golden beaches that tourists like to visit in late spring and summer. A popular vacation spot is Hilton Head.

★★★★★★★★★★★★★★★★★★★★★★★

260

South Dakota: The Mount Rushmore State

Look at an atlas or map of South Dakota. Add the names of the following places to the map below.

★ Citibank headquarters is here
★ two of the world's longest caves
★ home of Allen Neuharth
★ Yankton Indian Reservation
★ Badlands National Park
★ the world's largest drugstore is here

★ Devil's Gulch, a 20-foot wide canyon
★ hometown of Hubert Humphrey
★ South Dakota's capital
★ Wounded Knee Creek
★ Waubay Lake

Size: 77,116 square miles
Population: 732,000

• Eureka
Waubay Lake
Wallace •

★ Pierre

Devil's Gulch

Jewel Cave
Wind Cave
• Wall
Badlands National Park
Wounded Knee Creek

Sioux Falls •

Yankton Indian Reservation

262

© 2001 McGraw-Hill. All Rights Reserved.

South Dakota: The Mount Rushmore State

Draw a line to match the dates on the left with the events on the right.

1889 — The La Vérendrye brothers find Missouri River.
1743 — Massacre at Wounded Knee Creek kills 300 Sioux.
1876 — South Dakota becomes a state and Sioux are moved onto reservations.
1874 — Crazy Horse, Sitting Bull and Gall attack at Little Bighorn.
1890 — Gold is found in the Black Hills.

Imagine that you are a Sioux child. What was it like to be a Sioux child before the Europeans arrived? Write a journal entry about your customs, culture and beliefs.

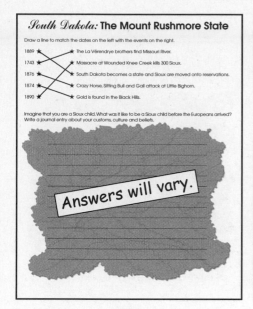

Answers will vary.

263

Tennessee: The Volunteer State

Look at an atlas or map of Tennessee. Add the names of the following places to the map below.

★ the capital of Tennessee
★ the easternmost and largest city in Tennessee
★ the city which is home to the Tennessee Aquarium
★ Elvis Presley's home
★ the river which creates Tennessee's western border
★ the river which flows through Nashville
★ the river which flows through Knoxville
★ the eight states that border Tennessee

Size: 42,144 square miles
Population: 4,897,000

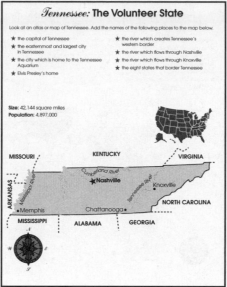

265

Tennessee: The Volunteer State

Read the clues. Write the answers on the lines. Then, read the boxed letters to find out where the Grand Ole Opry is.

1. What national park is found in Tennessee?
2. Who developed an alphabet?
3. What entertainer is known as the King of Rock and Roll?
4. Who wrote historical novels?
5. What is the name of the war hero Gary Cooper portrayed?
6. On what Cherokee word is the name Tennessee based?
7. What was the first name suggested for Tennessee?
8. Who was the eleventh president of the United States?
9. Who was the "coonskin cap" frontiersman?

1. SMOKEY MOUNTAIN
2. SEQUOYAH
3. ELVIS PRESLEY
4. ALEX HALEY
5. ALVIN YORK
6. TANASI
7. FRANKLIN
8. JAMES POLK
9. DAVY CROCKETT

Where is the Grand Ole Opry Radio Show? ___Nashville___

There are three stars on the flag of Tennessee. Find out what each represents.

The three stars represent the three different landforms in Tennessee: the mountains, the highlands and the lowlands.

Tennessee is nicknamed the "Volunteer State." Find out how the state got that name.

The nickname came from the War of 1812 when volunteer soldiers, under the leadership of General Andrew Jackson, fought bravely in the Battle of New Orleans.

266

Texas: The Lone Star State

Look at an atlas or map of Texas. Add the names of the following places to the map below.

★ the city where the Alamo is located
★ the city where the first two missions were built
★ the location of the Texas Rangers Hall of Fame
★ the capital of Texas
★ the city where John F. Kennedy was assassinated
★ the location of the Lyndon B. Johnson Space Center
★ the country to the south
★ the state to the north
★ the Rio Grande River
★ the Gulf of Mexico

Size: 266,807 square miles
Population: 17,060,000

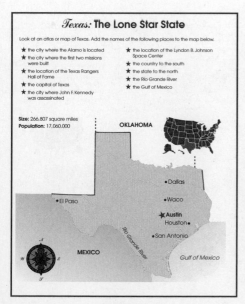

268

Texas: The Lone Star State

Complete the crossword puzzle below.

Across
3. The area south of Texas
6. The coast of Texas is on this body of water
7. A famous battle occurred here
9. Where astronauts report
10. John F. Kennedy was assassinated here

Down
1. This river is the boundary between Texas and Mexico
2. Texas Rangers Hall of Fame is here
4. You could find historical missions here
5. The Spanish built these when they claimed Texas
8. The president of Texas when it was a country

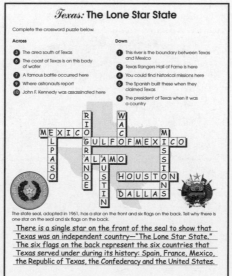

The state seal, adopted in 1961, has a star on the front and six flags on the back. Tell why there is one star on the seal and six flags on the back.

There is a single star on the front of the seal to show that Texas was an independent country—"The Lone Star State." The six flags on the back represent the six countries that Texas served under during its history: Spain, France, Mexico, the Republic of Texas, the Confederacy and the United States.

269

Utah: The Beehive State

Look at an atlas or map of Utah. Add the names of the following places to the map below.

★ Merlin Olsen is from here
★ the other states making the "four corners"
★ Utah's capital
★ a freshwater lake
★ where racecar records are set
★ a town near Utah Lake
★ many Western movies are filmed here
★ you can float in this lake
★ see dinosaur bones here

Size: 84,899 square miles
Population: 1,728,000

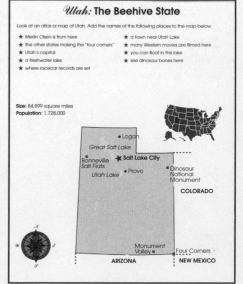

271

© 2001 McGraw-Hill. All Rights Reserved.

Appendix

Utah: The Beehive State

Write the letter from column B next to the matching phrase in column A.

A		B
1. **C** he led Mormons to Utah		**A** the Utes
2. **E** this lake has water you can drink		**B** New York
3. **A** these people were unhappy when the Mormons came		**C** Bringham Young
4. **B** Mormons originally came from here		**D** Colorado
5. **D** this state is another part of the "four corners"		**E** Utah Lake
6. **F** you can find these kinds of bones		**F** dinosaur

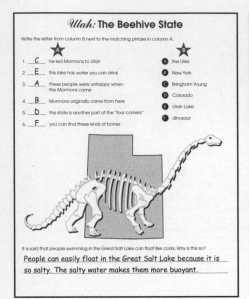

It is said that people swimming in the Great Salt Lake can float like corks. Why is this so?

People can easily float in the Great Salt Lake because it is so salty. The salty water makes them more buoyant.

272

Vermont: The Green Mountain State

Look at an atlas or map of Vermont. Add the names of the following places to the map below.

★ a lake named after an explorer
★ the capital of Vermont
★ a place near the first English settlement
★ a site where granite is quarried
★ the Green Mountains
★ the state which once claimed Vermont and now borders it to the east

★ the place where the Green Mountain Boys met
★ the state's largest city
★ the river that forms the border between New Hampshire and Vermont
★ Mount Mansfield
★ the birthplace of Chester Arthur

Size: 9,614 square miles
Population: 565,000

274

Vermont: The Green Mountain State

Use the words in the Word Bank to complete each sentence.

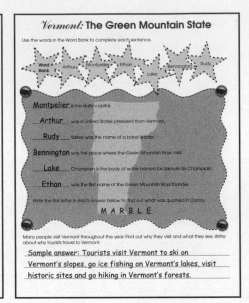

Word Bank: Arthur   Montpelier   Ethan   Lake   Bennington   Rudy

Montpelier is the state capital.

Arthur was a United States president from Vermont.

Rudy Vallee was the name of a band leader.

Bennington was the place where the Green Mountain Boys met.

Lake Champlain is the body of water named for Samuel de Champlain.

Ethan was the first name of the Green Mountain Boys founder.

Write the first letter in each answer below to find out what was quarried in Danby.

M A R B L E

Many people visit Vermont throughout the year. Find out why they visit and what they see. Write about why tourists travel to Vermont.

Sample answer: Tourists visit Vermont to ski on Vermont's slopes, go ice fishing on Vermont's lakes, visit historic sites and go hiking in Vermont's forests.

275

Virginia: Old Dominion

Look at an atlas or map of Virginia. Add the names of the following places to the map below.

★ the capital of Virginia
★ the site of the Civil War surrender
★ Thomas Jefferson's home, Monticello
★ George Washington's home, Mount Vernon
★ the site of the first permanent English colony

★ Arlington National Cemetery
★ the site of the British surrender
★ the Chesapeake Bay Bridge-Tunnel
★ the five states that border Virginia
★ the ocean to the east

Size: 40,767 square miles
Population: 6,217,000

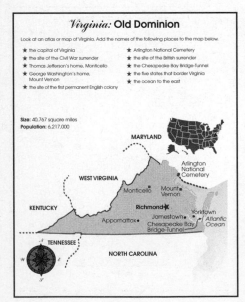

277

Virginia: Old Dominion

Use the words in the Word Bank to complete the sentences.

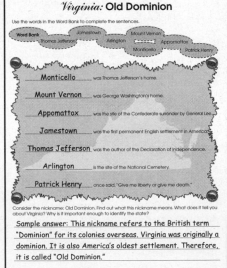

Word Bank: Jamestown   Mount Vernon   Thomas Jefferson   Arlington   Appomattox   Monticello   Patrick Henry

Monticello was Thomas Jefferson's home.

Mount Vernon was George Washington's home.

Appomattox was the site of the Confederate surrender by General Lee.

Jamestown was the first permanent English settlement in America.

Thomas Jefferson was the author of the Declaration of Independence.

Arlington is the site of the National Cemetery.

Patrick Henry once said, "Give me liberty or give me death."

Consider the nickname: Old Dominion. Find out what this nickname means. What does it tell you about Virginia? Why is it important enough to identify the state?

Sample answer: This nickname refers to the British term "Dominion" for its colonies overseas. Virginia was originally a dominion. It is also America's oldest settlement. Therefore, it is called "Old Dominion."

278

Washington: The Evergreen State

Look at an atlas or map of Washington. Add the names of the following places to the map below.

★ a software company's headquarters is near this city
★ a National Park that includes seashore and rainforests
★ a volcano that erupted in 1980
★ a large river that creates much of the border with Oregon
★ the capital of Washington
★ a tall glacier-covered mountain

★ a city, named for a Native American tribe, that began as a Canadian trading post
★ a city named after a British officer and a Hudson Bay fort
★ the settlement set up by missionary Marcus Whitman
★ the city where 747 aircraft are built
★ the bay mapped by George Vancouver

Size: 68,139 square miles
Population: 4,888,000

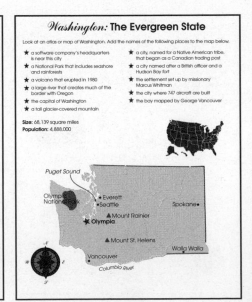

280

Appendix

348

© 2001 McGraw-Hill. All Rights Reserved.

Washington: The Evergreen State

Complete the crossword puzzle below.

Across
1. the capital city
3. an American fort
6. the name of a British explorer and a modern city
8. a famous cartoonist
9. a television pioneer

Down
2. the name of a Native American tribe
4. the Hudson Bay Company and the Americans wanted this
5. Mount St. Helens is one, so is Mount Rainier
7. an important forest resource

Crossword answers:
O L Y M P I A
O K A N O G A N
V A N C O U V E R — F U R S
L A R S O N
T I M B E R — M U R R O W

How many of Washington's major cities were built along the Columbia River? Write about why you think settlers chose to live along the river.

Sample answer: At least five of Washington's larger cities were built along the Columbia River: Longview, Vancouver, Pasco, Richland and Wenatchee. People built alongside rivers because the river was one of the main means of transportation. The banks of the river also provided fertile soil, fish and water.

281

West Virginia: The Mountain State

Look at an atlas or map of West Virginia. Add the names of the following places to the map below.

★ a one time capital of West Virginia
★ the state to the north and west of West Virginia
★ West Virginia used to be a part of this state
★ beautiful mountains in the east
★ city near Kentucky
★ the capital of West Virginia
★ the state to the north and east
★ this river forms a border between West Virginia and Ohio
★ a one time confederate state to the south and west
★ John Brown raided this place

Size: 24,232 square miles
Population: 1,802,000

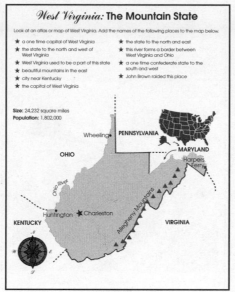

283

West Virginia: The Mountain State

Complete the sentences using facts about West Virginia.

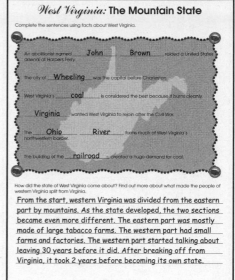

An abolitionist named **John** **Brown** raided a United States arsenal at Harpers Ferry.

The city of **Wheeling** was the capital before Charleston.

West Virginia's **coal** is considered the best because it burns cleanly.

Virginia wanted West Virginia to rejoin after the Civil War.

The **Ohio** **River** forms much of West Virginia's northwestern border.

The building of the **railroad** created a huge demand for coal.

How did the state of West Virginia come about? Find out more about what made the people of western Virginia split from Virginia.

From the start, western Virginia was divided from the eastern part by mountains. As the state developed, the two sections became even more different. The eastern part was mostly made of large tabacco farms. The western part had small farms and factories. The western part started talking about leaving 30 years before it did. After breaking off from Virginia, it took 2 years before becoming its own state.

284

Wisconsin: The Badger State

Look at an atlas or map of Wisconsin. Add the names of the following places to the map below.

★ this is a "super" Great Lake
★ the capital of Wisconsin
★ this bay feeds into Lake Michigan
★ this state is between Wisconsin and Canada
★ this state is to the south
★ this city is home to a pro football team
★ a large lake in Wisconsin
★ this river makes up the southwestern border
★ a large city on the banks of Lake Michigan
★ part of this state is wedged between the Great Lakes and Wisconsin
★ the only Great Lake to be entirely in the United States

Size: 56,153 square miles
Population: 4,907,000

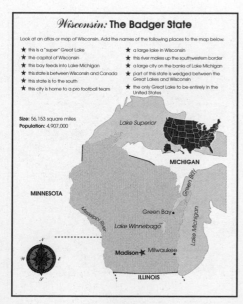

286

Wisconsin: The Badger State

Complete the crossword puzzle below.

Across
2. not a "great" lake
5. visit this city near Lake Michigan
6. a nickname for Wisconsinites
7. not just a city, a body of water, too

Down
1. It's the only Great Lake entirely in the United States
3. this city has a different-colored bay
4. an inland city

Crossword answers:
W I N N E B A G O
M I L W A U K E E
M A D I S O N — G R E E N — B A D G E R S
G R E E N B A Y
L A K E M I C H I G A N

Why do you think Wisconsin is called America's Dairyland?

Sample answer: Wisconsin produces more milk than any other state. Wisconsin also produces lots of cheese and other dairy products.

287

Wyoming: The Equality State

Look at an atlas or map of Wyoming. Add the names of the following places to the map below.

★ this city is just east of central Wyoming
★ the capital of Wyoming
★ a city in northwest Wyoming
★ this river passes through the Grand Teton National Park
★ the first national park
★ these beautiful mountains are in their own national park
★ this river passes by Casper
★ a city near Cheyenne
★ this state is to the west and borders Montana
★ this mountain range divides North America
★ this state is to the east and borders Colorado
★ the Continental Divide

Size: 97,809 square miles
Population: 456,000

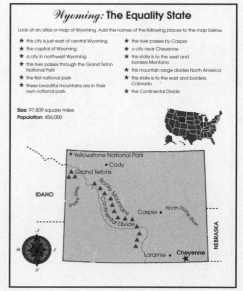

289

© 2001 McGraw-Hill. All Rights Reserved.

Appendix

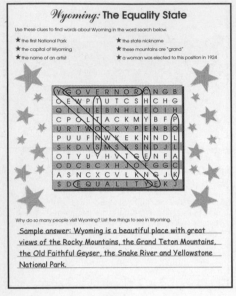

Wyoming: The Equality State

Use these clues to find words about Wyoming in the word search below.

★ the first National Park
★ the capital of Wyoming
★ the name of an artist
★ the state nickname
★ these mountains are "grand"
★ a woman was elected to this position in 1924

Word search grid with answers circled.

Why do so many people visit Wyoming? List five things to see in Wyoming.

Sample answer: Wyoming is a beautiful place with great
views of the Rocky Mountains, the Grand Teton Mountains,
the Old Faithful Geyser, the Snake River and Yellowstone
National Park.

290

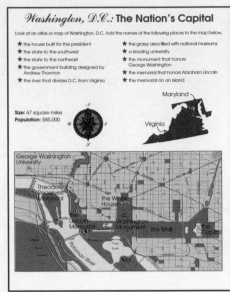

Washington, D.C.: The Nation's Capital

Look at an atlas or map of Washington, D.C. Add the names of the following places to the map below.

★ the house built for the president
★ the state to the southwest
★ the state to the northeast
★ the government building designed by Andrew Thornton
★ the river that divides D.C. from Virginia
★ the grassy area filled with national museums
★ a leading university
★ the monument that honors George Washington
★ the memorial that honors Abraham Lincoln
★ the memorial on an island

Size: 67 square miles
Population: 585,000

Map of Washington, D.C. with labeled landmarks.

292

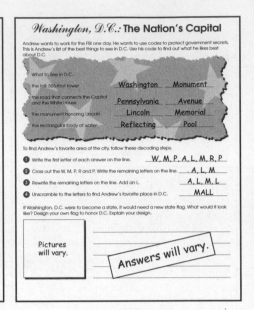

Washington, D.C.: The Nation's Capital

Andrew wants to work for the FBI one day. He wants to use codes to protect government secrets. This is Andrew's list of the best things to see in D.C. Use his code to find out what he likes best about D.C.

What to See in D.C.:		
the tall, 555-foot tower	Washington	Monument
the road that connects the Capitol and the White House	Pennsylvania	Avenue
the monument honoring Lincoln	Lincoln	Memorial
the rectangular body of water	Reflecting	Pool

To find Andrew's favorite area of the city, follow these decoding steps.

1. Write the first letter of each answer on the line.   W, M, P, A, L, M, R, P
2. Cross out the W, M, P, R and P. Write the remaining letters on the line.   A, L, M
3. Rewrite the remaining letters on the line. Add an L.   A, L, M, L
4. Unscramble to the letters to find Andrew's favorite place in D.C.   MALL

If Washington, D.C. were to become a state, it would need a new state flag. What would it look like? Design your own flag to honor D.C. Explain your design.

Pictures will vary.

Answers will vary.

293

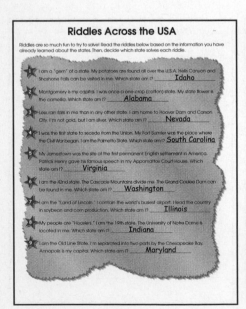

Riddles Across the USA

Riddles are so much fun to try to solve! Read the riddles below based on the information you have already learned about the states. Then, decide which state solves each riddle.

★ I am a "gem" of a state. My potatoes are found all over the U.S.A. Hells Canyon and Shoshone Falls can be visited in me. Which state am I?   Idaho

★ Montgomery is my capital. I was once a one-crop (cotton) state. My state flower is the camellia. Which state am I?   Alabama

★ Less rain falls in me than in any other state. I am home to Hoover Dam and Carson City. I'm not gold, but I am silver. Which state am I?   Nevada

★ I was the first state to secede from the Union. My Fort Sumter was the place where the Civil War began. I am the Palmetto State. Which state am I?   South Carolina

★ My Jamestown was the site of the first permanent English settlement in America. Patrick Henry gave his famous speech in my Appomattox Court House. Which state am I?   Virginia

★ I am the 42nd state. The Cascade Mountains divide me. The Grand Coulee Dam can be found in me. Which state am I?   Washington

★ I am the "Land of Lincoln." I contain the world's busiest airport. I lead the country in soybean and corn production. Which state am I?   Illinois

★ My people are "Hoosiers." I am the 19th state. The University of Notre Dame is located in me. Which state am I?   Indiana

★ I am the Old Line State. I'm separated into two parts by the Chesapeake Bay. Annapolis is my capital. Which state am I?   Maryland

294

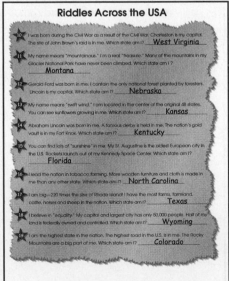

Riddles Across the USA

10. I was born during the Civil War as a result of the Civil War. Charleston is my capital. The site of John Brown's raid is in me. Which state am I?   West Virginia

11. My name means "mountainous." I'm a real "treasure." Many of the mountains in my Glacier National Park have never been climbed. Which state am I?   Montana

12. Gerald Ford was born in me. I contain the only national forest planted by foresters. Lincoln is my capital. Which state am I?   Nebraska

13. My name means "swift wind." I am located in the center of the original 48 states. You can see sunflowers growing in me. Which state am I?   Kansas

14. Abraham Lincoln was born in me. A famous derby is held in me. The nation's gold vault is in my Fort Knox. Which state am I?   Kentucky

15. You can find lots of "sunshine" in me. My St. Augustine is the oldest European city in the U.S. Rockets launch out of my Kennedy Space Center. Which state am I?   Florida

16. I lead the nation in tobacco farming. More wooden furniture and cloth is made in me than any other state. Which state am I?   North Carolina

17. I am big—220 times the size of Rhode Island! I have the most farms, farmland, cattle, horses and sheep in the nation. Which state am I?   Texas

18. I believe in "equality." My capital and largest city has only 50,000 people. Half of my land is federally owned and controlled. Which state am I?   Wyoming

19. I am the highest state in the nation. The highest road in the U.S. is in me. The Rocky Mountains are a big part of me. Which state am I?   Colorado

295

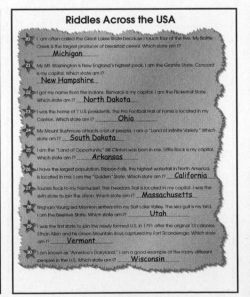

Riddles Across the USA

20. I am often called the Great Lakes State because I touch four of the five. My Battle Creek is the largest producer of breakfast cereal. Which state am I?   Michigan

21. My Mt. Washington is New England's highest peak. I am the Granite State. Concord is my capital. Which state am I?   New Hampshire

22. I got my name from the Indians. Bismarck is my capital. I am the Flickertail State. Which state am I?   North Dakota

23. I was the home of 7 U.S. presidents. The Pro Football Hall of Fame is located in my Canton. Which state am I?   Ohio

24. My Mount Rushmore attracts a lot of people. I am a "Land of Infinite Variety." Which state am I?   South Dakota

25. I am the "Land of Opportunity." Bill Clinton was born in me. Little Rock is my capital. Which state am I?   Arkansas

26. I have the largest population. Ribbon Falls, the highest waterfall in North America, is located in me. I am the "Golden" State. Which state am I?   California

27. Tourists flock to my Nantucket. The Freedom Trail is located in my capital. I was the sixth state to join the Union. Which state am I?   Massachusetts

28. Brigham Young led Mormon settlers into my Salt Lake Valley. The sea gull is my bird. I am the Beehive State. Which state am I?   Utah

29. I was the first state to join the newly formed U.S. in 1791 after the original 13 colonies. Ethan Allen and his Green Mountain Boys captured my Fort Ticonderoga. Which state am I?   Vermont

30. I am known as "America's Dairyland." I am a good example of the many different peoples in the U.S. Which state am I?   Wisconsin

296

© 2001 McGraw-Hill. All Rights Reserved.

Riddles Across the USA

31. I am the biggest state. The highest peak in the U.S., Mt. McKinley, is located in me. Which state am I? **Alaska**

32. I contain the Grand Canyon. Phoenix is my capital. Without irrigation, half of me would be desert. Which state am I? **Arizona**

33. I am the Garden State. My Atlantic City offers lots of exciting things for visitors to do. The purple violet is my flower. Which state am I? **New Jersey**

34. I am the First State. I was named for Lord De La Warr. I was the first state to ratify the new constitution in 1787. Which state am I? **Delaware**

35. I am the first state in the U.S. to greet the sun each day. I lead the nation with my lobster catch. Ninety percent of my land is covered with woods. Which state am I? **Maine**

36. In 1610, I was founded by the Spanish. I am the "Land of Enchantment." My Santa Fe is the oldest seat of government in the nation. Which state am I? **New Mexico**

37. My Hartford is known as "Insurance City." The first constitution in the New World was adopted in me in 1639. Which state am I? **Connecticut**

38. I can "show" you a lot. Jefferson City is my capital. In the summer of 1993, much of my land flooded. Which state am I? **Missouri**

39. I lead the nation in banking and wholesale trade. I contain the nation's largest city. I am the Empire State. Which state am I? **New York**

40. I am "the land where tall corn grows." I lead the nation in literacy. Des Moines is my capital. Which state am I? **Iowa**

297

Riddles Across the USA

41. Portland is my largest city. My Columbia River Gorge attracts many tourists. There is year-round skiing at my Mount Hood. Which state am I? **Oregon**

42. I am the Gopher State. My Mesabi Range contains much iron ore. St. Paul is my capital. Which state am I? **Minnesota**

43. I am the tiniest state. Roger Williams founded me in 1636. I produce the most costume jewelry in the world. Which state am I? **Rhode Island**

44. My name is an Indian word meaning "red people." The Five Civilized Tribes wanted me to become the state of Sequoyah in 1905. Instead, I am the Sooner State. Which state am I? **Oklahoma**

45. La Salle claimed my area for France in 1682. The U.S. bought me from France in 1803. I am the 18th state. Which state am I? **Louisiana**

46. Elvis Presley was born in my Tupelo. I am the Magnolia State. Jackson is my capital and largest city. Which state am I? **Mississippi**

47. You probably love my peaches. My most famous peanut farmer is Jimmy Carter. I am the Empire State of the South. Which state am I? **Georgia**

48. I was the second state to ratify the Constitution. I was the center, or "keystone," of the original 13 colonies. Which state am I? **Pennsylvania**

49. I am the 50th state. My Pearl Harbor is very famous. Diamond Head is one of my most famous extinct volcanoes. Which state am I? **Hawaii**

50. I have an east, a middle and a west. My state capital is the home of country music. I am the Volunteer State. Which state am I? **Tennessee**

298

Abbreviate Those States!

When you mail something to someone, the state in the address is always abbreviated using two letters. See how many postal abbreviations you know!

AL Alabama	LA Louisiana	ND North Dakota
AK Alaska	ME Maine	OH Ohio
AZ Arizona	MD Maryland	OK Oklahoma
AR Arkansas	MA Massachusetts	OR Oregon
CA California	MI Michigan	PA Pennsylvania
CO Colorado	MN Minnesota	RI Rhode Island
CT Connecticut	MS Mississippi	SC South Carolina
DE Delaware	MO Missouri	SD South Dakota
FL Florida	MT Montana	TN Tennessee
GA Georgia	NE Nebraska	TX Texas
HI Hawaii	NV Nevada	UT Utah
ID Idaho	NH New Hampshire	VT Vermont
IL Illinois	NJ New Jersey	VA Virginia
IN Indiana	NM New Mexico	WA Washington
IA Iowa	NY New York	WV West Virginia
KS Kansas	NC North Carolina	WI Wisconsin
KY Kentucky		WY Wyoming

299

Going Crossword Crazy!

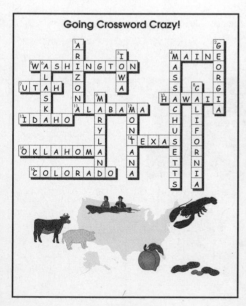

301

Going Crossword Crazy!

303

The Northeast

Label the states in the Northeast region. Draw and label the Hudson River. Answer the questions below the map.

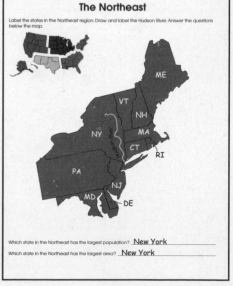

Which state in the Northeast has the largest population? **New York**

Which state in the Northeast has the largest area? **New York**

304

© 2001 McGraw-Hill. All Rights Reserved.

Appendix

The Southeast

Label the states in the Southeast region. Draw and label the Tennessee and Savannah Rivers. Answer the questions below the map.

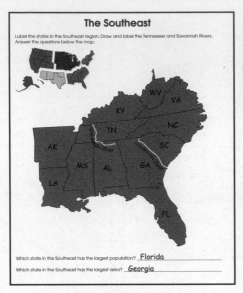

Which state in the Southeast has the largest population? __Florida__

Which state in the Southeast has the largest area? __Georgia__

305

The Midwest

Label the states in the Midwest region. Draw and label the Missouri and Mississippi Rivers. Answer the questions below the map.

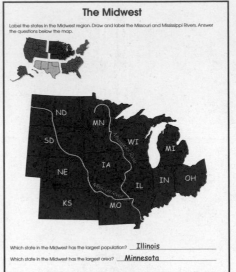

Which state in the Midwest has the largest population? __Illinois__

Which state in the Midwest has the largest area? __Minnesota__

306

The Southwest

Label the states in the Southwest region. Draw and label the Rio Grande River. Answer the questions below the map.

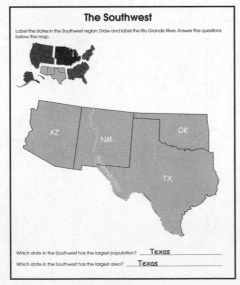

Which state in the Southwest has the largest population? __Texas__

Which state in the Southwest has the largest area? __Texas__

307

The West

Label the states in the Western region. Draw and label the Colorado and Columbia Rivers. Answer the questions below the map.

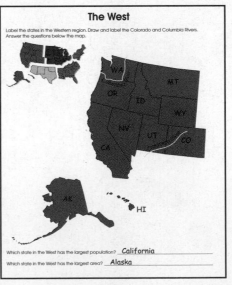

Which state in the West has the largest population? __California__

Which state in the West has the largest area? __Alaska__

308

© 2001 McGraw-Hill. All Rights Reserved.